Economics and Management of Franchising Networks

Contributions to Management Science

H. Dyckhoff/U. Finke
Cutting and Packing in Production and Distribution
1992. ISBN 3-7908-0630-7

R. Flavell (Ed.)
Modelling Reality and Personal Modelling
1993. ISBN 3-7908-0682-X

M. Hofmann/M. List (Eds.)
Psychoanalysis and Management
1994. ISBN 3-7908-0795-8

R.L. D'Ecclesia/S. A. Zenios (Eds.)
Operations Research Models in Quantitative Finance
1994. ISBN 3-7908-0803-2

M.S. Catalani/G.F. Clerico
Decision Making Structures
1996. ISBN 3-7908-0895-4

M. Bertocchi/E. Cavalli/S. Komlósi (Eds.)
Modelling Techniques for Financial Markets and Bank Management
1996. ISBN 3-7908-0928-4

H. Herbst
Business Rule-Oriented Conceptual Modeling
1997. ISBN 3-7908-1004-5

C. Zopounidis (Ed.)
New Operational Approaches for Financial Modelling
1997. ISBN 3-7908-1043-6

K. Zwerina
Discrete Choice Experiments in Marketing
1997. ISBN 3-7908-1045-2

G. Marseguerra
Corporate Financial Decisions and Market Value
1998. ISBN 3-7908-1047-9

WHU Koblenz – Otto Beisheim Graduate School of Management (Ed.)
Structure and Dynamics of the German Mittelstand
1999. ISBN 3-7908-1165-3

A. Scholl
Balancing and Sequencing of Assembly Lines
1999. ISBN 3-7908-1180-7

E. Canestrelli (Ed.)
Current Topics in Quantitative Finance
1999. ISBN 3-7908-1231-5

W. Bühler/H. Hax/R. Schmidt (Eds.)
Empirical Research on the German Capital Market
1999. ISBN 3-7908-1193-9

M. Bonilla/T. Casasus/R. Sala (Eds.)
Financial Modelling
2000. ISBN 3-7908-2282-X

S. Sulzmaier
Consumer-Oriented Business Design
2001. ISBN 3-7908-1366-4

C. Zopounidis (Ed.)
New Trends in Banking Management
2002. ISBN 3-7908-1488-1

U. Dorndorf
Project Scheduling with Time Windows
2002. ISBN 3-7908-1516-0

B. Rapp/P. Jackson (Eds.)
Organisationand Work Beyond 2000
2003. ISBN 3-7908-1528-4

M. Grossmann
Entreprencurship in Biotechnology
2003. ISBN 3-7908-0033-3

H.M. Arnold
Technology Shocks
2003. ISBN 3-7908-0051-1

T. Ihde
Dynamic Alliance Auctions
2004. ISBN 3-7908-0098-8

Josef Windsperger · Gérard Cliquet
George Hendrikse · Mika Tuunanen
Editors

Economics and Management of Franchising Networks

With 16 Figures
and 69 Tables

Springer-Verlag Berlin Heidelberg GmbH

Series Editors
Werner A. Müller
Martina Bihn

Editors

Ass. Prof. Dr. Josef Windsperger
University of Vienna
Center for Business Studies
Brünner Straße 72
1210 Vienna
Austria
josef.windsperger@univie.ac.at

Prof. Dr. Gérard Cliquet
University of Rennes 1
Center for Research on Economics
and Management
11 rue Jean Macé
CS 70803
35708 Rennes Cedex
France
gerard.cliquet@univ-rennes1.fr

Prof. Dr. George Hendrikse
Erasmus University Rotterdam
Rotterdam School of Management
Office F3-51
Burg. Oudlaan 50
3000 DR Rotterdam
The Netherlands
ghendrikse@fbk.eur.nl

Mika Tuunanen
Research Fellow
University of Jyväskylä
School of Business & Economics
P.O. Box 35 (MaE)
40351 Jyväskylä
Finland
mptuunan@econ.jvu.fi

Funding from the Austrian Ministry for Education, Science and Culture
is gratefully acknowledged.

ISSN 1431-1941
ISBN 978-3-7908-0202-3 ISBN 978-3-7908-2662-3 (eBook)
DOI 10.1007/978-3-7908-2662-3

Bibliographic information published by Die Deutsche Bibliothek
Die Deutsche Bibliothek lists this publication in the Deutsche Nationalbibliografie; detailed bibliographic data is available in the Internet at <http://dnb.ddb.de>.
Library of Congress Control Number: 2004103845

springeronline.com

Originally published byPhysica-Verlag Heidelberg in 2004

Softcover design: Erich Kirchner, Heidelberg

SPIN 10994009 88/3130/DK-5 4 3 2 1 0 – Printed on acid-free paper

Contents

Introducing 'Economics and Management of Franchising Networks' 1
George Hendrikse and Josef Windsperger

Part A: Theoretical Views of the Franchise Governance Structure

Towards a More General Theory of Franchise Governance 17
Seth Norton

The Organizational Choice Decision in Business Format Franchising: An Empirical Test 38
Janet Bercovitz

Part B: Plural Forms and Other Hybrid Organizational Forms

The Dual Network Structure of Franchising Firms: Property Rights, Resource Scarcity and Transaction Cost Explanations 69
Josef Windsperger

Successful Franchising Using the Plural Form 89
Thomas Ehrmann and Georg Spranger

Innovation Management with the Plural Form Network 109
Gérard Cliquet and Minh-Ngoc Nguyen

Franchising and Alternative Forms of Contract to Organize Vertical Restraints: Evidence from French Networks 126
Magali Chaudey and Muriel Fadario

Part C: Contract Design and Compensation

The Use of Up-front Fees, Royalties and Franchisor Sales to Franchisees in Business Format Franchising 145
Luis Vázquez

Contract Design and Range of Services in Franchising: An Empirical Contribution to the Effect of Incentives and Reputation 160
Thomas Ehrmann

Franchising Public Services: An Analysis of the Duration of Passenger Rail Franchises in Great Britain 174
Anne Yvrande-Billon

Part D: Knowledge and Strategic Management Issues

Understanding Exploration and Exploitation in Franchising and Other Forms of Commercial Cooperation 191
Evelien Croonen

The Importance of Time Management for the Performance of Franchising Networks 211
Rozenn Perrigot and Gérard Cliquet

Relocate, Render and Renovate: A Framework for Marketing Implementation across Franchise Networks 223
Mukul Gupta

Part E: International Market Entry Through Franchising

Franchising and the Choice of International Entry Mode 243
Krista Duniach-Smith

The Choice of Foreign Entry Mode by the Franchiser: Case Studies of Lithuanian Franchisers Entering Latvia 264
Regina Jarmalaite and Irina Sekundo

Part F: Country Studies

Exploring the Anatomy of Franchising: A Cross-National Examination of US and Finnish Franchise Contract Provisions 287
Mika Tuunanen

A Comparison of Finnish and United States Franchisee Satisfaction 312
Frank Wadsworth, Mika Tuunanen and Doug Haines

Finnish Franchisee Training Program - Findings from the First Ten Programs 1999 – 2001 320
Jenni Torikka

Part G: Regulation of Franchise Agreements

Antitrust Implications of Franchise Agreements 343
Kai Hüschelrath

List of Contributors 363

Introducing 'Economics and Management of Franchising Networks'

George W. J. Hendrikse

Erasmus University Rotterdam
Rotterdam School of Management
PoBox 1738
3000 DR Rotterdam
The Netherlands
ghendrikse@staf.fbk.eur.nl

Josef Windsperger

Center for Business Studies
University of Vienna
Brünner Str. 72
A-1210 Vienna
Austria
josef.windsperger@univie.ac.at

The increasing economic significance of networks has fuelled rapid growth in research at the intersection of economic and management disciplines (Brickley et al. 2002; Hendrikse 2003). The first international conference on Economics and Management of Networks (***EMNET***) took place at the Center for Business Studies, University of Vienna, from June 26 to June 28, 2003. ***EMNET***-conferences should serve in promoting communication and awareness among researchers in economics and management and should provide a forum to present current research and to discuss issues of common interest, such as relevant developments in organizational economics and management. The content of future conferences will include all forms of networks, such as franchising, joint ventures, virtual organizations, strategic alliances, cooperatives, clusters, venture capital relations and other forms of hybrids.

The purpose of the Viennese conference was to provide an international discussion forum for the research in economics and management of franchising networks. A selection of theoretical, conceptual and empirical papers from many areas in economics and management of franchising are published in this book.

The Status of Franchising Research and the Aim of this Book

Franchising research is one of the fields in economics and management of networks most subjected to new theoretical developments in the last two decades. Most of the *theoretical frameworks* used to explain the institutional structure of franchising networks focus on two main research questions (Penard, Reynaud,and Saussier 2003): The first question refers to the explanation of the degree of vertical integration and the mix between franchised and company-owned outlets. Starting from the ownership redirection approach in marketing (Oxenfeldt and Kelly 1968-69; Dant, Paswan, and Kaufman 1996), the following theories were developed in the last two decades: Transaction costs theory (Williamson 1985; Minkler and Park 1994), agency theory (Brickley and Dark 1987; Martin 1988; Lafontaine 1992), signalling theory (Gallini and Lutz 1992), search cost theory (Minkler 1992), incomplete contract theory (Lutz 1995; Maness 1996). More recently Lewin-Solomon (1999) explained the dual structure as a governance mechanism to promote innovations in the network. In addition, Bai and Tao (2000) presented a multi-task model of the existence of franchised and company-owned outlets. Moreover, Bradach (1997, 1998), Cliquet (2000a, b), and Sorenson and Sorensen (2000) proposed the plural form hypothesis. Bradach, Cliquet and Sorenson and Sorensen argue that the dual structure is the result of synergistic effects between franchised and company-owned outlets. According to this strategic management approach, franchised outlets are more efficient at the 'exploration' and company-owned outlet at the 'exploitation' of the profit potential of the network. In addition, Michael (2000) presented the tapered integration hypothesis. Tapered integration raises the bargaining power of the franchisor by improving the franchisor's local market information and by signalling to franchisees that the franchisor is committed to quality.

The second research question focuses on explaining the structure of franchise agreements. The fee structure (initial fees and royalties) has been comprehensively investigated. The agency cost explanation initiated by Rubin (1978), extended by Mathewson and Winter (1985), Lal (1991), Bhattacharyya and Lafontaine (1995), and tested by Brickley and Dark (1988), Norton (1988) as well as Lafontaine (1992) tries to show that franchising, characterized by revenue or profit-sharing contracts, has agency cost advantages compared to company ownership. A further explanation is offered by the screening theory (Dnes 1992). According to this theory, fixed fees and specific investments have a screening function by attracting competent franchisees. The higher the initial fees and specific investments, the more likely franchisees with high entrepreneurial capabilities are selected. An alternative explanation of the initial fees is offered by the transaction cost model of Klein (1980) and Williamson (1985). They show that the initial fee serves as a hostage in the franchise relationship. The payment of the initial fee prevents the franchisee from ex post opportunistic behaviour, i.e. from expropriating quasi rents generated by the franchiser's system-specific assets. In addition to these approaches, Gallini and Lutz (1992) present a signalling theory. High variable fees serve as a device to signal high quality investments of the franchiser in his brand name. More recently, Windsperger (2001) explains the relationship between royalties and initial fees by using the property rights theory.

In the last years some authors have studied interaction effects between contract provisions. Wimmer and Garen (1997) have shown that more specific assets act as an implicit bond and substitutes for a reduced royalty rate in inducing franchisees efforts. In addition, Brickley (1999) presented an agency cost explanation of the complementarities between mandatory advertising and area development plans, restrictions on franchisee's outside activities and area development plans, and between mandatory advertising and restrictions of outside activities. Further, Bercovitz (1999) applies transaction cost reasoning to analyse interactions between contract provisions. She found that the initial fee and the duration of franchise contracts are significant larger, the larger the relationship-specific investments. In addition, she argued that including termination conditions could increase the hostage function of specific investments. By extending Klein's self-enforcement view of contract provisions (Klein 1995), Lafontaine and Raynaud (2001) examined complementarities between residual claimancy rights and self-enforcement mechanisms, such as exclusive territory clauses, multi-unit ownership guarantees, contract renewal and termination rights. Finally, Arrunada et al. (2001) and Windsperger (2003) went further than the previous literature in that they analyzed the entire system of the allocation of decision rights and incentive mechanisms. They found some complementarities and substitutabilities between contract provisions.

The current trend in franchising research is twofold: On the one hand, there is a strong tendency toward theoretical approaches developed in economics and management, such as property rights theory, agency theory, signalling theory, transaction costs theory, strategic management approaches (especially resource-based theory), and population ecology theory. On the other hand, there is also a strong tendency toward the application of new empirical methods, such as case study methods, discrete choice models, time series and panel studies as well as survival analysis. Empirical studies focus on a large number of research questions. Especially investigations regarding international market entry through franchising, multiple unit franchising, contract duration, knowledge, strategic management and marketing issues, franchisee satisfaction, and organizational mortality are new empirical research directions.

Starting from this status of franchising research the current book has two aims: First, the book emphasizes franchising research as a theory-driven field by offering new theoretical perspectives on the degree of vertical integration and the contract design. Second, the book is an effort to present new research results on knowledge and strategic management issues, international market entry through franchising, influence of country characteristics on franchising, and regulation of franchise agreements. Hence the papers focus on the following topics:

Theoretical views on franchise governance structure
Plural forms and other hybrid organizational forms
Contract design and compensation
Knowledge and strategic management issues

International market entry through franchising
Country studies
Regulation of franchise agreements

Theoretical Views of the Franchise Governance Structure

Norton examines the nature of franchising and various business practices in terms of economic governance systems. Markets versus hierarchies, problems of collective action, and tournaments and adaptive imitation are linked to alternative types of franchise organization. Norton highlights some of the comparative advantages of alternative governance systems and derives some conclusions for marketing channel strategy.

Bercovitz investigates the franchising make-or-buy decision providing a comprehensive test of the economizing perspective of organizational choice while controlling for the potential influence of resource scarcity factors. The study extends the extant empirical franchising literature in three ways. First, it takes the outlet as the unit of analysis and explores organizational choice within the franchise system. Second, the analysis is more inclusive, simultaneously accounting for both of the component elements of the free-riding hazard. And third, it provides one of the rare empirical investigations of the adoption of multi-unit franchising – the ownership of two or more outlets by a single franchisee. The econometric analysis, using discrete choice methods, provides strong support for the hypothesis that ownership mode of individual outlets (single-unit franchise, multi-unit franchise or company-owned outlet) turns on the relative levels of the contracting hazards present.

Plural Forms and Other Hybrid Organizational Forms

Bercovitz' make-or-buy analysis is the bridge to this chapter. The plural form hypothesis is examined under different theoretical perspectives. In addition, the question of efficiency advantage of franchise contracts compared to other network forms (licence, concession and commission-affiliation) is addressed.

Windsperger formulates and tests various hypotheses from various theories regarding the dual network structure of franchising firms. By applying the property rights theory Windsperger argues that the contractual mix between company-owned and franchised outlets depends on the distribution of intangible assets between the franchisor and franchisee. Second, Windsperger compares these results with the resource scarcity and transaction cost view. According to the resource scarcity view, the proportion of company-owned outlets varies negatively with the franchisor's restraints in financial, informational and management resources. In addition, transaction cost theory states that the franchisee's specific investments mitigate the hold-up risk for the franchisor resulting in a lower degree of vertical integration. These hypotheses are tested by using data from the Austrian franchise sector. The empirical results are generally supportive of the property rights hypothesis. In addition, the informational restraint hypothesis is compatible with the property rights hypothesis regarding the influence of franchisee's local market know-how advantage on the percentage of company-owned outlets.

According to *Ehrmann and Spranger the* evolution and existence of the dual form cannot be explained along a pure principal-agent-view. They argue that the plural form may benefit from cost reduction, quality enhancement, growth stimulation and optimized risk control in contrast to pure franchise chains. Based on data of 240 franchise systems in the German franchise sector they found empirical support for the quality argument of the plural form. By running company-owned stores as well as independent franchised outlets, chains force themselves successfully into cooperative and less opportunistic behavior towards their franchisees.

Cliquet and Nguyen deals with innovation management within the plural form network. They argue that network operators face difficulties in managing innovation in networks. In addition, they address the question as to why the plural form could facilitate innovation. Finally, they establish innovation process models that highlight how innovations are made and managed in the plural form network. Data for analysis are obtained by interviews with network operators in France. On the whole, Cliquet and Nguyen‘s paper tends to show the superiority of the plural form.

Chaudey and Fadario shows that, as far as France is concerned, franchising is one of the four types of contracts within networks (license, concession, franchising, commission-affiliation) sharing the same brand name. There is a hierarchy among these four categories of contracts in accordance with the degree of restriction imposed on the retailer. They address the question as to why networks choose franchising contracts and more precisely why they opt for this degree of vertical integration. Chaudey and Fadario conduct an econometric study on French data to test the agency-theoretical argument in explaining the degree of restriction within vertical contracts.

Contract Design and Compensation

Vazquez empirically investigates the determinants of compensation provisions included in franchise contracts. The results support for both the optimal allocation of risk and double-sided moral hazard explanations for franchise contracts. The results also reveal that the value of both the initial and ongoing services provided by franchisors to franchisees strongly affects the compensation arrangements, which implies that a capital goal of these arrangements is to recover the costs of the services offered by franchisors.

Ehrmann investigates the influence of contract design and range of services offered by the franchisor on the success of the franchisor and the franchisee. The study interprets the consequences of contract design in franchising networks in terms of sales. A data set on German franchise systems generated first empirical results concerning the relation between the royalty rate and initial lump sum fee, on the one hand, and the degree of organization and sales, on the other hand. Furthermore the influence of initial investments and the degree of entrepreneurial freedom on sales was investigated. The results show that high fixed fees combined with low variable fees and a certain degree of freedom for franchisees are positive indicators for a high individual revenue of the franchisee.

Yvrande-Billon applies the transaction cost reasoning to the question of the duration of the passenger rail franchise contracts in Great Britain. For two decades, the procurement of public utilities has been engaged in a process of intensive reform. One type of organizational change that has been massively introduced is the use of franchise agreements for the provision of public services. This is the choice adopted by the reformers of the British railways, who decided to franchise the passenger rail service. But, whereas the theory on utilities restructuring recommends to turn to long-term contracting, the British policy makers have chosen to rely on short-term franchise agreements. Yvrande-Billon examines the relevance of these contractual choices. Referring to transaction cost economics, she investigates the determinants of franchise contracts duration. The results of the econometric tests show that the British reformers' contractual choices are not consistent with the theoretical propositions.

Knowledge and Strategic Management Issues

Croonen presents and illustrates a framework for understanding how and why franchise partners and partners in other forms of commercial cooperation deal with the paradox of exploration and exploitation in their relationships through time. Two levels of analysis are distinguished: the level of strategic characteristics of the franchise system and the level of relationships between the franchisor and the franchisees that are part of the franchise system. For the level of the system, it is argued that franchise systems have to balance exploration and exploitation in order to survive and prosper in their environment. The following five strategic characteristics of franchise systems reflect the franchisor's exploration and exploitation objectives: the positioning of the franchise system, the "hardness" of the franchise system, the system's entrepreneurial orientation, the degree of strategic participation of franchisees in the system and growth objectives for the system. On the relationship level, the franchise relationship between the franchisor and its franchisees is considered a specific form of strategic alliance. The following variables are distinguished for understanding both franchise partner's response strategies towards each other: the degree of strategic compatibility between the franchise partners, the degree of operational compatibility, the evaluation of available alternatives, and switching costs.

Perrigot and Cliquet show that network performance is very important both for the franchisor, who wants to promote his network, and the prospective franchisees, who want to invest in a store operated under a national or international brand name. Nevertheless, this network performance often presents some difficulties to be evaluated. This paper examines the importance of time management for the performance of franchising network, both for the franchisor and the franchisees. In addition, the difficulties linked to longitudinal studies are discussed and the survival analysis is presented as an adequate methodology.

Gupta argues that marketing organizations must establish processes to manage firm-customer connectivity across boundaries of their franchisees. Franchisees are selected based on their competencies in the specialized and task-dependent forms of activity domains designed and prescribed for them by the marketing strategists at the firm. Franchisees may excel at their domains but that may not necessarily result in optimal firm-customer connectivity since the strength of the connectivity is only as much as the strength of the weakest link. To address this challenge, an integrative framework is developed that identifies and integrates the value of different approaches to managing marketing channels that are often presented as incompatible in the literature. The framework describes three progressively complex types of peripheries: course, concept and conduct. The examples from gasoline, mobile telephony, health care, credit cards, fast food, school education, and automobile industry from the Indian market are presented to illustrate the conceptual strength of this framework

International Market Entry Through Franchising

Duniach-Smith examines the international entry mode choice in a franchise setting. Based on the market entry mode and international franchising literature, she argues that both organizational and environmental determinants influence the franchisor's choice of entry mode (direct franchising, foreign direct investment, area development agreement, joint venture and master franchising). Expert opinions are used to identify the most influential determinants of entry mode choice by international franchisors. However, the results of the Delphi panel composed of 35 international franchising experts show that the determinants of the international franchising entry mode differ somewhat from those identified for entry mode choice in general. The findings suggest that a specific conceptual framework is needed to explain entry mode choice by international franchisors.

The paper of *Jarmalaite and Sekundo* is the first attempt to find reasons for decision-making factors related to the international expansion of Lithuanian franchise companies. On the basis of two case studies concerning Lithuanian franchisors that have entered the Latvian market in order to expand their franchising network, they investigate the motivating factors and their influences on the market entry mode. Twelve factors are identified and critically evaluated, and five propositions that reflect the decision-making considerations for Lithuanian franchisers regarding the choice of entry mode to Latvia are developed.

Country Studies

Tuunanen describes and compares the provisions of the franchise contracts and pre-sale disclosures to prospective franchisees in the USA and Finland. A fact that makes the investigation especially interesting is that no franchising specific legislation exists in Finland. Whereas in the USA franchisors are by a directive of the Federal Trade Commission required to publicly disclose key information on their franchise systems. Two separate samples are developed for the study. The member franchisors of the *International Franchise Association* and franchisors listed in *Entrepreneur Magazine's* "Franchise 500" are sampled for the US data and in Finland the member franchisors of the *Finnish Franchising Association* are surveyed. The obtained data sets from the two countries are combined and statistically analyzed to reveal differences and similarities between franchise contract characteristics. The empirical results indicate significant differences in franchise contract provisions.

Wadsworth, Tuunanen and Haines investigate differences between franchisee satisfaction in Finland and the United States. They compare Finnish and American franchisee satisfaction levels across eight dimensions of franchisee satisfaction. Results show franchisees in Finland and the United States are overall equally satisfied. Data analysis revealed that for four of the eight dimensions, a statistical difference exists between franchisee perceptions in the two countries. United States franchisees are more satisfied than Finnish franchisees with the financial, entrepreneurial control, communication and franchise contract dimensions. A multiple regression model of franchisee satisfaction is able to explain 89 percent of the variation of franchisee general satisfaction with the variation of seven dimensions: financial, relation, support services, brand image, entrepreneurial control, contract and training.

Torikka analyzes the effectiveness of the Finnish franchisee-training program. The program aims to find people interested in franchising and to give them the essential skills and knowledge a franchisee needs. Additional goal is to help the trainees to choose a franchise. In total, more than 200 trainees graduated from the first ten programs held in 1999-2001. The graduates comprise the sample of the current study. The paper analyzes the effectiveness of the franchisee-training program by describing the career shifts of the trainees.

Regulation of Franchise Agreements

Hueschelrath argues that franchise agreements can be an efficient way to solve the firm's distribution problem with certain products, services or concepts in certain environments. Hueschelrath discusses the essential antitrust implications of franchise agreements. First, he gives a brief overview of the evolution of antitrust regulations concerning franchise agreements in the United States and the European Union. In addition he argues, why and how firms choose certain franchise agreements including certain restrictions (the so-called 'vertical restraints') to distribute their products. Furthermore, he shows why and under which circumstances such agreements might get into difficulties with antitrust regulations. Finally Hueschelrath discusses the implications for antitrust policy.

Future Research Topics

There are many ways to extend the current body of knowledge regarding franchising. We grasp the opportunity at the end of the introduction to this volume to identify a few directions/topics for future research. A number of issues regarding the governance of franchises and the different degrees of coverage by the business format will be addressed. We will focus on bottom-up franchises, Gibrat's law, cognition, and complementarity.

Bottom-up Franchises

Research regarding the plurally organized franchisor usually positions it between the franchise consisting entirely of company-owned outlets and the franchise consisting entirely of franchised outlets. A common feature of these three governance structures is that the franchisor has residual rights of control (Hart and Moore 1990; Rajan and Zingales 1998). However, governance structures other than the top-down franchise are possible regarding a business format relationship. Hart and Moore (1990) suggests a bottom-up franchise, i.e. a franchise where the downstream franchisees jointly own the upstream franchisor, for incentive purposes. Their theory predicts that the allocation of asset ownership will be downstream when the assets at the downstream stage of production are more important than at the upstream stage. The question is why these bottom-up franchises are hardly observed. A bottom-up franchise may provide protection and countervailing power for small franchisees against a powerful, and potentially opportunistic franchisor. More generally, a bottom-up franchise may create value because '...many franchisees place value on both security and independence' (Hennessy 2003, p 460). One problem of bottom-up franchises will be collective decision making. However, this cannot be the entire story. There are for example many agricultural cooperatives, where many small farmers own jointly an enterprise at a downstream stage of production. Further research is desirable.

A characteristic feature of franchising is that it usually specifies a method of operating. This is called the business format. Many variations exist regarding the extent and direction of the coverage of the business format. A crude distinction is trade name franchising and business format franchising. Trade name franchising is franchising without a business format, while business format franchising entails a specification of the method of operating in addition to the trade name. Does the efficient coverage of the business format differ between company-owned and franchised outlets?

Gibrat's Law

One of the amazing features of franchising is the huge variation in the number of outlets of various franchises. For example, Ehrmann and Spranger report in this volume that McDonald's had 26,236 outlets in 2001, whereas Purified-Water-to-Go had just 51 in 2001. This raises not only questions regarding the equilibrium size distribution of franchises, but also regarding the pattern of franchise growth. The seminal study regarding (the evolution of) firm size distribution is Gibrat (1931). Expected firm growth rates are believed to be independent of firm size, i.e. Gibrat's Law, and the equilibrium size distribution of firms is approximately log-normal. Recent empirical evidence (Cabral and Mata 2003) questions both beliefs, which is based on more complete data sets than used in the past. Selection as well as age play a role in the evolution of firm size distribution, but financing constraints dominate according to Cabral and Mata. However, there is also the empirical result by Johnson et al. (2002, p 1336)) that '... secure property rights are both necessary and sufficient to induce investment by entrepreneurs.' Weak property rights seem to be a tighter constraint on private sector investment than limited access to external finance. This seems to be in line with the scepticism of economists about the franchise form as a vehicle for financing expansion. The abundant data regarding franchises may provide a fertile source to select out these positions.

Cognition

The limited cognitive capacities of humans have to deal with a world they cannot grasp entirely. Humans reduce the complexity of the world by focusing on the local world surrounding them and the structure in this local world. A franchise structures and simplifies the local world by the adoption of a business format. It specifies an operation method imposing (some) uniformity across franchisees. This has substantial advantages in terms of communication with the outside world. However, there are also several disadvantages. A well-known concern regarding the business format is that the imposed uniformity might stifle innovation. This is obvious when certain choices are not allowed. The choice of business format is still not innocuous when there is choice, because information will be channeled in certain directions. It will therefore to a certain extent direct the process of exploration and exploitation.

Problems in organizations are often related to information. There may be asymmetric information, a lack of information, or wrong information. We illustrate the latter by an example regarding the relationship between the way organizations are structured and the generation of wrong information. There are usually several ways in which information can be channeled from franchisees to the franchisor (Hammond 1994). The channeling of information is important because nobody can all by himself process all the available information. Information is compressed in the decision making process in such a way that it can be comprehended. An important insight is that every business format, or every slicing of the incredible amount of information, entails inevitably a certain bias in the provision of information. A specific business format is only sensitive to certain kinds of information. This inevitability implies that the choice of business format is a choice between different kinds of biases. Research regarding the cognitive aspects of business formats is desired in order to become aware of them and to take some precautions against the biases generated by it.

Complementarity

Organizations are complex mechanisms for coordinating and motivating individuals' activities. An example of a complex mechanism for the motivation of individual activities in franchises is the plural form. It entails that the franchise consists of a mix between company-owned and franchised outlets. The contracting externalities (Holmström and Milgrom 1991; 1994) between these two different allocations of authority in one organization is not well understood. A question regarding the fit between decision authority and the intensity of incentives in the plural form regards the synergy between the contract mix and the contract terms, i.e. does a company-owned outlet have the same royalty and fee structure as a franchised outlet? The synergy between these attributes probably breaks the symmetric treatment of company-owned and franchised outlets.

Providing the right incentives to invest is an important issue in organizational design, but there is much more to organizations. A richer approach considers also work practices, strategy, products and services, supplier and customer relationships. The fit between organizational, accounting, communication, financial, production, logistics and marketing attributes of franchises becomes important. Increasing synergies between these attributes will have an impact on the investment decisions of each party. Investments in one part of the franchise must be coordinated with investments in other parts to obtain optimal performance. Such an approach requires a system of attributes view (Milgrom and Roberts 1990). The crucial concept regarding the relationship between the various instruments is complementarity. Complementarity entails that doing more of one activity increases the return to doing more of the other activity. It gears the attention towards the interdependencies between these various attributes of franchises, and results in the identification of viable combinations of attributes.

References

1. Arrunada B, Garicano L, Vazquez L (2001) Contractual Allocation of Decision Rights and Incentives: The Case of Automobile Distribution. Journal of Law, Economics and Organization 17:256 – 283
2. Bai CE, Tao Z (2001) Contract Mix in Franchising, Journal of Economics and Management Strategy. 9:85 – 113
3. Bercovitz J (1999) An Analysis of Contract Provisions in Business Format Franchise Agreements: In J Stanworth, D Purdy (eds.), Proceedings of the Conference of the 13th Conference of the International Society of Franchising

4. Bhattacharyya S, Lafontaine F (1995) Double-Sided Moral Hazard and the Nature of Share Contracts. RAND Journal of Economics 26:761 – 781
5. Bradach JL (1997) Using the Plural Form in the Management of Restaurant Chains, Administrative Science Quarterly. 42:276 – 303
6. Bradach JL (1998) Franchise Organizations. Boston
7. Brickley JA, Dark. FH (1987) The Choice of Organizational Form: The Case of Franchising. Administrative Science Quarterly 42:276 - 303
8. Brickley JA (1999) Incentive Conflicts and Contractual Restraints: Evidence from Franchising. Journal of Law and Economics 42:745 - 774
9. Brickley JA, Smith CW, Zimmerman JL (2002) Managerial Economics and Organizational Architecture, McGraw Hill, Irvin
10. Cabral LM, Mata J (2003) On the Evolution of the Firm Size Distribution: Facts and Theory. American Economic Review 93: 1075 – 1090
11. Cliquet G (2000a) Plural Forms in Store Networks: A Model for Store Network Evolution. International Review of Retail, Distribution and Consumer Research 10:369 - 387
12. Cliquet G (2000b) Plural Form Networks and Retail Life Cycle, An Explorative Investigation of Hotel Franchised/Company-owned Systems in France. Journal of Business and Entrepreneurship 12:75 – 98
13. Dant RP, Paswan AK, Kaufman PJ (1996) What we Know about Ownership Redirection in Franchising: A Meta-Analysis. Journal of Retailing 72:429 - 444
14. Dnes AW (1992) Unfair Contractual Practices and Hostages in Franchise Contracts. Journal of Institutional and Theoretical Economics 148:484 – 504
15. Gallini N, Lutz N (1992) Dual Distribution and Royalty Fees in Franchising. Journal of Law, Economics and Organization 8:471-501
16. Gibrat R (1931) Les Inegalites Economiques. Applications: Aux Inegalites des Richesses, a la Concentration des Entreprises, aux Populations des Villes, aux Statistiques des Familas, etc., d'une Loi Nouvelle: La Loi de l'Effect Proportionelle, Sirey, Paris
17. Hammond TH (1994) Structure, Strategy, and the Agenda of the Firm, in Rumelt RR. and DE Schendel (eds.), Fundamental Issues in Strategy. Harvard Business School Press, Boston, pp 97-154
18. Hart O, Norms and the Theory of the Firm, in Brousseau E and Glachant J (eds.), The Economics of Contract in Prospect and Retrospect. Cambridge University Press, Cambridge, forthcoming
19. Hart OD, Moore J (1990) Property Rights and the Nature of the Firm. Journal of Political Economy 98:1119-1158
20. Hendrikse GWJ (2003) Economics and Management of Organizations. McGraw Hill, London
21. Hennessy DA (2003) Property Rights, Productivity, and the Nature of Noncontractible Actions in a Franchise System. Journal of Economic Behavior and Organization 52:443 – 468
22. Holmström BR, Milgrom P (1991) Multitask Principal-Agent Analysis: Incentive Contracts, Asset Ownership, and Job Design. Journal of Law, Economics, and Organization 7:S24-52
23. Holmström BR, Milgrom P (1994) The Firm as an Incentive System. American Economic Review 84:972-991
24. Johnson SJ, McMillan, Woodruff C (2002) Property Rights and Finance. American Economic Review 92:1335 - 1356
25. Klein B (1980) Transaction Cost Determinants of 'Unfair' Contractual Arrangements. American Economic Review 70:356 – 362
26. Klein B (1995) The Economics of Franchise Contracts. Journal of Corporate Finance 2: 9 – 38

27. Klein B, Crawford R, Alchian A (1978) Vertical Integration, Appropriable Rents, and the Competitive Contracting Process. Journal of Law and Economics 21:297 – 326
28. Lafontaine F (1992) Agency Theory and Franchising: Some Empirical Results. RAND Journal of Economics 23:263 - 283
29. Lafontaine F, Shaw KL (2001) Targeting Managerial Control: Evidence from Franchising. RAND Journal of Economics (in print)
30. Lafontaine F, Raynaud E (2000) Créances Résiduelles et Flux de Rentes comme Mecanisms Incitatifs dans les Contrats de Franchise: Complements ou Substituts. Revue d' Economie Industrielle 92 :255 – 276
31. Lal R (1990) Improving Channel Coordination Through Franchising. Marketing Science 9:299 - 318
32. Lewin-Solomon SB (1999) Innovation and Authority in Franchise Systems: An Empirical Exploration of Plural Form. Working Paper, Iowa State University, July
33. Lutz NA (1995) Ownership Rights and Incentives in Franchising. Journal of Corporate Finance 2:103 - 130
34. Maness R (1996) Incomplete Contracts and the Choice Between Vertical Integration and Franchising. Journal of Economic Behaviour and Organization 31:101 – 115
35. Martin RE (1988) Franchising and Risk Management. American Economic Review 78:954 - 968
36. Mathewson F, Winter R (1985) The Economics of Franchise Contracts. Journal of Law and Economics 28:503 - 526
37. Michael SC (2000) Investments to Create Bargaining Power: The Case of Franchising. Strategic Management Journal 21:497 – 514
38. Milgrom P, Roberts J (1990) The Economics of Modern Manufacturing: Technology, Strategy, and Organization. American Economic Review 80: 511-528
39. Minkler AP (1992) Why Firms Franchise: A Search Cost Theory. Journal of Institutional and Theoretical Economics 148:240 - 259
40. Minkler A, Park TA (1994) Asset Specificity and Vertical Integration in Franchising. Review of Industrial Organization 9: 409 – 423
41. Norton SW(1988) An Empirical Look at Franchising as an Organizational Form. Journal of Business 61:197 – 219
42. Oxenfeldt AR, Kelly AO (1968-69) Will Successful Franchise Systems Ultimately Become Wholly-owned Chains?, Journal of Retailing 44:69 - 83
43. Pénard T, Raynaud E, Saussier S (2003) Théorie des Contrats et des Réseaux de Franchise: Analyse et Enseignement. Working Paper, CREREG, Université de Rennes 1
44. Rajan R, Zingales L (1998) Power in a Theory of the Firm, Quarterly Journal of Economics 113:387- 432
45. Rubin P (1978) The Theory of the Firm and the Structure of the Franchise Contract. Journal of Law and Economics 21:223 - 233
46. Sorenson O, Sorensen JB (2001) Finding the Right Mix: Organizational Learning, Plural Forms and Franchise Performance. Strategic Management Journal 22:713 – 724
47. Williamson OE (1985) The Economic Institution of Capitalism. New York
48. Wimmer BS, Garen JE (1997) Moral Hazard, Asset Specificity, Implicit Bonding, and Compensation: The Case of Franchising. Economic Inquiry 35:544 – 554
49. Windsperger J (2001) The Fee Structure in Franchising: A Property Rights View. Economics Letters 73:219 - 226
50. Windsperger J (2003) Complementarities and Substitutabilities in Franchise Contracting: Evidence from the German Franchise Sector. Journal of Management and Governance 7:291 – 213

Part A:

Theoretical Views of the Franchise Governance Structure

Towards a More General Theory of Franchise Governance

Seth W. Norton

Wheaton College, Department of Business and Economics
Wheaton, IL 60187 USA
Seth.Norton@Wheaton.edu

Abstract. This chapter examines the nature of franchising and various business practices in terms of economic governance systems. Markets versus hierarchies, problems of collective action, and tournaments and adaptive imitation are linked to alternative types of franchise organization using established franchising taxonomies and previous research on franchise organization. Common activities of franchised operations are examined in light of governance systems. The chapter highlights some of the comparative advantages of alternative governance systems. The chapter also includes some implications for marketing channel strategy.

1 Introduction

Franchising is a remarkable organizational form. In common economic parlance, it is a hybrid organizational form (Brickley and Dark 1987; Norton 1988a; Shane 1996). In a related vein, Coughlan, Anderson, Stern, and El-Ansary (2001) describe franchising as an "inherently contradictory marketing channel." There is ambivalence to independent firms acting in consort both in investing in relationship specific assets and carrying out continuously coordinated routine business

Franchising is also remarkable in its success. As a marketing channel, it thrives in North American and Europe and is emerging in many nonwestern economies. Coughlan et. al. (2001) indicate that more than 40 percent of retail sales in the US pass through some franchised operations and some observers project the fraction will soon exceed 50 percent. Moreover, after a much later introduction in Europe, franchising is now surging there as well. Indeed, there is considerable evidence that franchising as an organizational form is flourishing globally.

It is noteworthy that scholars of franchising have made remarkable progress in the past few decades in understanding franchising. Important theoretical and empirical studies have provided coherent explanations for the existence of franchised marketing channels and understanding the conditions that promote its existence. Moreover, related research has enlightened our understanding of various features of franchising—its fundamental economic organization, the choice between franchised and non-franchised channels, the choice between company-owned and franchisee-owned units, the structure of franchise contracts, the determinants of franchise fees and royalties, the nature of termination procedures, the role of capital structure, and others (Brickley and Dark 1987; Dnes 1993; Lafontaine 1992; Mathewson and Winter 1985; Minkler 1992; Norton, 1988a, 1988b, 1995; Rubin 1978; Sen 1993; Shane 1996).

Despite the prodigious quantity of research on franchising, some important gaps exist in our understanding of this organizational form. Moreover, continuing evolving markets create new challenges to understanding franchised marketing channels. One important gap that is a foundation of evolving franchised arrangements is the nature of franchise system governance. While some progress has been made in this area, governance remains a fertile area for franchise research. For example, Bradach's (1998) study of five major restaurant chains that use franchised marketing channels provides considerable detail regarding governance issues, identifying who has the right to make strategic and tactical decisions and how those decisions are made. Similarly, Windsperger (2003) examines the link between decision rights in franchised systems and the incidence of intangible knowledge assets of franchisors and franchisees. However, a unifying framework for analyzing the governance of franchised systems does not exist. The intent of this paper is to examine several types of alternative franchise governance arrangements in light of core concepts in the new institutional economics and related literature. Besides expanding our understanding of alternative forms of franchising, the framework attempts to add to our understanding of the evolution of individual franchise systems over the course of a franchise system's life and in response to innovations.

It is essential to recognize that although governance issues are often linked to ownership, they are not identical. Indeed, Hansman (1996) documents numerous cases where they are separate. Consider the largely publicly owned corporation. Ownership rights to residual income rest with shareholders, yet the overall governance rests with directors and managers. In franchised arrangements, ownership and governance often coincide for franchisees but numerous decision rights affecting franchisees are in the franchisors' purview. Thus, while much franchise research addresses the distribution of company owned versus franchisee owned outlets, the issue of governance is much broader and subtler than the determinants of the dichotomous ownership issue.

The remainder of the chapter is organized as follows. Section 2 identifies three different forms of franchising and their dominant characteristics. Section 3 identifies three governance arrangements that are foundational to the core of modern economies and describes the coordinating role of the respective governance systems. Section 4 links the governance arrangements with the franchise taxonomies and operations. Section 5 discusses some implications for marketing channel strategy. Section 6 contains a summary and conclusions.

2 Forms of Franchising

Franchising is a common term in daily life, business discourse, and the law. Nevertheless, the term is used in different contexts and with different meanings. Coughlan, Anderson, Stern, and El-Ansary (2001, p 546) employ the European Union's description of franchising as a "...package of industrial or intellectual property rights." The EU identifies three features of franchising—a common name or sign with a uniform presentation of the premises, communication of know-how from franchisor to franchisee, and continuing provision of commercial or technical services by the franchisor to the franchisee.

Coughlan, et. al. (2001) point out that the EU description may be too restrictive. Franchising has been associated with a variety of institutional arrangements. In US business history, franchising has been the declared form of distribution in numerous prominent industries—e.g. automobiles, farm equipment, and sewing machines. Accordingly, Coughlan et. al. (2001) note that when franchising is conceived more broadly than the EU description, the border between franchising and other marketing channels is not clear.

Despite potential ambiguity, scholars have developed taxonomies for franchising. Stern and El-Ansary (1988) describe some of these. Some taxonomies focus on the type of business—e.g. accounting and tax services, ice cream stores, vending machines, etc. Other taxonomies focus on a contractual feature—leasing, co-ownership, co-management, etc. For tractability, Coughlan, et. al. (2001) provide a simple, workable dichotomy—authorized franchised systems and business format franchising.[1]

2.1 Authorized Franchised Systems

Authorized franchised systems are also known as product and trade name franchising. Sellers are known as dealers, distributors, resellers and agents. These selling units can operate at the wholesale or retail level. Wholesale examples include soft drink bottlers or distributors of electrical and electronic equipment. Retail examples include appliances, automobiles, computers, household furniture, televisions, and tires.

Products are sold through the respective resellers, but there is considerable control by the manufacturer regarding the product presentation, and manufacturers can provide substantial business support for business operations, product specific training, technical support, advertising, and selecting outlet locations.

---

[1] Vaughn (1979) identifies four types of channels. The first three would fall under the authorized franchised system, but differ by the members of the channel. Type I is manufacturer-retailer systems—e.g. gasoline service stations; type II is manufacturer-wholesaler systems—e.g. soft drink syrup manufacturers and bottlers; type III is wholesale-retailer systems—e.g. drug or paint stores. Type IV is "trademark/trade name" licensor-retailers and fits closely with the business format category.

2.2 Business Format Franchising

Business format franchising is the form of franchising most commonly associated with the franchise concept (Coughlan et. al. 2001). A franchisor licenses an entire way of doing business under a brand name. This variety of franchising is prevalent in accounting services, auto accessories, auto rentals, campgrounds, cleaning systems, fast food, food retailing, motels/hotels, real estate, and schools.[2] Business format franchising involves packaging a mode of business, attracting a supply of capable and dedicated entrepreneurs, selecting superior prospects, training them in the minute details of the business operations, providing assistance in setting up the business at specific outlets, and maintaining an ongoing business that is profitable for the franchisor and the collective franchisees. The relationship entails continued provision of beneficial services such as advertising and new product development by the franchisor and continued provision of royalties from the franchisees to the franchisors, as well as new product development and local promotion by the franchisees.

2.3 Franchisee Confederations

Franchisees are noted for their independent spirits and style (Bradach 1998), but they certainly recognize the value of collective action in communicating with the franchisor organization and in concerted efforts when some business action warrants activity on a scale greater than that of individual franchisees. Consequently, franchisees often organize themselves into confederations.

Franchisee organizations are common both for authorized franchised systems (Pashigian 1961) and business format franchising (Vaughn 1979). Moreover, franchisors treat them seriously, due to the potentially adversarial relationship and due the enormous potential gains from franchisor and franchisee cooperation (Enrico and Kornbluth 1986; Bradach 1998).

In addition to franchisee associations that deal collectively with the franchisors, franchisees also organize themselves collectively for common business purposes (Bradach 1998). For example, franchisees operate purchasing cooperatives to obtain supplies for franchisees. Advertising and group marketing activities are often run through franchisee cooperatives. For example, Love (1995) reports that regional franchise advertising cooperatives emerged somewhat spontaneously in the McDonald's system so that by 1967 (only 12 years after Ray Kroc, the chain's founder, entered the franchise business) all major regional markets had them. Bradach (1998) notes that KFC, Pizza Hut, and Hardee's also relied on franchisee cooperatives.

---

[2] Note that business format franchising includes both products—e.g. fast food, and services—e.g. cleaning services, and that authorized franchised systems uniformly entail product sales.

3 Economic Governance Systems

All economic organizations, ranging from households to nation-states, must decide what is to be produced, how to produce the selected output, and how to divide the benefits of what is produced (Stigler 1987). Production is treated in the broadest possible sense to include all valuable human endeavors and treated as equal to the value of consumption. In contemporary economics, the new institutional economics approach examines institutions that address these basic economic decisions. Two institutions are particularly salient in modern economies—markets or the "price mechanism" and firms or "hierarchy." Both governance arrangements provide answers to the three questions and thus both entail the coordination of human behavior.

3.1 Markets/Price Mechanism

Solving the coordination of human effort and answering the basic economic questions through the price mechanism is somewhat mysterious because it involves multiple interactions that are not so evident. Adam Smith's term "the invisible hand" captures the mystery. Exploring the means by which markets coordinate human effort is important to delineate the roles prices play in influencing human behavior. The coordinating function of the price mechanism relies on two features of prices—prices as incentives and prices as reporters.

3.1.1 Prices as Incentives

Prices direct both buyers and sellers. Prices are a powerful means to encourage buyers and sellers to cooperate so that maximum value is attained. Prices induce producers to use inputs and technology such that costs are minimized and prices induce consumers to use products so that buyers economize on more expensive goods. Prices compel economic agents to use more expensive resources sparingly. The compulsion is paradoxical because the price system functions on mutual benefits for buyers and sellers. However, in the mystery of the invisible hand, the compulsion occurs because the parties bear the cost of not economizing and reap the benefits from doing so. Accordingly, it is common to associate the price mechanism with leading to strong motivation for people to respond sensibly and profoundly to the benefits and costs implied by the price system.

It merits noting that more than just price is captured in the price system. Despite some observers' tendency to render "quantity" decisions as in the domain of firms, quantity is well within the domain of the price mechanism. Profit maximizing behavior, either in a "perfectly competitive" market or in an oligopoly with rivals using Cournot conjectures, focuses on quantity choices. Yet these choices are central to the functioning of the price system. Simply stated, quantity decisions are strictly related to price decisions.

Similarly, product quality variations (Chamberlin 1933 or Rosen 1975) fall under the rubric of the price mechanism as do variations in the value of time to both producers and consumers (Becker 1965). In all cases, prices of commodities or implicit prices for product characteristics or the value of time, serve to compel economic agents to make choices that recognize the relative costs of their options.

The price mechanism is always subject to market failure, such as monopoly power, but the coordinating role of prices is still present. Moreover, value maximizing behavior is plausible under a wide variety of circumstances. Milgrom and Roberts (1992) state the case simply:

A vast amount of recent research in economics, both theoretical and experimental, has focused on the behavior that is induced by the incentives that arise under various market institutions. Related studies try to determine when this behavior will lead (approximately) to the efficient outcome identified by the neoclassical model. The theoretical work employs many different approaches, but the common conclusion is that in most economies with sufficiently large number of participants, competition between agents will eliminate monopoly and result in essentially competitive prices and outcomes. Furthermore, the experimental work indicates the number of participants necessary to make a market tolerably competitive need not be unrealistically large.

The incentive effects of the price mechanism constitute an important set of issues regarding marketing channel design.

3.1.2 Prices as Reporters

Prices play a second role in coordinating economic behavior. Prices have informational content regarding the willingness of buyers to acquire goods or the willingness of sellers to sell goods. The point pertains to observed transactions prices, but it also pertains to ask and bid prices. Potential buyers or sellers reveal their subjective values and their assessment of their production costs. These values or assessments ultimately may lead to market exchange.

Friedrich Hayek's interpretation of prices as reporters of information content is particularly relevant for central questions regarding economic coordination. Hayek addressed the role of the information content of prices (broadly defined) in the mid-20th century debate with Keynes and other advocates of central planning regarding the role of markets versus centralized planning in coordinating economic life—addressing the basic economic questions posed above. Some critics of market coordination stressed the lack of realism in the perfect competition model and concluded that the resultant market failure rendered central planning a superior way to direct an aggregate economy as opposed to the decentralized direction implied by the invisible hand.

Hayek did not deny the absence of perfect information in actual markets. Instead, Hayek compared the quality of information in an admittedly imperfect, decentralized price system with the quality of information for decisions rendered by a centralized planner. Hayek asserted that the imperfect information dispersed among decentralized decision makers in a price mechanism led to superior outcomes than those based on aggregations of data employed by central planners who used summary data to direct the basic economic decisions of decentralized decision makers.

Hayek's contention points to possible "aggregation bias" as the term is used in statistics but more importantly it points to a decision making relevancy gap. Because producers have heterogeneous endowments and deal with heterogeneous potential consumers, production and consumption decisions rest critically on *local* decisions. Remote central planners have the wrong data and hence cannot make the right decisions. Hayek's argument is amplified by the consideration that *change* characterizes all economic life and hence localized information is even more important. Hayek's (1945) argument is straightforward.

> If we agree that the economic problem of society is mainly one of rapid adaptation to changes in the particular circumstances of time and place, decisions must be left to the people who are familiar with these circumstances, who know directly of the relevant changes and the resources immediately available to meet them. We cannot expect that this problem will be solved by first communicating all this knowledge to a central board which, after integrating all knowledge, issues its orders. We must solve it by some form of decentralization.

Jensen and Meckling (1991) extend Hayek's point to questions of organizational design. They distinguish between general knowledge that is transferred at low costs and specific knowledge that is costly to transfer. In the latter case, Jensen and Meckling argue for the co-location of the specific knowledge with decision-making rights and authority to act upon the specialized knowledge.

3.2 Hierarchy

Williamson (1975) synthesizes some important themes in disparate and sometimes ignored writings on economic organization. Williamson presents markets and hierarchies as alternative instruments in organizing economic production. The concept had foundations in Barnard's (1938) observations that authority is employed in organizations to solve complex problems in coordination and adaptations as well as in Simon's (1951) assertion that the authority concept is foundational to the employment relationship and ultimately to wide ranges of problem solving in human organizations (Simon 1962). Williamson's contributions point to both the nature of hierarchy and its comparative advantage in basic economic coordination.

3.2.1 Fiat

Williamson (1996) characterizes hierarchy or internal organization as governance by fiat. Fiat means one party directs another. To be sure, voluntary acceptance of a relationship governed by the fiat of anther party means that the fiat will be circumscribed in a world with reasonable mobility and opportunities for those who are willing to accept such a relationship. Simon (1976) refers to the limits of fiat as "zones of acceptance." Moreover, government by fiat requires some doctrinal forbearance on the part of the parties involved and the legal system (Williamson 1996).

It is noteworthy that hierarchy entails a superior-subordinate relationship that is asymmetrical (Casson 1994). The roles cannot be reversed. Hierarchy is strongly linked with specialization. Hierarchy typically means unity of command—one person at the top, spanning—several subordinates for one superior, and stacking—one person's subordinate is another person's superior (clearly only with reference to the middle ranks). At the core of hierarchical operations are the practices of monitoring and control. Superiors observe and evaluate subordinates and circumscribe subordinates behavior to conform to the ultimate strategy of the hierarchy.

Hierarchy is an unpopular term in the contemporary world. The term *command, fiat*, or *order* is widely viewed as anachronistic in an egalitarian age. Nevertheless, the ubiquity of hierarchies in economies with free exchange indicates people's willingness to accept employment in hierarchies and attests to the long run efficiency of hierarchical governance; the arrangement survives. Moreover, hierarchies in practice contain many features that are decidedly not fiat-like. Some of these entail compensation policies based on motivation by reward (Simon 1951) and hence resemble coordination by the price mechanism. However, governing through hierarchy also typically involves employee loyalty and organizational identification. Hierarchies develop cultures that promote achievement of the fundamental goals of the hierarchies.

3.2.2 *Incentives versus Adaptability*

Williamson (1996) provides additional insights into the nature of hierarchy. While hierarchy has "low powered" incentives compared to market coordination, hierarchy permits greater cooperation and less conflict under various circumstances. While the price mechanism is more effective in dealing with adaptation to changes in demand and supply so individuals can adjust to changing conditions as Hayek argued, hierarchy is the better governance system for dealing with adaptation where group cooperation is valued. Moreover, the comparative advantage of hierarchy in cooperative adaptation is likely to occur when the costs of using the price mechanism—transactions costs, are relatively high. Williamson (1985) attributes that condition to situations where the market participants have invested in specialized assets. Demsetz (1995) and Spulber (1999) identify transactions costs with the process of exchanging information. In either case, when transactions costs are present, hierarchy offers coordination advantages.

3.3 The Logic of Collective Action and Problems of Social Choice

While markets and hierarchies are foundational to all economic systems, they do not exhaust the set of foundational institutions common to all of life, especially to marketing channel design and franchising. Two problems—the "free riding" incentives associated with varieties of public goods (Olson 1965) and the difficulties agreeing on group action when individuals have different preference for alternative actions (Arrow 1963) impede cooperative behavior and its attendant benefits.

The logic of collective action addresses problems associated with the supply of public goods, i.e. goods where the benefits are nonexcludable—available to all and nonrival—the same good is consumable by multiple parties. For example, the benefits of mine-sweeping operations in an international waterway are nonexcludable and nonrival. Public goods have the undesirable property of being undersupplied because self-interested parties have an incentive to free ride on other people's provision. If that practice is prevalent and enough people do free ride, the good will be undersupplied. Despite the discouraging prospects of suboptimal provision, public goods can be supplied at closer to optimal levels if decision makers use "selective incentives" and various "institutional designs." Considerable human ingenuity focuses on developing incentives and institutions that at least partially solve the undersupply problem.

It is also noteworthy that varieties of the collective action problems exist with imperfect public goods. These include goods that are nonrival but excludable, such as concerts, or goods that are nonexcludable but rival, such as underground pools of crude oil. In these cases, the problem of collective action leads to congestion or excessive depletion.

The problem of social choice (Arrow 1963) provides some related difficulties for collective action when multiple potential strategies exist. When group members have well specified preferences or rankings of the strategies, but the parties in the group are sufficiently diverse in their preferences or rankings, an agreed-upon strategy may be impossible. In Miller's (1992) terms, an organization of. "... instability, indecisiveness, inefficiency, or manipulability" could result. Majority rule would not help. A "dictatorship" may be the only means to instill a consistent course of action.

4 Governance Arrangements and Franchised Systems

4.1 Optimization and Governance Alignment

To examine the relationship between a franchise governance system and basic economic decisions, consider the simple example of single local retail outlet. The manager must decide the quantity of labor to use—the mix between labor and capital. The simplified textbook optimization problem is

$$\underset{K,L}{Max.}\, Q_f = \alpha_f K^{\beta} L^{\delta} + \lambda(rK + wL - C) \tag{1}$$

where Q is output, K and L are the quantities of capital and labor, r and w are the prices of capital and labor, α, β, and γ are conventional parameters in the Cobb-Douglas production function, and C equals total costs. The subscript, f, is used to denote that the local outlet is owned by a franchisee. α_f is commonly identified as a technological state parameter, but it is just as easy to view it as governance parameter, or as a technological parameter embedded in a governance context.

The first order conditions imply[3]

$$\frac{MP_{L_f}}{w_f} = \frac{MP_{K_f}}{r_f} \qquad (2)$$

where MP_L and MP_K are the marginal products of labor and capital. The alignment governance issue would occur if the central planner—in this case the centralized franchisor, would impose its standard of labor intensity leading to

$$\frac{MP_{L_c}}{w_c} \neq \frac{MP_{K_f}}{r_f} \qquad (3)$$

where the subscript c refers to the franchisor.[4] The inequality holds unless

$$\frac{MP_{L_c}}{W_c} = \frac{MP_{L_f}}{w_f} \qquad (4)$$

If the optimal ratios of the marginal products of labor to wages for the company owned outlets are not the same as those of a franchisee owned local outlet, a governance arrangement that imposed the franchisor's optimum on the franchisee would mean that the franchisee would operate at a suboptimal level. Of course, if the franchisor knew the appropriate mix of labor and capital for the local franchised outlet, the franchisor would have no reason to mandate a misaligned arrangement. However, Hayek's point is that central planners, the franchisor in this case, are often ignorant of local variations in economic conditions and thus his perspective implies possible mandated misalignment if the franchisor imposed a uniform standard that differed from local conditions.

Some evidence indicates that franchisor determined levels of labor utilization are not much different from market determined ones. Bradach (1998) reports that the nature of the business operation largely determines labor utilization. Centralized restaurant chains develop "labor grids" with a fixed amount of labor utilization. Franchisees also often follow the same grid. However, there is also evidence (Bradach 1998) that franchisee operations are sometimes more labor intensive than company owned operations. At both Hardee's and KFC, franchisees tend to add extra labor and to reconfigure operations so that more labor is required. However, the relevant point is not more or less labor, it is the fact that a hierarchically imposed operating configuration can lead to suboptimal operations if local conditions vary from the franchisor's uniform standard.

These examples are simplistic and only illustrate the basic problem. In more complex examples, not only the cost side of the production process, but also the

---

[3] $MP_{L_f} = \delta\alpha_f K_f^{\beta} L_f^{\delta-1}$ and $MP_{K_f} = \beta\alpha_f K_f^{\beta-1} L_f^{\delta}$

[4] $MP_{L_c} = \delta\alpha_c K_c^{\beta} L_c^{\delta-1}$

revenue side and the integration of the revenue and cost sides, are governance issues. Consider the introduction of Hardee's breakfast biscuits, an enormously popular and profitable product innovation (Bradach 1998). The biscuit was the product of a franchisee's innovation. The chain experimented with the product and wanted to introduce it in a prepared format whereas the franchisee innovation entailed homemade, i.e. locally made, biscuits. The latter process was far more labor intensive but seemingly preferred by customers. Eventually, the chain adopted the franchisee version. However, the story underscores the possible existence of differences in operations that are linked to governance systems. The more general point is that different governance systems have different features that affect franchise operations. An important part of successful marketing channel design is applying the governance systems in a value maximizing manner. Considerations of the salient features of governance systems, the core features of forms of franchising, and various features of business activities underlie the basics of franchising strategy.

A central task facing the franchisor in designing and adapting a franchise system is to structure a governance system that combines elements of the governance systems identified above. Focusing just on the optimal input mix on the cost side, the maximizing task facing the managers of the franchise system is shown in equation (5).

$$\underset{K,L}{Max.}\, Q_{System} = Q_{f_1} + Q_{f_2} + Q_{f_3} + ... + Q_N + \sum_{j=1}^{M} Q_C = \sum_{i=1}^{N} \alpha_{fi} K_f^{\beta} L_f^{\gamma} + \sum_{j=1}^{M} \alpha_{cj} K_c^{\beta} L_c^{\gamma} \quad (5)$$

subject to the corresponding cost constraints for each unit as in equation (1).

Much franchising research has dealt with issues that determine the relative size of M and N—the proportion of franchised and company-owned units and the distribution of those alternative forms within franchised systems. Incentive issues, information issues and resource constraints are prominent in that literature. The governance issue is related, but focuses on determining the nature of the relationship, including important features related to the revenue side of business—advertising, pricing, new product development, and others. Designing a governance system for the franchisees and the interaction of the franchisees with company-owned operations must be a subtle as well as a difficult task. The existing literature suggests that system design must blend the net benefits of the governance systems and match the governance system to various market parameters, technology, the nature of the business, and others.

4.2 Analogs with Franchised Systems

Observed franchised systems reflect different governance systems that the franchisors deem appropriate for their franchisees. These can be described in terms of the three governance systems described above.

4.2.1 Authorized Franchised Systems

The dominating feature of authorized franchised systems is coordination by the price mechanism. The observation is borne out by examples in the literature. The examples relate to the two coordinating roles of the price mechanism—incentives and local information advantages.

Pashigian (1961) provides an exhaustive account of the economics and institutional details of franchised automobile dealer system in the US. An important marketing channel coordination issue is the "double marginalization" problem of excessive dealer markups. The net effect is that manufacture profits and the sum of manufacturer and dealer profits are reduced by excessively high dealer markups. The simple solution historically used in the US auto industry was "dealer forcing"—the use of dealer quotas to compel dealers to lower their margins.

A second example is in soft drink bottling. Enrico and Kornbluth (1986) describe Pepsico's strategy in dealing with high domestic prices for sugar during 1983. Pepsico raised the price of concentrate syrup sold to their franchised bottlers. To offset that price increase, bottlers were permitted to substitute high fructose corn syrup for up to 50 percent of the sugar they had purchased. While the control of the type of sweetener is a hierarchical feature, the control mechanism is still strongly linked to the price mechanism—prices and quantities.

In the automobile industry, the manufacturer's ability to pursue that simple strategy may have been circumscribed by court decisions and legislation, but the existence of that simple contractual device combined with selling products at a wholesale or "dealer" price provides a powerful incentive mechanism to coordinate franchised dealers behavior. Other contractual arrangements also exist, but the role of prices as incentives, i.e. use of the wholesale price plus related stipulations, serves to govern the relationship.

The US auto industry also provides an example of local information in market coordination for the franchised dealer system. One explanation put forth for the existence of the franchised system of automobile distribution was the existence of trade-ins of used cars. Used cars come in considerable variety of condition and resale value. Trade-in values which affect the net price paid by the consumer of a new automobile and the net price received by the local automobile dealer are likely to vary. The local seller is the one closest to that transaction and hence the one with localized knowledge in the Hayekian sense. Following the Jensen-Meckling (1991) prescription of locating decision making authority with the party with the specific local information—automobile trade-in values in this case, means that the local dealer should have authority to negotiate trade-in values for new automobile purchases (Williamson 1985).

Distribution in the automobile franchised network illustrates the concept of coordination between the manufacturer and the dealer through the price mechanism. Other governance elements in those relationships are no doubt present. The ubiquitous purchasing requirements exemplify hierarchy and important franchisee organizations exemplify confederations. However, the role of the governance via the price mechanism is dominant compared to business format franchising. The coordinating role of the wholesale price and related terms and co-location of local authority with trade-in values illustrate the dominance of market driven coordination in authorized franchised systems.

4.2.2 Business Format Franchising

All types of governance arrangements are evident in business format franchising. Price mechanism coordination exists in business format franchising. The most evident examples are the roles that franchise fees and royalties play in coordinating the incentives between the franchisor and franchisees. The common business format franchisor practice of leasing local outlets to franchisees is also an example of governance through the price mechanism. Similarly, collective action and social choice governance mechanisms are also evident in business format franchising. Bradach describes voting procedures and assessment policies to finance marketing promotions for franchisees in business formant franchising. Both illustrate common mechanisms to address the problems of collective action.

The most striking feature of business format franchising, however, is the role of hierarchy as a governing system. This assertion may seem erroneous because evidence shows considerably more hierarchical behavior among company-owned units than franchised arrangements. Indeed, Bradach (1998) documents substantially more hierarchical governance within the franchisor organization than between chain management and franchisees. However, that conclusion simply illustrates greater hierarchy with full vertical integration. The proposition is nearly tautological.

The more relevant comparison is business format franchising versus authorized franchised systems and versus nonfranchised marketing channels—spot market channels and other nonfranchised relational, contractual forms of marketing channels. In these comparisons, the more hierarchical arrangement of business format franchising is clear. The powerful role of monitoring franchisees (albeit not as intensively as company-owned operations), the heavy fixed investment made by franchisees, the large potential loss via termination that renders monitoring more than a perfunctory exercise, and more generally, the great efforts franchisors expend at compelling system uniformity, all attest to hierarchy. Franchisees are not employees. Franchisee relationships with chain managers imply "zones of acceptance" that are more narrow than the relationships within the chain management hierarchy. However, in comparison with other channels or authorized franchised systems, the relationship for franchisees is decidedly more hierarchical.

4.2.3 Franchisee Confederations

The discussion of authorized franchised systems and business format franchising indicates that franchisee confederations are foundational to both of those types of franchising even though price governance plays a bigger role in the former and hierarchy plays a bigger role in the latter arrangements. One notable issue is that while it is conventional to treat the price mechanism and hierarchies as alternative arrangements, i.e. substitutes, it is appropriate to treat collective action as complementary to both governance arrangements. The accounts of Bradach (1998) and

Enrico and Kornbluth (1986) indicate that confederations enhance communication and the flow of information. Thus, confederations lower the costs of decision making and thereby make coordination via both markets and hierarchies more effective.

4.3 System Governance: Tournaments and Imitation

Additional governance issues focus on the long-term evolutionary characteristics of franchised systems. Two relevant economic governance devices are tournament theory and imitation. Strictly speaking, applying both concepts to the franchise context entails an extension well beyond their conventional application. Tournaments are market mediated compensation devices within hierarchies and are components of that governance system. Imitation represents a particular form of economic behavior that is applicable to a wide variety of contexts. Moreover, it can certainly *reflect* governance systems. However, both tournaments and strategies that encourage adaptive imitative behavior can be used in the franchise context to enhance franchise system performance.

4.3.1 Tournament Theory

Compensation in contemporary firms involves some unique practices. One concept derived from Lazear and Rosen (1981) is designing a compensation strategy that uses the possibility of future promotion to motivate intense effort on current job assignments. Compensation via tournaments typically entails prizes fixed in advance, evaluation of relative not absolute performance, and effort levels linked to the size of the prize.

Franchised systems seem to employ the tournament approach. However, the details vary between the franchisor organization and the franchisee organization (Bradach 1998). In the former case, the tournament is similar to any firm. It is internal to the firm. Workers simply expend considerable effort in seeking promotion. In the franchise case, franchisees are motivated to expend effort to acquire additional franchises and in turn obtain the pecuniary rewards of owning multiple units.

4.3.2 Imitation as a Competitive Device

Optimization, or choosing the best solution given the circumstances, is a difficult proposition when there is uncertainty about what circumstances exist or will prevail (Alchian 1950). In such a world, formal models of decision making hold limited value. Alchian suggests two alternative strategies—using trial and error and hoping to converge to some optimal condition or observing the behavior of other decision makers and following the strategies of those that appear to be succeeding. These two strategies rest on the assumption that success is based on results and not motivation. Survival is the standard of success. Of the two strategies, Alchian argues that imitation is the most promising, because the conditions for trial and error leading to an optimum can fail as the environment changes unpredictability.

5 Implications for Marketing Channel Strategy

The most relevant application of the governance frameworks described above is the design of franchise systems and adjusting to changes that occur in a dynamic marketplace. A misaligned governance system will threaten the survival of individual units and the franchisor. Inability to adjust to changes in the marketplace will attenuate the growth and prosperity of the franchisees and the franchisor. It could also threaten a system's viability. The governance frameworks lead directly to some implications for marketing channel strategy—conditions where one of the governance systems seems more appropriate.

5.1 Setting Up Franchise Systems

Franchisors take the lead in setting up franchise systems. In so doing, franchisors rely little on franchisee confederations because if those organizations exist, they are embryonic. Franchisors do rely on markets in the process of screening franchisee applications and selling franchise rights. However, the dominant governance scheme is hierarchy. The training and system design has a strong asymmetry. The parties cannot change roles. The authoritative essence of hierarchy is present. The point is quite evident for business format franchise systems, but it is also present for authorized franchised systems. For example, Coughlan et. al. (2001) document the hierarchical nature of Goodyear Tire franchise program for new members.

5.2 Operating Franchised Systems

Bradach (1998) identifies four management challenges associated with operating franchised restaurant chains. Presumably these challenges are generally present in business format franchising. Moreover, at least four additional dimensions of operating franchised systems entail governance issues.

5.2.1 Growth by Adding Units

Bradach notes that sales growth for individual units is severely constrained by the size and competitive nature of local markets. Thus, sales growth is primarily driven by adding new units. The growth tends to be disproportionately driven by awarding franchised units to existing franchisees. In this process, the awarding of units clearly puts the chain owners in charge and renders the relationship dominantly hierarchical. It also employs tournament like motivation for the franchisees to seek new units and hence perform well with their existing units.

5.2.2 Uniformity

Franchise chains devote enormous effort to standardize operations. Common menus, prices, store designs, operating procedures, and supply sources are examples. These efforts are successful. Bradach's data indicate remarkable uniformity across outlets. Chain managers monitor and control company-owned outlets with stringent performance measures and base rewards upon achieving those measures. The control and monitoring of franchisees is decidedly less intense and thus less hierarchical, even though those activities do exist. However, the limited degree of control and monitoring combined with the compensation system of franchisees results in roughly comparable degrees of uniformity among franchisees and throughout the system as a whole. The limited hierarchy for franchisees seems to be sufficient to ensure the requisite uniformity.

5.2.3 Local Responses

Bradach documents numerous examples where franchisees use the freedom in their business relationships and use their localized knowledge to adapt their business to local markets. The use of localized menus (e.g. KFC) or adjusting prices to meet local competitive standards are illustrative (e.g. KFC and Pizza Hut). Whereas setting up a franchise system and ensuring uniformity are more hierarchical, local response is clearly a market driven mechanism. It entails prices as incentives—e.g. meeting local competition in the Pizza Hut example as well as a Hayekian or local knowledge approach in the case of localized menus—e.g. KFC. Similarly, Love (1995) describes McDonald's franchisees as being particularly sensitive to *local labor market* conditions.

5.2.4 System Adaptation

Bradach devotes considerable attention to system adaptation—a dynamic form of competition. The two themes in the system governance framework above are certainly evident in this application. The restaurant chain ownership structure competes with the franchisee structure. The chain (franchisor) employees' drive for promotion competes with the franchisees' drive for growth by adding franchised units. The tournament effect is present. Moreover, the competing structures tend to *imitate* successful strategies of the other entity. Bradach uses the term "mutual learning" for the two components of the system. He argues that the net effect of this "plural form"—the presence of both company owned and franchisee-owned local outlets, is more successful adaptation to the competitive environment and more innovation than exclusively company-owned or franchisee-owned systems would be. The important point, however, is that his account points to success through the tournament structure and the competitive imitation.

5.2.5 Advertising

Advertising presents classic public goods problems for franchised operations and hence addresses the difficulties associated with collective action. The issue is that advertising entails economies of scale at least for the local television market area. Consequently, any individual franchisee or the franchisor-owned outlets in the same markets are subject to free-rider incentives. Franchised systems have developed basic collective action devices, such as exclusionary behavior—franchisees are required to contribute a percentage of sales for national television advertising otherwise they cannot be franchisees. Similarly, franchisees create local or regional marketing cooperatives in which clearly specified voting arrangements are used to determine the required regional or local advertising. In short, the free rider problem is often at least partially solved.

The history of McDonald's (Love 1995) is instructive. Franchisees in the Minneapolis, Washington, D.C. and Cleveland areas experimented with radio and television advertising. The strategy was a radical innovation for the chain restaurant business. Sales and profits rose notably. Franchisees in other cities imitated the strategy. However, Chicago area franchisees engaged in conspicuous free riding and thus franchisee based advertising did not emerge quickly despite the fact that the market was particularly well suited for such advertising programs. Eventually, sustained enhanced profitability from local advertising across the nation led to full coverage of franchised based local advertising in the McDonald's system. By 1992, McDonald's had 165 regional advertising cooperatives.

5.2.6 Pricing

Pricing is characterized by substantial differences in governance arrangements. Franchisor owned outlets emphasize uniformity of price and adhere to strict hierarchy—almost no local discretion. Some franchised units follow a market driven approach and hence adjust prices to meet local competition or to meet the unique demands of local consumers. Bradach (1998) reports substantial price dispersion for sales of the same product between company owned outlets and franchised outlets and between different franchised outlets. Moreover, he reports some franchised outlets cut prices to met local competitive threats. Thus, franchised operations reflect a more Hayekian approach than is the case for company-owned outlets. The arrangement attests to room for heterogeneity of strategies within aggregate franchise systems. Alternative governance arrangements can peacefully coexist for pricing strategy and tactics.

5.2.7 New Products

In authorized franchised operations, new product generation may be completely centralized. For example, motor vehicle manufacturers can directly query consumers and develop new products that fit with consumer preferences and production realities. The franchised dealers seem unimportant in design of new products. However, the cooperative efforts between manufacturers and franchised dealers means that franchisees need to accept the innovations with enthusiasm. In the soft drink business, Roger Enrico experienced a similar effect in franchisee relations when Pepsi sought acceptance of aspartame sweetened Diet Pepsi (Enrico and Kornbluth 1986).

The situation is dramatically more complex in business format franchising (Bradach 1998). Given local variations in consumer preferences, the experimental nature of franchisees, and the push for system uniformity, new products involve challenges to all parties and particularly to system adaptation. Innovations occur both locally and through centralized franchisor operations. While the record of innovation by franchisees is impressive, especially for McDonald's (Love 1995), franchisors also successfully develop new products (e.g. McDonald's Chicken McNuggets). Moreover, the task of standardizing innovative products and bringing them to market across an entire franchise system is a daunting feat of collective action. Collective decision-making is involved in dealing with approval of new products and encouraging enthusiastic support. In short, new products present a challenge for discrete governance schemes. No single mechanism can coordinate the development, promotion, and launching of new products. The tasks require system integration. All governance systems seem to play a role.

5.2.8 Multiunit Franchisees

The existence of multiunit franchise operations is numerically impressive. For example, Bradach (1998) reports that only three percent of Hardee's franchisees own 50 percent the franchises. Bradach argues that researchers have tended to ignore multiunit franchising. Accordingly, addressing this common practice is an important task.

The collective action and social choice governance arrangements may be particularly useful in examining the multiunit franchise phenomenon. Two basic issues in the logic of collective action are noteworthy. First, Olson (1965) argues that as group size increases collective failure is more likely and public goods are less likely to be provided.[5] However, this effect could be offset somewhat if a privileged group rather than a latent group exists or emerges. A privileged group is one where there exists at least one member of the group for whom the benefit from the collective action exceeds the cost and hence would single-handedly supply the public good.

In applying the logic to business format franchising, unit growth should lead to collective action problems due to more units and more incentive to free ride. If public goods exist for the franchisees, then the public goods are less likely to be voluntarily provided as the number of franchisees increases. However, if one franchisee is sufficiently larger than the others, then the entity (all franchisees) is more likely to be a privileged group. Hence, the existence of a larger franchisee within the group of all franchisees raises the probability that the public good will be provided. Because local marketing or advertising promotions are likely to be public goods and other public goods for the group of franchisees may exist, having a lar-

[5] See Sandler (1992) for more recent treatment of Olson's themes.

ger franchise raises the chances that public goods will be provided—desirable collective action will occur.[6] The application to multiunit franchising is straightforward. That arrangement should increase the provision of public goods. Accordingly, we might expect franchised business with substantial public goods and a large number of franchisees to increase the likelihood of multiunit franchisees.

The problem of social choice also presents an explanation for the existence of multiunit franchising. If heterogeneous preferences prevent a decision from occurring or a stable strategy existing—e.g. adoption of a certain type of new product among several alternatives, or the size or theme of an advertising campaign, then a dictator may be the only solution (Miller 1992). In that case, one way to have a "dictator" is to give ownership rights to a single franchisee that in effect becomes a franchisor for a given geographic territory. Bradach's (1998) observation that multiunit franchisees tend to mimic the hierarchy of the chain's management is certainly consistent with this explanation. If the social choice problem leads to multiunit franchising, then we should expect to find multiunit franchising existing where potential franchisees' preferences are heterogeneous.

6 Conclusions

Franchising presents a variety of governance arrangements. These in-turn provide benefits and costs and a wide range of potential applications. Market mediated governance seems to dominate for authorized franchised systems while a combination of governance systems with special reliance on hierarchy seems to dominate business format franchising. Collective action and social choice governance systems are complementary to both market mediated and hierarchically directed governance. Marketing channel design needs to be directed toward fitting the appropriate governance system with the nature of the business and the nature of local markets.

Understanding franchise governance constitutes a central research agenda for scholars studying franchising just as the appropriate governance arrangement is a central strategic factor facing franchisors. Identifying the roles of market and organizational factors and the appropriate strategic fit between those factors and governance arrangements should be forthcoming.

References

1. Alchian AA (1950) Uncertainty, Evolution, and Economic Theory. Journal of Political Economy 58:211-21
2. Arrow K (1963) Social Choice and Individual Values. Wiley, New York

[6] Even the costs of communicating preferences to the franchisor can be viewed as a public good.

3. Barnard CI (1938) The Functions of the Executive. Harvard University Press, Cambridge
4. Becker, GS (1965) A Theory of the Allocation of Time. Economic Journal 75:493-517
5. Bradach JL (1998) Franchise Organizations. Harvard Business School Press, Boston
6. Brickley J, Dark F (1987) The Choice of Organizational Form: the Case of Franchising. Journal of Financial Economics 18:401-420
7. Casson M (1994) Why are Firms Hierarchical? International Journal of Economics of Business 1:47-76
8. Chamberlin EH (1933) The Theory of Monopolistic Competition. Harvard University Press, Cambridge
9. Coughlan, AT, Anderson E, Stern LW, El-Ansary A (2001) Marketing Channels 6th edn, Prentice-Hall, Upper Saddle River
10. Demsetz H (1995) The Economics of the Business Firm. Cambridge University Press, Cambridge
11. Dnes AW (1993) A Case-study Analysis of Franchise Contracts. Journal of Legal Studies 22:367-93
12. Enrico R, Kornbluth J (1986) The Other Guy Blinked. Bantam, New York
13. Hansman H (1996) The Ownership of Enterprise. Belknap Press of Harvard University Press, Cambridge
14. Hayek FA (1945) The Use of Knowledge in Society. American Economic Review 35:519-30
15. Jensen M, Meckling W (1991) Specific and General Knowledge and Organizational structure. In: Werin L, Wijkander H (eds) Main Currents in Contract Economics. Blackwell, Oxford, pp 251-274
16. Kaufman P, Lafontaine F (1994) Costs of Control: the Sources of Economic Rents for McDonald's franchisees. Journal of Law and Economics 37:417-54
17. Klein B (1980) Transaction Cost Determinants of 'Unfair' Contractual Arrangements. American Economic Review 70:356-62
18. Klein B, Saft L (1985) The Law and Economics of Franchising Tying Contracts. Journal of Law and Economics 28:345-61
19. Lazear EP Rosen S (1981) Rank Order Tournaments as Optimum Labor Contracts. Journal of Political Economy 89:841-64
20. Lafontaine F (1992) Agency Theory and Franchising: Some Empirical Results. Rand Journal of Economics 23:263-83
21. Love JF (1995) McDonald's: Behind the Arches. Bantam Books, New York
22. Mathewson GF, Winter R (1985) The Economics of Franchise Contracts. Journal of Law and Economics 28:503-26
23. Milgrom P Roberts J (1992) Economics, Organization, and Management. Prenctice-Hall, Englewood Cliffs
24. Miller GJ (1992) Managerial Dilemmas. Cambridge University Press, Cambridge
25. Minkler, A (1993) Why Firms Franchise: a Search Cost Theory. Journal of Institutional and Theoretical Economics. 148:240-49
26. Norton SW (1988a.) An Empirical Look at Franchising as an Organizational Form. Journal of Business 61: 197-218
27. Norton SW (1988b) Franchising, Brand Name Capital, and the Entrepreneurial Capacity Problem. Strategic Management Journal 9:105-114
28. Norton SW (1995) Is Franchising a Capital Structure Issue? Journal of Corporate Finance 2:75-101
29. Olson M (1965) The Logic of Collective Action. Harvard University Press, Cambridge
30. Pashigian, BP (1961) The Distribution of Automobiles: an Economic Analysis of the Franchise System. Prentice-Hall, Englewood Cliffs

31.Rosen S (1975) Hedonic Prices and Implicit Markets: Product Differentiation in Pure Competition. Journal of Political Economy 82:33-45
32.Rubin PH (1978) The Theory of the Firm and the Structure of the Franchise Contract. Journal of Law and Economics 21:223-33
33.Sandler T (1995) Collective Action. University of Michigan Press, Ann Arbor
34.Sen KC (1993) The Use of Initial Fees and Royalties in Business-Format Franchising. Managerial and Decision Economics 12:190-210
35.Shane S (1996) Hybrid Organizational Arrangements and Their Implications for Firm Growth and Survival: a Study of New Franchisors. Academy of Management Journal 39:216-34
36.Simon H (1951) A Formal Theory of the Employment Relation. Econometrica 19:293-305
37.Simon, H (1976) Administrative Behavior. 3rd edn. Free Press, New York
38.Simon H (1962) The Architecture of Complexity. Proceedings of the American Philosophical Society 106:467-82
39.Spulber DF (1999) Market Microstructure. Cambridge University Press, Cambridge
40.Stern LW, El-Ansary A (1988) Marketing Channels. 3rd edn. Prentice-Hall, Englewood Cliffs.
41.Stigler GJ (1987) The Theory of Price, 4th edn. Macmillan, New York
42.Vaughn CL (1979) Franchising, 2nd edn. Lexington Books, Lexington
43.Williamson OE (1975) Markets and Hierarchies. Free Press, New York
44.Williamson OE (1985) The Economic Institutions of Capitalism. Free Press, New York
45.Williamson OE (1996) The Mechanisms of Governance. Oxford University Press, New York
46.Windsperger J (2003) Centralization of Franchising Networks: Evidence from the Austrian Franchise Sector. Journal of Business Research, forthcoming

The Organizational Choice Decision in Business Format Franchising: An Empirical Test

Janet E. L. Bercovitz

The Fuqua School of Business
Duke University
Box 90120
Durham, NC 27708 0120

Abstract. This paper empirically investigates the franchising make-or-buy decision providing a comprehensive test of the economizing perspective of organizational choice while controlling for the potential influence of resource scarcity factors. The study reported here extends the extant empirical franchising literature in three ways. First, this study takes the outlet as the unit of analysis and explores organizational choice within the franchise system. Second, the analysis is more inclusive, simultaneously accounting for both of the component elements of the free-riding hazard. And third, this study provides one of the rare empirical investigations of the adoption of multi-unit franchising – the ownership of two or more outlets by a single franchisee. The econometric analysis, using discrete choice methods, provides strong support for the hypothesis that ownership mode of individual outlets (single-unit franchise, multi-unit franchise or company-owned outlet) turns on the relative levels of the contracting hazards present.

1 Introduction

The rapid growth of franchising over the past twenty years has spurred extensive study of this phenomenon by academic researchers.[1] One simple question – "Why franchise?" – has, in itself, served as the impetus for numerous investigations. For the most part, academics have hypothesized that franchising is adopted as a means to either (1) economize on the agency/governance costs associated with internal organization or (2) overcome capital and managerial constraints.

This paper empirically investigates the franchising make-or-buy decision providing a comprehensive test of the economizing perspective of organizational choice while controlling for the potential influence of resource scarcity factors. The study reported here addresses the three key weaknesses of the extant empirical franchising literature. First, this study takes the outlet as the unit of analysis

[1] In a recent survey of franchising research, Elango and Fried (1997) found close to 100 relevant articles that had been published during the last twenty years. These articles appear within numerous disciplines including economics, law, management, marketing, and management science.

and explores organizational choice within the franchise system. Second, the analysis is more inclusive, simultaneously accounting for both of the pertinent contractual hazards – shirking and free-riding – that underlie the central economizing trade-off. Further, this study probes the potential interaction effects of the component elements of the free-riding hazard. No other study has examined this effect. And third, this study provides one of the rare empirical investigations of the adoption of multi-unit franchising – the ownership of two or more outlets by a single franchisee.

The empirical tests in this paper use a unique set of data drawn directly from a sample of franchise disclosure documents, known as the uniform franchise offering circulars (UFOCs). As compared to previous studies which generally draw their data from published franchised guides or government census reports, this source has the advantage of providing more extensive and more detailed system-level and unit-level information. The econometric analysis, using discrete choice methods, provides strong support for the hypothesis that ownership mode of individual outlets (single-unit franchise, multi-unit franchise or company-owned outlet) turns on the relative levels of the contracting hazards present.

This paper proceeds as follows. Section 2 provides a brief summary of the key theoretical perspectives that have been put forth to explain organizational choice – the decision whether to franchise or company-own units – in the franchising arena. Section 3 reiterates the central economizing trade-off and sets forth specific testable hypotheses. Section 4 describes the data and methodology. Results are summarized and discussed in Section 5. Section 6 concludes.

2 Summary of Existing Theoretical Perspectives

Two distinct theoretical frameworks have been put forth in the literature to explain organizational choice in the franchising arena. These are: (1) the Agency Cost/Transaction Cost Economizing Perspective and (2) the Resource Scarcity Perspective.[2] The first portrays franchising as an economizing response to the incentive problems of internal organization. The second depicts franchising as a means for overcoming capital and managerial constraints. In the following section, I briefly review the main elements of these two perspectives.[3]

[2] Recent authors have also adopted a property rights lens to explore the organizational choice issue (see, for example, Windsperger in this volume). In many respects the economizing approach highlighted here and the property rights approach are complementary. The property rights perspective emphasizes the need to allocate ownership according to the distribution of intangible assets that generate rents. The economizing perspective evaluates ownership options in terms of the hazards associated with these important intangible assets.

[3] See Dnes (1996) for a more extensive survey of the theoretical literature on franchising.

2.1 Economizing Perspective

Currently, the most accepted explanations for franchising are based on an economizing logic. Following this logic, the company-own (make) versus franchising (buy) decision for distributing goods and services is argued to turn on the comparative costs of operating under the two alternative organizational forms. This type of argument has been put forth in three different, but closely related, bodies of literature: (1) the agency theory literature (Fama and Jensen 1983; Mathewson and Winter 1985; Brickley and Dark 1987; Lafontaine 1992; Bhattacharyya and Lafontaine 1995); (2) the self-enforcing agreement literature (Klein 1980, 1995; Klein and Saft 1985; Klein and Murphy 1988); and (3) the transaction cost economics literature (Rubin 1978, 1990; Williamson 1985, 1991).

The main elements of the arguments in all three strands of literature are similar. First, hazards associated with the alternative forms of organization are highlighted. In general, it is agreed that shirking and/or perquisite consumption by employees is a central problem associated with company-ownership (Brickley and Dark, 1987, p 407; Klein 1995, p 22; Rubin 1978, p 226) while free-riding on the common brand name is a key hazard of franchising arrangements (Brickley and Dark 1987, p 406; Klein 1980, pp 358-59; Rubin 1978, p 228; Williamson 1985, p 181).

The susceptibility of these different organizational forms to these different hazard types is due, in part, to the unique incentives of each structure.[4] Managers of company-owned stores are generally compensated through fixed salaries.[5] Operating under such low-powered incentives, salaried managers are more likely to engage in shirking behavior as they do not bear significant costs of such opportunistic action (Alchian and Demsetz 1972; Jensen and Meckling 1976). To mitigate this hazard, the franchisor can either (1) monitor the employee-manager's behavior (an input control mechanism), or (2) opt to franchise and provide the manager with the higher-powered incentives of residual claimant rights (an output control mechanism) (Ouchi 1979; Fama and Jensen 1983; Anderson and Oliver 1987). Both of these options have costs. Direct monitoring requires the development and implementation of oversight mechanisms. Such administrative apparatus can require significant investments on the part of the franchisor. Franchising, on the other hand, circumvents the need to incur shirking-related monitoring costs. Rather, this organizational form alleviates shirking hazards by replacing low-powered incentives with high-powered incentives – having residual claimant rights, the franchisee now bears a greater share of the shirking costs, and thus has less incentives to shirk. Unfortunately, these high-powered incentives also have the perverse effect of increasing free-riding costs. Specifically, franchisees are believed to be more likely to engage in quality debasement and/or free-riding behavior as they, unlike salaried employees, are able to pocket the savings of such op-

[4] Alternative governance forms also differ in terms of administrative controls and contract law supports. (Williamson 1991).

[5] In a study of wages in the fast food industry, Krueger found that the practice of paying managers of company-owned outlets a fixed salary that does not directly depend on their performance or their restaurants' profitability to be quite common. (Krueger 1990, p 5)

portunistic actions (Klein 1980, 1995; Brickley and Dark 1987; Carney and Gedajlovic 1991).

The choice of organization form is thus hypothesized to be driven by attempts to choose the least cost mode of governance. Namely, company-ownership will be preferred when the free-riding costs of franchising exceed the shirking costs of integrated distribution. Conversely, franchising will be selected if shirking costs are expected to be greater than free-riding costs.

2.2 Resource Scarcity Perspective

An alternative explanation for franchising – put forth by Oxenfeldt and Kelly 1968-69; Oxenfeldt and Thompson 1968-69; Ozanne and Hunt 1971; Caves and Murphy 1976; Norton 1988; and Shane 1996 – is that franchising arises as a solution to the capital and managerial constraints faced by franchisors. With respect to capital needs, it has long been argued that franchisors look to franchisees for the capital needed to expand in the early stages of their business when the value of the system's trademarks have yet to be firmly established. Specifically, by paying franchise fees and shouldering the costs of constructing new outlets, franchisees provide an attractive, low-cost, external source of capital.[6] With respect to managerial needs, franchising is offered as a solution to adverse selection challenges.

The capital scarcity argument remains quite controversial. Rubin (1978, p 225) took issue with this perspective arguing that "in light of modern capital theory" the contention that franchising is adopted as a means to raise capital is clearly "fallacious." Rubin points to a central flaw with the capital constraint argument: Since investing in a single outlet is much riskier than investing in shares of the franchise chain (which allows for diversification across outlets), than the cost of raising capital on the market (or from offering managers shares). As such, he concludes, capital constraints clearly do not justify franchising. Rubin's argument, while compelling, has shortcomings of its own. First, Rubin's strong conclusion runs counter to accepted industry wisdom. In separate surveys, Lafontaine (1992b) and Dant (1995) both find that franchisors of all sizes consistently cite capital acquisition as a key reason for franchising. Second, and perhaps more importantly, Rubin's argument is based upon a restrictive assumption of zero transaction costs. In conjunction with positive financing-related transaction costs, it is feasible that franchisees may indeed provide funds at a cost comparably lower than that of traditional capital markets. As such, the capital constraint argument once again emerges as a reasonable hypothesis (Lafontaine 1992; Norton 1995; Combs and Ketchen 1999).[7]

[6] Initial franchise fees generally range from $20,000 to $40,000. Total initial investment required is normally much higher, averaging $272,000 in the fast-food sector and $162,300 in the retail sector (Bond 1997).

[7] Each of these authors highlight different potential financing-related transaction costs. Lafontaine (1992) considers the influence of downstream incentive problems, Norton (1995) considers the monitoring costs associated with the investments in intangible as-

The managerial constraints rationale for franchising builds from Penrose's (1959) observation that a firm's growth is constrained by the speed and efficiency by which it can expand its managerial capacity (Shane 1996). Opening a new unit in a franchise system is a complex and time-consuming task. Activities required include: site identification and qualification, new employee hiring and training, supplier relationship initiation, leasehold improvement and equipment installation oversight, and local marketing program implementation (Bradach 1998). Given a limited internal stock of managerial resources, growing franchise systems generally find it necessary to hire additional managers from the outside labor market to complete these tasks. If the skill levels of potential employees are not easily observable, applicants may overstate their capabilities in the hopes of securing positions. Such opportunistic behavior on the part of potential employees increases the firm's need for (and relatedly the costs of) candidate screening and, given imperfect screening, the subsequent cost of new employee training. In theory, such costs can be reduced by the use of incentive-based contracts which promote the efficient self-selection of managers (Akerlof 1970; Demski and Feltham 1978; Holmstrom 1982). Wage packages that tie rewards to outputs effectively shift the risks and costs of underperformance to the employee and thus reduce the benefits of misrepresenting one's abilities. Franchising, with its high-powered incentives, is thus hypothesized to offer a lower-cost means to reduce the screening costs associated with internal growth (Norton 1988; Shane 1996).[8]

2.3 Unexplained Phenomenon – Multi-Unit Franchising

One lapse in the existing economic research on franchising is a failure to explore the phenomenon of multi-unit franchising. In most previous theoretical and empirical work, the franchisee is depicted as an individual that owns and manages a single-unit operation. However, this characterization is somewhat unrealistic as franchise systems are rarely composed solely of single-unit, owner-operated outlets and franchisor company-owned stores. Rather, the practice of multi-unit franchising, the ownership of two or more outlets by a single franchisee, is widespread. For example, in a national survey of the franchised fast-food restaurant

sets, and Combs and Ketchen (1999) consider adverse selection problems that confront lenders and stockholders.

[8] This rationale is, in truth, a low-cost screening argument which can feasibly be classified under the economizing rubric. Likewise, the capital scarcity argument of organizational choice could be interpreted from an economizing perspective: the choice whether to own or franchise a particular unit turns on the relative cost of local (franchisee) capital versus corporate (franchisor) capital. In this section, I discuss the resource scarcity perspective separately from the traditional agency economizing perspective to reflect the historical divide between these two theoretical camps. However, the underlying economizing theme between these camps suggests that these perspectives may be best treated as complements rather than substitutes.

industry, Kaufmann and Dant (1996) found that 88% of the 152 franchisors surveyed had multi-unit franchisees within their systems.

Though rarely directly addressed, two views regarding multi-unit franchising emerge from a close reading of the literature. These views broadly mirror the economizing and scarcity perspectives discussed above. In general, the existence of multi-unit franchising is rationalized as either (1) a means to raise capital and promote system growth or (2) a mechanism to control free-riding hazards. The first camp focuses on the relative disability of this organizational form (as compared to single-unit franchising) to mitigate shirking hazards. In theory, franchising relieves the shirking problem by making the franchisee an owner-manager whose compensation is tied to the residual returns of his particular outlet. With multi-unit franchising, however, the owner-manager tie and the resultant beneficial incentives are weakened when the franchisee hires employee-managers to oversee operations at the individual outlets in his mini-chain. As such, theorists in this camp argue that multi-unit franchising can not as easily be justified by economizing logic and thus, must arise for another reason.[9] Alleviating resource constraints is generally the alternative rationale offered.[10] Specifically, it is argued that multi-unit franchising is adopted to exploit previously qualified external sources of funds, to leverage the managerial skills of talented franchisees, and to take advantage of specialization economies. (Darr, Argote, and Epple 1995; Kaufmann and Dant 1996)

The second camp, while acknowledging the increased shirking problems, argue that adoption of multi-unit franchising may be justified by the increased capabilities of this form to reduce free-riding hazards. In theory, the effective level of demand externalities will be diminished under multi-unit franchising as a franchisee owning numerous outlets will be forced to internalize a greater fraction of the costs accruing to his input decisions. (Brickley and Dark 1987)

---

[9] The viability of this argument hinges on the size of the mini-chain. An individual that owns two outlets may still be able to take a hands on approach at both his outlets with little to no loss of efficiency. Expected efficiency losses will vary with the size and geographical dispersion of the mini-chain.

[10] For example, Kaufmann and Dant (1996, p 347) assert, "Unfettered franchisee expansion produces wide spans of control (in some cases reaching into the hundreds), too wide to assume that franchisee monitoring can efficiently solve store level incentive problems. In those cases, franchisee holdings take on all of the trappings of company-owned chains. The only reasonable explanation for these franchised mini-chains is the access to capital that they afford."

3 Hypotheses

The starting point for the empirical analysis is the economizing central trade-off:

> The probability of franchising a given unit varies directly with the shirking costs of integrated distribution and negatively with the free-riding costs of franchising.

More specifically, given the differing competencies of the alternative governance forms, it is expected that:

H1: Less hierarchical governance modes will be chosen as shirking-related monitoring costs increase, *ceteris paribus*.

H1a: The probability that a particular outlet will be franchised will be positively related to the level of shirking-based monitoring costs, *ceteris paribus*.

H1b: Given franchising, the probability that a particular franchised outlet will be one of several owned by an individual franchisee will be negatively related to the level of shirking-based monitoring costs, *ceteris paribus*.

And that:

H2: More direct ownership of outlets will be chosen as free-riding hazards increase, *ceteris paribus*.

H2a: The probability that a particular outlet will be franchised will be negatively related to the level of the free-riding hazard, *ceteris paribus*.

H2b: Given franchising, the probability that a particular franchised outlet will be one of several owned by an individual franchisee will be positively related to the level of the free-riding hazard, *ceteris paribus*.

The prototypical free-riding hazard associated with franchising is the threat of free-riding on the brand name by the outlet manager. Brand names convey information as to expected product and service quality, aid in differentiating company offerings and, thus, provide a means to generate positive (above competitive) returns (Keller 1997). If consumers cannot detect the quality of a product before purchasing, the outlet manager may free-ride on the system's brand name and substitute cheaper, lower quality inputs in order to lower their store's operating costs. The outlet manager bears only a portion of the costs of such chiseling as the effects of consumer dissatisfaction will be shared with the franchisor and other outlet managers in the system. Note that the level of the free-riding hazard at each outlet will depend both on the strength of the system's brand name and on the proportion of dissatisfaction the focal manager can dissipate to others in the system. That is, the level of the free-riding hazard will be a function of both the value of the shared specific investment and the spillover potential. This dual component nature of the free-riding hazard leads to the following hypothesis:

H3: There is an interaction effect: The relationship between governance mode choice and one component of the free-riding hazard, is amplified by the level of the other component of the free-riding hazard, *ceteris paribus*.

H3a: The predicted negative relationship between the use of franchising and brand name value (spillover potential) will become more negative as the level of the spillover potential (brand name value) increases, *ceteris paribus*.

H3b: Given franchising, the predicted positive relationship between the use of multi-unit franchising and brand name value (spillover potential) will become more positive as the level of the spillover potential (brand name value) increases, *ceteris paribus*.

4 Data and Methodology

4.1 Data Source

The Federal Trade Commission requires franchisors to furnish prospective franchisees with detailed disclosure documents. Generally provided via a Uniform Franchise Offering Circular (UFOC), these disclosure documents contain information on 20 different aspects of the franchise offering, the franchisor's financial statements, and copies of all pertinent contracts including a current franchise agreement.

As there is no requirement for these documents to be filed with the FTC, UFOCs are not readily available to the general public. There are however, thirteen states, including California, in which franchisors are required to register and file UFOCs before offering franchises for sale in that state.[11] To build my data base, I have gathered franchise circulars from those on file at the San Francisco, Los Angeles and San Diego offices of the California Department of Corporations as well as UFOCs from non-filing franchisors by request.[12] For the analysis in this

[11] The thirteen states that require registration and filing are California, Hawaii, Illinois, Indiana, Maryland, Minnesota, New York, North Dakota, Rhode Island, South Dakota, Virginia, Washington, and Wisconsin. Two other states have disclosure laws but do not require filing: Oregon and Michigan.

[12] Non-filing franchisors include those companies that do not sell units in California and thus are not required to place their UFOCs on file with the California Department of Corporations. Note, the majority of the franchisors that file in California also operate units in other states.

paper, I am using data from the UFOCs of 64 franchise systems (with a total of 5,219 outlets) in the fast-food and general retail sectors.

4.2 Dependent Variables

Ownership mode is the dependent variable in this study. In the franchising arena, there are three possible outlet ownership modes: (1) Company-Owned Units; (2) Multi-Unit Franchised Outlets; and (3) Single-Unit Franchised Outlets. In general, choice of outlet organizational form occurs as a sequential decision. In the first stage, franchisors decide whether the outlet will be company-owned or franchised. Given a decision to franchise, a second stage choice as to whether the outlet will be offered to a new or an existing franchisee (i.e., single-unit vs. multi-unit) is then made. Discussions with several franchisors confirm this two-stage decision process.[13]

To reflect this two stage process, the organizational choice decision is represented first by a binomial choice model of whether to company-own or franchise the outlet. In this stage, the dependent variable is coded 1 if the unit is franchised, and 0 if the unit is company-owned. For those outlets for which franchising is selected, a second binomial choice model is run where the dependent variable is coded as 1 if the unit is one of several owned by an individual franchisee, and 0 if the outlet is the sole unit owned by the franchisee. Information as to the ownership of individual outlets is drawn from the list of current franchisees which is generally included as an appendix to Item XX (List of Outlets) of the UFOC.

4.3 Shirking-Related Independent Variables

In this study, I use two proxies to capture shirking-related monitoring costs: (1) the importance of local input and (2) principal-agent dispersion. The argument with respect to the first element is quite simple: The greater the importance of local input, the more extensive and thus, more costly, the monitoring task. While all franchise systems push some responsibility to the outlet-level, the relative importance of these downstream inputs varies substantially across systems. In some cases, the possible discretion at the outlet-level is limited as the franchisor provides the outlets with near-final goods. This practice is common in the specialty retail sector – home furnishings, specialty foods, and hobby stores, for example – where inputs purchased directly from the franchisor (or from a set of designated suppliers) account for a large proportion of the outlet's ongoing operating costs. In other cases, such as franchise systems in the maintenance sector (i.e., residential cleaning services, pest control services, and carpet and upholstery cleaning services) the scope of the outlet manager's jurisdiction is much broader – inputs pur-

[13] This two-step decision sequence is in-line with the decision process uncovered by Slade (1996) in her study of organizational choice in gasoline retailing.

chased from the franchisor account for only a small portion of operating costs.[14] It is the extent of the "discretionary" outlet-level inputs required that indicates the importance of local input. When this variable is small, the importance of outlet-level incentive intensity and the related behavior monitoring costs are relatively low. As it increases, shirking-related monitoring costs (and incentive intensity) are expected to become more of an issue.

Item VIII of the UFOC details, as a percentage of the franchisee's ongoing operating costs, the franchisee's obligation to purchase inputs from designated sources – either the franchisor, its affiliates, or specific suppliers. This value is used to create a measure of "discretionary" outlet-level inputs. Specifically, the level of discretionary inputs is calculated as a percentage of the total operating costs of the outlet. Given $T = P + D$, where T equals total operating costs, P equals the costs of inputs the outlet manager is required to purchase from the franchisor or from a source designated by the franchisor, and D equals the costs of all other inputs, the level of discretion, d, is represented by the ratio D/T. Manager's span of control, and thus the importance of local input, is argued to increase as d increases.

As compared to local input measures used in previous studies, the proxy described above has two distinct advantages. First, using information provided in the UFOC, I am able to build system-specific measures of local input whereas, given data limitations, many of the earlier studies (e.g., Caves and Murphy 1976; Norton 1988; Lafontaine 1992) were forced to rely upon industry-level information to create the related measure. Second, unlike many of the other studies, I have sufficient information to represent this construct using a continuous, rather than dichotomous, variable.

Following prior studies (Brickley and Dark 1987; Norton 1988; Lafontaine 1992; Scott 1995), a measure of geographical dispersion is used to capture within-system shirking-related cost differences. The logic (originally put forth in Rubin 1978) is simple: Direct monitoring can be used to increase the observability of outlet-level behavior. However, the cost of monitoring, and thus viability of dampening shirking, increases with the distance the monitor must travel to conduct inspections. Distances between outlets and the nearest monitoring headquarters were found using Power ZipFind geographic information software. This software is used to match outlet and headquarter zip codes with their latitude and longitude coordinates and then, based on these coordinates, calculates the geographical distance between points. The address of the franchisor's headquarters is specified in Item I (The Franchisor, Predecessors and Affiliates) of the UFOC. Addresses for all outlets in the system are often provided in attachments to Item XX of the UFOC. Additionally, calls were made to each franchisor to ascertain the location of all additional company offices from which on-site monitoring is conducted. Typically, monitoring personnel were located at the main headquarters and/or the district offices of each franchise.

---

[14] On average, discretionary outlet-level inputs for franchise systems in the retail sector is calculated to be 62% of total operating costs, while discretionary outlet-level inputs in the above mentioned maintenance segments averaged 82% of total operating costs.

Using a geographic dispersion variable that provides observations at the outlet-level is essential to illuminate within-system organizational choice – the selection of particular units to be franchised vs. company-owned. To date, only two other studies (Brickely and Dark 1987; Minkler 1990) have employed such unit-specific data in the operationalization of this distance measure.

4.4 Free-Riding Related Independent Variables

There are two component elements that contribute to the level of the free-riding hazard. These are: (1) the shared specific investment at stake and (2) the spill-over potential. Broadly, the investment at stake is the reputation or "brand name" of the franchise system (Klein and Leffler 1981; Klein 1995). Information about the quality of a system's offering is conveyed to customers through the brand name. Investing in the development of a strong brand name enables the system to sell its products and/or services at premium prices. As all outlets in a system operate under the common brand name, each outlet stands to benefit from investments in brand name capital. Brand name capital is, however, a transaction-specific asset (Williamson 1985, 1996). As with other forms of asset specificity, an increase in this asset increases the associated level of quasi rents, which in turn, increases the possible gains to, and thus risk of, opportunistic behavior.

The actual gains to free-riding on a system's brand name are determined by the spillover potential. Specifically, the returns to quality shading (i.e., the substitution of cheaper, lower quality inputs) that an individual outlet manager can capture are dependent on the degree to which the resultant customer dissatisfaction is dispersed across other outlets in the system. If negative reputation effects are shared broadly across outlets, the direct effect for each unit will be a small decrease in perceived brand name value. Thus, whereas the cost savings from quality shading accrue to the quality-shading unit, the adverse effects on the brand name are spread across the system. Accordingly, the threat of free-riding will be high. If, on the other hand, spillover is low and the focal unit is forced to internalize a greater portion of the quality debasement costs, the returns to cheating will be minimal. As such, the threat of free-riding will be small.

A proxy for brand name value (the investment at stake) is created based on the advertising expenditures of each franchise system. Specifically, the brand name proxy (BN) is calculated using advertising expenditure data from the three most recent years with BN = Year(0) expenditures + (0.9*Year(-1) expenditures) + (0.9*0.9* Year(-2) expenditures).[15] The reasoning is straight forward: Brand name value is assumed to increase as more people are exposed to the brand. The

[15] This formula is based on the historic cost method for valuing intangible assets (Reilly 1996; Ason 1996). This method calls for the summation of the investments made in developing the asset of interest less an obsolescence term. Based on conversations with marketing faculty, I use a 10% annual obsolescence rate. I have also calculated this term using a 20% annual obsolescence rate. This different formulation did not substantially change the econometric results.

number of people exposed to the franchise's brand name, in turn, increases with the level of advertising.[16] Advertising expenditure data is drawn from the *AD $ Summary* , published yearly by LNA/Media Watch. This source tracks the yearly advertising expenditures of individual brands spending more than $25,000 annually for advertising placement.[17]

A measure of outlet density is used as a proxy for spillover potential. Spillover potential is thought to increase when outlets are in close proximity to one another as the effects of actions taken by an individual franchisee are more likely to be dispersed to others in the system when customers are shared. Customers are more likely to frequent multiple outlets if these outlets are located in the same general vicinity. Attachments to Item XX (List of Outlets) of the franchise circular details outlet locations. I measure the spillover proxy as the inverse of the average distance between the focal outlet and the three outlets that are closest to this outlet. Distances between outlets are derived using Power ZipFind geographic information software.

This spillover proxy offers a much finer-grained measure of potential demand externalities than the traditional repeat vs. non-repeat customer categorization (Brickley et. al 1987, 1991). As calculated, I am able to differentiate outlets based upon the unique retail environment in which that particular unit resides. It is not possible to differentiate between individual franchise systems, let alone specific outlets, using the traditional categorization variables.

Both of these factors – brand name value and spillover potential – contribute to the free-riding hazard. Further, the level of each of these components is believed to moderate the effects of the other. For example, the relationship between brand name value and the organizational choice decision is expected to differ, depending upon whether the potential of spillover is high or low. Specifically, at a given level of brand name, the free-riding hazard is heightened as the spillover potential increases, thus increasing the probability – at that level of brand name – that the unit will be company-owned. I include the term (brand name value) * (spillover potential) to investigate this hypothesized interaction effect.

4.5 Control Variables

In addition to the independent variables specified in the economizing hypotheses, four control variables are included in the model. The first two are added to explore resource scarcity influences. First, a market segment age variable is added to provide a more germane test of the long-standing argument that franchising is

[16] Prior studies (Lafontaine 1992; Agrawal and Lal 1995), have used the total number of outlets in the franchise system as a proxy for brand name value – the investment at stake. Though simple to obtain, there are significant problems with using number of outlets as a proxy for brand name value – namely, the inability to isolate (and control for) the influence of system size.

[17] In years that the franchise system is not listed in the *AD $ Summary*, the brand name proxy is calculated using the minimum expenditure of $25,000 for that year.

adopted by the franchisor as a means to overcome binding capital constraints (Oxenfeldt and Kelly 1969; Ozanne and Hunt 1971; Caves and Murphy 1976). Under the capital requirement logic, it is argued that franchisors who are short on cash are forced to look to franchisees for the capital needed to expand. Though belief in the capital acquisition rationale for franchising is common among industry players (Kaufmann and Dant 1996; Lafontaine 1992b), previous studies have found little statistical support for this conclusion. For example, in studies by Brickley and Dark (1987), Brickley, Dark and Weisbach (1991), and Lafontaine (1992) a negative relationship between the amount of capital needed to open a franchise outlet and the use of franchising was found.

It is possible that this lack of support is due to oversimplification rather than a lack of underlying validity in the capital acquisition-franchising relationship. Specifically, all franchise systems probably will not face the same difficulties in acquiring capital through financial markets, banks, and/or other financial institutions. For example, it is more likely that an active capital market will exist to support franchisors operating in established market segments. On the other hand, franchisors exploiting truly innovative franchise ideas (i.e., applying franchising to new market segments), may have difficulty raising money in the capital market and thus may turn to franchising to generate funds to expand. A negative relationship between the age of a segment and the propensity to franchise thus is expected.[18]

A market segment age variable is added to the model to test this hypothesis. The market segment age variable for each franchise system (calculated as the average number of years systems in that sub-sector have been franchising) is determined using *Entrepreneur* Magazine's Annual Franchise 500 list which provides information on franchising history for numerous classes of franchises. The segment age variable used here has advantages over the required investment variables used in many of the earlier examinations of the capital constraint hypothesis. Specifically, by focusing on the franchisor's access to external capital rather than on the required level of expenditures in isolation, this variable better reflects the "capital constraint" attribute of interest.

Second, a system growth rate variable, operationalized as one-half the difference in the log of the number of outlets in year 3 and year 1, is included to further explore resource scarcity rationales for franchising.[19] Under the resource scarcity hypothesis, franchising is held to provide a means for overcoming the capital *and* managerial constraints faced by the franchisor. As system growth intensifies the

---

[18] The capital scarcity perspective does not distinguish between generating funds through the sale of outlets to "new" franchisees or through the sale of additional outlets to existing franchisees. The argument could go either way: (1) sell to existing franchisees as they are a proven and qualified financial source; or (2) sell to new franchisees as, having yet to invest, they are less likely to face "binding" capital constraints. Ex ante, the influence of the segment age variable on the choice between adding outlets as single-units or as part of a multi-unit chain is ambiguous.

[19] This operationalization of the growth rate mirrors that used by Norton 1988 and Lafontaine 1992.

franchisor's need for both types of resources, it is predicted that a positive relationship between system growth and the use of franchising will be observed (Norton 1988; Shane 1996).

Adding this control variable to the model in conjunction with the refined "access to capital" proxy (segment age), offers a preliminary cut at isolating the effect of managerial constraints on organizational choice. If the segment age variable picks up the influence of capital constraints on the franchising make-or-buy decision, any subsequent significance on the growth term should reflect the influence of human capital needs. Numerous other studies have found a positive relationship between system growth and the use of franchising, and in many cases, have held this finding to represent the ability of franchising to relax managerial limitations to growth.[20] These conclusions are premature, however, as none of these studies have effectively controlled for the related capital constraint influence.[21]

Third, for each outlet I include a dummy variable that indicates whether the outlets is located in a state having franchise termination laws. These laws, by requiring the franchisor to meet the standard of "good cause", make it more difficult to terminate a franchisee. Practitioners as well as researchers have argued that such laws, by muting the franchisor's ability to punish and thus deter franchisee cheating, raise the cost of franchising. In line with this reasoning, previous studies (Beales and Muris 1995; Brickley, Dark, and Weisbach 1991) have shown that franchisors choose to company-own outlets at a higher rate in termination states than in non-termination states.

Finally, I include a sector dummy – coded as 0 for fast-food and 1 for retail – to control for any industry difference in the propensity to franchise that is not captured by the unit-level and system-level independent variables. Given the catch-all nature of this control, the expected sign is ambiguous. One caveat, this industry dummy mirrors the repeat customer/non-compete customer categorization variable used by Brickley et al (1987, 1991) to proxy potential free-riding hazards.

---

[20] The relative competencies of single-unit franchising vs. multi-unit franchising as vehicles for relaxing managerial constraints is ambiguous. Though it can be argued that sequential multi-unit franchising (i.e., the granting of additional units on a merit basis to existing franchisees) may reduce the adverse selection costs associated with qualifying a new franchisee, not all multi-unit chains are built sequentially. Some franchisors offer area development agreements, in which they grant a "new" franchisee the right to open multiple stores in a specific region. Adverse selection in this context is still problematic (Kaufmann and Dant 1996). In my sample I do not know which multi-unit franchising form was used. As such, I can not predict the sign on the growth term in the multi-unit/single-unit choice model.

[21] In her model, Lafontaine (1992) does include both a growth variable and an "access to capital" variable. However, access to capital is represented using an extremely blunt dummy variable indicating whether or not the franchisor provides financing to its franchisees. (as compared to the continuous segment age "access" variable proposed here.) Not surprisingly, the financial dummy variable is insignificant while the growth variable is positively and significantly related to the use of franchising. In her discussion, she concludes that her growth-related findings are more supportive of the capital needs argument than the managerial needs argument.

If this dummy variable truly captures this hazard, one would expect its coefficient to be positive as retail locations are assumed to service repeat customers and thus face low free-riding hazards.

The independent variables, with source information and hypothesized signs, are summarized below in Table 1.

Table 1. Summary of Variables – Choice of Ownership Mode

Independent Variable	**Source**	**Predicted Sign Stage 1:** Ownership Choice Co-Own vs. Fran 1=Franchised 0=Company-Own	**Predicted Sign Stage 2:** Ownership Choice Single vs. Multi 1=Multi-Unit 0=Single-Unit
Shirking:			
Local Input Importance	UFOC: VIII	+	-
Distance from HQs	UFOC: I & XX	+	-
Free-Riding			
Brand Name Value	AD$ Summary	-	+
Spillover Potential	UFOC: XX	-	+
(Brand Name*Spillover)		-	+
Control Variables			
Resource Scarcity			
Segment Age	Entrepreneur Mag.	-	n/a
System Growth	UFOC: XX	+	n/a
Termination State		-	n/a
Industry Dummy		n/a	n/a

4.6 Exogeneity of Independent Variables

For the econometric model, franchise system characteristics are assumed to be exogenous. In business-format franchising, the first task of the franchisor is to develop and codify a unique business concept. Once defined, this concept, and the supporting core elements of the business model, are generally held invariant over time. According to franchisors, changes to established models are limited in order to ensure image consistency and contain the costs of maintaining uniformity across the system (Kaufmann and Eroglu 1999).[22] One of the proxies used to op-

[22] To maintain uniformity, any proposed change to the business model must be adopted both by new units and all existing units. This can be challenging as it is difficult to per-

erationalize shirking-related monitoring costs – Required Local Input – is an established element of the business concept. By law, required purchases are limited to items that support "market identity" by preserving the distinctiveness, uniformity, and quality of the franchisor's product.[23] As these core "identity" items are determined during business concept development, the required local input variable – which is a function of the required purchases (D = T- P) – is held to be exogenous to subsequent ownership decisions. Unfortunately, prior to 1996, franchisors were not required to document the franchisee's obligation to purchase from designated sources in the UFOC. Thus, I am not able to review older UFOCs to confirm the constancy of this value. However, I did track the initial investment requirements – another established element of the business concept – in a small sampling of UFOC documents over time and found little variation. The annual UFOC documents of both Wienerschnitzel and Taco Bell, for example, specify the same expenditure categories of required initial investments, with only slight increases in levels of expenditures (within the realm of inflation) within these categories, over a ten year period. Brand name specificity, which is accrued over time, is also held to be exogenous to ownership decisions.

While at first glance, the two locational proxies (geographical dispersion and spillover potential) appear to present endogeneity challenges, these concerns are mitigated when system dynamics are considered. Specifically, outlet turnover is remarkably fluid in business-format franchising. In the sample used for this study, I find that approximately 10% of existing outlets change ownership each year.[24] As, on average, the systems in this sample have been actively franchising for close to fifteen years, it is fair to assume that, in general, ownership choice follows location selection. Thus, we have grounds to treat the locational proxies as exogenous.

4.7 Descriptive Statistics

Table 2 reports the descriptive statistics for the current sample of 5,219 outlets from 64 franchise systems drawn from fast-foods and general retail sectors. Table 3 shows the correlation matrix for the independent variables. None of the key variables are highly correlated. The strongest correlation is the positive correla-

suade established franchisees to invest additional funds and/or effort in format changes (Bradach, 1998).

[23] See the note, "Quality Control and Antitrust Laws in Trademark Licensing" in 15 U.S.C. Sections 1055, 1127.

[24] In Item XX of the UFOC, franchisors are required to report the number of outlets that have been terminated, not-renewed, transferred, reacquired, converted to franchisee ownership or have left the system in each of the previous three years. The 10% turnover number cited above is derived by summing transfers, reacquisitions, conversions and 50% of the terminations. This is a conservative calculation of turnover as franchisors are notoriously loathe to close outlets preferring to resell the outlets of terminated franchisees.

tion of 0.54 between the free-riding interaction term and spillover potential – one of the component elements of this term.

Table 2. Descriptive Statistics for Ownership Choice Analysis

Variable	Mean	Std Dev	Minimum	Maximum
Ownership 0 = Company-Owned Outlet (N=696) 1 = Multi- or Single-Unit Franchisee (N=4523)	0.866	0.340	0	1
Multi-Unit – Single-Unit 0 = Single Unit Franchisee (N=2161) 1 = Multiple Unit Franchisee (N=2362)	0.522	0.499	0	1
Importance of Local Input Discretionary Inputs as % of Total	0.804	0.173	0.35	1.00
Shirking-Related Monitoring Costs Miles to Monitoring HQ (100s)	5.32	6.17		48.62
Brand Name Value Advertising Expenditures ($M)	0.756	1.158	0.048	3.489
Spillover Potential 1/Ave. Distance to 3 Closest Units	0.115	0.221	0.0004	5.882
Free-Riding Hazard Interaction Term (Brand Name) * (Spillover)	0.092	0.255	3.3×10^{-5}	3.837
Sector Age Average Years Franchising	11.13	6.42	2.00	39.00
Growth Rate	0.087	0.122	-0.088	0.557
% Outlets Located in a Termination State 0 = No 1 = Yes	0.397	0.489	0	1
Sector 0 = Fast-Food 1 = General Retail	0.194	0.395	0	1

Table 3. Correlation Matrix for Independent Variables

	1	2	3	4	5	6	7	8
1 Local Input Impt.	1.00							
2 HQ Distance	-0.17**	1.00						
3 Brand Name Value	-0.03	-0.02	1.00					
4 Spillover	0.02	-0.16**	0.02	1.00				
5 Free-Riding Inter.	-0.04*	-0.05**	0.54**	0.39**	1.00			
6 Sector Age	0.10**	-0.23**	0.35**	0.11**	0.24**	1.00		
7 Growth Rate	-0.10**	0.04*	-0.40**	-0.03	-0.22**	-0.48**	1.00	
8 Termination State	0.01	0.07**	-0.09**	0.06**	-0.01	-0.01	-0.01	1.00
9 Sector	0.05**	0.11**	-0.02	-0.11**	-0.13**	-0.06**	-0.12**	0.03

**p < 0.001; *p < 0.01

5 Results and Discussion

5.1 Stage One Organizational Choice: Company-owned vs. Franchised

Results of four binomial logit estimations relating ownership mode (company-owned versus franchised) to the independent variables are reported in Table 4. Model 1, in the first column, provides coefficient estimates for the baseline model which contains only the linear variables featured in the economizing hypotheses. Model 2a and 2b, in the second and third column, add the free-riding interaction term.[25] Model 3 provides estimations for an expanded model which includes the control variables as well.

Overall, there is strong support for the overarching economizing hypotheses. All four of the specific hazard-related variables have the predicted sign and are highly significant. Consider first the shirking-related hypothesis (H1a). The estimated coefficient on the local input variable, an indicator of across-system variation in behavioral monitoring costs, is positive and highly significant ($p<0.01$). This finding supports the contention that outlets in which managers have broad spans of control (i.e., outlets that would require relatively extensive, and therefore relatively expensive, monitoring) are more likely to be franchised than company-owned. A related interpretation of this finding, (one offered and supported in

[25] Several franchise systems in the sample did not report number of units for past years. As such, I was not able to calculate a growth rate term in all cases. Thus, Model 2b and Model 3 use a smaller data set consisting of 4,803 units in 56 systems for which growth rate is known.

studies of franchising by Cave and Murphy 1976; Lafontaine 1992) is that as the outlet-level activities of agents become more important, use of high-powered incentives, and thus franchising becomes increasingly necessary, and thus, more likely.

Table 4. Binomial Logit Estimations: Ownership Mode Dependent Variable: Franchised Outlet =1 Company-Owned Outlet = 0

Variable	Model 1	Model 2a	Model 2b	Model 3
Intercept	0.6512*** (0.2048)	0.6143*** (0.2058)	0.5027** (0.2149)	1.2247*** (0.2606)
Importance of Local Inputs	1.1.8774*** (0.2420)	1.8475*** (0.2428)	2.0518*** (0.2550)	2.1838*** (0.2640)
Distance to HQ	0.0227*** (0.0077)	0.0242*** (0.0077)	0.0283*** (0.0083)	0.0223*** (0.0084)
Brand Name Value	-0.2207*** (0.0328)	-0.1398*** (0.0420)	-0.1578*** (0.0441)	-0.0907* (0.0504)
Spillover Potential	-1.3237*** (0.1917)	-0.9427*** (0.2234)	-1.0704*** (0.2305)	-0.9271*** (0.2334)
(BN)* (Spillover)		-0.5638*** (0.1764)	-0.5307*** (0.1793)	-0.5038*** (0.1788)
Sector Age				-0.0510*** (0.0103)
Growth Rate				-0.3788 (0.4561)
Termination State				-0.6227*** (0.0897)
Sector				0.1421 (0.1341)
Chi-Square for Covariates	168.561***	179.074***	196.715***	275.715***
% Outcomes Predicted Correctly	65.1%	65.7%	67.6%	69.6%
Sample Size	5,219	5,219	4,803	4,803

*** $p < 0.01$; ** $p < 0.05$; * $p < 0.10$

The estimated coefficient on the geographical distance variable, an indicator of within-system variation in behavioral monitoring costs, is also positive and highly significant. This result, which is in-line with findings in several previous studies of the franchising make-or-buy decision (e.g., Brickley and Dark 1987; and Minkler 1990), indicates that less hierarchical modes are the preferred organizational form for distant, and thus harder to monitor, outlets. In sum, the positive and significant coefficients on these two variables reflects a tendency for systems to reduce their reliance on behavior (input) monitoring, and increase their reliance on residual claims (and output monitoring) as shirking-related monitoring costs increase.

Next, consider the free-riding hazard hypothesis (H2a). The estimated coefficient on the brand name variable, the shared system attribute that is vulnerable to free-riding, is negative and significant. This negative finding is consistent with the economizing hypothesis.[26] The direct effect of the spillover potential variable is also negative and significant, supporting the argument that company-ownership will be the preferred governance form when the possibility of demand externalities is high. This strong finding bolsters the economizing perspective as, hampered by the use of blunt customer transience proxies, previous empirical studies have reported mixed findings with respect to the relationship between this component element of the free-riding hazard and the use of franchising.

In Model 2a and 2b, I add the free-riding interaction term to the main effects economizing model. As hypothesized, the coefficient on this interaction term is negative and significant. To test the value of including this interaction term, a likelihood ratio test comparing Model 2a to the main effects model, Model 1, was run. The difference between the two models was significant yielding a p-value less than 0.01. To illuminate the impact of the free-riding interaction term on the propensity to adopt different ownership modes (company-owned or franchised), the predicted probabilities at different brand name values (advertising levels) and with different spillover potential are calculated. Table 5 reports the predicted probabilities for different levels of brand name value given significant spillover potential and average values of all other hazard variables. Similarly, Table 6 presents the predicted probabilities for low, average, and high levels of spillover potential given significant brand name value and average values of all other hazard variables. In both cases, as either spillover potential increases or as brand name value increases, the probability a unit will be franchised (single and/or multi unit) decreases while the probability of units being company-owned increases. In sum, and in support of hypothesis H3a, the model indicates that more hierarchical governance forms are preferred as the free-riding interaction term increases.

---

[26] The negative coefficient found here relating brand name value and the use of franchising is also consistent with findings in the extant empirical literature (Lafontaine 1992; Minkler and Park 1994; Thompson 1994; Fladmoe-Linquist and Jacque 1995).

Table 5. Predicted Probabilities for Different Brand Name Values Probability of Franchising

Brand Name Level	Pr(Company-Owned)	Pr(Franchised)
Low	0.3436	0.6564
Medium	0.3976	0.6024
High	0.4423	0.5577

Now consider Model 3 which includes the economizing variables along with resource scarcity and other control variables. One of the two resource scarcity control variables was found to be significant in this estimation. Specifically, a negative relationship between the propensity to franchise and segment age was found. This result provides some support for the argument that franchising (multi/single) is adopted by the franchisor as a means to overcome financial constraints in situations where acquiring funds through the capital market is relatively difficult. The coefficient for the growth rate variable was negative and non-significant. This finding calls into question arguments that franchising is adopted to economize on the managerial screening and selection costs associated with high growth. Interestingly, when the sector age variable is omitted from Model 3, the coefficient on the growth variable becomes positive and, though still not significant, has a much larger Wald Chi-Square. Results of this manipulation show the importance of controlling for capital scarcity before drawing conclusions as to the relationship between growth, managerial needs, and franchising.

Table 6. Predicted Probabilities for Different Levels of Spillover Probability of Franchising

Spillover Potential Level	Pr(CompanyOwned)	Pr(Franchised)
Low	0.3097	0.6903
Medium	0.3486	0.6514
High	0.4423	0.5577

Only one of the remaining two control variables was significant. As predicted, a negative relationship between propensity to franchise and the presence of state termination laws was found. This finding suggests that laws restricting the franchisors' ability to terminate a franchisee effectively increase the costs of franchising and shift the make-or-buy calculus towards hierarchy. Finally, the coefficient on the sector variable while positive is not significant. There does not appear to be any industry difference in the propensity to franchise that has not been adequately captured by the more specific unit-level and system-level independent variables.

5.2 Stage Two Organizational Choice: Use of Multi-Unit vs. Single-Unit Franchising

Table 7 reports the results of four binary logit estimations – the main effects economizing model, the main effects plus interaction term economizing models, and the expanded model – relating franchising mode (multi-unit/single unit) to the independent variables. Again, strong support for the economizing hypotheses were found. All of the hazard-related variables are significant, and three of the four have the expected sign. Additionally, the overall predictive power of the model is strong: Model 1 correctly predicts the organizational form of 61.7% of the outlets in the sample. This is significantly better than a random assignment which would be expected to be correct for only 50.1% of the outlets.

Consider each hazard-related variable in turn. First, the sign on the local input variable (a measure of across-system behavioral monitoring costs) is in the expected direction (negative), and is statistically significant. This finding supports hypothesis H1b which argues that more market-like governance forms (i.e., single-unit franchising) will be favored as shirking-related costs increase. On the other hand, the estimated coefficient on the geographical distance variable (a measure of within-system behavioral monitoring costs) is in the opposite direction than was hypothesized, and is significant at the 1% level. This contrary result, which suggests that increased distance from franchisor headquarters is positively related to the use of multi-unit governance, makes sense if the franchisor delegates direct monitoring responsibilities of multi-unit outlets to the owner of that multi-unit chain.[27] In this case, distance from franchisor headquarters is no longer the relevant measure for within-system shirking related monitoring costs for both single-unit and multi-unit outlets. Rather, the geographical distance measure should reflect the location of the appropriate monitor-the franchisor for single unit franchisees and the multi-unit owner for outlets in a multi-unit chain. Such coding would allow the reported findings to be disaggregated. It is quite possible that H1b will then be supported with less hierarchical governance forms being positively related to increasing (appropriate) monitor-outlet dispersion, even as distance between outlets in a multi-unit chain and franchisor headquarters increase. Unfortunately, most UFOCs do not report operating headquarters for multi-unit franchisors. As such, I was unable to test the above proposition. Further data collection and empirical testing is needed in this area.

---

[27] Bradach (1997, p 285) finds evidence of such delegation in his case study of five fast-food franchises. Specifically he finds, "The chain's relatively wide spans of control over franchisees are attributable in part to the presence of franchisee-owned and operated mini-hierarchies, which exercised control over franchise units and enabled the chain to devote fewer resources to controlling these units."

Table 7. Binomial Logit Estimations: Multi-Unit/Single Unit Franchising
Dependent Variable: Multi-Unit Franchise = 1 Single-Unit Franchise = 0

Variable	Model 1	Model 2a	Model 2b	Model 3
Intercept	0.6106*** (0.1581)	0.6529 *** (0.1581)	0.7556*** (0.1640)	0.8334*** (0.1898)
Importance of Local Inputs	-1.2339*** (0.1793)	-1.1959*** (0.1796)	-1.2981*** (0.1861)	-1.1027*** (0.1896)
Distance to HQ	0.0171*** (0.0053)	0.0163*** (0.00524)	0.0145*** (0.0055)	0.0184*** (0.0057)
Brand Name Value	0.2794*** (0.0277)	0.1316*** (0.0360)	0.1312*** (0.0384)	0.1814*** (0.0417)
Spillover Potential	1.9580*** (0.2394)	1.1409*** (0.2530)	1.3785*** (0.2722)	1.3793*** (0.2777)
(BN) * (Spillover)		1.9648*** (0.3441)	2.1359*** (0.3784)	1.8419*** (0.3725)
Sector Age				-0.0114* (0.0065)
Growth Rate				0.0557 (0.3044)
Termination State				-0.0592 (0.0678)
Sector				-0.7658*** (0.0874)
Chi-Square for Covariates	237.207***	280.548***	298.046***	385.446***
% Outcomes Predicted Correctly	61.7%	62.2%	63.8%	67.1%
Sample Size	4,523	4,523	4,172	4,172

*** $p < 0.01$; ** $p < 0.05$; * $p < 0.10$

Results with respect to H2b – predicting a positive relationship between the use of multi-unit franchising and increasing levels of the component elements of the free-riding hazard – are encouraging. The coefficients on both the brand name variable and the spillover potential variable are positive and significant. These finding are consistent with the economizing argument that multi-unit franchising mitigates the free-riding threat. Individuals owning multiple units know they will internalize a greater share of quality debasement costs and thus have less incentive to cheat. As shown in Model 2, the coefficient on the free-riding interaction term, is highly significant and positive. Further, the likelihood ratio test comparing this model containing the free-riding interact term with Model 1 in which this variable was omitted was highly significant yielding a p-value of less than 0.01. To facilitate interpretation of the free-riding variable, I again compute the predicted probabilities at different brand name values (advertising levels) and with different spillover potentials. (See Tables 8 and 9) In both cases, as either spillover potential increases or as brand name value increases, the probability a unit will be part of a multi-unit franchise chain increases while the probability of the outlet being a single-unit franchise decreases. In sum, and in support of hypothesis H3b, the model indicates that, in certain instances, multi-unit franchising provides a cost-effective way to mitigate free-riding hazards.

Table 8. Predicted Probabilities for Different Brand Name Values Multi-Unit/Single Unit Franchising

Brand Name Level	Pr(Single-Unit)	Pr(Multi-Unit)
Low	0.7452	0.2548
Medium	0.6248	0.3752
High	0.5163	0.4837

Table 9. Predicted Probabilities for Different Levels of Spillover Multi-Unit/Single Unit Franchising

Level of Spillover Potential	Pr(Single-Unit)	Pr(Multi-Unit)
Low	0.7891	0.2109
Medium	0.7173	0.2827
High	0.5163	0.4837

A comparison of Tables 6 and 7 with Tables 8 and 9, respectively, highlights an interesting detail about the influence of free-riding hazards on organizational choice. Namely, there is a greater propensity to shift from single-unit franchising to multi-unit franchising than from single-unit franchising to company ownership of units given comparable increases in the free-riding hazard. This finding is logical as the shirking-related penalty of such ownership shifts are expected to be much less in the first case than in the second.

Now consider Model 3. Again, one of the two resource scarcity variables is significant. The probability of multi-unit franchising (as compared to single-unit franchising) is negatively related to sector age. This result is not particularly surprising. One would anticipate that systems in new sectors are relatively new themselves and, as such, have not yet grown to the point where multi-unit franchising presents a significant option. The coefficient on the system growth variable is positive and insignificant regardless if the model is run with or without the sector age variable. The estimated coefficient on the termination state variable while negative is insignificant. Again, this result is not surprising as the inability to freely terminate franchise agreements would be expected to discourage single-unit and multi-unit franchising at similar rates. Finally, the coefficient on the sector dummy is negative and significant. As compared to retail outlets, fast-food outlets are more likely to be operated as part of a multi-unit chain.

6 Conclusion – Future Research

The make-or-buy analysis reported in this chapter extends the extant empirical franchising literature. Leveraging a unique and detailed data set compiled directly from franchise disclosure documents (UFOCs), this study has the advantage of working with proxies – built at the system-level as well as unit-level – that more precisely capture the theoretical constructs of interest. Thus, the study is able to add to the literature in three specific ways. First, the analysis is more inclusive. The comprehensive models tested simultaneously account for the direct effects of both pertinent contractual hazards – shirking and free-riding – hypothesized to underlie the central economizing trade-off, explores the potential interaction effects of the component elements of the free-riding hazard, and controls for the possible influence of resource scarcity factors. Second, the study takes the outlet as the unit of analysis and is thus able to investigate within-system organizational choice – the likelihood that a specific outlet will be organized as a franchise unit rather than as a company-owned outlet. And third, this study provides one of the rare empirical investigations of the adoption of multi-unit franchising – the ownership of two or more outlets by a single franchisee. Given the pervasiveness of this practice, such studies are critical for building a true understanding of "what's going on" in the franchising arena.

Overall, the results reported here provide strong support for the economizing perspective of organizational choice. As set forth in H1a-H3a, I find that the probability a unit will be franchised increases with the level of shirking-related costs and decreases with the intensity of the free-riding hazard. Similarly, the choice between multi-unit franchising and single-unit franchising is found to turn on the relative level of these two hazards. Further, using an innovative proxy to capture the franchisor's capital constraints, I find support for the resource scarcity argument that a shortage of capital shifts the make-or-buy decision calculus towards franchising. In sum, this study illuminates the complementary nature of the economizing and resource scarcity perspectives and highlights the benefits of applying both to increase our understanding of organizational choice in the franchising arena.

Even with these contributions, there is still room for further research. As alluded to several times in the text, our understanding of the factors that drive direct monitoring costs remain underdeveloped. While the commonly used proxy of geographical distance has merit, it provides an incomplete measure. Additional research is needed to more fully characterize other elements – such as demographic distance, organization size, and/or observability – that influence direct monitoring costs. Further, there are questions as to the viability of different types of monitoring procedures (alternatives to direct monitoring) in controlling shirking behavior and/or free-riding behavior. Are different types of monitoring more effective in repressing different types of opportunistic behavior? A study investigating variations in monitoring practices at company-owned stores and franchised outlets may provide insight into these questions.

With respect to the resource scarcity perspective, questions about the influence of managerial limitations on the decision to franchise remain unresolved. The development of proxies that better capture the franchisor's need for, and access to, managerial resources are required to clarify this issue. Future research opportunities beckon.

References

1. Agrawal D, Lal R (1995) Contractual Arrangements in Franchising: An Empirical Investigation. Journal of Marketing Research 32:213-221
2. Akerlof G (1970) The Market for 'Lemons': Quality Uncertainty and the Market Mechanism. Quarterly Journal of Economics 84:488-500
3. Alchian AA, Demsetz H (1972) Production, Information Costs, and Economic Organization. American Economic Review 62:777-795
4. Aldrich J, Nelson F (1984) Linear Probability, Logit, and Probit Models Number 07-045 in Sage University Paper Series on Quantitative Applications in the Social Sciences. California: Sage Publications
5. Anderson E, Oliver R (1987) Perspectives on Behavior-Based Versus Outcome-Based Sales Control Systems. Journal of Marketing 51(October):76-88
6. Anson W (1996) Ways to Put Value on a Trademark. Corporate Finance 144:36-39
7. Beales HJ III, Muris TJ (1995) The Foundations of Franchise Regulation: Issues and Evidence. Journal of Corporate Finance 2:157-197
8. Bhattacharyya S, Lafontaine F (1995) Double-Sided Moral Hazard and the Nature of Share Contracts. Rand Journal of Economics 26(4):761-781
9. Bond RE (1997) Bond's Franchise Guide 1997 Edition. Source Book Publications, Oakland, CA
10. Bradach J (1997) Using the Plural Form in the Management of Restaurant Chains. Administrative Science Quarterly 42(2):276-303
11. Bradach J (1998) Franchise Organizations. Boston, MA: Harvard University Press
12. Brickley JA, Dark FH (1987) The Choice of Organizational Form: The Case of Franchising. Journal of Financial Economics 18:401-20
13. Brickley JA, Dark FH, Weisbach SW (1991) An Agency Perspective on Franchising. Financial Management 20:27-35

14.Carney M, Gedajlovic E (1991) Vertical Integration in Franchise Systems: Agency Theory and Resource Explanations. Strategic Management Journal 12:607-629
15.Caves RE, Murphy WF II (1976) Franchising: Firms, Markets, and Intangible Assets. Southern Economic Journa, 42:572-586
16.Combs J, Ketchen D Jr. (1999) Can Capital Scarcity Help Agency Theory Explain Franchising? Revisiting the Capital Scarcity Hypothesis. Academy of Management Journal 42(2):196-207
17.Dant R (1995) Motivations for Franchising: Rhetoric Versus Reality. International Small Business Journal 14(1):10-32
18.Darr E, Argote L, Epple E (1995) The Acquisition, Transfer, and Depreciation of Knowledge in Service Organizations: Productivity in Franchises. Management Science, 41(November):1750-1762
19.Demski JS, Feltham GA (1978) Economic Incentives in Budgetary Control Systems. The Accounting Review 53(2):336-359
20.Dnes AW (1996) The Economic Analysis of Franchise Contracts. Journal of Institutional and Theoretical Economics 152:297-324
21.Elango B, Fried V (1997) Franchising Research: A Literature Review and Synthesis. Journal of Small Business Management 35(3):68-81
22.Entrepreneur Magazine. Annual Franchise 500. January, 1996; January, 1997; and January, 1998
23.Fama EF, Jensen MC (1983) Separation of Ownership and Control. Journal of Law and Economics 26:301-326
24.Fladmoe-Lindquist K, Jacque L (1995) Control Modes in International Service Operations: The Propensity to Franchise. Management Science 41(7):1238-1249
25.Holmstrom B (1982) Moral Hazard in Teams. Bell Journal of Economics 13:324-341
26.Jensen MC, Meckling WH (1976) Theory of the Firm: Managerial Behavior, Agency Costs, and Ownership Structure. Journal of Financial Economics 3:305-360
27.Kaufmann PJ, Dant RP (1996) Multi-Unit Franchising: Growth and Management Issues. Journal of Business Venturing 11:343-358
28.Kaufmann PJ, Eroglu S (1999) Standardization and Adaptation in Business Format Franchising. Journal of Business Venturing 14(1):69-86
29.Keller K (1997) Strategic Brand Management. Upper Saddle River, N.J.: Prentice Hall
30.Klein B (1980) Transaction Cost Determinants of Unfair Contractual Arrangements, American Economic Review Papers and Proceedings 70:356-362
31.Klein B (1995) The Economics of Franchise Contracts. Journal of Corporate Finance 2: 9-37
32.Klein B, Leffler KB (1981) The Role of Market Forces in Assuring Contractual Performance . Journal of Political Economy 89:615-641
33.Klein B, Murphy K (1988) Vertical Restraints as Contract Enforcement Mechanisms. Journal of Law and Economics 31:265-297
34.Klein B, Saft LF (1985) The Law and Economics of Franchise Tying Contracts. Journal of Law and Economics 28:345-361
35.Krueger AB (1990) Ownership, Agency and Wages: An Examination of Franchising in the Fast Food Industry. NBER Working Paper No. 3334
36.Lafontaine F (1992) Agency Theory and Franchising: Some Empirical Results. RAND Journal of Economics 23(2):263-283
37.Lafontaine F (1992b) How and Why Do Franchisors Do What They Do, in PJ Kaufmann (Ed.) *Franchising: Passport for Growth & World of Opportunity*, 6th Annual Proceedings of the Society of Franchising, University of St. Thomas
38.Leading National Advertisers/Media Watch. 1992-1998. AD $ Summary. New York, NY: LNA

39. Liao TF (1994) Interpreting Probability Models: Logit, Probit, and Other Generalized Linear Models. Number 07-101 in Sage University Paper Series on Quantitative Applications in the Social Sciences. California: Sage Publications
40. Mathewson GF, Winter RA (1985) The Economics of Franchise Contracts. Journal of Law and Economics 28:503-526
41. Minkler AP (1990) An Empirical Analysis of a Firm's Decision to Franchise. Economic Letters 34:77-82
42. Minkler AP, Park TA. (1994) Asset Specificity and Vertical Integration in Franchising. Review of Industrial Organization 9:409-423
43. Norton SW (1988) An Empirical Look at Franchising as an Organizational Form. Journal of Business 61(2):197-218
44. Norton SW (1995) Is Franchising a Capital Structure Issue? Journal of Corporate Finance 2(1-2):75-101
45. Ouchi WG. (1979) A Conceptual Framework for the Design of Organizational Control Mechanisms. Management Science 25(9):833-848.
46. Oxenfeldt AR, Kelly AO (1968-69) Will Successful Franchise Systems Ultimately Become Wholly-Owned Chains? Journal of Retailing 44(4):69-83
47. Oxenfeldt AR, Thompson DN (1968-69) Franchising in Perspective. Journal of Retailing 44(4):3-13
48. Ozanne UB, Hunt SD (1971) The Economic Effects of Franchising, Prepared for the Small Business Administration
49. Penrose E (1959) The Theory of the Growth of the Firm. New York, NY: Wiley
50. Reilly R (1996) The Valuation of Intangible Assets. The National Public Accountant. 41(7):26-40.
51. Rubin PH (1978) The Theory of the Firm and the Structure of the Franchise Contract. The Journal of Law and Economics 21:223-233
52. Rubin PH (1990) Managing Business Transactions. New York, NY: The Free Press
53. Scott FA (1995) Franchising vs. Company Ownership as a Decision Variable of the Firm. Review of Industrial Organization 10:69-81
54. Shane SA (1996) Hybrid Organizational Arrangements and Their Implications for Firm Growth and Survival: A Study of New Franchisors, The Academy of Management Journal 39(1):216-234
55. Slade ME (1996) Multitask Agency and Contract Choice: An Empirical Exploration. International Economic Review 37(2):465-486
56. Thompson RS (1994) The Franchise Life Cycle and the Penrose Effect. Journal of Economic Behavior and Organization 24(2):207-218
57. Williamson OE (1985) The Economic Institutions of Capitalism. New York, NY: The Free Press
58. Williamson OE. (1991) Comparative Economic Organization: The Analysis of Discrete Structural Alternatives. Administrative Science Quarterly 36:269-296
59. Williamson OE (1996) The Mechanisms of Governance. New York, NY: Oxford University Press

Part B:

Plural Forms and Other Hybrid Organizational Forms

The Dual Network Structure of Franchising Firms: Property Rights, Resource Scarcity and Transaction Cost Explanations

Josef Windsperger

Center for Business Studies
University of Vienna
Brünner Str. 72
A-1210 Vienna
Austria
josef.windsperger@univie.ac.at

Abstract. This paper formulates and tests various hypotheses from various theories regarding the dual network structure of franchising firms. First, by applying the property rights theory we argue that the contractual mix between company-owned and franchised outlets depends on the distribution of intangible assets between the franchisor and franchisee. The more important the franchisor's system-specific assets relative to the franchisee's local market assets for the generation of residual income, the more ownership rights should be transferred to him, and the higher is the percentage of company-owned outlets. Second, we compare these results with the resource scarcity and transaction cost view. According to the resource scarcity view, the proportion of company-owned outlets varies negatively with the franchisor's restraints in financial, informational and management resources. In addition, transaction cost theory states that the franchisee's specific investments (as bonding mechanism) mitigate the hold-up risk for the franchisor resulting in a lower degree of vertical integration. These hypotheses are tested by using data from the Austrian franchise sector. The empirical results are generally supportive of the property rights hypothesis. In addition, the informational restraint hypothesis is compatible with the property rights hypothesis regarding the influence of franchisee's local market know-how advantage on the percentage of company-owned outlets. On the other hand, the financial restraint and transaction cost hypotheses are not supported by our data.

Acknowledgements: I gratefully acknowledge financial support by the Austrian National Bank. A first version of the paper was presented at the International Society of Franchising Conference, Orlando, February 2002, the Research Seminar at the University of Vienna and the **EMNET**-Conference, June 2003, in Vienna. I want to thank Askin Yurdakul, Technical University of Vienna, for his comments and assistance.

1 Introduction

One of the main characteristics of franchising firms is the dual ownership structure (Lafontaine and Shaw 2001; Lewin-Solomon 1999; Bradach 1997; Dahlstrom and Nygaard 2000; Cliquet 2001; Penard et al. 2002). From a property rights view the mix of franchisor-owned and franchised outlets improves the organizational efficiency by combining intangible system-specific assets and local market assets to generate the residual income stream. The franchisee's intangible assets refer to outlet-specific knowledge and capabilities that generates residual income, and the franchisor's intangible assets refer to the system-specific know-how and brand name assets. Since investments in these assets cannot be specified in the contract, asset ownership critically influences the residual income stream of the network (Hart and Moore 1990; Hart 1995; Windsperger 2002b). According to the property rights approach, the allocation of residual income rights should encourage investments in system-specific and local market assets to create a large residual income stream. If the system-specific assets are very important for the generation of residual income relative to the local market assets, the franchisor´s investment incentive is critical for the success of the network, and hence more residual income rights are transferred to the franchisor by a higher proportion of company-owned outlets. Consequently, under the strong know-how position of the franchisor the intention is to control the network by relatively more company-owned outlets compared with a situation in which local market assets are critical for the creation of residual income.

The present article focuses on a property rights explanation of the relationship between company-owned and franchised outlets. Based on the property rights approach, we derive the dual structure hypothesis that the mix between company-owned and franchised outlets depends on the distribution of intangible assets between the franchisor and the franchisee. The higher the franchisor‘s portion of intangible assets relative to the franchisee's, the more ownership rights should be allocated to the franchisor, and the higher the proportion of company-owned outlets is. This hypothesis is tested in the Austrian franchise sector. As suggested by our data, noncontractible system-specific and local market assets influence the contractual mix between company-owned and franchised outlets. Finally, we compare our results with the resource scarcity and transaction cost view. According to the resource scarcity view, the proportion of company-owned outlets varies negatively with the franchisor's restraints in financial and informational resources. In addition, transaction cost theory states that the franchisee's specific investments (as bonding mechanism) mitigate the hold-up risk for the franchisor resulting in a lower degree of vertical integration. The empirical result about the informational restraint hypothesis is compatible with the property rights hypothesis regarding the influence of franchisee's local market know-how advantage on the percentage of company-owned outlets. On the other hand, our data do not support the financial restraint and transaction cost hypotheses.

Our main contribution to the franchising literature is to apply the property rights theory to explain the dual network structure of the franchising firm. Contrary to the existing literature, we argue that the mix between company-owned and franchised outlets depends not only on the brand name assets of the franchisor – as argued by Azevedo and Silva 2001, Penard et al. 2002 and Lafontaine and Shaw 2001 – but also on the importance of the intangible local market assets of the franchisee for the creation of residual income.

The paper is organized as follows: Section two presents a literature review. Section three develops a property rights view of the allocation of residual income rights in franchising. In section four we derive the dual structure hypothesis that the mix of franchised and company-owned outlets depends on the distribution of the intangible assets between the franchisor and the franchisee. Finally we test the hypothesis in the Austrian franchise sector.

2 Literature Review

The coexistence of franchised and company-owned outlets was examined from different perspectives. Starting from the ownership redirection hypothesis in marketing (Oxenfelt and Kelly 1968-69; Dant et al. 1996), an increase of the proportion of company-owned outlets was predicted during the organizational life cycle because scarcity of franchisor's resources (managerial and financial resources and local market knowledge) declines in later stages of the cycle. According to this resource scarcity view, the mix of franchised and company-owned outlets arises because it allows firms to obtain access to scarce financial, managerial and information resources (Norton 1988; Minkler 1990; Thompson 1994). In the 1980s and 1990s, agency-theoretical and transaction cost explanations were developed (Klein 1980, 1995; Williamson 1985; Brickley and Dark 1987; Brickley et al. 1991; Dnes 1992; Lafontaine 1992; Berkovitz 1999). According to these theories the decision between company ownership and franchising depends on the individual characteristics of the outlets (Lafontaine and Shaw 2001). The agency theory offers the following explanation: Under low monitoring costs company-owned outlets as low-powered incentive mechanism are more efficient than franchised outlets. When the monitoring costs rise due to local market uncertainty and opportunism, franchised outlets are more efficient due to their high-powered incentive effects. In addition, Gallini and Lutz (1992) developed a signalling model. At the beginning of the franchise business company-owned outlets signal high quality to potential franchisees and a commitment to protect the value of the brand name assets. When the value of the brand name is established that signals quality, company-ownership is less required resulting in a higher proportion of franchised outlets. Conversely, the transaction cost explanation is based on the assumption that differences in asset specifity, frequency and uncertainty may explain the ownership of the individual outlets. Primarily, the influence of transaction specifity on the tendency toward vertical integration by company-owned outlets was investigated. Due to the hostage effect of the outlet-specific investments, the franchisor's opportunism risk is reduced resulting in a lower proportion of company-owned outlets. More recently Lewin-Solomon (1999) explained the dual structure as a governance mechanism to promote innovations in the network. In addition, Bai and Tao (2000) presented a multi-task model of the existence of franchised and company-owned outlets. Moreover, Bradach (1997), Cliquet (2001), Sorenson and Sorensen (2000) and Michael (2000) proposed the plural form hypothesis. Bradach, Cliquet, and Sorenson and Sorensen argue that the dual structure is the result of synergistic effects between franchised and company-owned outlets. According to this strategic view, franchised outlets are more efficient at the 'exploration' and company-owned outlet at the 'exploitation' of the profit potential of the network (Sorenson and Sorensen 2000). Further, due to the complementarities between franchised and company-owned outlets, the organizational capability and hence the rent-generating capacity of the dual structure is higher than under the pure franchised or company-owned forms. Recently, Michael (2000) presented the tapered integration hypothesis. Tapered integration raises the bargaining power of the franchisor by improving the franchisor's local market information and by signalling to franchisees that the franchisor is committed to quality. This result is compatible with the synergistic view of the plural form.

Although these approaches and hypotheses offer explanations of different aspects of the ownership structure of franchising firms, the following deficits exists: *First*, the agency and transaction cost theory cannot explain the dual network structure under homogenous outlet characteristics. In addition, in a strictly methodological sense, the agency theory cannot explain the allocation of ownership rights as residual rights of control, due to the complete contracting assumption (Hart 1995; Masten 2000; Brousseau and Glachant 2003; Hart 2002; Hendrikse 2003). Under the property rights approach this assumption is critical for the explanation of asset ownership. As Baker and Hubbard (Baker and Hubbard 2001, 2002, 2003) argued, increasing the contractibility of assets may explain changes in the ownership structure. Furthermore, Whinston (2000, 2001) criticized the asset specifity theory developed by Williamson (1979) and Klein et. al (1978), because it does not differentiate between the various types of specifity that matter for integration decisions - for instance between contractible and noncontractible specific assets. *Second*, with the exception of the resource scarcity hypothesis, these theories do not take into account the influence of local market assets upon the optimal mix between franchised and company-owned outlets.

Starting from these theoretical deficits, the objective of this paper is to develop a property rights approach of the dual network structure. Contrary to the resource scarcity view, our approach differentiates between intangible and tangible resources. Only intangible resources can explain the ownership structure. In addition, compared to the agency and transaction cost theory, our approach does not require the assumption of heterogeneous outlet characteristics. Given the same outlet characteristics, our approach may explain the dual network structure by differences in organizational capabilities (as intangible assets) between the franchisor and franchisee.

3 The Allocation of Ownership Rights in Franchising Firms

According to the property rights approach, the structure of ownership rights depends on the distribution of intangible assets that generate the firm's residual surplus (Barzel 1997; Hart and Moore 1990; Hart 1995; Brynjolfsson 1994). In franchising, intangible knowledge assets refer to the brand name and system-specific assets of the franchisor and the local market assets (know-how) of the franchisee. Based on the property rights view, the allocation of residual income rights should encourage investments in system-specific and local market assets to create a large residual income stream. The more important the franchisor's intangible assets are for the creation of residual income relative to the franchisee, the higher the franchisor's portion of ownership rights is. The franchisor's residual income rights consist of two components: Fees and company-owned outlets.

(I) Initial fees are the remuneration for the system-specific know-how transferred to the franchisee at the beginning of the contract period. The higher the franchisor's intangible system-specific assets at the beginning of the contract period, the higher the rents generated by his system-specific know-how, and the higher the initial fees. In addition, the more important the franchisor's system-specific investments relative to the franchisees's intangible investments during the contract period, the higher the fraction of residual income created by him, and the higher the royalties (Rubin 1978; Brickley and Dark 1987; Lutz 1995). Conversely, the more important the franchisee‘s intangible local market investments are relative to the franchisor's intangible investments, the higher his fraction of the residual income should be, and the lower the royalties to provide the necessary incentive for the franchisees. Empirical results from the Austrian franchise sector support this property rights view of the fee structure (Windsperger 2001). (II) In addition, since the franchisor′s residual income rights are diluted by the transfer of outlet rights to the franchisee, his incentive to untertake system-specific intangible investments is lower and accordingly, the lower the fees are. On the other hand, the fees serve as incentive mechanism for the franchisee to untertake investments in intangible local market assets. The lower they are, the larger the franchisee's fraction of residual income rights is. Hence, to increase the franchisor′s residual income position and his investment incentive without mitigating the franchisee′s investment incentive by raising the fees, the percentage of company-owned outlets (PCO) must be increased. Consequently, fees and the proportion of company-owned outlets must be simultaneously determined to establish an efficient governance structure.

4 A Property Rights View of the Dual Network Structure

4.1 Franchised versus Company-owned Outlets

According to empirical studies, the organizational life cycle of franchising networks is characterized by two stages (Lafontaine and Shaw 2001; Azevedo and Silva 2001): The transitory period refers to the early stage of the life cycle in which an unstable mix between franchised and company-owned outlets exists, and the stable period refers to the stage of the life cycle with a relatively stable mix of franchised and company-owned outlets. How can we explain the ownership structure in both stages?

(a) Unstable Contractual Mix
In the transitory period no stable mix between franchised and company-owned outlets exists. Empirical studies find a significant decrease in company ownership during the first years of franchising (Lafontaine 1992; Scott 1995; Thompson 1994; Martin 1988; Minkler and Park 1994). There are different approaches to explain the transitory contractual mix: According to the signalling theory, the franchisor may maintain some company-owned outlets with the major role of signalling the value of the brand name assets to potential franchisees (Gallini and Lutz 1992). This may explain the higher percentage of company-owned outlets in the early period of organizational life cycle. On the other hand, a rise of company ownership was proposed and extensively tested in the marketing literature (Oxenfeldt and Kelly 1968-69; O'Hara and Thomas 1986; Padmanabhan 1989; Dant et al. 1998). Based on this resource scarcity view, ownership redirection results from resource constraints (financial, local information and management resources) in the early period of franchising. With more franchise experience, the percentage of company-owned outlets rises because the franchisor could already improve its financial position and also acquire outlet-specific knowledge and capabilities. However, the empirical results of these studies are mixed (Dant et al. 1996; Lafontaine and Kaufmann 1994).

How can the property rights theory explain the unstable contractual mix? Baker, Hubbard and Wernerfelt (Baker and Hubbard 2001; Baker and Hubbard 2003; Wernerfelt 2002) argue that changes in asset ownership result from changes in contractibility. Applied to franchising, changes in asset ownership are based on changes in intangibility of assets due to organizational learning of the franchisor who acquires local market knowledge during the organizational life cycle. According to Nonaka's knowledge spiral model (Nonaka 1994; Nonaka and Takeuchi 1995; Nonaka et al. 2001), organizational learning triggers a knowledge conversion process that changes the nature of local market knowledge from tacit to more explicit knowledge. Therefore, contractibility of local market assets rises during the transitory period that changes the bargaining power between the franchisor and franchisee. Under more contractible (less intangible) local market assets of the franchisees, the franchisor's system specific assets are more important for the creation of residual surplus of the network. Hence ownership rights must be transferred to the franchisor to secure the franchisor's investments in system-specific assets and to prevent the franchisee from hold-up. Consequently, due to this knowledge conversion from tacit to more explicit knowledge the PCO should rise during the organizational life cycle. This result is compatible with the resource scarcity view which states that the scarcity of information resources decreases during the organizational life cycle.

(b) Stable Contractual Mix

Empirical studies show that the percentage of company-owned outlets stabilizes after the decline in the early stage of the organizational life cycle (for instance Lafontaine and Shaw 2001; Penard et al. 2002). Similar results are found in the Austrian franchising sector (see Windsperger 2002). How can we explain the dual network structure? According to the property rights theory, the allocation of residual income rights depends on the distribution of intangible system-specific and local market assets between the franchisor and the franchisee. The higher the fraction of the franchisor's intangible assets relative to the franchisee's for the generation of residual income, the more property rights must be transferred to him, and the higher the percentage of company-owned outlets is. Hence, if the intangible system-specific assets of the franchisor are relatively important compared to the intangible local market assets, the PCO should be relatively high; and if the local market assets of the franchisee are relatively important compared to the brand name assets, the PCO should be relatively low. In addition, how can we explain the stabilizing effect of the dual structure? Based on the property rights theory, the distribution between contractible and noncontractible assets may result in a certain ownership structure. If the local market assets become fully contractible, the franchising firm will no longer exist. In this case, ownership redirection results in a vertically integrated firm with only company-owned outlets. If, on the other hand, both the franchisor and the franchisees have noncontractible assets to create the residual surplus, ownership cannot be completely redirected. Therefore, the necessary condition to explain the dual structure is a stable distribution of noncontractible assets between the franchisor and the franchisees. Depending on the importance of both parties'noncontractible assets to generate the residual income of the network, the percentage of company-owned outlets is higher or lower.

For instance, differences in the distribution of noncontractible assets between the franchisor and the franchisees may explain sectoral differences in the percentage of company-owned outlets. As shown by Lafontaine and Shaw (2001), the PCO in product franchising is much higher than in the service sector. This is also the case in the Austrian franchise sector; the PCO is 23,87 % in services and 31,04 % in product franchising. In product franchising the franchisor's intangible system-specific assets are more important for the generation of residual income of the network than the local market assets of the franchisee. On the other hand, in services the PCO is relatively lower due to the higher importance of noncontractible local market assets for the creation of residual surplus. To summarize, after a transitory period, a stable contractual mix between franchised and company-owned outlets results from a certain distribution of complementary intangible system-specific assets and local market assets.

4.2 Interaction between Company-owned Outlets and Royalties

Since residual income rights are allocated to the franchisor and franchisee, ownership rights include both residual income rights of franchised outlets (royalties and fees) and residual income rights of company-owned outlets. Given the initial fees, royalties and the proportion of franchisor-owned outlets are negatively related. The lower the royalties, the higher the PCO to maintain the franchisor's incentive to invest in intangible system-specific assets. This may be explained by the dual incentive effects of royalties (Scott 1995). Royalties are the residual income for the franchisor to invest in system-specific assets, but setting a positive royalty rate dilutes the incentive effect for the franchisee to invest in local market assets. To secure the franchisor's investment incentive under a low royalty rate, residual income rights are transferred to him by increasing the proportion of company-owned outlets. Consequently, contrary to the agency-theoretical view (Lafontaine 1992; Penard et al. 2002), company-owned outlets function as a substitute for the diluted residual income rights of franchised outlets.

Which factors influence the relationship between royalties and the PCO? According to the property rights view, the interaction effect between PCO and royalties depends on the importance of intangible system-specific assets relative to the local market assets for the creation of residual surplus. (a) If the system-specific assets are very important for the generation of residual income, a high fraction of ownership rights must be transferred to the franchisor. In this case the diluted residual income rights of the franchised outlets are compensated by a relatively high PCO. (b) On the other hand, if the local market assets and the system-specific assets are very important for the creation of residual surplus, more residual income rights must be transferred to the franchisee. Compared to (a), the franchisee pays relatively lower royalties and the dilution of the franchisor's residual income rights is compensated by a higher PCO. Therefore, under a more equal know-how distribution between the franchisor and the franchisee, the negative relationship between royalties and PCO is higher than under a strong know-how position of the franchiser, because in this case the franchisor' and the franchisee's investment incentives are very important for the creation of the residual surplus. In sum, we may conclude that the negative interaction between royalties and PCO depends on the bargaining power of the franchisor and the franchisee, i. e. on the importance of intangible system-specific assets relative to the local market assets for the creation of residual surplus of the network.

As a result, we summarize the property rights propositions of the dual network structure:

Proposition I: Stable contractual mix

The more important the franchisor's (franchisee's) intangible assets (know-how) relative to the franchisee's to generate the residual surplus, the more ownership rights should be transferred to the franchisor (franchisee), and the higher (lower) the percentage of company-owned outlets is.

Proposition II: Transitory contractual mix

The larger the knowledge conversion effect relative to the signaling effect during the early stage of the organizational life cycle, the more likely ownership redirection occurs.

Proposition III: Interaction between royalties and PCO

Royalties and PCO are substitutes. The more important the franchisee's intangible local market assets to generate the residual surplus, the more residual income rights should be transferred to the franchisee, and the larger the negative relationship between royalties and PCO is.

The following testable hypotheses can be derived from this property rights approach:

> *H1: The percentage of company-owned outlets is positively related to the franchisor's intangible system-specific assets and negatively related to the franchisee's intangible local market assets.*
>
> *H2: The larger the franchise experience, the lower the negative relationship between local market assets and PCO, and the higher is the positive relationship between system-specific assets and PCO.*
>
> *H3: PCO and royalties are negatively related.*

5 Empirical Analysis

5.1 Sample

The empirical setting for testing these hypotheses is the franchising sector in Austria. A national mail survey was used to collect the data from all franchise systems in Austria that were registered at the Austrian Franchise Association in 1997. The database identified a total of 216 franchise systems in Austria representing more than 90 % of all franchise systems in Austria. The data set was collected in 1997-98. After several preliminary steps in questionnaire development and refinement, including in-depth interviews with franchisers in Vienna and representatives of the Austrian franchise association, the final version of the questionnaire was protested with 6 franchisers. The questionnaire took approximately 20 minutes to complete on average. The revised questionnaire, which incorporated the alterations suggested by the pretest, was mailed to 216 franchisers in Austria. We received 83 completed and usable responses with a response rate of 38,4%. To trace non-response bias, it was investigated whether the results obtained from analysis are driven by differences between the group of respondents and the group of non-respondents. Non-response bias was measured by comparing early and late responders (Amstrong and Overton 1977). The non-responding group includes the firms, which completed the questionnaire four weeks after the first group. No significant differences emerged between the two groups of respondents.

5.2 Measures

Intangible Assets

They refer to the noncontractible system-specific assets of the franchisor and the local market assets of the franchisee. The franchisor's intangible assets are operationalized by the number of annual training days of the franchisee and its employees. The assumption behind this measure is that as the franchisor's intangible assets increases, so does the number of days of face-to-face interaction (Simonin 1999; Daft and Lengel 1986; Darr et al. 1995). Intangible assets of the franchisee refer to the franchisee's local market know-how. The local market know-how refers to the franchisee′s local marketing, human resources, quality control and innovation capabilities. The higher the intangible local market assets of the franchisee, the larger the local market knowledge advantage of the franchisee compared to the manager of a company-owned outlet. Therefore, we use the local market know-how advantage of the franchisee as indicator of his intangible outlet-specific assets. Furthermore, according to the resource scarcity view, this variable is a proxy for the franchisor's constraints on local market knowledge during the organizaitonal life cycle. In the questionnaire the franchisors were asked to rate on a five-point scale to evaluate franchisee's local market assets (see appendix). We used a three-item scale to measure the local know-how advantage of the franchisee compared to the manager of a company-owned outlet. The three-item measure was extracted by employing factor analysis. All variables had a loading in excess of 0,59. The total amount of variance explained by the factor solution is 58,04 percent. The reliability of this scale was assessed by Cronbach's alpha (0,63) which is compatible with the generally agreed upon lower limit of 0,6 for exploratory research (Nunnally 1978; Hair et al. 1998).

Residual Income Rights

These refer to the royalties and the percentage of company-owned outlets.

Control Variables

We controlled for two variables that might affect the mix of company-owned and franchised outlets:

(1) Initial investments: According to the resource-scarcity view, initial investments are an indicator for the financial constraints of the franchisor when he intends to increase the number of outlets (Brickley et al. 1991). The higher the initial investments, the more financial resources are required to extend the network, and the higher the tendency toward franchised outlets is. In addition, according to the

transaction cost theory, the tendency toward vertical integration is negatively related to the extent of transaction specific investments of the franchisees, because high outlet-specific investments reduce the hold-up risks for the franchisor (Klein 1980; Williamson 1985). Hence franchisee's intial investments are a proxy for transaction specific investments.

(2) Sectoral variable: Because the know-how intensity of franchising firms varies between product franchising and service firms (Zeithaml et al. 1985; Lafontaine and Shaw 2001), we include a sectoral variable to control for sectoral effects. 0 refers to product franchising and 1 to the services sector. Since the product franchising sector is characterized by a higher fraction of intangible system-specific assets of the franchisor relative to the intangible local market assets of the franchisees, the product franchising firm should have a higher proportion of company-owned outlets compared to a firm in the service sector.

5.3 Results

1) Descriptive Results

Table 1 presents descriptive data for the sample. More than 26,9% of the outlets are company-owned. If we differentiate between services and product franchising, the percentage of company-owned outlets is 23,8 % in the service sector and 31,04 % in the product franchising sector.

Table 1. Franchise Systems in Austria

	N	Minimum	Maximum	Mean	Standard Deviation
Initial Fees	79	,00	218023 (EUR)	11797,60	25326,5000
Franchisee's Local Market Knowledge Advantage	71	1,00	5,00	3,8732	1,2754
Franchisee's Quality Advantage	70	1,00	5,00	2,7857	1,3925
Franchisee's Innovation Advantage	69	1,00	5,00	3,5072	1,3572
Annual Training Days	73	,00	60,00	15,1370	12,8941
Percentage of Company-owned Outlets	79	,63	87,50	26,9613	22,7747
Advertising Fees (Percent of Sales)	67	,00	9,00	1,2806	1,7042
Total Number Outlets	82	1,00	400,00	30,3293	59,4983
Royalties	73	,00	20,00	4,2305	4,2682

2) Regression Analysis

To test the property rights hypotheses (H1, H2 and H3), we conducted a regression analysis with the percentage of company-owed outlets (PCO) as an independent variable. The explanatory variables refer to the annual training days of the franchisee and its employees (BNA), franchisee's local market know-how advantage (LMA), the initial investment (INV), royalties (FEE), and the sectoral variable (SEC). In addition, we include a dummy variable (DUM) for the franchise experience. Table 2 presents the correlation matrix between the independent variables. We only find colinearity indication for the correlations between royalties and annual training days (0,452) and between the sectoral variable and annual training days (0,319). Hence we estimated the model both with and without the annual training days-royalties and annual training days-sector interactions. The model demonstrated a high degree of stability without any significant changes in the coefficients. Furthermore, heteroscedasticity tests do not show heteroscedasticity indication.

The regression analysis was conducted in two steps: (a) Regression without and (b) with the interaction effect between the proportion of company-owned outlets (PCO) and royalties (FEE). In (a) we applied ordinary least squares (OLS) and ordinal regression analysis, and in (b) we conducted OLS, ordinal and two-stage least squares (2SLS) regression analysis. Under OLS and 2SLS regressions, the dependent variable (PCO) was modelled as the natural log of the ratio of the percent company-owned divided by the percent franchised outlets. Shane (1998) and Norton (1988a) also use this variable. Under ordinal regression analysis, we divided the PCO variable into three groups (Chu and Anderson 1992): Systems with a relatively low PCO (smaller than 15), systems with a medium PCO (15 – 40), and systems with a relatively high PCO (larger than 40).

Table 2. Correlations between Explanatory Variables

	Royalties	Initial Investments	Local Market Knowledge	Annual Training Days	Sector	Number of Outlets	Initial Fees
Royalties	1,000	-,067	,086	,452	,306	-,031	,233
Initial Investments	-,067	1,000	,030	,076	,073	-,009	-,081
Local Market	,086	,030	1,000	,022	,121	-,164	,096
Annual Training Day	,452	,076	,022	1,000	,319	-,259	,155
Sector	,306	,073	,121	,319	1,000	-,275	,286
Number of Outlets	-,031	-,009	-,164	-,259	-,275	1,000	-,240
Initial Fees	,233	-,081	,096	,155	,286	-,240	1,000

Ad (a):

In the first step, we estimate the following regression equation without the PCO-FEE-interaction (MODEL 1):

$$PCO = \alpha + \beta_1 BNA + \beta_2 LMA + \beta_3 INV + \beta_4 (BNA*DUM) + \beta_5 (LMA*DUM) + \beta_6 SEC + \varepsilon$$

Based on our property rights hypotheses, the PCO is higher, the higher the number of annual training days (BNA), and the lower the local market knowledge advantage of the franchisees (LMA). Hence β_1 has a positive and β_2 a negative sign. In addition, INV represents the financial scarcity and the transaction costs explanation. According to the resource scarcity hypothesis (Oxenfelt and Kelley 1968-69, Caves and Murphy 1976; Dant et. al 1996), franchisors are exposed to financial constraints resulting in more franchisees that finance the network expansion. In addition, transaction cost theory states that intial investments of the franchisees are negatively related to vertical integration. Hence β_3 has a negative sign both under the resource scarcity and the transaction cost view. Furthermore, two dummy variables are included representing the knowledge conversion effect due to the franchise experience. The property rights theory suggests that the influence of the local market assets upon PCO is lower and the influence of the brand name assets upon PCO is higher, the larger the franchise experience is. Therefore, for younger systems (first franchised units founded after 1990) the negative relationship between PCO and local market assets (LMA) is higher and the positive relationship between PCO and brand name assets (BNA) is lower than for older systems. Since product franchising firms have a higher fraction of intangible assets of the franchisor, the PCO should be higher than under service firms; hence β_6 should have a negative sign.

Table 3. OLS and Ordinal Regression (Model 1)

Variables	OLS	Ordinal Regression
	Intercept	Threshold Constants
	-1,33***	-0,8**
	(0,195)	(0,33)
		1,246***
		(0,36)
BNA (System-specific Assets)	1,677**	2,759**
	(0,64)	(1,222)
LMA (Local Market Assets)	1,098***	2,021**
	(0,394)	(0,933)
INV (Initial Investments)	-0,112	-0,27
	(0,162)	(0,387)
BNA*DUM	-1,179**	-2,064**
	(0,548)	(1,015)
LMA*DUM	-1,093**	-2,347**
	(0,468)	(0,994)
SEC (Sectoral Variable)	-0,173	-0,884***
	(0,208)	(0,319)
N = 54	F = 3,041	Model Chi-Square = 19,257
	R-Square = 0,275	-2 Log likelihood = 99, 026
		Nagelkerke R-Square = 0,334

*** P < 0,01; ** P < 0,05; *P < 0,1; values in parentheses are standard errors.

We conducted an OLS and ordinal regression analysis (see table 3). The results are consistent with the property rights hypotheses (H1, H2). The coefficients of BNA and DUM*BNA ($\beta_1 + \beta_4$) show that the impact of the franchisor's system-specific assets upon the PCO rises during the life cycle, and the coefficients of LMA and DUM*LMA ($\beta_2 + \beta_5$) indicate that the impact of franchisee's outlet-specific assets upon the PCO declines during the organizational life cycle indicating a tendency toward ownership redirection. However, for older franchise systems (first franchised unit founded before 1990) the influence of LMA upon the PCO is positive. In addition, the coefficient of INV is negative but not significant, indicating that financial constraints and the transaction cost hypotheses are not supported by our data. The coefficient of SEC is negative and significant in the ordinal regression model.

Table 4. OLS, Ordinal and 2SLS Regressions (Model 2)

Variables	OLS	Ordinal Regression	2SLS
	Intercept -1,215*** (0,185)	Threshold Constants -1,061*** (0,375) 1,365*** (0,399)	Intercept -1,309*** (0,245)
BNA (System-specific Assets)	1,861*** (0,638)	3,327** (1,312)	2,558*** (0,932)
LMA (Local Market Assets)	0,998*** (0,366)	1,693* (0,918)	0,778* (0,433)
INV (Initial Investments)	-0,146 (0,151)	-0,412 (0,485)	-0,094 (1,17)
BNA*DUM	-1,329** (0,531)	-2,347** (1,063)	-1,778** (0,698)
LMA*DUM	-1,184** (0,442)	-2,225** (0,999)	-0,979* (0,524)
SEC (Sectoral Variable)	-0,161 (0,199)	-0,798** (0,343)	-0,069 (0,266)
FEE (Royalties)	-0,213 (0,214)	-0,664* (0,358)	-0,903$^+$ (0,567)
N = 50	F = 3,131 R-Sqaure = 0,338	Model Chi-Square = 24,203 -2 Log likelihood = 85,487 Nagelkerke R-Square = 0,428	F = 2,733 Pseudo R^2 = 0,353

*** P < 0,01; ** P < 0,05; *P < 0,1; $^+$P < 0,12; values in parentheses are standard errors.

Ad (b):
In the second step, we estimate the regression equation with FEE as additional explanatory variable (MODEL 2).

$$PCO = \alpha + \beta_1 BNA + \beta_2 LMA + \beta_3 INV + \beta_4 (BNA*DUM) + \beta_5 (LMA*DUM) + \beta_6 SEC + \beta_7 FEE + \varepsilon$$

According to our property rights hypothesis (H3), PCO and FEE are negatively related; hence β_7 has a negative sign. Since simultaneity may exist due to the correlation between the error term and the royalties as explanatory variable, we conducted a Hausmann specification test and a 2SLS regression analysis (Pindyck and Rubinfeld 1991). The specification test did not confirm simultaneity indicating that the coefficients of the OLS regression are unbiased. Based on OLS and ordinal regressions, the data only provide partial support for the hypothesis that the PCO and FEE are substitutes (see table 4). In addition, the fit of the model increased by including the royalty rate in the regression model. Furthermore, based on 2SLS regression analysis, the significance of the coefficient of FEE is slightly higher than under OLS regressions. As a result, the data provide some support for the property rights hypotheses H1 and H2, but only very weak support for the substitutability hypothesis (H3).

5.4 Discussion

This study presents empirical evidence from the Austrian franchise sector that the dual ownership structure in franchising firms can be explained by the distribution of system-specific and local market assets between the franchisor and franchisee. As suggested by our data, noncontractible system-specific and local market assets influence the contractual mix between company-owned and franchised outlets. In addition, our data suggest that the impact of system-specific assets relative to the local market assets upon the percentage of company-owned outlets is higher, the larger the franchise experience is. This may indicate that the knowledge conversion from tacit to more explicit local market knowledge during the organizational life cycle improves the franchisor's bargaining power and explains the tendency toward ownership redirection. Moreover, the data provide only very weak support for the substitutability hypothesis between royalties and the proportion of company-owned outlets. In addition, we compare the property rights results with the resource scarcity and transaction cost view. According to the resource scarcity view, the proportion of company-owned outlets varies negatively with the franchisor's restraints in financial and informational resources, and the transaction cost theory states that the franchisee's specific investments are negatively related to the degree of vertical integration. The empirical results are only supportive of the information scarcity hypothesis measured by the impact of the franchisee's local market knowledge advantage on the PCO. This hypothesis is consistent with our property rights hypothesis regarding the influence of franchisee's local market assets on the percentage of company-owned outlets. On the other hand, the financial scarcity hypothesis is not supported by our data. This may be due to the fact that, contrary to the property rights approach, the resource scarcity view does not differentiate between intangible (noncontractible) and tangible resources. According to Hart and Moore (Hart and Moore 1990; Hart 1995), only intangible resources explain the structure of ownership rights. Since financial resources are more contractible due to a relatively low degree of intangiblility, this may explain their insignificant impact on the proportion of company-owned outlets. On the other hand, the empirical results are not consistent with the asset specifity hypothesis. This may be due to the unsolved problem in transaction cost economics that specific but contractible assets may not explain asset ownership (Whinston 2000; Woodruff 2001).

This study is not without limitations: It used cross-sectional data instead of panel data to explain the mix between franchised and company-owned outlets. In addition, the study used proxy variables to measure some of the constructs. Especially the proxy variable to measure intangible local market assets might be critizised because this measure was based on the franchisor's perception. In future research the operationalization of franchisee's intangible assets should be improved by collecting data from franchisees. In addition, multi-item constructs should complement the proxy for the franchisor's intangible assets.

This study also has managerial implications. First, in accordance with Lafontaine and Shaw (2001), we may conclude that the ownership structure of franchising firms is an important managerial control factor. Franchising firms set a target level of company ownership which depends on the distribution of intangible system-specific and local market assets between the franchisor and the franchisee. Second, based on our property rights view, this target level must be adjusted during the organizational life cycle when the contractibility of assets changes. For instance, if the contractibility of local market assets increases, the importance of system-specific assets for the creation of residual income increases resulting in an increase of the franchisor's bargaining power. In order to secure the incentive to invest in intangible system-specific assets, the franchisor has to increase his fraction of ownership rights in the network. Third, given the distribution of intangible assets between the franchisor and franchisee, the franchisor may exercise managerial control by determining the 'optimal' mix between the proportion of company-owned outlet and the royalties. Due to the dual incentive effects of royalties, the proportion of company-owned outlets and the royalty rate are substitutes.

5 Conclusions

The paper offers a property rights explanation for the dual ownership structure in franchising networks. We argued that the percentage of company-owned outlets depends on the distribution of intangible assets between the franchisor and franchisee. The franchisee's intangible assets refer to the local market assets and the franchisor's intangible assets to the system-specific assets. The more important the franchisor's and the franchisee's intangible assets are for the generation of residual income, the more residual income rights should be transferred to both, and the higher the percentage of company-owned outlets and the lower the royalties should be. Therefore, company-owned outlets compensate the disincentive effect of the diluted residual income rights of franchised outlets and, in turn, they enable the transfer of more residual income rights to the franchisees by charging lower royalties. Further, we presented empirical results using data collected in the Austrian franchise sector. The data provide some support for the hypothesis that the dual network structure is determined by the distribution of intangible assets of the franchisor and franchisee. In addition, the empirical results support the information scarcity hypothesis, but do not support the financial scarcity and asset specifity hypotheses.

References

1. Armstrong JS, Overton TS (1977) Estimating Non-Response Bias in Mail Surveys. Journal of Marketing Research 14:396 – 402
2. Azevedo PF, Santos Silva VL (2001) Contractual Mix Analysis in the Brazilian Franchising. ISNIE Conference, Berkely, September 2001
3. Bai CE, Tao Z (2001) Contract Mix in Franchising. Journal of Economics and Management Strategy 9:85 – 113
4. Baker GP, Hubbard TN (2001) Empirical Strategies in Contract Economics: Information and the Boundary of the Firm. American Economic Review, 91:189 – 194
5. Baker GP, Hubbard TN (2002) Make versus Buy in Trucking: Asset Ownership: Job Design and Information. NBER Working Paper, January 2000
6. Baker GP, Hubbard TN (2003) Contractibility and Asset Ownership: On-Board Computers and Governance in U.S.Trucking. NBER Working Paper, April 2003
7. Barzel Y (1997) Economic Analysis of Property Rights. New York
8. Berkovitz J (1999) An Analysis of Contract Provisions in Business Format Franchise Agreements: In J. Stanworth, D. Purdy (eds.), Proceedings of the Conference of the 13th Conference of the International Society of Franchising
9. Bradach JL (1997) Using the Plural Form in the Management of Restaurant Chains. Administrative Science Quarterly 42:276 – 303
10. Brickley JA, Dark FH (1987) The Choice of Organizational Form: The Case of Franchising. Administrative Science Quarterly 42:276 - 303
11. Brickley JA, Dark F, Weisbach M (1991) An Agency Perspective on Franchising. Financial Management 20:27 – 35
12. Brousseau E, Glachant J-M (2003) Economics of Contracts and Renewal of Economic Analysis, In : E. Brousseau, J.-M. Glachant (eds.), The Economics of Contracts (forthcoming)
13. Brynjolfsson E (1994) Information Assets, Technology, and Organization. Management Science 40:1645 - 1662
14. Caves RE, Murphy WF II (1976) Franchising: Firms, Markets, and Intangible Assets. Southern Economic Journal 42:572 - 586
15. Chu W, Anderson EM (1992) Capturing Ordinal Properties Categorial DependenVariables. International Journal of Research in Marketing 9:149 – 160
16. Cliquet G (2001) Plural Forms in Store Networks: A Model for Store Network Evolution, International Review of Retail, Distribution and Consumer Research. 10:369 - 387

17. Daft RL, Lengel RH (1986) Organizational Information Requirements, Media Richness and Structural Design. Management Science 32:554 - 571
18. Dahlstrom R, Nygaard A (1999) Ownership Decisions in Plural Contractual Systems. European Journal of Marketing (forthcoming).
19. Dant RP, Paswan AK, Kaufman PJ (1996) What we Know about Ownership Redirection in Franchising: A Meta-Analysis. Journal of Retailing 72:429 - 444
20. Dant RP, Kaufman PJ, Robicheaux RA (1998) Changes in the Mix of Company-Owned and Franchised Outlets: Ownership Redirection Revisited. Proceedings of the International Society of Franchising Conference, Las Vegas
21. Darr ED, Argote L, Epple D (1995) The Acquisition, Transfer, and Depreciation of Knowledge in Service Organizations: Productivity in Franchises. Management Science 41: 1750 - 1762
22. Dnes AW (1992) Unfair Contractual Practices and Hostages in Franchise Contracts. Journal of Institutional and Theoretical Economics 148:484 – 504
23. Gallini N, Lutz N (1992) Dual Distribution and Royalty Fees in Franchising. Journal of Law, Economics and Organization 8:471-501
24. Hair JF, Anderson RE, Tathan RL, Black WC (1998) Multivariate Data Analysis, Prentice Hall
25. Hart O (1995) Firms, Contracts and Financial Structure. Oxford
26. Hart O (2002) Incomplete Contracts and Public Ownership: Remarks and Application to Public-Private Partnerships. Working Paper, Harvard University, July 2002
27. Hart O, Moore J (1990) Property Rights and the Nature of the Firm. Journal of Political Economy 98:1119 - 1158
28. Hendrikse G (2003) Economics and Management of Organization. London
29. Klein B (1980) Transaction Cost Determinants of 'Unfair' Contractual Arrangements. American Economic Review 70:356 – 362
30. Klein B (1995) The Economics of Franchise Contracts. Journal of Corporate Finance, 2: 9 – 38
31. Klein B, Crawford R, Alchian A (1978) Vertical Integration, Appropriable Rents, and the Competitive Contracting Process. Journal of Law and Economics 21:297 – 326
32. Lafontaine F (1992) Agency Theory and Franchising: Some Empirical Results. RAND Journal of Economics 23:263-283
33. Lafontaine F, Kaufmann PJ (1994) The Evolution of Ownership Patters in Franchise Systems. Journal of Retailing 70:97 – 113
34. Lafontaine F, Shaw KL (2001) Targeting Managerial Control: Evidence from Franchising. Working Paper, University of Michigan Business School.
35. Lewin-Solomon SB (1999) Innovation and Authority in Franchise Systems: An Empirical Exploration of Plural Form. Working Paper, Iowa State University, July
36. Martin RE (1988) Franchising and Risk Management. American Economic Review, 78: 954 - 968
37. Masten SE (2000) Contractual Choice. Encyclopedia of Law and Economics, B Boukaert, G DeGeest (eds.), Edard Elgar Publishing.
38. Michael SC (2000) Investments to Create Bargaining Power, The Case of Franchising. Strategic Management Journal 21:497 – 514
39. Minkler AP (1992) Why Firms Franchise: A Search Cost Theory. Journal of Institutional and Theoretical Economics 148:240 - 259
40. Minkler A, Park TA (1994) Asset Specificity and Vertical Integration in Franchising. Review of Industrial Organization 9:409 – 423
41. Nonaka I (1994) A Dynamic Theory of Organizational Knowledge Creation. Organization Science 5:14 – 37
42. Nonaka I, Takeuchi H (1995) The Knowledge Creating Company. New York

43. Nonaka I, Toyama R, Konno N (2001) SECI, Ba and Leadership: A Unified Model of Dynamic Knowledge Creation. in: I Nonaka, DJ Teece (2001) Managing Industrial Knowledge. New York, pp 13
44. Norton SW (1988a) An Empirical Look at Franchising as an Organizational Form. Journal of Business 61:197 – 219
45. Norton SW (1988b) Franchising, Brand Name Capital, and the Entrepreneurial Capacity Problem. Strategic Management Journal 9:103 - 114
46. Nunnally JC (1978) Psychometric Theory. New York
47. O'Hara MJ, Thomas WL (1986) Franchise Systems: The Internal Dynamics of Sales Growth and Dual Distribution. International Society of Franchising Conference
48. Oxenfeldt AR, Kelly AO (1968-69) Will Successful Franchise Systems Ultimately Become Wholly-owned Chains?. Journal of Retailing, 44:69 -83
48. Padamanabhan KH (1989), Franchise Evolution: A New Look at the Debate. Proceedings of the International Society of Franchising Conference, Bal Harbor, January
49. Penard T, Raynaud E, Saussier S (2002) Dual Distribution and Royalty in Franchised Chains: Empirical Analysis Using French Data. Journal of Marketing Channels (forthcoming)
50. Pindyck RS, Rubinfeld DL (1991) Econometric Methods and Economic Forecasts. New York
51. Rubin P (1978) The Theory of the Firm and the Structure of the Franchise Contract. Journal of Law and Economics, 21:223 - 233
52. Scott FA (1995) Franchising vs. Company Ownership as Decision Variable of the Firm. Review of Industrial Organization 10:69 – 81
53. Shane S (1998) Explaining the Distribution of Franchised and Company-owned Outlets in Franchise Systems. Journal of Management 24:717 – 739
54. Simonin BL (1999), Transfer of Marketing Know-how in International Strategic Alliances. Journal of International Business Studies 30:463- 490
55. Sorenson O, Sorensen JB (2001) Finding the Right Mix: Organizational Learning, Plural Forms and Franchise Performance. Strategic Management Journal 22:713 – 724
56. Thompson RS (1994) The Franchise Life Cycle and the Penrose Effect. Journal of Economic Behavior and Organization 24:207 - 218
57. Wernerfelt B (2002) Why Should the Boss Own the Assets?, Journal of Economics and Management Strategy 11:473 – 485
58. Whinston MD (2000) On the Transaction Cost Determinants of Vertical Integration. Working Paper, Northwestern University, Feb. 2000
59. Whinston MD (2001) Assessing the Property Rights and Transaction Cost Theories of Firm Scope. American Economic Review, 91:184 – 188
60. Williamson OE (1979) Transaction Costs Economics: The Governance of Contractual Relations. Journal of Law and Econmics 22:233 - 262
61. Williamson OE (1985) The Economic Institution of Capitalism. New York
62. Windsperger J (2001) The Fee Structure in Franchising: A Property Rights View. Economics Letters 73:219 - 226
63. Windsperger J (2002a) The Dual Structure of the Franchising Firms. 17th ISOF Conference Proceedings, Orlando, FL
64. Windsperger J (2002b) The Structure of Ownership Rights in Franchising: An Incomplete Contracting View. European Journal of Law and Economics, 13:129 – 142
65. Woodruff C (2001) Non-Contractible Investments and Vertical Integration in the Mexican Footwear Industry. Working Paper, UCSD Working Paper 92093-0519
66. Zeithaml VA, Parasuraman A, Berry LL(1985) Problems and Strategies in Services Marketing, Journal of Marketing 49:33 – 46

Appendix: Measures of Variables

Proportion of Company-owned Outlets (PCO)
Annual Training Days (BNA): Number of annual training days (franchisee and his employees)
Fees (FEE): The royalty rate (including advertising) is measured as the ongoing percentage of gross sales that franchisees must pay to franchisors.
Franchisee's Intangible Knowledge Assets:

LMA (three items; Cronbach alpha = 0,63)

Franchisee's know-how advantage compared to the manager of a company-owned outlet, evaluated by the franchisor (no advantage 1 – 5 very large advantage)

1. Innovation
2. Local market knowledge
3. Quality control

Initial Investment (INV): $ value of franchisee's start-up investments to open an outlet.
Sectors (SEC): 0 = Product franchising firms; 1 = Services firms
DUM: 1 for franchise systems which opened the first franchised outlet between 1990 and 1998, and 0 for systems which opened the first franchised outlet before 1990.

Successful Franchising Using the Plural Form

Thomas Ehrmann, Georg Spranger

Center for Entrepreneurship, University of Muenster
Leonardo-Campus 18, 48149 Muenster, Germany
www.ug.uni-muenster.de

Abstract. Many successful franchise companies consist - other than their name might suggest - of more than just the system's headquarter and its associated franchisees. Besides independent franchise outlets, the majority of chains operates a significant number of company-owned stores run by employed store managers. The evolution and constant existence of these hybrid organizational forms cannot be explained along a pure principal-agent-view and deserves further analysis. As this article explores, plurally organized franchisors may benefit from effects of cost reduction, quality enhancement, growth stimulation and optimized risk control in contrast to pure franchise chains. Within our sample of 240 franchise systems we found strong empirical support for the quality argument of the Plural Form. Compared to pure franchise companies, plurally organized chains are superior in sending out positive signals to any external community containing internal information and thus in reducing costly agent uncertainty. By running company owned stores as well as independent franchise outlets, chains force themselves successfully into cooperational and less opportunistic behavior towards their franchisees.[1]

1 Introduction

In principle, the manufacturers of a product or the providers of a service (as principals) have a choice between numerous solutions regarding the organizational design of their distribution channels. The extreme positions are marked by a company-owned distribution system, on the one hand, and a distribution through independent external subjects on the other. Within this broad spectrum, franchising takes up a middle position as principals interact with vastly independent franchisees on a fixed contract basis. The choice between company-owned and independent distribution clements depends on the contractual appropriateness of the solution as well as on the visibility of certain in- and output variables. First, the franchisor – being the principal – has to decide whether the agent is able to influence the outlet's output significantly, for instance by changing input variables such as his personal work effort. Sometimes the agent's influence on the store's output by increasing individual input is very small (e.g. in supermarkets). In cases

[1] We gratefully acknowledge financial support from the Konrad-Adenauer-Foundation and the University of Muenster Graduate Fund for this research.

like this, franchisors will rarely decide to franchise outlets (Maness 1986), but place the control of distribution in the hands of company-owned outlets. With increasing agent influence on an outlet's output, the franchisor then has to decide whether the agent's individual extra input leading to extra output is observable as well as controllable by and through the franchisor. The better a franchisor is able to steer the agent's specific input and thus the outlet's extra output, the more likely he will again prefer company-owned stores over franchisees (and vice-versa). If it is easier for the franchisor (or his only option) to control the agent's output - for instance through observing his revenues - without having power over the agent's input variables, franchising becomes the superior distribution mode (Lafontaine and Slade 1998). Some researchers (e.g. Shelton 1967; Oxenfeldt and Kelly 1968) have argued that franchisors would eventually turn their organizations either into wholly franchised or wholly company-owned systems in the long run. In reality, however, for the majority of franchise systems we observe a relatively stable coexistence of franchised and company-owned outlets within one chain – a phenomenon defined as the dual or the plural form (Bradach 1997; Gallini and Lutz 1992; Lewin-Solomons 1998). In an attempt to identify the advantages that legitimize the plural form, our paper starts with an examination of the basic characteristics of the plural form providing an overview over the organizational settings of 240 large franchise chains (2). Then we specify several theories which try to explain the coexistence we find in reality and, afterwards, derive hypotheses concerning the advantages of plurally organized over pure franchise firms (3). These hypotheses are then tested along our sample (4). The paper closes with an interpretation of our empirical results (5).

2 The Plural Organizational Structure of Franchise Chains

2.1 The Origin of the Plural Form

Hybrid firm structures are a combination of distinct parameters of firm organization and are not a new phenomena in organization science. Generally speaking, hybrid structures combine a mixture of the organizational methods "price" and "hierarchy" with the organizational institutions "markets" and "firms" (Ouchi 1980). The various ways of possible matches result in a broad spectrum of potential organizational constellations. We talk about the plural form as soon as we observe a side by side mix of price and hierarchy within one single firm (Hennart 1993). Cases where two different organizational methods exist within one institution have to be distinguished from firms that present one organizational form as a mixture of both prices and hierarchy. Many companies employ a sales force as part of their sales department and manage independent salesmen as freelancers simultaneously. Others, for example companies in the automotive sector, produce a pre- or final-product by themselves and, at the same time, buy the same part from external suppliers. What attracted our research interest are franchise chains that employ fixed-paid managers to run company-owned outlets as well as vastly independent franchisees operating franchised stores. Whereas the first one can be controlled by the franchisor through hierarchical relationships, the latter, bearing rather a great entrepreneurial risk by investing money in a chain, is more likely to be governed through monetary incentives than through authority. Within this complex organization the employed managers represent the hierarchical branch, whereas the independent and risk-bearing franchisees belong to the price-steered fraction of inter-firm subjects.

It is crucial for our further analysis to distinguish between three possible developments leading to such a plural form. First, plural forms can be the results of a continuous process of selecting the individually best method for the current situation of the firm. Thus we can speak of a case-by-case decision between the best fit of either the price or the hierarchy method for a given situation and environment.[2] Second, from the perspective of the entire firm, a mixture of both methods can be appropriate to create an organization that contains "the best of both worlds" in one structure.[3] We will come across this approach again when looking at the plural form's function of actively managing risk exposures. And third, some researchers argue that the plural form arises due to the intention of realizing certain synergies that would not exist if just one method were used without the other.[4] All three options become more visible when we discuss the arguments for the existence of the plural form in part 3.

2.2 The Design of the Plural Form

As a basis to analyze the organization of franchise chains, we used the data of 240 franchised chains, published in the yearly *Franchise500* report by the *Entrepreneur Magazine.* A self-restriction to 240 systems minimizes - from our point of view - the downward distortion of empirical figures, which results from the rapidly decreasing system size of companies with lower rankings. This effect seems to be detrimental in earlier studies by Lafontaine and Shaw (2001) and by Pénard, Raynaud and Saussier (2002), where much larger samples of 4842 and 581 franchise chains were analyzed. The high degree of heterogeneity already inherent in our sample of 240 chains is shown in table 1 below. In particular, we compare companies like McDonald's, founded in 1955 and with 28.236 outlets in 2001 the largest chain of the sample, with systems like Purified-Water-to-Go, ranked number 190, founded 40 years later in 1994 and representing the smallest system of our sample with a total of just 51 outlets in 2001. In order to analyze a chain's organizational set-up, we compute the degree of plural organization (λ) as the per-

[2] This line of argumentation is used by Brickley and Dark (1987), Caves and Murphy (1976), Lafontaine and Slade (1996) and Walker and Weber (1984).

[3] Cf. Hennart (1993), p 538. This statement does not stand in conflict with our definition of the plural form, as each business unit is either a franchised or a company-owned outlet.

[4] Cf. Bradach (1997) and Lewin-Solomons (1998), p 1-2.

centage of franchised units out of the number of all outlets under a chain's trademark. As the mean degree of plurality of our sample we calculate 91%, with a standard deviation of 17%. Whereas, for instance, McDonald's is truly plurally organized with a share of 25% of company-owned outlets, Purified-Water-to-Go has no company-owned outlets at all.

Table 1. Descriptive Statistics

Parameter	Sample	Mean	Std. Dev.	Min.	Max.
Total Outlets	240	1.297	3.205	51	28.236
Number of franchised units	240	1.159	2.849	41	24.695
Number of company units	240	138	639	0	6.918
Percent franchised	240	91 %	17 %	15 %	100 %
Royalty rate in %	215	6 %	3 %	0 %	20 %
Franchise fee in T$	235	27	17	0	130
Minimum investment in T$	240	525	2.084	1	22.000
Maximum investment in T$	240	1.202	4.551	13	44.800
Years in business	240	28	19	5	137
Years of franchise experience	240	20	12	4	69

Corresponding results are presented by the two studies already mentioned. Pénard, Raynaud and Saussier (2002) extract the following means and standard deviations (in brackets) out of a sample of 581 French franchise chains: number of all outlets 74 (158), percentage franchised: 67 (68), royalty rate in percent: 4,4 (3,9), franchise fee in T$: approx. 15 (13), years in business: 24 (29), years of franchise experience: 14 (12). Lafontaine and Shaw (2001) analyzed 4842 US-American franchise systems and present the following means and standard deviations: number of all outlets: 207 (788), percentage franchised: 78 (71), years in business: 17 (15), years of franchise experience: 11 (10). As stated above, we believe the results of both studies to be distorted downwards because of the rapid decrease in firm sizes in larger samples. Nevertheless, the figures suffice in order to have an idea of franchise chain organizational design. According to the three studies, one can expect franchise chains to be plurally organized in a range between 91% (this study) over 78% (Lafontaine and Shaw 2001) up to 67% (Pénard, Raynaud and Saussier 2002). Thus we expect plural systems to have a realistic share of company-owned outlets of about 9-33%.

Fig. 1. The Organizational Dynamics of the Franchise240

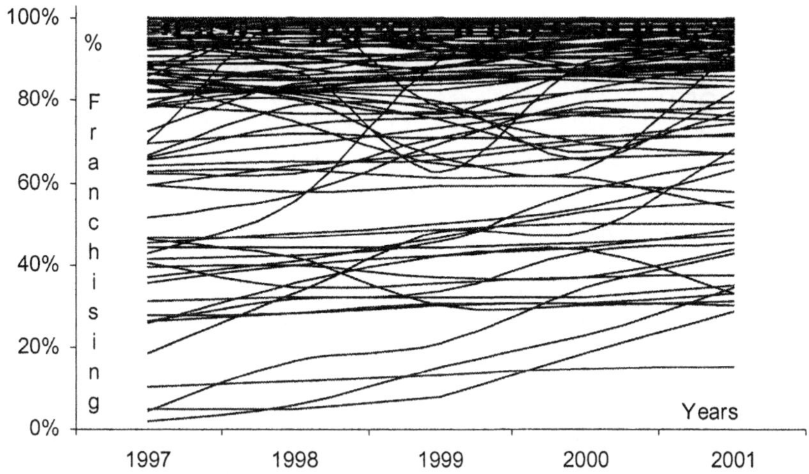

Adding to this rather static analysis we looked at the organizational development of our sample over the period observed providing a dynamic component to our plural form arguments. As displayed in figure 1, we find a relatively dense concentration of systems with a high λ, i.e. systems, that have a rather small share of company units against a large proportion of franchised outlets. In 1997 83% and in 2001 85% of our sample firms show a λ of at least 80%, which seems to serve as a lower limit concerning the organizational constellations. Both in 1997 as well as in 2001 about 37% of our sample represent pure franchise chains without any company-owned units. A significant majority of 63% is more or less plurally organized throughout the 5-year period. Although figure 1 does not provide up-front evidence for changes towards one single organizational mode, there appears to be a trend towards the λ-limit of 80% for those companies holding vastly more company-owned units prior to and in the beginning of 1997.[5]

Summarizing the findings above, we conclude that our sample reflects a broad variety of different organizational solutions. Assuming a similar business strategy for all systems, e.g. the maximization of revenue and profit, the motives for organizing the systems appear to be manifold and ambiguous. Therefore, we first want to explore the arguments put forward by researchers justifying the existence of the plural form. As will be shown, plurally organized chains may realize advantages in costs, quality, growth and risk control over singular organized pure franchise

[5] For an in-depth analysis on possible correlations between age and organizational setting refer to part 4.

chains. In a second step, we test these apparent benefits on our sample and attempt to explore the true reason(s) for the wide use of the plural form.

3 Theoretical Arguments for the Existence of the Plural Form

3.1 Cost Benefits

In a world of asymmetrically distributed information, costs arise as soon as a principal (i.e. the franchisor) tries to contract with an agent (i.e. the franchisee or the company-unit manager). Depending on whether such a situation exists before, during or after the signing of a contract, one deals with uncertainty of the contract's quality, uncertainty concerning the other party's behavior or uncertainty in regard of the expected outcome of the contract. While a franchisor can test the quality of his agent ex-ante via intense selection processes and the outcome of the contract by controlling the agent's output ex-post (for instance by checking his revenues), it is difficult to observe and control the agent's true behavior while he himself enforces the contract according to his own will. For maintaining system quality and protecting the trademark, the franchisor needs to ensure the agent's compliance with the contracted rules. Choosing the right organizational structure may be an option to reduce this kind of costly behavior uncertainty. The costs for controlling the agent have to be considered against the costs arising through inefficient investment, through cheating against the system and through free-riding on behalf of other system members.

Managers of company-owned units are generally employed on a fixed-wage basis and thus have little influence on raising their salary (i.e. their output) by increasing personal work input. Thus an opportunistic company-unit manager may tend to maximize his input-output-balance by reducing work input while maintaining his output i.e. his position and salary. To prevent this kind of shirking the franchisor will have to monitor the manager closely and punish misbehavior either by ending the contract or by reducing the agent's salaries.

Franchisees, on the other hand, accept a significant risk when investing into a franchise unit with the intention to improve personal income by influencing the outlets' revenues and costs through increased personal work effort. The franchisees, therefore, will rarely tend to shirk, which means monitoring costs are kept low. The franchisee will rather maximize his income-output-balance by improving financial output and not by minimizing work input. Reducing costs by lowering the offered quality or offering discounts unapproved of the franchisor are just two possible actions that franchisees could exert without any control by the franchisor. Through free-riding on the system's trademark and quality, cheating on other system members and thus hurting the chain as a whole, the franchisee is able to maximize his personal income. Franchisees may also try to avoid those chain-wide measures that drive up the franchisee's costs without delivering an instant reward, but which benefit the entire chain and the common trademark. From the perspective of the franchisor, such resistance results in avoidable opportunity costs for necessary improvements not carried out. In contrast to the managers of company-units, franchisees thus cause costs for the franchisor because of free-riding on the trademark's value and because of resistance to necessary investments.

Other than pure franchise chains, plurally organized systems have the choice between franchised and company-owned units and thus between two different sources of costs. For every location they (could) weigh up the costs of monitoring against those of free-riding and inefficient investment and choose the individual best solution (Brickley and Dark 1987).

Besides agency costs, franchisors gather knowledge about local markets in order to maximize profits from their trademarks. Although the acquisition of such information is quite costly, the franchisor needs to know local market preferences in order to adjust his decentral production and distribution facilities under the restrictions of system wide uniformity and standardization. As Minkler (1992) has stated, the need and costs to acquire such knowledge are likely to grow with increasing unfamiliarity, heterogeneity and volatility of local markets as well as with the decreasing half-life of the information collected.

The franchisee as the receiver of the residual income will have a much stronger motivation to collect and use local information in order to raise his personal output than the fixed-paid manager of a company-owned unit. As an alternative to the information gathering franchisee, the franchisor would first have to engage in costly market research himself and then, secondly, would have to force and to control his company-units in using the information and maximizing the chains profits. Besides the cost component, franchisors would have a problem identifying and collecting the kind of implicit knowledge that franchisees win and collect through experiments and experiences. Even if a franchisor could manage to do this, he probably would still lag behind the franchisees and loose information when implementing the knowledge within the company units. Thus in gathering and using local information, franchisees should always be a step ahead and should succeed over employed unit managers in maximizing profits out of the local knowledge. With this in mind Minkler (1992) has demonstrated that plurally organized franchise chains optimize their search costs for local information by setting up franchise units where the acquisition of local knowledge is necessary and costly and where their extra effort has a greater impact on the outlets' output. At the same time, the cost- conscious franchisor setting up company-owned units in the direct neighborhood of these franchisees is able to transfer this knowledge to his own outlets and to benefit from the franchisees' initiative and commitment. According to Minkler's (1992) analysis, franchisors should develop new business areas by first installing franchise units exploring the new local market.

As the system matures and regional headquarters are built, distances between the principal and its monitored agents decrease and monitoring costs become less critical. Now the franchisor could focus on company-owned units (whose monitoring costs decrease with expansion), using the local information gathered by the adjacent franchisees. Thus we ask whether Franchisors use the plural form in order to optimize the inner system costs of searching and transferring important local information. This being the case, our sample data should validate the following hypothesis:

H1: The older the franchise chain, the higher (smaller) should be the fraction of company-owned units (franchise units).

Both aspects perceive the plural form to be an applicable solution to the reduction of organizational costs (Posselt 1998, p 368). With increasing size of the system and decreasing distances between monitoring and monitored subjects, monitoring costs and therefore the specific advantages of the plurally organized system become less important. At the end of such a development, we should observe a wholly owned chain.

3.2 Growth Benefits

The success of franchise chains depends largely on their ability to grow as quickly as possible, thereby attaining a high visibility and building a strong and widely recognized trademark. Probably because of their strategy of fast international expansion, companies like Burger King and McDonald's belong to the 100 strongest brands worldwide.[6] The two most common factors which limit a new venture's growth are a restricted access to investment capital and a limited availability of qualified human resources. Franchise systems, in contrast to traditionally organized new ventures, solve this shortage by contracting with franchisees who provide the necessary funds (Caves and Murphy 1976; Mathewson and Winter 1985) as well as the management talent (Thompson 1994), i.e. themselves, to open new outlets and to help the system grow.

The franchisee, as a cautious investor, will only invest in such locations that promise a benefit high enough to compensate for the inherent risk of that specific investment. Starting in new markets may require the opening of outlets at highly visible locations (e.g. at airports or train stations), that positively impact the system's brand development but, at the same time, scare franchisees because of high above-average costs (i.e. lower than average profitability). Pure franchise systems would either have to franchise such a location or leave it undeveloped. Plurally organized chains are flexible enough to install company units quickly wherever necessary, handing them over to franchisees once profitability has been established, or otherwise running them on their own because of a positive effect on the chain and the trademark as a whole. With the choice of company-owned and franchised units, plurally organized chains theoretically gain an advantage in flexibility over singularly organized systems when it comes to the fast development of new and important markets. Thus we analyze whether franchisors use the plural form to succeed over restricted access to capital and human resources and at the same time can stay flexible enough to develop strategic locations more quickly and easily. Our data should therefore test the following hypothesis:

---

[6] Cf. the survey „Interbrand 2002": http://www.wuv.de (April 28th, 2003).

H2: The stronger the franchise chain's growth, the higher (smaller) the fraction of company-owned units (franchise units)should be.

Up to this point we have only listed such arguments which solve the franchisor's agency- and resource shortage problems. The needs and reactions of franchisees towards opportunistic franchisor behavior have been completely neglected so far. The following chapter will therefore focus on a rather cooperative understanding of the franchisor-franchisee-relationship, which could positively effect the system's overall quality.

3.3 Quality Benefits

According to current theories, a plurally organized chain can benefit from the following impacts on its system's quality: The plural form signals internal franchisor information to the franchisee, thus overcoming inefficiencies arising from asymmetrical information (Gallini and Lutz 1992; Michael 2000); it aligns and thus harmonizes the interests of the principal (franchisor) and his potential agents (franchisees) (Lewin-Solomons 1999); it promotes innovation processes and speeds up internal change (Sorenson and Sørensen 2001) and it finally creates a competitive environment, where benchmarking of both franchisees and managers of company units can lead to increased system performance (Bradach 1997). These propositions are now to be investigated step by step

Especially young and small franchise chains without a great financial record have difficulty in convincing potential franchise partners of their new system's profitability. As Gallini and Lutz (1992) point out, one option for franchisors to overcome this dilemma may be the installation of company-owned units. Through self-investing into company units a franchisor can signal commitment and faith in the profitability of the business concept to external subjects. Thus the franchisor tries to overcome the uncertainty concerning a project's quality. The amount of money invested and thus the number of company outlets owned vary with the strength of the signal the franchisor wants or needs to send out.[7] The underlying argument assumes that a franchisor would not raise his financial risk by investing upfront into company-owned outlets unless he was convinced about the system's profitability. Such a franchisor would rather try to transfer the initial risk to franchisees by attracting them with comparably low entrance fees, and charging a royalty-fee as soon as they are successful with their business. Thus risk-conscious franchisees would more likely join those franchisors who commit themselves credibly to the system. Plural elements within chains could help to overcome such information asymmetries, convince external partners of the system's success and support franchisors to find franchisees especially during the start-up and growth phases of the system.

Another important issue the plural form could improve is the existence of divergent interests between the franchisor and his franchisees, based on their indi-

[7] Cf. Leland and Pyle (1977), p 376; Cho and Kreps (1987), p 179 f.

vidual income situation. The franchisee's income generally consists of the residual of revenues and costs, whereas the royalty rate paid to the franchisor belongs to the latter, too. The franchisor of a pure franchise system could be tempted to favor strategies that maximize the outlets' revenues, as he participates via charging the royalty rate, neglecting the action's effects on the outlets' costs. As the franchisee would enjoy the revenue increase only by bearing the increased costs, he might oppose actions attractive to the franchisor that seem inefficient from the perspective of the single franchisee. Including the outlet's costs into the calculation of the royalty rate could solve this conflict. Since most franchisees administer their accounting system strictly by themselves, they report only financial key-figures, such as the monthly revenue, to the franchisor and rarely announce detailed costs calculation. The proposition to change the royalty rate calculations would therefore require stronger ties to the franchisor, probably an unacceptable step to most of the franchisees and thus unrealistic to impose (Lewin-Solomons 1999). As proposed by Lewin-Solomons (1999) the franchisor could align divergent interests alternatively by running company units himself, now bearing the full consequences of system-wide strategies enforced by himself. Thus the franchisor of a plural system would overcome detrimental opportunistic behavior uncertainty and signal the willingness to cooperate and to harmonize interests to his franchisees. He will then restrain from decisions with a negative revenue-cost-increase balance and gain trust from current (and potential) franchisees.

Besides performance and inner-system opportunism, the power of innovation is another important aspect for (future) partners, which is initially not visible to them. The decentralization of franchise systems impedes the right balance between centralization/standardization, on the one hand, and adaptation to local market specifics, on the other. As March (1989) has pointed out, innovative businesses successfully combine the improvement and efficient use („Exploitation") of existing and the search and development („Exploration") of new resources and technologies. Systems that lose or neglect one of the challenges will either operate below their maximal efficiency ("Doing things wrong") or below their maximal effectiveness ("Doing wrong things"). As March (1989) concludes, „maintaining an appropriate balance between exploration and exploitation is a primary factor in system survival and prosperity"[8].

Recently, Sorenson and Sørensen (2001) have demonstrated the advantage of plurally organized chains in installing such a balance through their distinct structures of motivation. Managers of company-owned units, on the one side, are paid for controlling and for optimizing existing processes. As they do not participate monetarily in the realization of new processes or products, they will mainly "exploit" the system at its status-quo. Franchisees, on the other side, add an entrepreneurial, local market perspective and participate directly via their residual income when improving the system through adding new and better processes or products. Therefore, franchisees are generally an important source of innovation within the system. At the same time, the franchisor will have a centrally organized division of research and development and will develop innovations via this channel, too.

[8] March (1991), p 71.

Nevertheless, when testing the new products or processes becomes an issue, the franchisor will heavily rely on the franchisees practical opinion again (Ehrmann 2002). This interplay between exploration and exploitation through the complementary role of both the franchisees and the company managers was first introduced by Bradach (1997). Just as automotive companies keep their competence of innovation and simultaneously realize decreasing costs by buying and producing ("Make-and-Buy") identical parts, it seems to be as important for franchisors to keep the right balance between franchised and company-owned units and thus the balance between exploration and exploitation. Lewin-Solomons (1997) concludes that those franchise chains are the most innovative ones where „λ is high enough to make franchisees feel important but low enough that the chain has a significant stake in the innovation process"[9]. Sorenson and Sørensen (2001) even demonstrate that a franchisor's success depends heavily on the organizational mix of company and franchised units. Therefore, plurally organized chains take a critical organizational lead over pure franchise systems, especially in markets of high competition.

A fourth argument in favor of the plural form is brought up by Bradach (1997) and deals with the positive effects of increased interfirm competition established through benchmarking. Franchisors of singularly arranged systems lack a neutral third party that checks the results of and sets new standards for its franchisees. According to Bradach (1997), company-owned units provide this information, enabling franchisors to judge and to guide the performance of the franchised units. As company-owned unit's operations are influenced by the franchisor through authority, and their results are easily accessible through management-information-systems, they supply the necessary figures to set performance standards for the franchisees. Generally, reaching these goals does not seem problematic to the franchisees (Bradach 1997; Kaufmann and Lafontaine 1994) as, in a study by Boeckenholt and Wiens (2001), they were able to beat the goals by about 20%. These new results are then used by the franchisor to define the new standards for all company units. Besides pure financial figures, franchisors frequently add non-monetary goals as, for instance, enhanced cleanliness or customer friendliness to this benchmarking process. The challenge between company and franchised units within this process of benchmarking is based on the self identification of the company-managers and the franchisees as two competing teams. Thus by arranging company units side by side with franchisees, the franchisor may learn to understand the problems of franchisees, gain an (indirect) insight into their financial and non-financial operations and install a performance-increasing, challenging benchmark process.

All the four aspects mentioned above are generally positive for both the franchisor as well as for the (potential) franchisees, whereas the benefits of costs and growth are positive for the franchisor only. Thus it could be in a (potential) franchisee's interest that his (future) franchisor commits himself to the system through self-investing, that he aligns his interests with those of his franchisees, that he provides a balanced climate for innovations and that he uses benchmarking to enable an interfirm challenge enhancing the system's overall performance. These as-

[9] Lewin-Solomons (1997), p 43.

pects therefore exceed the pure profitability signal (Gallini and Lutz 1992) proposing that plural elements enable franchisors to credibly send out signals of cooperation and high system quality. Such action will be especially valuable to chains operating in very competitive markets, as franchisors compete for the limited amount of qualified and cooperative franchisees (Ehrmann 2002). Testing the evidence of these proposed aspects, we question our data with the following hypotheses:

> *H3: The higher the one time franchise fee, the higher (smaller) the fraction of company-owned units (franchise units) should be.*

> *H4: The lower the ongoing royalty rate, the higher (smaller) the fraction of company-owned units (franchise units) should be.*

Depending on the business field and model, franchisors require their franchisees to invest significantly different initial investment volumes.[10] According to the reasoning above, we should observe a stronger reliance on quality aspects as the amounts of investment and thus the individual risk exposures increase.

> *H5: The higher the investment volume, the higher (smaller) the fraction of company-owned units (franchise units) should be.*

Assuming our data supports one or more of the listed potential benefits (on costs, growth, quality), the plural form could be expected to have a positive impact on a franchise chain's overall performance. Since the *Entrepreneur Magazine* evaluates each chain according to several, both financial and non-financial figures, we believe the *Franchise500* ranking to be an appropriate instrument to reflect a system's success.[11] In order to analyze a potential influence of the plural form in a chain's performance, we should find support for the following hypothesis connecting the organizational structure with the system's success:

> *H6: The better the ranking within the Franchise240, the higher (smaller) the fraction of company-owned units (franchise units) should be.*

3.4 Risk Benefits

A fourth argument for the existence of the plural form is formulated by Martin (1988), who states that the choice between company and franchised units enables the franchisor to adjust his personal risk profile as economic settings change. He assumes every location to have it's own individual risk factors upon which individual revenues depend heavily. These specific revenue risks are determined by factors such as the location's geographic situation and extension, the size of the catchment area and the income structure of people living in it. A risk averse franchisor behaving opportunistically could now hand over all doubtful locations to

---

[10] Cf. table 1.

[11] The evaluation process of the *Franchise500*: http://www.entrepreneur.com/Your_Business/YB_Static/1,4557,about_franchise500,00.html, (Feb. 20th, 2002).

franchisees, keeping the less risky as his own company-units to secure profits on them. A franchisor objecting to the risks of unprofitable but strategically important locations would now develop these as franchise units and not - as stated above (cp "Growth Benefits") - as company units. As Martin (1988) has pointed out, even a risk neutral franchisor would act in this opportunistic way since the costs of monitoring rise at high-risk locations as well. Just as portfolio managers shift their assets to maintain the level of investment risk, a franchisor could act similarly by simply adjusting the mix of franchised and company-owned units within his system. A rational franchisee, who would then expect to be offered a location with higher than average risk, would consequently have to demand additional rents from the franchisor to compensate the increased risk. The fact that one of the biggest and most successful franchise systems in the world, McDonald's, offers it's franchisees additional and more than expected ex-ante as well as ex-post rents (Ehrmann 2002; Kaufmann and Lafontaine 1994) could be an indication of the existence of such a strategy. As a risk management motivation contradicts the idea of cooperational behavior between a franchisor and his franchisees, we can state for this aspect:

> *H7: The higher the support for the quality signaling effects, the less likely do franchisors manage a chain along risk aspects.*

A rational franchisee with a long-term focus, having the choice between a franchisor trying to optimize his position of risk or another one trying to signal cooperation to his franchisees, would probably have to decide in favor of the latter one.

4 Empirical Issues

As stated in part 2, we used the data of the top 240 franchise chains of the *Entrepreneur Magazine's 2001* survey to test our hypotheses. As the λ-values of our sample systems are not distributed normally, we apply the non-parametric Mann-Whitney-Test instead of the common t-test to verify significant differences between the various variables. This requires the two groups tested to belong to the same single sample. Thus both groups were first treated as one entity and ranked according to the tested variable. Then the rank sum of the first group was compared to that of the second. A significantly similar (different) rank sum in both groups reveals similarity (difference) in the pattern of the tested variable. To enhance exactness, we tested each hypothesis on three different quantiles ((2x120, 3x80 and 4x60 systems), meaning that the importance of a supported or rejected hypothesis increases with smaller quantile size.

As outlined (compare part 2.2), franchisees as well as company-owned units make costs for the franchisor because of behavior uncertainty. According to both costs aspects, the franchisor could use the plural form to minimize this costly uncertainty. Whereas the costs caused by franchisees are nearly constant over time, the ones caused by company units diminish as regional headquarters are installed and distances between monitoring headquarters and monitored units shrink. From a pure agency perspective we should observe a substitution of company-owned units to the disadvantage of franchised units as the system matures and exploitation of already explored regions begins. A similar development should be observable if the information costs aspect applies, as franchisors would start more company units neighboring the franchised outlets, transferring and profiting from the gathered local knowledge.

Thus we actually test the thesis of ownership-redirection, brought up by Oxenfeldt and Kelly (1969) and summarized well by Dant, Paswan and Kaufmann (1996) as the question: „Do franchisors use franchisees to open markets, develop consumer acceptance and preference for the franchisors' trademarks and then appropriate that brand equity by terminating or otherwise ending the franchisees' rights to continue to operate the business?"[12] As we show in table 2, we could not find significant support for this thesis in our sample.

Table 2. Plural Form and System

	QU120*	**QU80***		**QU60***		
	λ	λ	λ	λ	λ	λ
	Q1<Q2	Q1<Q2	Q1<Q3	Q1<Q2	Q1<Q3	Q1<Q4
Z-Value	0.25	0.35	-0.35	0.06	1.12	-0.56
Sig. (1-side)	0.5991	0.6387	0.3639	0.5251	0.8682	0.2872
Probability	40.09%	36.13%	63.61%	47.49%	13.18%	71.28%

*Table 2 summarizes the tests on three different quantiles, i.e. QU120 (2x120), QU80 (3x80) and QU60 (4x60). In each test the entire sample was ranked according to the tested variable (AGE in table 2), e.g. for QU60 Q1 contains the 60 oldest systems and Q4 the 60 youngest ones. We then tested correlations between the quantiles using the Mann-Whitney-U-Test.

Our analysis demonstrates that the differences in the percentage franchised, displayed as λ, depending on the age of the system, were not significant at either one of the quantiles. None of the three tests showed a significant smaller λ and thus a higher percentage of company-owned units at the older systems (in quantile 1) compared to the younger systems (in the quantiles 2, 3 and 4). A correlation between age and organizational form of the system could not be supported through this test. Looking at our entire data, we found that only 21% of the systems displayed a decreasing λ in favor of company units within the five years covered. Whereas 41% of the systems did not change their λ over the period at all, 38% slightly increased λ by about 8% on average. As the average age of the first group of systems is about 20 years, and that of the last one is about 18.8 years, we conclude that franchisors do not change their λ significantly as soon as franchise contracts expire (which happens after about 10-15 years in general).

[12] Dant, Paswan and Kaufmann (1996), p 429.

These findings are supported by studies of Lafontaine and Kaufmann (1994), Lafontaine and Shaw (1999) and Pénard, Raynaud and Saussier (2002), who cannot find indications for the existence of ownership redirection tendencies either, even when researching much larger samples.[13] Even Oxenfeldt and Kelly (1969) - being the first to state this correlation - remark at the beginning of their study: „Frankly, we are not fully convinced that the hypothesis we propound is valid. Certainly the arguments advanced by advocates of franchising have force, but we are not persuaded by them."[14] Thus with the rejection of the ownership-redirection thesis we reject H1 as a plausible argument for the existence of the plural form phenomenon.

Since H2 is concerned with resource shortages and the advantages of flexibility, the plural form should have positive impact on the systems growth. Plurally organized chains therefore should be able to realize over-proportional company growth compared to singular arranged systems. The results on a potential correlation between the organizational structure and the absolute growth of outlets over the period covered are displayed in table 3.

Table 3. Plural Form and System Growth

	QU120*	QU80*		QU60*		
	λ	λ	λ	λ	λ	λ
	Q1<Q2	Q1<Q2	Q1<Q3	Q1<Q2	Q1<Q3	Q1<Q4
Z-Value	-0.67	-0.76	-1.40	-0.72	-0.55	-1.07
Sig. (1-side)	0.2510	0.2233	0.0814	0.2344	0.2926	0.1421
Probability	74.90%	77.67%	91.86%	76.56%	70.74%	85.76%

* Q1 contains the fastest growing systems, Q2/3/4 the weaker growing ones

Again we cannot observe that the differences of λ between the strong growth systems (quantile 1) and the less growing ones (quantiles 2, 3 and 4) is significant on a acceptable confidence level. In the case that H2 applied, one would expect the differences in λ between the first and the other quantiles to be significantly different on a confidence level between 5% and 1%. As we cannot show that plurally organized systems grow faster than singular ones, we reject H2, too.

Laying out the arguments that led to H3 to H5, we have already pointed out the character distinguishing the background of these arguments from the ones used in

---

[13] Cf. Lafontaine and Kaufmann (1994), p 11; Lafontaine and Shaw (1999), p 1073 ff.; Pénard, Raynaud and Saussier (2002), p 21 ff., Dant, Paswan and Kaufmann (1996), p 431 f. Contradicting these findings are the results of a recent study by Dant and Kaufmann (2003) making the authors state (p 63) that „ there is some evidence of a greater tendency to permanently convert existing franchised outlets to company-owned outlets as fast food systems mature and gain greater access to resources".

[14] Cf. Oxenfeldt and Kelly (1969), p 69.

the hypotheses before. Whereas H1 and H2 assumed the plural form to be an appropriate means for the franchisor to use opportunistic freedom granted to him by the system of franchising, the quality aspects in H3 to H5 are based on the idea of long-term cooperation between the franchisor and his franchisees. We outlined that such a cooperation is nurtured on continuous profitability, homogeneous interests, balanced streams of innovation and fair interfirm competition. Since aspects like these are difficult to recognize for outsiders, a franchisor can try to send out signals of credibility to make these inside facts visible from outside. The franchisor of a pure franchise system (λ=1), could now offer low franchise fees to ease the system entry and simultaneously demand high royalty rates to demonstrate his dependence from the franchisees long-term success. The franchisor of a plurally organized chain (e.g. λ=0,8) is able to send out the same signal just by running a certain number of units himself, thereby leaving franchise fees relatively high and keeping royalty rates relatively low. Our data strongly supports these two genuine strategies. Tables 4 and 5 clearly show that chains charging the highest franchise fees and lowest royalty rates are significantly more plurally organized than the ones with lower entrance and higher ongoing fees.

Table 4. Plural Form and Franchise Fees

	QU120*	**QU80***		**QU60***		
	λ	λ	λ	λ	λ	λ
	Q1<Q2	Q1<Q2	Q1<Q3	Q1<Q2	Q1<Q3	Q1<Q4
Z-Value	-2.80	-1.88	-3.61	-1.50	-2.29	-3.00
Sig. (1-side)	0.0026	0.0300	0.0002	0.0667	0.0109	0.0014
Probability	99.74%	97.00%	99.98%	93.33%	98.91%	99.86%

* Q1 contains the systems with the highest, Q2/3/4 the ones with the lowest franchise fees.

Table 5. Plural Form and Royalty Rates

	QU120*	**QU80***		**QU60***		
	λ	λ	λ	λ	λ	λ
	Q1<Q2	Q1<Q2	Q1<Q3	Q1<Q2	Q1<Q3	Q1<Q4
Z-Value	-2.46	-0.42	-1.66	-1.15	-0.56	-1.48
Sig. (1-side)	0.0070	0.3361	0.0488	0.1255	0.2888	0.0697
Probability	99.30%	66.39%	95.12%	87.45%	71.12%	93.03%

* Q1 contains the systems with the lowest, Q2/3/4 the ones with the highest royalty rates.

Gallini and Lutz (1992) present similar results and explain the two strategies: „...a sufficiently large number of the company-owned stores gives the high-demand franchisor enough stake in the product's success to deter the low-demand franchisor from misleading franchisees; the franchisor does not need to claim an additional stake through a royalty to convince them of the product's demand. The high-demand franchisor offers the efficient contract, charging a zero royalty on sales and using the fixed fee to extract all profits from the franchisee."[15]

Testing H5, we have to compare the strength and the effectiveness of either one signal. As explained in part 3.3, the more a franchisee invests, the higher his risk exposure will be and the more he will be concerned about the franchisor's correct behavior. As investment volumes increase, the barriers to enter such a high-volume system grow together with the necessity for the franchisor to credibly signal his willingness to cooperation. Thus in our analysis we concentrated on the reduction of this costly behavior uncertainty and looked at franchise systems that demand high investments from their franchisees.

As table 6 demonstrates, so called high-volume-franchisors are significantly more plurally organized than low-volume franchisors. Thus we conclude the signal of cooperation and quality sent out by plural elements to be more important to franchisees (and thus to franchisors) than the ones sent out by an alternative structure of entrance and ongoing fees.

Table 6. Plural Form and Investment Volumes

	QU120*	**QU80***		**QU60***		
	λ	λ	λ	λ	λ	λ
	Q1<Q2	Q1<Q2	Q1<Q3	Q1<Q2	Q1<Q3	Q1<Q4
Z-Value	-5.15	-1.96	-5.36	-1.35	-3.01	-4.72
Sig. (1-side)	0.0000	0.0253	0.0000	0.0878	0.0013	0.0000
Probability	100%	97.47%	100%	91.22%	99.87%	100%

* Q1 contains the systems with the highest, Q2/3/4 the ones with the lowest investment volumes demanded from franchisees.

A pure franchise system may be able to signal profitability through relatively high royalty rates, demonstrating strong dependence on the franchisee success. Plurally organized systems, though, are further able to signal the harmonization of divergent interests, the balance of innovation and the installation of an interfirm competition based on fair benchmarks. Especially the fact that high-volume franchisors with an increased shortage in capital own a larger part of company-owned units than low-volume systems with a lesser resource problem, is an additional indication for the signaling function of the plural form.

Finally we tested H6, showing in table 7 that the highest ranking systems in our sample are significantly more plurally organized than the ones that received lower rankings.

[15] Cf. Gallini and Lutz (1992), p 482 f.

Table 7. Plural Form and System Success

	QU120*	QU80*		QU60*		
	λ	λ	λ	λ	λ	λ
	Q1<Q2	Q1<Q2	Q1<Q3	Q1<Q2	Q1<Q3	Q1<Q4
Z-Value	-1.38	-1.71	-1.28	-1.14	-1.67	-1.45
Sig. (1-side)	0.0833	0.0433	0.1003	0.1274	0.0470	0.0737
Probability	91.67%	95.67%	89.97%	87.26%	95.30%	92.63%

* Q1 contains the highest ranking systems, Q2/3/4 the lowest ones.

The results presented here strongly support (H6) the notion that franchisors use the plural form to signal continuous, overall and above average system quality and that, at the same time, they end up being more successful than systems less plurally or singular organized. We conclude from this that hypothesis 7, assuming the plural form to be a tool for active risk management, has to be rejected. A franchisor, running his system like a portfolio manager, uses practically all freedom of opportunistic behavior and obstructs any opportunity of cooperation. The risk-managing franchisor as seen by Martin (1988) does not match at all the idea of a cooperational franchisor outlined as essentially important in the quality arguments. As has been demonstrated, successful franchisors use the plural form not against, but rather in favor of, the franchisees in order to create a system of cooperative and high-quality interaction.

5 The Plural Form as an Element of Successful Franchise Chains

As this analysis has revealed, a broad variety of strategies exists on how to best organize a fast-growing franchise system. The spectrum we find in reality starts with pure franchise systems without any company-owned units, on the one side, and ends with chains that hold one company-owned unit for every two franchised outlets. Therefore, we have aimed at outlining the theoretical arguments in favor of the plural form, and at testing them empirically against the behavior of real world franchisors.

We illustrated that the franchisor of a plurally organized system is theoretically able to realize positive effects on costs, growth and risk of the system using the freedom of opportunistic behavior. In our sample, however, we could not find significant support for strategies such that generally are exercised at the expenses of the franchise partners. Therefore, we concluded that franchisors do not use the plural form to realize cost reduction, growth increase or risk control. As our empirical analysis has verified, the advantage of the plural form seems to be the option for plurally organized franchisors to credibly demonstrate to existing and future franchisees their positive intent towards a long-term and cooperational partnership Such partnerships develop as the outcome of two processes, a combination of reciprocity and repeated interaction by which a good franchise relationship is strongly influenced. Both actors, the principal and his agents, are initially motivated to act in cooperation because of the repeated interaction. Then the reciprocity, i.e. the mutual strengthening of this positive behavior, helps to institutionalize these positive efforts building a basis for long-term and trustful partnerships. Looking at the *Franchise240* we found that the systems which ranked highest were those that had been able to activate such a process using the plural form. One reason for the absence of major organizational changes towards pure franchise chains or towards ownership redirection could be due to the shifting of priorities of the franchisor over time. Young and relatively unknown franchise systems have to attract new system partners and need to overcome quality uncertainty first. Once the chain matures, behavior uncertainty becomes the major issue to solve for growth oriented franchise systems. With its functions of signaling profitability, harmonizing divergent interests, balancing innovation streams and boosting interfirm competition, the plural form is neither an early nor a late stage business tool only, but rather a permanent management instrument for long-term strategic franchising.

References

1. Boeckenholt I, Wiens R (2001) Fuehrung einer Franchise-Organisation am Beispiel des Mischsystems der Blume 2000 GmbH & Co. KG. Ahlert (Ed.) (2001) Handbuch Franchising & Cooperation, Neuwied, pp 175 -184
2. Bradach J (1997) Using the Plural Form in the Management of Restaurant Chains. Administrative Science Quarterly 42:276-303
3. Brickley J, Dark F (1987) The Choice of Organizational Form - The Case of Franchising. Journal of Financial Economics, 18:401-420
4. Caves R, Murphy W (1976) Franchising - Firms, Markets and Intangible Assets. Southern Economic Journal 42:572-586
5. Cho I, Kreps D (1987) Signaling Games and Stable Equilibria. Quarterly Journal of Economics, 102:179-221
6. Dant R, Kaufmann P, Paswan A (1996) What we know about Ownership Redirection in Franchising - A Meta-Analysis. Journal of Retailing 72(4):429-444
7. Dant R, Kaufmann P (2003) Structural and Strategic Dynamics in Franchising. Journal of Retailing 79:63-75
8. Ehrmann T (2002) Reale Franchisesysteme, begrenzter Opportunismus und kooperative Elemente. Zeitschrift für Betriebswirtschaft 72(11):1133-1153
9. Gallini N, Lutz N (1992) Dual Distribution and Royalty Fees in Franchising. The Journal of Law, Economics and Organization 8(3):471-501
10. Hennart J (1993) Explaining the Swollen Middle - Why Most Transactions are a Mix of "Market" and "Hierarchy". Organization Science 4:529-547
11. Kaufmann P, Lafontaine F (1994) Costs of Control – The Source of Economic Rents for McDonald's Franchisees. Journal of Law and Economics 37:417-453
12. Lafontaine F, Kaufmann P (1994) The Evolution of Ownership Patterns in Franchise Systems. Journal of Retailing 70(2):97-114

13. Lafontaine F, Shaw K (1999) The Dynamics of Franchise Contracting - Evidence from Panel Data. Journal of Political Economy 107(5):1041-1080
14. Lafontaine F, Shaw K (2001) Targeting Managerial Control - Evidence from Franchising. NBER Working Paper No. W8416, http://papers.nber.org/papers/w8416.pdf (Oct. 17th, 2001)
15. Lafontaine F, Slade M (1996) Retail Contracting and Costly Monitoring - Theory and Evidence. European Economic Review 40:923-932
16. Leland H, Pyle D (1977) Informational Asymmetries, Financial Structure and Financial Intermediation. Journal of Finance 32(2):371-387
17. Lewin-Solomons S (1997) Innovation and Authority in Franchise Systems - Toward a Grounded Theory of the Plural Form. Dissertation, http://www.econ.cam.ac.uk /dae/people/lewin/thesis.pdf (Oct. 11th, 2001)
18. Lewin-Solomons S (1998) The Plural Form in Franchising - A Synergism of Market and Hierarchy. Working Paper, Iowa State University, http://www.econ.cam.ac.uk/dae /people/lewin/pluralA4.pdf (Oct. 11th, 2001)
19. Lewin-Solomons S (1999) Innovation and Authority in Franchise Systems - An Empirical Explanation of the Plural Form. Working Paper, Iowa State University, http://www.econ.cam.ac.uk/dae/people/lewin/empiricalA4.pdf (Oct. 11th, 2001)
20. Maness R (1986) Incomplete Contracts and the Choice of Vertical Integration and Franchising. Journal of Economic Behavior and Organization 31(1):101-115
21. March J (1991) Exploration and Exploitation in Organizational Learning. Organization Science 2:71-87
22. Martin R (1988) Franchising and Risk Management. American Economic Review 78(5):954-968
23. Mathewson G, Winter R (1985) The Economics of Franchise Contracts. Journal of Law and Economics 28:503-526
24. Michael S (2000) The Effect of Organizational Form on Quality - The Case of Franchising. Journal of Economic Behavior and Organization 43(3):295-318
25. Minkler A (1992) Why Firms Franchise -A Search Cost Theory. Journal of Institutional and Theoretical Economics 148:240-259
26. Ouchi W (1980) Markets, Bureaucracies and Clans. Administrative Science Quarterly 25:129-140
27. Oxenfeldt A, Kelly A (1969) Will Successful Franchise Systems Ultimately Become Wholly-Owned Chains? Journal of Retailing 44:69-83
28. Pénard T, Raynaud E, Saussier S (2002) Dual Distribution and Royalty Rates in Franchised Chains - An Empirical Analysis Using French Data. Journées de Microéconomie Appliquées, Rennes-Saint Malo
29. Posselt T (1998) Das Design vertraglicher Vertriebsbeziehungen am Beispiel Franchising. Zeitschrift für Betriebswirtschaft 69(3):347-376
30. Shelton J (1967) Allocative Efficiency vs. "X-Efficiency" – A Comment. American Economic Review 57, October:1252-1258
31. Sorenson O, Sørensen J (2001) Finding the Right Mix - Franchising, Organizational Learning and Chain Performance. Strategic Management Journal 22:713-724
32. Thompson R (1994) The Franchise Life Cycle and the Penrose Effect. Journal of Economic Behavior and Organization 24:207-218
33. Walker G, Weber D (1984) A Transaction Cost Approach to Make-or-Buy Decisions. Administrative Science Quarterly 29:373-391

Innovation Management within the Plural Form Network

Gérard Cliquet, Minh-Ngoc Nguyen

Center for Research on Economics and Management, University of Rennes 1
IGR-IAE, 11 rue Jean Macé CS, 70803 RENNES Cedex 7, France
gerard.cliquet@univ-rennes1.fr

Center for Research on Economics and Management, University of Rennes 1
IREIMAR - Campus de Beaulieu, Bât 1, 263, av. du Général Leclerc, 35042 Rennes, France
nguyenminhngoc@netcourrier.com

Abstract. Nowadays, most retail chains are organized in a network structure, which operates under the principals of mutual communication and cooperation for lower overhead cost, increased responsiveness and flexibility, and greater operational efficiency (Lozenzoni and Baden 1995). In addition, thanks to interfaces between many units, the network is a powerful tool to foster innovation. However, networks can also block innovation because of the divergence of interests among units (Hagedoorn 1995). A franchised network is an illustration of this, due to the fact that franchisees, as independent small business owner, have the right not to adopt all the modifications proposed by the franchiser. A solution is to use the plural form, associating franchise and company arrangements. In reality, the plural form is increasingly used in retailing; it has advantages over the pure franchised and wholly owned chains in terms of innovation.

This paper deals with innovation management within the plural form network. Firstly, difficulties in managing innovation faced by network operators are pointed out. Secondly, why the plural form could facilitate innovation is explained. Finally, the innovation process models are established, which highlight how innovations are made and managed in the plural form network. Data for analysis are obtained by interviews with network operators in France.

On the whole, this work tends to show the superiority of the plural form and has a practical purpose to help the plural form network to optimize the management of innovation projects.

1 Introduction

Innovation is increasingly seen as a powerful way of securing competitive advantage and one of the key factors in a firm's strategy for survival (Drucker 1985). Innovation is not easy to manage due to its characteristics of complexity, change and uncertainty. For a network organization that possesses geographically dispersed business units, the management of innovation is more complex and thus requires more effort. The purpose of this paper is to investigate how innovation is made and managed within business networks, especially focusing on the retail and service sectors. Retail and service networks may operate as unique forms chains (i.e. purely franchised and wholly owned chains) or plural form networks associating frequently franchise and company arrangements.

Overall, this paper deals with innovation management within the plural form network. It is hypothesized that the plural form could be a better organizational option for point-of-sale network in terms of developing innovation. The paper is structured as follows. Section 2 provides a brief summary of the literature on advantages and disadvantages of network structure, difficulties faced by retail network operators in the innovation management are pointed out. Section 3 discuses the reasons why the plural form having both franchise and company arrangements could facilitate innovation. Our analysis is based on interviews with French franchisors in various sectors of activity and on the results of past research (Bradach 1998; Lewin-Solomons 1998). Section 4 proposes the models of innovation process, which are expected to help the plural form network operators to optimize the management of their innovation projects. Section 5 offers some concluding remarks including implications and suggested directions for future study.

2 Innovation and Network Organization

Nowadays, it is observed that a growing number of retail chains are organized in a network structure. This organizational form seems to provide potential sources of competitive advantages (Wilkinson and Young 2002) but also poses challenges to the management (Håkansson and Ford 2002). This section presents in the first place a brief literature review of the advantages of networks regarding innovation development. Then, it is important to show difficulties in innovation management within a network, particularly in the franchised network.

2.1 Advantages of the Network Structure in Terms of Innovation

The term "network", by definition, refers to a set of business units and relationships which connect them (Fombrun 1982). Networks operate under the principals of mutual communication and cooperation for lower overhead cost, increased responsiveness and flexibility, and greater operational efficiency (Lozenzoni and Baden 1995). They allow companies to gain access to complementary resources and competence, which are not available internally. Networks are dynamic and flexible structures subject to change (Hagedoorn 1995).

Innovation could be fostered more thanks to interfaces between two or more parties. In other words, innovation could be seen as an efficient process stemming from a network of several actors. Various network attributes which influence the innovation capability can be considered, such as *flexibility*, *speed* and *network learning system*.

- The network structure provides chains with the *flexibility* to respond to continuous evolution and revolution in products, technologies and markets. Empirical investigations have shown that alliances of small firms can archive higher flexibility and efficiency than a single-plant enterprise (Semlinger 1993). A greater organizational flexibility permits greater ability to adapt to the changing market conditions (Cliquet 2000), and therefore to a better accommodation of novelty, innovation and local responsiveness.
- *Speed* is viewed as an advantage of networks; speed is also essential for successful innovation. With the co-operation's mechanism in the strategic development, networks have generally an ability to respond to customer needs faster than a single unit does. Hence, networks promote a means to reduce the time of the innovation process. Moreover, speed offers three majors payoffs (Cooper 1993).
  - *Speed yields competitive advantage.* The ability to respond to customer needs and changing markets faster than competitors and to beat competitors to market with a new product is often the key to success.
  - *Speed yields higher profitability.* The revenue from the sale of the product is realized earlier, and the revenues over the life of the product are higher, given a fixed window of opportunity and hence limited product life.
  - *Speed means fewer surprises*. The short timeframe reduces the odds that market conditions will change dramatically as development proceeds.

  Speed appears to be really a competitive weapon of the network structure.
- Co-operation offers companies the availability of a wide range of resources almost immediately. Under the current competitive circumstances, the two basic resources are knowledge and relationships. Pooling those resources is necessary for a business network to get stronger. The network organization form increases learning (Håkansson et al. 1999), by providing linkages with external learning partners in long-term relationships that facilitate information sharing. The diversity of information that resides in a network is greater than that in a single firm. In fact, the network as a *learning system* provides skills to organizations by creating, acquiring and transferring knowledge and modifying their behavior in order to figure out new perspectives (Garvin 1993).

Networks are powerful tools to foster innovation in company and industry-wide (Gomez Arias 1995). As for the retail and service sectors, it is observed that this type of organization is more generally used and also enhances many activities including innovation.

In this paper, we concentrate on retail and service sectors. There are various network structures that are popular in retailing. Bradach (1998) has proposed three types of network: a centralized company-owned system, a decentralized franchise system and a plural form network that associates both franchise and company arrangements. The first kind of system is the basic hierarchical network where there is a center (operator) with dependent units. Managers of these units are employees of the chain operator and they work under the instructions of that operator. On the contrary, the franchising system is a decentralized business network, which incorporates elements of both market and hierarchy (Williamson 1991) and was called by Shane (1996) the hybrid organization. Indeed, the franchisor retains the ownership and authority over the use of a trade name, the know-how in contracting with independent franchisees. The operator-franchisee relationship is a partnership between owners. Thirdly, the plural form network associates the strictly hierarchical mechanism of the company arrangement and the hybrid market/ hierarchy of business format franchising. Today, many retail chains adopt this organizational structure because the plural form provides a significant number of advantages in terms of marketing (Cliquet 2002), of management (Bradach 1997, 1998), of network performance (Sorenson and Sørensen 2001) and survival ability (Cliquet and Perrigot 2002).

2.2 Some Problems Related to Innovation Faced by Retail Networks

However, networks have some major drawbacks. The higher the number of units with different objectives and strategic agendas are involved, the more time-consuming the process of decision-making is. Therefore, close attention must be given to the trade-off between faster implementation and slower decision-making. Required relationships and norms entail drawbacks and hazards such as increasing complexity, less autonomy, information asymmetry (Hagedoorn 1995).

If network structure can promote innovation, it can also block it. It will be more complicated for the network to manage innovation. In reality, the operators of retail networks frequently have to confront this problem:

- The network management is different from the management of a single unit in the fact that the network operator has to control the set of geographically dispersed units. Many difficulties result from this characteristic of the network organization. First, the operator hardly knows the events which happen at local units, so may lose some control, especially over remote units. When an innovation occurs, the problem is how to implement the innovation while maintaining the uniformity of the network. Bradach (1998) defined uniformity as a key element of the business format chain. The objective of every chain is to build the good image of its concept and keep it identical across all units (Lafontaine and Shaw 1999). The evolution of the concept is essential for the network to survive in competitive circumstances, but it also makes the maintenance of uniformity a major challenge for network operator.
- It is difficult for the franchisor to have his concept deeply evolved in a pure franchised chain when this evolution requires an important investment of franchisees. The franchisor can not impose everything on his franchisees but rather persuade them to follow innovation. In reality, implementing an innovation on company-owned units does not cause problem. However, this requires efforts to diffuse innovation to franchised units. One of the drawbacks of franchising is the fact that franchisees have the right not to adopt all the modifications required by the franchisor in their own stores. The franchisor sometimes has to persuade his franchisees and stays very flexible. In reality, there are many solu-

tions: *Catena* (French do-it-yourself network) provided financial help for its franchisees to set up a new commercial brand with a new logo; *Sweetlit* (French home furnishing network) gave its franchisees a certain period to completely implement an innovation. In the worst case, as in the case of *Galler Chocolat* (Belgium confectionery network), if franchisees do not want to implement a new concept, they can stay as they are and continue to work as they used to do. So, in chains that have a rigid concept and where uniformity is highly required, it is necessary to maintain a right proportion of franchised and company-owned units, which can influence the chain performance (Sorenson and Sørensen 2001).

- The same thing happens with the system-wide adaptation. When an innovation is proposed, the network operator has to adapt it in all different contexts, particularly while there are points of sale abroad. The adaptation of a given innovation must be different from one country to another, from one region to another or even from one unit to another. We agree with Bradach (1998) in stating that system-wide adaptation is the most complex and difficult of all management challenges facing retail networks.

It is stated that in retailing, the plural form organizations, composed of franchised and company-owned units, can more or less deal successfully with the obstacles mentioned above. The next section will show how the plural form could facilitate innovation. Our qualitative analysis is based on results of past research in the fast-food industry by Bradach (1997) and Lewin-Solomons (1998) completed by our interviews with a number of French franchisors in various sectors of activity.

3 Discussion: Influence of the Plural Form on Innovation

The plural form associating franchise and company arrangements seems to enhance the network's ability to innovate. In the following, the influence of the plural form will be discussed successively in three stages of an innovation project: innovation generation, innovation programming and innovation implementation. Some French networks in several sectors of activity (e.g. do-it-yourself, home furnishing, car accessories, etc.) are used as our empirical illustration.

3.1 Idea Generation

Generating ideas is the first stage of any innovation process. The plural form seems to produce a greater variety of ideas than either arrangement could do by itself. By mixing a company arrangement with expert staff and a franchise arrangement with its business-experienced franchisees, the plural form benefits from two possible sources of information. Ideas for new products or services can be developed in two ways: by the franchisor and his company staff and by individual franchisees.

Within a plural form network, the franchise arrangement positively affects the system-wide development. With their experience in local markets, the franchisees play an important role in the ideas generation stage. They are regularly in contact with consumers. They can give local information feedback, if they want to, in order to help the chain's operator make decisions.

"Yes, franchisees are a significant source of innovation because, thanks to them, we have the feedback on consumer behavior. This enables us to adjust our concept of product or service according to the consumer's demand". (French franchisor *Sweetlit,* home furnishing)

"If franchisees come up with an idea, it should be taken. Franchisor and franchisees always work in groups. There are not two separated entities". (French franchisor *Sweetlit*)

"We appreciate franchisees ideas because these ideas came from the local market. We have some franchisees of high level who can reason, seek for and bring innovation ideas. It is one of the great forces of franchising". (French franchisor *Feu Vert*, car accessories)

Bradach's study has shown that local managers in the company arrangement, as a franchisor's employee, rarely came up with innovative ideas. By contrast, everyone agreed that franchisees were an important source of ideas, regarding the quantity of information and the quality as well. Explanations for this can be found while analyzing two fundamental differences between a company unit and a franchisee: *incentives* and *initiatives* (Lewin-Solomons 1998). Franchisees have strong incentives to manage their own business as well as possible because they are independent entrepreneurs who keep the profits produced by them, once the royalty payment is made. They are responsible for the results of their units, so take part in the network management and innovation activities. On the contrary, the company manager's incentives are lower-powered because they operate as employees within a standard corporate hierarchy. As far as initiatives are concerned, franchisees are much more independent than company managers are. They exercise a great deal of initiatives to make their business successful. Whereas company managers have to recognize authority, do not like taking risk and depend on the chain operator's decisions, franchisees have freedom in acting on their own. These kinds of incentives and initiatives demonstrate that a franchised outlet tends to perform better than company unit in generating innovations. For their own profits, franchisees regularly think about making the network more efficient. Ideas from franchisees once shared and accepted by other units will be converted into true and profitable projects. Sometimes, owing to the presence of franchisees, company managers become more dynamic and motivated. Through a *mutual learning process*, company units will be aware of their responsibility to daily develop the network (Bradach 1997).

Bradach (1998) cites franchisor arguments as illustrations. "If franchisees see a competitor doing something, they will quickly call us and want to do it themselves." (Franchisor *Hardee,* fast food). According to the *Kentucky Fried Chicken* CEO, franchisees accelerated the process of identifying opportunities for innovation: "Ultimately we would identify these issues, but franchisees sometimes enable us to see things earlier. "Franchisees are good at focusing on things that really hit the bottom line". From our own study on French franchisors, we can also notice: "Sometimes, franchisees come up with ideas that we have never thought of before" (Franchisor *Feu Vert,* car accessories).

In short, within the plural form structure, franchisees will develop their capabilities to influence network performance in terms of innovation. For instance, franchisee local responses push company units to be more dynamic, encourage the chain operator to develop more new products/services or evolve the existing concept. Franchisors often rely on the information, which comes up from local markets, to define their policies. This flow of information is rich qualitatively speaking because its stems from the direct contacts of local units with consumers.

3.2 Test and Evaluation of Ideas

After having innovative ideas, it is important for the operator to evaluate whether the innovation projects work as expected. Franchisees rarely participate in the formal testing and evaluating process, mainly because the characteristics of a franchise contract have nothing to do with field-testing. They are not ready to bear the risk of testing new ideas in their units. Therefore, it is easier to work with company units. In every network we studied, innovation ideas are conceived by the franchisor before being realized and diffused in the whole network. Franchisees rarely participate in this stage because the project's programming is part of the network operator's mission and tests for a new concept will be firstly carried at company-owned outlets. Still, franchisees do play a certain role in testing and evaluating innovation ideas. The independent thinking of franchisees is very valuable for the franchisor to check and balance before making decisions. In other words, the franchisor listens to his franchisees and acts according to their feedback. Franchisees tend to say exactly what they think, either good or bad things. These obvious and frank opinions are helpful to the franchisor to adjust the new concept and make good decisions. "We have franchisee committees for many aspects like advertisement, information… We cannot do anything without their opinion" (according to the director of *Catena*'s expansion department).

3.3 Implementation of Innovation

In a plural form network, each arrangement has an effect on the way the other arrangement works. A *reciprocal influence* positively affects the behavior of local units toward innovation. The chain operator can persuade franchisees to adopt an innovation by firstly implementing it in company units. The company's adaptation will directly affect the decision-making process of franchisees. The network operator can also use the company's data to demonstrate the viability of the proposed innovations. When new ideas are successfully adapted to company units, why not implement them in franchised stores? So, the convergence of interest created by the plural form can encourage the franchisee's acceptance. In his turn, the franchisee also provides feedback. The chain operator can use the franchisee performance to put pressure on company units or to set performance benchmarks for them.

In short, the relative weakness of a pure company arrangement is a function of few locally generated innovations, low-powered incentives to innovate, the absence of initiatives and experience, and the low level of local pressure on the franchisor to develop innovation. A franchise arrangement provides these four things lacking in a company arrangement. First, franchisees are an important source of local ideas. Second, franchisees have strong incentives to generate new ideas for the network's competitive advantage. Third, franchisees are someone who has a good intuition based on their experience. Finally, franchisees serve as a strong constituency pushing forward company managers and the chain operator to be more dynamic and to generate more ideas. Generally, the innovation programming (comprising innovation test and evaluation) is not composed of formal tasks for franchisees but it is at the franchisor's charge. However, the franchisee feedback is valuable for the network operator to check and adjust an innovation project. The speed of implementing an innovation is very high in pure company chains, but low in pure franchise arrangements, and considered as medium in plural form networks. Actually, the plural form enables accelerating the decision and implementation processes in franchised units, mainly because of the use of company units as screens for persuading franchisees to adopt innovations. In summary, the plural form seems to be a better option in terms of supporting innovation, in comparison to the purely franchised and wholly owned chains.

4 Innovation Process Modeling

One of the purposes of the present research is to study the innovation process and to conceptualize a model for the plural form network. This section starts with a summary of literature on innovation process research, followed by the proposition of two process models.

4.1 A Literature Review on Innovation Process Research

There are two streams of research on the innovation process (Wolfe 1994). The first, called stage model research (Ettlie 1980; Perl 1983), conceptualizes innovation as a series of stages that unfold over time. The purpose of stage model research is to determine whether innovation process involves identifiable stages and, if so, to try to nominate and place these stages in the right order. The second approach involves in-depth and longitudinal research conducted to fully describe the sequences of innovation process and the conditions that determine the innovation process. This paper deals with the first approach.

An impressive number of innovation process models have been described in the literature. A typology has been proposed according to various types of innovation (Saren 1984):

- Departmental-stage models consider the innovation process in relation with operational department of the innovative firm (R&D, design, technique, production, marketing).
- Decision-stage models are related to the series of decisions made (collecting information, evaluating information, taking decision, identifying uncertainty)
- Conversion process models deal with the innovation development as a process of transformation of raw materials and information (input) into end product (output)
- Response models are built as a function of the firm's responses to both internal and external stimuli (market demands, new product ideas, conception, acceptation or rejection of innovation…)
- Activity-stage models define an innovation process as the succession of stages or activities

As noted above, stage model research places a premium on the temporal sequence of activities in the development and implementation of innovation. The models by activity are mostly considered. Table 1 shows different models proposed in the literature.

Table 1 synthesizes many activity-stage models of innovation process, and it is noted that there is significant overlap among the models. Therefore, it is possible to describe an innovation process in the following general pattern: a generation of an idea, a decision-making unit becomes aware of an innovation idea, an evaluation considering a problem or opportunity matched to the innovation, a test through which the innovation costs and profits are appraised, a decision to adopt or reject innovation, an implementation of innovation, a review of the innovation decision and a confirmation, a diffusion of innovation.

The management of innovation within networks has its specific points. It is interesting to focus on the process for how innovation is made and managed within network structure. Until now, no innovation process model for retail networks exists. The following tends to describe our attempt towards building such a model.

Table 1. Stage Models of Innovation Process. (Adapted from Wolfe 1994)

Authors	1	2	3	4	5	6	7	8	9	10
Zalman, Duncan, Holbek (1973)		Knowledge/ awareness	Attitude formation			Decision	Initial implementation		Sustained implementation	
Daft (1978)	Idea conception				Proposal	Adoption/ rejection	Implementation			
Ettlie (1980)		Awareness	Evaluation	Trial		Adoption/ rejection	Implementation			
Tornatsky et al. (1983)		Awareness	Matching /selection			Adoption /rejection	Implementation		Routinization/ commitment	
Rogers (1983)		Knowledge			Persuasion	Decision	Implementation	Confirmation		
Meyer & Goes (1988)		Knowledge/ awareness	Evaluation / choice			Adoption	Implementation		Expansion	
Cooper & Zmud (1990)		Initiation (push / pull)				Adoption	Adapt/develop/ install	Acceptance/ usage	Incorporation/ routinization	Infusion
Jallat (1994, 1999)	Idea generation		Selection	Test			Development	Test/ confirmation		Diffusion
Bradach (1998)	Idea generation		Evaluation			Decision	Implementation			
Composite	**Ideas generation**	**Awareness**	**Evaluation**	**Test**	**Persuasion**	**Adoption decision**	**Implementation**	**Confirmation**	**Routinization**	**Diffusion**

4.2 Innovation Process Model for the Plural Form Network

Application field of this research

Innovation in retailing refers to two fundamentally different activities: radical innovation of the business system or sudden innovation and gradual improvements or regular innovation within the current structure (Liebmann 2003). Radical innovation in retailing means the current structure undergoes fundamental change. To a certain extent, the firm will be transformed in the future, e.g., a new commercial system such as a supermarket, e-business, etc.

The present research focuses more on the second type of retail innovations: gradual and continuous innovations. In this case, innovations mean improvements to existing operations in day-to-day business, i.e. new store concepts or services, new presentation and function of existing products, new distribution channel, new marketing systems (Barreyre 1980), cost reduction programs, more efficient logistics processes (Leibmann 2003). It is noted that this type of innovation is often made in retail networks. So, we decided to choose this type of innovation as the application field of our conceptual models.

Proposition of two innovation process models

Studying the issue of innovation within a plural form network, we find that it is possible to build an innovation process more efficiently applied to the plural form organizations. During our interviews with franchisors, we found out that there is a the need for communications between franchisor, franchisees and company units for more successful innovation.

Rogers (1983) defined *communication* as the process by which participants create and share information with one another in order to reach a mutual understanding. The pivotal role of effective communication has been substantiated in many innovation studies. In fact, many scholars in the field of innovation management have argued that innovation processes are essentially communication and information processing activities (Allen 1985; Brown and Utterback 1985; Ebadi and Utterback 1984; Fidler and Johnson 1984; Souder and Moenaert 1992; Tushman 1979; Tushman and Nadler 1980).

In a plural form network, because of the problem of divergent interests, the *communication stage* is needed to make an innovation project more profitable for every unit. Indeed, in the communication stage, franchisor, franchisees and company managers will meet each other and discuss the feasibility of innovation ideas. When the new ideas are accepted by a majority of people, the chance to succeed in following stages and in the whole innovation project will be higher. So, we propose adding a communication stage in the innovation process. Consequently, the proposed model comprises five stages: *idea generation, communication, innovation project design, test and evaluation, and innovation diffusion*. In principle, the model is based on the innovation process models proposed in the literature. It essentially differs from others in the stage of communication. The position of this stage may be changed according to where the innovation ideas come from. Two cases are distinguished:

- Model 1 is considered when innovation comes from the franchisor (*the top down process*).
- Model 2 is applied if innovation is initiated by the franchisee (*the bottom up process*).

The models are composed of three parts: *stage, innovation process* and *place.* There are 5 stages in each model: ideas generation, communication, innovation project design, test and evaluation, and innovation diffusion. In the column of innovation process, there are, by chronological sequence, actions that should be taken at the place showed in the third column of the model.

In the top down process, *communication* is stage number 4. The innovation process consists of five steps. Firstly, thanks to the local unit feedback, the competitive intelligence and the market analyses, the franchisor can have some innovative ideas. The innovation project will then be programmed by the franchisor, technically and commercially. Next, the prototype will be tested at company units. If the test gives favorable results, there can be a switch to the communication stage. If not, there needs to be a return to the previous stage to review and make adjustments. The communication is made through committee meetings and at franchised units with the purpose of informing and persuading franchisees to adopt, to train and give technical and financial aids for the implementation. Finally, it is the innovation diffusion in which new product and services will be commercialized in all units.

Model 2, the bottom up process, differs from model 1 by the fact that *communication* is the second stage. This is because when the innovation idea comes from a franchisee, it must be transferred to other units for review before it comes to the elaboration step.

The two models are particularly designed for the plural form networks, which seem to be in the majority of retail and service networks in France. These preliminary models are based on our observations and on what the interviewees told us. We shall, in the near future, test and improve these models among several chain operators in France.

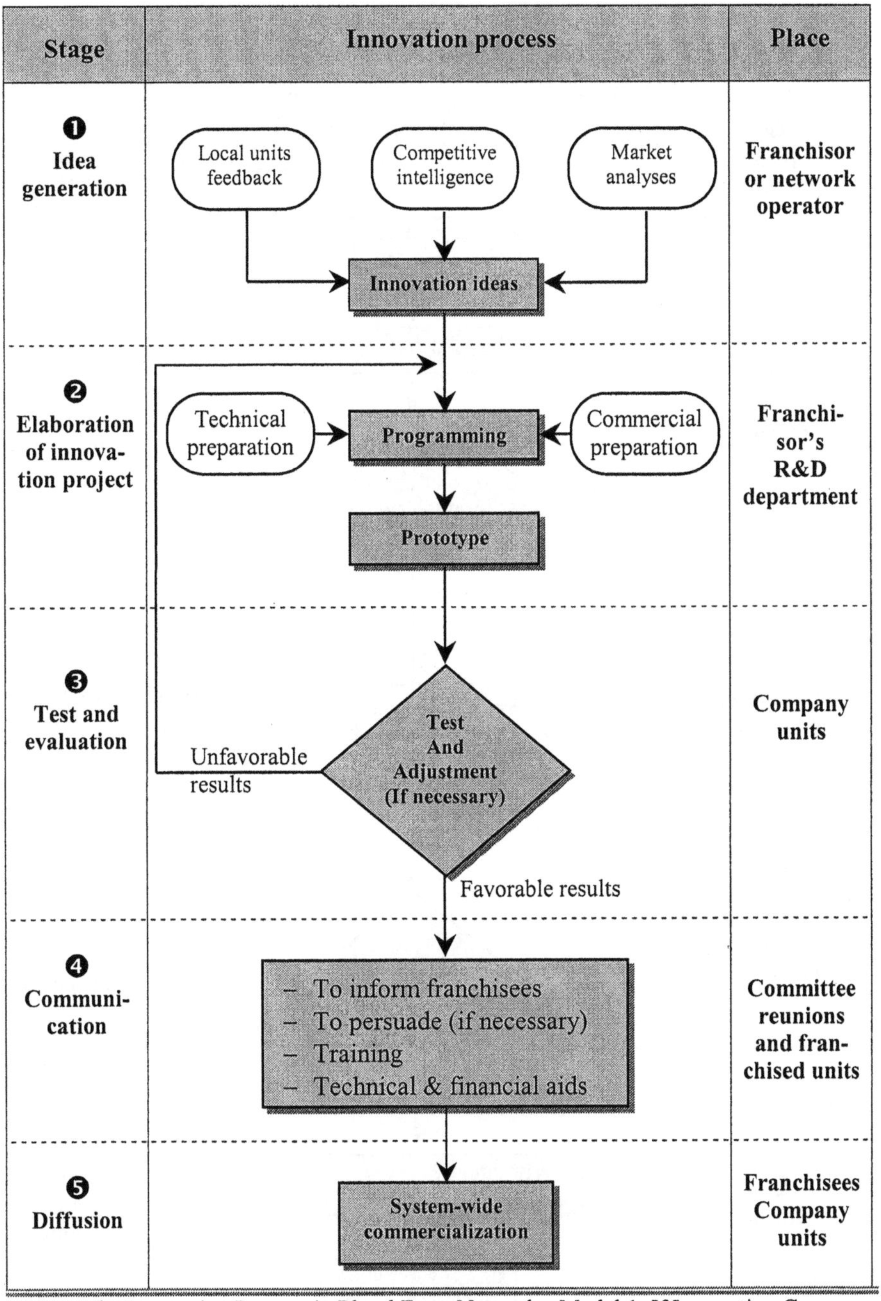

Fig. 1. The Innovation Process in Plural Form Networks. Model 1: If Innovation Comes from the Franchisor

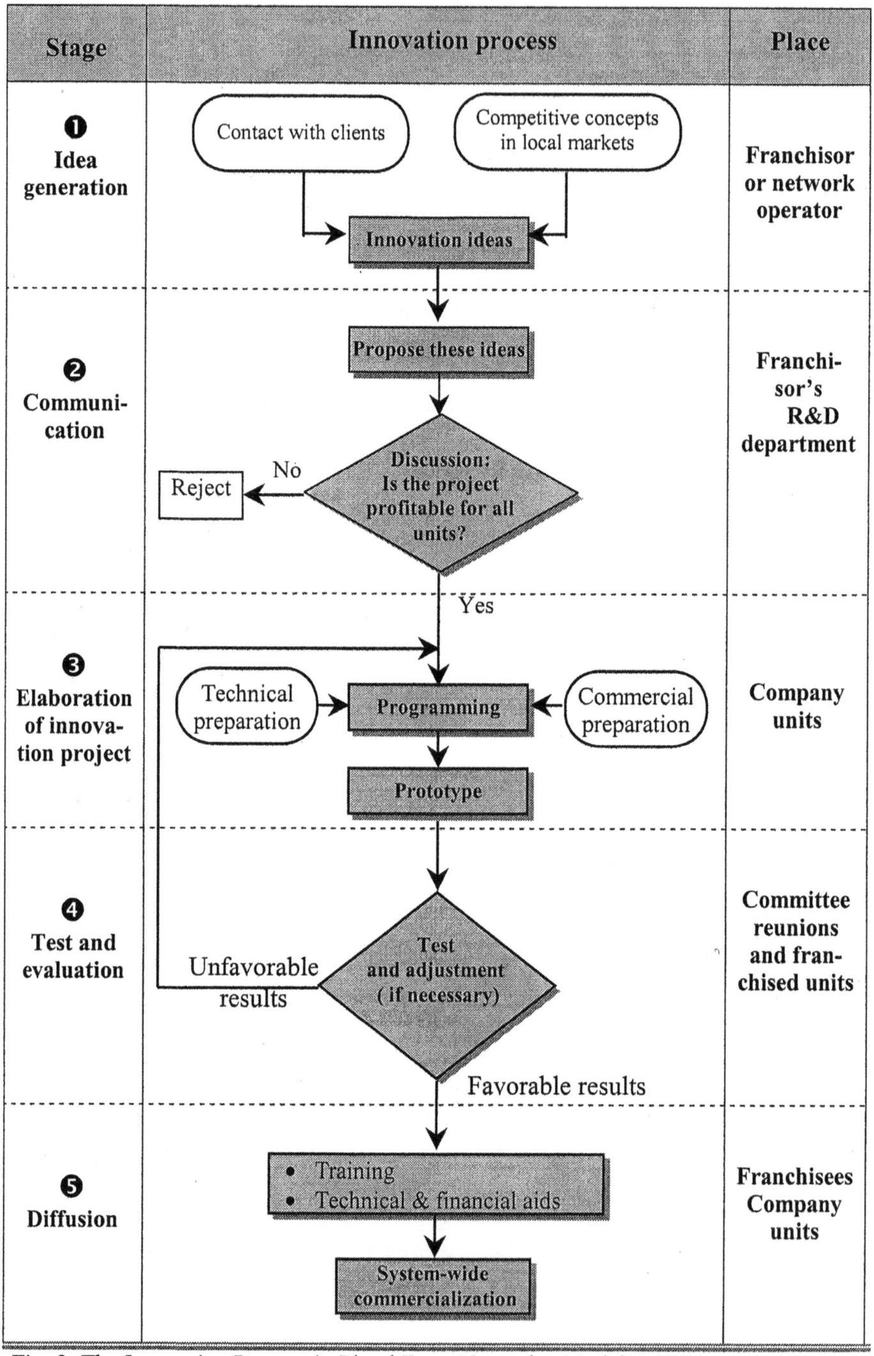

Fig. 2. The Innovation Process in Plural Form Networks. Model 2: If Innovation Comes from the Franchisee(s)

5 Conclusion

5.1 Contributions

This research offers a qualitative analysis of the influence of the plural form on innovation management. It couples different research on the plural form choice (Bradach and Eccles 1989; Bradach 1997, 1998; Lewin-Solomons 1998; Cliquet et al. 1998; Sorenson and Sørensen 2000; etc.) These authors have shown the superiority of the plural form over the unique form chains in terms of management, of marketing and network performance. We approached in this paper another advantage of the plural form regarding the innovation ability. Actually, the idea that the plural form seems to facilitate innovation was initiated by Bradach in 1998 and later raised by Lewin-Solomons in her studies on U.S. fast-food chains. We have strengthened this idea by examining it in others sectors and analyzing it in the different stages of the innovation process.

Identification of the role of plural form in terms of innovation development has important implications for practitioners in franchising. On the one hand, the network operators should consider the statutory choice while opening new sale outlets because the question "to franchise it or to own it ?" can, to some extent, affect the ability to innovate in the whole network. On the other hand, for a more innovative network, the network operators should pay attention to the positioning of franchised and company-owned units in a given territory taking care about the relative balance between the size of the franchise and company sectors.

The new contribution of our research is the proposition of two models of innovation process for plural form networks. The models that comprise operational stages are expected to be useful for network operators in managing their innovation projects.

5.2 Some Limitations and Directions for Future Research

There are some limitations associated with our empirical study. Our discussion is based on illustrations obtained by interviewing some French franchisors. The limitations of a small sample size and the qualitative analysis do not permit an affirmative conclusion. Consequently, the proposed models need more empirical examination in a larger sample. This constitutes one of our future works.

Our finding of a positive influence of the plural form on innovation management should be studied further because we found that the strength of the influence depends on the level of franchisees rate. It would be interesting to study the interaction between the innovativeness or the innovative climate of the network and its franchisees rate. Determining an adequate level of franchised and company owned units for more innovative networks would be a related issue for future research.

References

1. Allen TJ (1985) Managing the Flow of Technology: Technology Transfer and the Dissemination of Technological Information within the R&D Organization. The MIT Press, Cambridge, MA
2. Anchrol RS (1996) The Franchise as a Network Organization. Proceedings of the 10th Annual Conference of the International Society of Franchising, Honolulu, Hawaii
3. Barreyre PY (1980) Typologie des innovations. Revue Française de Gestion jan-feb:9-15
4. Bradach JL, Eccles RG (1989) Price, Authority and Trust: From Ideal types to Plural Forms. Annual Review of Sociology 15:97-118
5. Bradach JL (1997) Using Plural Form in the Management of Restaurant Chains. Administrative Science Quarterly 42, 2:276-303
6. Bradach JL (1998) Franchise organization. Harvard Business School Press
7. Brown JW, Utterback JM (1985) Uncertainty and technical Communication Patterns. Management Science 31, 3:301-11
8. Cliquet et al. (1998) Plural Form Networks: Franchise vs. Company Arrangements: Conflicting or Complementary organizations? Report on Research Contract Commissioned by the French Franchise Federation (FFF)
9. Cliquet G (2000) Plural Forms in Store Networks: A Model for Store Network Evolution. The International Review of Retail, Distribution and Consumer Research 10, 4:369-387
10. Cliquet G (2002) Les réseaux mixtes franchise/succursalisme : Apport de la littérature et implications pour le marketing des réseaux de points de vente. Recherche et Applications en Marketing 17, 1:57-73
11. Cliquet G, Perrigot R (2002) An Application of Survival Analysis to French Hotel Networks. Proceedings of the 16th Annual International Society of Franchising Conference, Orlando, Florida
12. Cooper RB, Zmud RW (1990) Information Technology Implementation Research: A Technological Diffusion Approach. Management Science 36:123-39
13. Cooper RG (1993) Winning at New Products. Accelerating the Process from Idea to Launch, Addison-Wesley, Reading, MA
14. Draf RL (1978) A Dual Core Model of Organizational Innovation. Academy of Management Journal 21:193-210
15. Drucker P (1985) Innovation and Entrepreneurship. Harper & Row, New York
16. Ebadi YM, Utterback JM (1984) The Effects of Communication on Technological Innovation. Management Science 30, 5:572-85
17. Ettlie JE (1980) Adequacy of Stage Models for Decisions on Adopting of Innovation. Psychological Reports 46:991-105
18. Fidler LA, Johnson JD (1984) Communication and Innovation Implementation. Academy of Management Review 9, 4:704-11
19. Fombrun CJ (1982) Strategies for Network Research in Organizations. Academy Management Review 7, 2: 280-91
20. Garvin DA (1993) Building a Learning Organization. Harvard Business Review, July-August:78- 91
21. Gomez Arias JT (1995) Do Networks Really Foster Innovation? Management Decision 33, 9:52-56
22. Hagedoorn J (1995) A Note on International Market Leaders and Networks of Strategic Technology Partnering. Strategic Management Journal 16:241-50

23.Håkansson H, Havila V, Pedersen AC (1999) Learning in Network. Industrial Marketing Management 28:443–452
24.Håkansson H, Ford D (2002) How Should Company Interact in Business Networks? Journal of Business Research 55:133-139
25.Jallat F (1994) Innovation dans les services : les facteurs de success. Décisions Marketing 2: 23-30
26.Jallat F (1999) Spécificités des processus et gestion de l'innovation dans les services. Market Management 4:31-42
27. Lafontaine F, Shaw KL (1999) Targeting Managerial Control: Evidence from Franchising. Working paper, University of Michigan Business School
28.Lewin-Solomons SB (1999) Innovation and Authority in Franchise System: An Empirical Exploration of the Plural Form. Journal paper no. J-18005 of the Iowa Agriculture and Home Economics Experiment Station, Project No. 3530
29.Lewin-Solomons SB (1998) The Plural Form in Franchising : A Synergism of Market and Hierarchy. Working paper, University of Cambridge and Iowa State University
30.Liebmann HP, Foscht T, Angerer T (2003) Innovation in Retailing : Gradual or Radical Innovations of Business Models. European Retail Digest 37:55-60
31.Lozenzoni G, Baden Fuller C (1995) Creating a Strategic Center to Manage a Web of Partners. California Management Review 37, 3: 146-63
32.Meyer AD, Goes JB (1988) Organizational Assimilation of Innovations: A Multilevel Contextual Analysis. Academy of Management Journal 31:897-923
33.Paswan AK, Wittman CM (2003) Franchise System and Knowledge Management. Proceedings of the 17th Annual International Society of Franchising Conference, San Antonio, Texas
34.Pelz DC (1983) Qualitative Case Histories of Urban Innovations: Are There Innovating Stage? IEEE Transactions on Engineering Management 30:60-7
35.Rogers EM (1983) Diffusion of Innovation. The Free Press, New York
36.Semlinger K (1993) Small Firms and Outsourcing as Flexibility Reservoirs of Large Firms. In: Graher G (ed) The Embedded Firm: On the Socioeconomics of Industrial Networks. Routledge, London New York
37.Saren MA (1984) A Classification and Review of Models of the Intra-firm Innovation Process. R&D Management 14, 1:11-24
38.Shane SA (1996) Hybrid Organizational Arrangements and Their Implications for Firm Growth and Survival: A Study of New Franchisors. Academy of Management Journal 39, 1:216-234
39.Sorenson O, Sørensen JB (2001) Finding the Right Mix: Organizational Learning, Plural Forms and Franchise Performance. Strategic Management Journal 22:713-724
40.Souder WE, Moenaert RK (1992) Integrating Marketing and R&D Project Personnel within Innovation Projects: An Information Uncertainty Model. Journal of Management Studies 29, 4:485-512.
41.Stanworth J, Price S, Purdy D, Zafiris N, Gandolfo A (1996) Business Format Franchising: Innovation and Creativity or Replication or Conformity? Proceedings of the 10th Annual conference of the International Society of Franchising, Honolulu, Hawaii
42.Stanworth J, Healeas S, Purdy D, Watson A, Stanworth C (2003) Entrepreneurial Teams, Intellectual Capital Acquisition and Knowledge Management-New Perspectives on Franchising as a Small Business Growth Strategy. Proceedings of the 17th Annual International Society of Franchising Conference, San Antonio, Texas

Franchising and Alternative Forms of Contract to Organize Vertical Restraints: Evidence from French Networks

Magali Chaudey*, Muriel Fadario*

CREUSET, Université Jean Monnet de Saint-Etienne
6, rue Basse-des-Rives, 42023 Saint-Etienne, cédex 2, France
chaudey@univ-st-etienne.fr
fadairo@univ-st-etienne.fr

Abstract. As far as France is concerned, franchising is one of the four types of contracts within networks sharing a same brand name. There is a hierarchy among these four categories of contracts, in accordance with the degree of restriction imposed on the retailer. The aim of this paper is to explain why networks choose franchising contracts, and more precisely why they opt for this degree of vertical integration. Section 2 highlights the relevance of the theory of incentives and the principal-agent paradigm to study franchising, and more generally speaking to study vertical restraints. Furthermore, this section provides an overview of the agency econometrics on franchising. Section 3 develops an econometrical study on French data to test the agency argument in explaining the degree of restriction within vertical contracts. Section 4 contains concluding remarks.

1 Introduction

Vertical constraints are defined as agreements binding companies located at various levels of the distribution chain: supplier and distributor, or wholesaler and retailer. Unlike subcontracting, which also involves a vertical relationship but concerns the production side, vertical restraints relate specifically to sales issues. These agreements are embodied in long-term commercial contracts, which restrict a distributor's field of action in areas such as the selling price, the quantities to be sold, the sales territory or even the product line and the method of supply. To be specific, we can distinguish: vertical restraints that concern i) the payment scheme such as non-linear prices, franchise fees, royalties, ii) vertical restraints that limit the distributor's rights such as price ceiling, price floors, quantity fixing, exclusive

* We are grateful to M. Debatisse, M. Normand, E. Raynaud, J. Windsperger, and the participants of the session "Competition between Network forms", ***EMNet***-Conference on "Economics and Management of Franchising Networks", Vienna, Austria, June 26 – 28 2003, for helpful comments. All remaining errors are ours.

dealing, tie-in, iii) vertical restraints that limit both parties' rights, such as exclusive territories (Rey and Caballero-Sanz 1996). These contracts do not belong to the traditional micro-economic framework of "linear" trade prices where the distributor pays the supplier an amount in proportion to the quantity purchased (Rey and Tirole 1986b). Franchising represents by far the most common form, but there are others that vary according to the variables in the relationship between the two companies.

As far as France is concerned, franchising is one of the four types of contracts within networks sharing the same brand name:

Licence: the independent retailer is authorized to use a brand name under some conditions ensuring the homogeneity of the network.

Concession: contract whereby a manufacturer offers the right to sell one or more products to a limited number of retailers. Concessions usually guarantee a double exclusivity: territory and supply.

Franchise: system whereby a franchisor puts a concept at the franchisee's disposal. This concept is perfected by the franchisor. In return, the franchisee remunerates the franchisor and respects the concept. The concept is based on some signs (brand), know-how, a line of products, some services and technologies.

Commission-affiliation: the commission-affiliation contract is similar to a franchise contract, except that the retailer does not own his stock and does not choose the resale prices. His remuneration is a percentage of the turnover.

These definitions underline a hierarchy among the four types of contracts, in accordance with the degree of constraint imposed on the retailer. This hierarchy can be explained as follows: regarding the Licence contract, the retailers only share the same trade name. Concession is like a licence contract, but in addition outlets also sell the same product manufactured by the upstream firm. Franchise is like Concession, but in addition firms also share the same concept and know-how. The Commission-affiliation contract has the same provisions as franchise, except that the upstream firm manages the downstream firm stock:

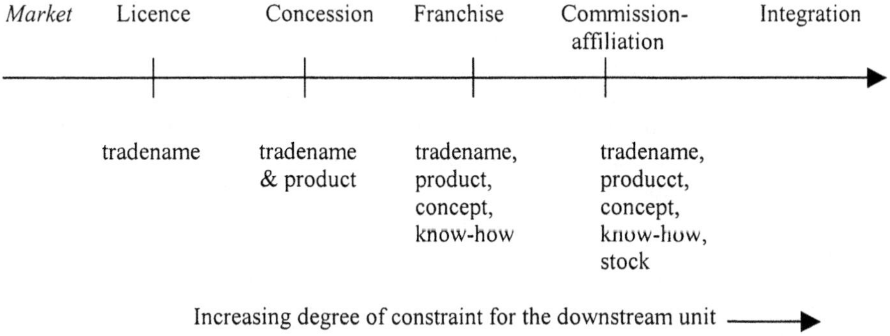

The aim of this paper is to use agency econometrics in order to highlight the conditions supporting the choice of a franchising contract to organise vertical relationships. The paper aims more precisely at explaining the reasons why networks opt for this particular degree of vertical integration.

The article is organized as follows: Section 2 highlights the relevance of the theory of incentives and the principal-agent paradigm to study franchising and, more generally speaking, to study vertical restraints. In addition, this section provides an overview of the agency econometrics on franchising. Section 3 develops an econometrical study on French data, thus allowing the test of the pertinence of agency arguments in explaining the degree of coercion in vertical contracts. Section 4 contains concluding remarks.

2 Agency Framework

2.1 Agency Argument for Franchising

The theory of incentives and the principal-agent paradigm are usually considered as the obvious framework to analyze franchising and vertical restraints in general (Rey and Tirole 1986b).

Two main agency problems arise when information is asymmetric: situations of "hidden action" cause a moral hazard problem, whereas occurences of "hidden information" cause an adverse selection problem (see notably Salanié 1994). The bilateral relation concerns, on the one hand, "the agent" (the informed party), who has access to private information that is of interest for the other party, and on the other hand, "the principal" (the non-informed party), who takes the initiative in contracting. In this context, the contract aims at settling the incentive mechanisms that encourage the informed party to reveal his information (adverse selection) or to behave in a way that is favorable to the non-informed party (moral hazard).

Analyzed within this framework, vertical restraints and franchising are justified by an initial asymmetry of information in favor of the downstream firm (the retailer – the agent). The upstream party (the manufacturer – the principal) initiates the contract and imposes a restriction which acts as an incentive system.

Within this theoretical context, a literature specifically dedicated to the private and social desirability of vertical restraints (their purpose, their welfare consequences) has, mainly since the mid 1980's, been developed. This literature formalizes the agency argument for vertical restraints. The vertical relationship is studied as a situation of moral hazard: i) the manufacturer is not able to observe the selling effort levels exerted by the retailers; ii) the retailers' actions affect the total profits.

This theoretical literature highlights a range of externalities under uniform-price contracts justifying the use of vertical restraints:

1/ The relation between producer-retailer is characterized by a « basic vertical externality» (Mathewson and Winter 1984; Tirole 1988) since the supplier's in-

[1] Dixit (1983); Gallini and Winter (1983); Mathewson and Winter (1983a), (1983b), (1984), (1985a), (1985b), (1988); Rey and Tirole (1986a); Tirole (1988).

come is related to the distributor's selling effort. To be more precise, the retailer's actions which are taken to increase demand improve the upstream profits. "Promotional" or "selling effort" can be understood in the general sense of the word, namely, information on the product, quality of the service, image of the product, accessibility of the product, etc. This includes all cum-sale services: highly trained sales staff, technical advisors, demonstrations, ambient atmosphere, quick delivery, convenient financing plans and post-sale services (Spiegel and Yehezkel 2002).

The double marginalization problem (Spengler 1950) is related to this vertical externality: it emerges in the case where a producer, in a monopolistic situation, sells a product by the intermediary of a unique distributor. In this situation of successive monopoly, each firm is incited to set a price higher than the unit cost of production. Finally, the resale price is higher than the monopoly price and the aggregate profit is sub-optimal.

2/ "Advertising spillovers" (Mathewson and Winter 1984) occur when a proportion of the advertising messages (and more generally of the selling efforts) from one outlet increases the demand at other outlets. This externality emerges within an intrabrand competition, which involves a network of retailers sharing the same brand: a distributor can free-ride (Telser 1960), and benefit from the other retailers' efforts to promote the brand, without bearing the costs. This horizontal externality at the distribution level is unfavorable to the producer because it results in a sub-optimal level of the promotional effort. More generally speaking, this externality leads to the problem of network protection, where several legally autonomous units share the use of the same brand or benefit simultaneously from a reputation. This case of moral hazard results in a deterioration of the brand.

3/ Symmetrically, a horizontal externality exists at the production level when a distributor has several suppliers. In this case, the downstream firm can behave in the same way with two producers whose promotional efforts are different. Here the free-riding problem arises at the upstream level. As in the preceding case, this results in a deficient promotional effort.

From this basis, the theory of incentives highlights the usefulness of vertical restraints as incentive mechanisms to restore the weak selling effort. It reveals how vertical devices make the retailers take the right actions. In this framework, vertical constraints are privately desirable as they allow a better control of the retailers. This literature defines the "minimal set of sufficient tools" (Rey and Tirole 1986a) that leads to perfect control over the downstream units by the manufacturer. Moreover, when helping to suppress the externalities associated with linear pricing rules, the restrictions increase the social welfare.

2.2 Agency Econometrics on Franchising

One main result of the theoretical literature is that the agency costs confronting firms are a major determining factor in the organizational choices, particularly within the producer-retailer relationships. However, the econometrical tests in the light of these theoretical developments remain scarce, mainly due to the lack of available data (Chiappori and Salanié 1997) and the difficulty for the incentive theory to generate testable implications: the incentive mechanism is always complex and highly variable according to the assumptions relative to the informational environment (Masten and Saussier 2000). Thus there is a contrast between the high level of sophistication reached by the theoretical models and the empirical results.

However, the methodological analysis which calls attention to the possibility and the way to test the theory of incentives can be stressed (Chiappori and Salanié 1997, 2000; Salanié 1999; Chiappori et al. 2002). Moreover, an econometrical literature on vertical restraints in the framework of agency arguments has been developed since the end of the 1980's (Brickley and Dark 1987, Norton 1988). This literature focuses on the United States. Most of the studies use a dataset compiling the information related to many industrial sectors, but some econometrical tests are based on sectorial data concerning the fast food industry (Krueger 1991; Kaufmann and Lafontaine 1994; Kaufmann and Dant 1996), or gasoline stations (Shepard 1993; Slade 1996). One of the main features of the existing agency econometrics on vertical restraints is that – except for in a few cases (Shepard 1993; Brickley 1999) – it focuses on franchising (Kaufmann and Lafontaine 1994, Kaufmann and Dant 1996; Lafontaine and Shaw 1999). This literature is part of the theory of franchising explaining the choice of this organisational form: explanations of franchising are discussed and tested. More specifically, the main concern of these studies is the following theme - franchising versus company ownership (Brickley and Dark 1987; Norton 1988; Minkler 1990; Brickley et al. 1991; Lafontaine 1992; Williams 1999). One main result is the strong support for the agency argument of franchising (it provides evidence that monitoring costs and moral hazard affect the choice between franchising and company ownership), particularly in comparison with the signalling theory (Lafontaine 1993), and the capital market theory (franchising as financial resources for the upstream firm; for instance Kaufmann and Dant 1996).

Agency econometrics on vertical restraints support the idea that the more the contract is near integration, the more the producer controls the retailer, and on the contrary when the contract is less constraining (near market) the producer will rather choose incentives to reduce the agency problems. This assumption - a set of choices between incentives and control for the upstream firm – is consistent with Shepard 1993. More generally, agency econometrics on franchising confirm that for the manufacturer, franchising downstream units is more interesting than owning when the monitoring costs are significant (Brickley and Dark 1987; Minkler 1990; Brickley et al. 1991).

From this basis, the four types of contracts organizing the French networks that share a trademark can be presented as follows:

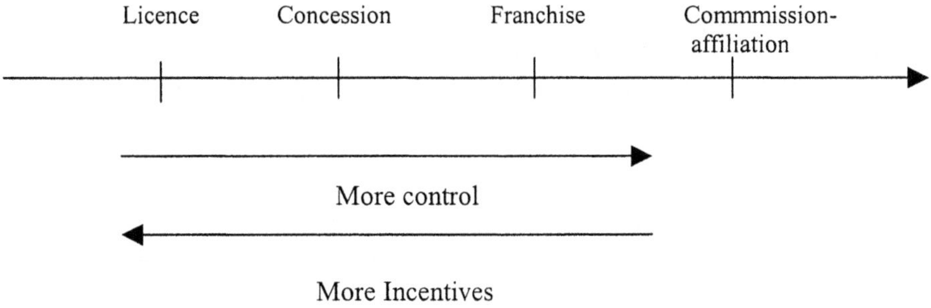

3 An Empirical Test of the Agency-theoretical Approach

3.1 Testable Predictions

To assess the agency theory empirical relevance in analyzing franchising, we focus here on the intra brand competition, thus on externalities that generate a potential free-riding problem between the retailers of the same network. Our point here concerns free-riding at the downstream level. The central goal for the producer confronting this problem is to homogenize his network of retailers.

Theory and previous empirical studies show that the vertical constraints can be a reaction from this agency problem: the contract imposing the restrictions solves the incentive problem relative to the selling effort. The general testable qualitative prediction from this theoretical framework is that the level of externalities between the retailers of the same network (sharing a brand name) determines the organisational structure of the vertical relationship. More precisely, we assume here that the level of the potential horizontal externality determines the degree of coercion of the contract between the upstream unit (the producer) and the downstream units (the retailers) within a network sharing a brand name.

The goal of the test is to assess how much the moral hazard problem – in this particular case the externalities between the retailers sharing the same brand name – explains the organizational form chosen within networks between the upstream firm and the retailers. Considering the impossibility of measuring those externalities directly, we use three proxy variables resulting from the following assumptions:

H_1: When the industry is more likely to be characterized by a high level of intrabrand externality, the probability of having a high degree of restriction increases (positive relation).

---

[2] As before seen, within a vertical relationship, this problem can also appear at the production level.

H_2: The bigger the network, the higher the level of the intrabrand externality, and the higher the probability of having a constraining contract (positive relation). But the other alternative is relevant as well: the bigger the network, the more difficult it is for the upstream firm to control the outlet; that is the reason why it chooses a less constraining - and more incentive - contract (negative relation).

H_3: When the exclusive territory is large, the potential externality between the retailers is low, so the contract is less constraining (negative relation). But the opposite case is possible: when the exclusive territory is large, the retailers are more independent and can more easily show a cheating behavior. As a result the upstream firm imposes a more constraining contract to control this potential behavior (positive relation).

The positive relations in H_1 and H_2 support the idea that vertical constraints are palliatives for externalities: more externality should result in more restraining contracts and therefore in a higher degree of vertical integration. The positive relation in H3 supports the theory, too: large exclusivity territory enables cheating behavior and more vertical restraints are therefore necessary.

The industrial proxy (related to *H1*) results from the intuition, according to which, the level of the intra brand externality varies with the type of industry. We assume that some industries are more likely to receive « non repeat customers » (versus « repeat customers ») more attached to a brand name than to a specific outlet. In this case, the consumers consider each retailer within a network as equivalent to the others: the network sells standard products. Therefore the behavior of one member of the network generates important consequences on the trademark and consequently on the whole network. Since Caves and Murphy (1976), such a type of industrial proxy is commonly used in the literature on franchising[3]. For instance: the travel related industries (hotels, fast-food chain restaurants, car rental agencies) are considered as high-externality industries because they are more likely to serve non-repeat customers.

In order to classify the industries (high externality sector versus low externality sector) we make the assumption of networks (retailers sharing a same brand name) without any vertical contract being defined. In other words, we appreciate the level of the potential intrabrand externality as if the contract between the upstream firm and the retailers did not include any vertical restraints.

This industrial proxy (industry) is coded 1, for high-externality industries, characterized by a strong attachment to the brand name, and 0 for the others (table 2).

3.2 The Data

The data for the current study were collected in the "yearbook of independent retailers networks[4]" published by the headquarters of the French "Chambres de

---

[3] Brickley and Dark (1987); Minkler (1990); Brickley (1999).

[4] «Annuaire des réseaux commerciaux d'indépendants».

Commerce et d'Industrie". Here "independent" means owning a business but belonging to a network organized by an upstream firm. The information included in the 2001 yearbook comes directly from the networks in a broad range of trade and service industries consulted at the end of 2000. Some additional data have been collected from specialized magazines.

The yearbook distinguishes ten categories of networks[5] in accordance with the organizational form of the vertical relationship. Our sample consists of all networks sharing a brand name. The four standard contractual forms previously presented (*licence*, *concession*, *franchise*, *commission-affiliation*) correspond to this criterion. Each of these contracts is characterized by a particular set of vertical restraints.

In our econometrical study, the dependent variable is the contract chosen by the upstream firm to organize the vertical relationships in the network. We assume that this qualitative multinominal variable has an ordinal nature. Only three types of contracts are taken into account in the test, as there are a few cases of licence contracts in our dataset[6]. The dependent variable (contract) is coded from 0 (concession) to 2 (commission-affiliation).

Table 1. Descriptive Statistics (439 Networks; Year 2001)

Variable Name	Mean	Standard Error	Minimum	Maximum
Contract	0.89	0.45	0	2
Industry	0.68	0.47	0	1
Network size	318.87	1432.65	1	20700
Exclusive territory	77301.5	77326.89	2000	600000
Ownership structure	0.27	0.29	0	100
Concentration	0.19	0.23	0	1
Entry duties	83770.98	84521.82	0	800000

[5] In French and in alphabetical order: affiliation, centrale d'achat, chaîne volontaire, commission-affiliation, concession, coopérative, franchise, licence d'enseigne ou de marque, groupement d'achats de détaillants, partenariat.

[6] Franchising is the most representative form of contracts in France (table 4).

Table 2. Descriptive Statistics for the Sample (439 Networks in 2001)

Industry	Network average size	Numbers of networks/ sector	% of Franchises	Network average turnover (million of €)	Inhabitants/outlet (on average for the sector)
HIGH-EXTERNALITY SECTORS					
Food					
Bakery-cake	89,3	11	82%	28.76	25 500
Frozen foods	20	1	100%	9.14	40 000
Miscellaneous foods	3	1	0%	0.53	15 000
Mini-market, self-service	3132,1	8	75%	310.20	4000
Popular stores	303	1	100%	Not available	50 000
Clothing / Textiles					
Women's apparel	145,4	23	39%	37.21	43 550
Men's apparel	86	5	80%	59.45	90 000
Unisex apparel and sportswear	142,8	10	40%	31.72	66 560
Children's apparel	134,8	9	67%	61.78	80 000
Maternity-child care	125,8	4	75%	34.9	77 500
Shirts	84	1	100%	Not available	100 000
Lingerie	120	3	33%	12.96	65 000
Shoes	184,3	8	88%	113.38	87 850
Luggage and leather goods	36,5	2	50%	9.83	40 000
Jewelery-clocks	43,4	5	80%	22.33	87 500
Custom jewelery	13,5	2	100%	5.5	100 000
Decoration and home equipment					
Home furniture and beds	73	25	68%	77.9	62 375
Floor and wall covering	10	1	100%	5.33	50 000
Home textiles	109	5	80%	19.8	157 000
Kitchen utensils	154,2	6	100%	28.73	67 500
Decoration	42,7	7	57%	23.78	70 000

Do-it-yourself materials	62	6	83%	182.47	94 160
Household linen	111,3	3	67%	71.64	130 000
Household appliances	276	2	100%	123.47	110 000
Miscellaneous home equipment	194	1	100%	Not available	Not available
Gifts	52,7	3	100%	6.25	60 000
Flowers and seeds	48,6	5	80%	24.15	73 000
Garden equipment	212	4	100%	234.37	16 000
Leisure					
Books	222	2	50%	38.11	50 000
Stationery	60	3	67%	Not available	49 160
Video and audio equipment	70	3	100%	45.73	73 300
Sports, camping	45	1	100%	19.82	Not available
Leisure	22	1	100%	Not available	100 000
Discount stores and secondhand	53,4	8	88%	70.51	52 500
Miscellaneous specialized trade	35	1	100%	3.49	Not available
Health and Beauty					
Beauty goods and perfumery	192	10	60%	60.42	36 110
Health and beauty store, pharmacy	27	1	100%	7.62	50 000
Hotels and restaurants					
Hotels	329,3	19	100%	21.43	41 000
Fast-food chains	1658,9	18	94%	71.12	101 600
Restaurants	73,8	5	80%	128.48	95 000
Thematic restaurants	47,5	6	83%	94.89	95 800
Thematic bars	28,8	4	50%	18.75	38 750
Miscellaneous personal services					
Telephony	25	1	100%	15.24	20 000
Video rentals	1769,7	3	33%	13.72	17 500

Developing	82,3	3	67%	14.48	60 000
Personal services	52,3	3	100%	1.83	45 000
Rapid services, keys, heels and printing	158,5	2	50%	49.54	28 750
Repair services	26	1	100%	15.24	120 000
Automotive parts (sales and repairs)	437,2	9	89%	141.41	96 875
Miscellaneous automotive services	403,9	7	100%	38.87	107 000
Vehicles rentals and sales					
Cycles and motorbikes	222,7	3	67%	24	100 000
Boats rentals and sales	15	2	100%	13.72	Not available
Vehicles rentals	1612,4	8	88%	163.8	60 700
Miscellaneous enterprises services					
Office suppliers	11	2	100%	15.78	65 000
Messenger and transport services	317,7	3	67%	46.15	100 000
Services for firms	222,8	9	67%	11.94	175 000
Miscellaneous services	2164	2	50%	11.9	190 000
LOW-EXTERNALITY SECTORS					
Delicatessen / Food					
Delicatessen and regional products	28,2	6	83%	10.75	190 000
Dietetic and natural foods/organic products	55,3	3	100%	22.1	36 600
Wine and drinks	135	4	100%	21.57	56 300
Confectionery, chocolate and ice-cream	119,3	7	86%	9.53	57 500
Tea and coffee	31	2	100%	8.86	175 000

Wedding apparel					
Wedding	116	2	100%	18.29	32 500
Specialized personal services					
Medical Articles	122	2	100%	30.49	65 000
Beauty salons	40,5	13	85%	8.53	63 660
Hair-dressing salons	159,9	29	100%	35.72	50 000
Sport Club/gym	72,3	3	67%	109.76	75 000
Binoculars and optical goods	143,6	5	80%	107.47	31 000
Transports, travel and tourism	160,3	3	100%	686.1	60 000
Estate agencies	795,9	10	90%	44.9	60 000
Removal firms	100	1	100%	58.38	300 000
Wedding bureau	62	3	67%	7.20	80 000
Grooming, miscellaneous pets services	150	1	100%	Not available	70 000
Training and teaching	29,2	5	80%	19	156 250
Laundry and dry-cleaning	205,7	6	67%	7.62	53 000
Others cleaning services	2140,8	4	50%	0.11	180 000
Building, personal services					
Kitchen and bathroom makers	153,7	9	44%	76.65	84 285
Miscellaneous specialized services	80,6	12	50%	29.41	123 636
Verandas	13	1	100%	26.67	100 000
Fireplaces	117	1	0%	62.5	Not available
Swimming-pools	19,5	2	50%	76.22	Not available
Detached house builder	101	1	100%	68.6	200 000
Building services and maintenance	31,3	4	100%	3.39	262 500

Specialized enterprises services					
Printing	32	1	100%	6.1	30 000
Publicity	55	2	50%	6.55	35 000
Press, publishing and radio	4	2	0%	0.29	Not available
Point-of-sale equipment	46	2	100%	Not available	300 000

Table 3. Correlation Matrix

	Network size	Concentration	Ownership structure	Entry duties	Exclusive territory
Network size	1,00	-0,01	-0,09	0,05	-0,04
Concentration	-0,01	1,00	0,02	0,06	0,05
Ownership structure	-0,09	0,02	1,00	0,11	0,08
Entry duties	0,05	0,06	0,11	1,00	0,00
Exclusive territory	-0,04	0,05	0,08	0,00	1,00

The correlation matrix shows that there is no collinearity problem between the quantitative explanative variables.

3.3 Econometric Model and Estimations

We assume that the dependant variable y^* represents the degree of constraint within the contract, which increases with the level of the intra brand horizontal externality, proxied by x_1, x_2, x_3,

$$y^* = \beta_1 x_1 + \beta_2 x_2 + \beta_3 x_3 + \beta_4 x_4 + \beta_5 x_5 + \beta_6 x_6 + \varepsilon \qquad (1)$$

where:

x_1 = dummy variable that equals 0 if the network belongs to a low-externality industry, and 1 if the network corresponds to a high-externality industry (see table 2);

x_2 = network size (number of outlets within the network);

x_3 = size of the exclusive territory (potential population of customers per outlet);

x_4 = ownership structure, more precisely the proportion of owned units within the network (number of owned units / number of outlets within the network; control variable);

x_5 = concentration (network turnover/sector turnover; control variable);

x_6 = amount of entry duties (control variable);

ε = error term.

y* exists with three types of contracts:

$y = 0$ Concession
$y = 1$ Franchise
$y = 2$ Commission-affiliation

Table 4 presents the ordered probit estimates.

Table 4. Estimates for Ordered Probit

Variables	Coefficients	Standard Error	Student value	Probability
Industry	0.462^{***}	0.128	3.545	0.0003
Network size	0.78^{E-04}	0.109^{E-03}	0.699	0.4519
Exclusive territory	0128^{E-05*}	0.751^{E-06}	1.698	0.0923
Ownership structure	1.498^{***}	0.240	6.141	0.0000
Concent	0.99	0.275	0.516	0.7204
Entry duties	0.16^{E-05*}	0.876^{E-06}	2.084	0.0804

* Significant at the 10 % level
** Significant at the 5 % level
*** Significant at the 1 % level

Table 4 shows that two explanatory variables are significant: the industry and the exclusive territory. In these two cases the correlation is positive between the level of externalities and the probability to have a more restricting contract. Two control variables are significant: ownership structure and entry duties. So hypotheses H1 and H3 are confirmed, H2 is not:

H1: when the externality level of the industry is high (non-repeat customers industry), the probability of having a high degree of vertical integration (by coercion) increases. This conclusion is consistent with Brickley and Dark (1987); Brickley et al. (1991); Brickley (1999). In our study the marginal effects show that a high level of externality reduces by 11.26% the probability of having a less constraining contract (concession);

H3: when the exclusive territory is large, the probability of having a high degree of vertical integration increases.

In addition, this table highlights two significant control variables:

1/ The higher the proportion of company-owned units (in this case there are few independent members in the network), the higher the probability of having a high degree of vertical constraint. We came across some conclusions of American studies (Lafontaine 1992, 1993) related to the explanatory ability of the property structure on the contract choice. More generally, this remark is consistent with the agency theory according to which the nature of property rights on an asset (and the rights on the residual income) induces a less opportunistic behavior.

2/ The " entry duties " control variable is significant. The relation is positive between the level of entry duties and the degree of coercion. This result confirms that the entry duties are one of the provisions that the upstream firm introduces to reinforce the control on the retailers.

4 Conclusion

In this paper, we argued that contract econometrics is useful to understand the choice of the degree of constraint in vertical contracts: our econometrical test stresses the impact of horizontal externalities on the probability for the upstream firm to choose - or not - a franchising contract.

This article confirms that agency econometrics is an interesting way to study franchising and more generally speaking to highlight what motivates these agreements. Contract econometrics within the principal-agent paradigm provides empirical evidence on the potential moral hazard within a contractual relationship, and on the presence of asymmetries in information in general.

Future lines of inquiry could focus on the antitrust perspective so as to understand whether vertical devices are mainly palliatives for market failures (agency argument) or strategic tools (implemented to reinforce a market power). In this case the main questions would be: is the restriction, and more precisely this particular form of vertical constraint, justified by an agency problem? In other words: is there an originally vertical coordination problem? What is the nature of this problem? Some answers should enable us to tackle what motivates the restrictions and then to highlight the status of such constraints. We believe that this point has a great relevance for antitrust policy within the ongoing debate concerning the competitive impact of vertical constraints.

References

1. Acfi (2001) L'Annuaire des Réseaux Commerciaux d'Indépendants, 19° Edition
2. Brickey J (1999) Incentive Conflicts and Contractual Restraints: Evidence from Franchising. Journal of Law and Economics 42:745-774
3. Brickey J, Dark F (1987) The Choice of Organisational Form: The Case of Franchising. Journal of Financial Economics 18:401-420
4. Brickey J, Dark F, Weisbach M (1991) An Agency Perspective on Franchising. Financial Management 20: 27-35

5. Caves R, Murphy W (1976) Franchising: Firms, Markets And Intangible Assets. Southern Economic Journal 42: 572-86
6. Chiappori P, Salanie B (1997) Empirical Contract Theory : The Case of Insurance Data. European Economic Review 41: 943-950
7. Chiappori P, Salanie B (2000) Testing Contract : A Survey of Some Recent Works. Invited Lecture, World Congress of Econometric Society, Seattle, August
8. Chiappori P, Jullien B, Salanie B, Salanie F (2002) Asymetric Information in Insurance: Some Testable Implications. Working Paper
9. Dixit A (1983) Vertical Integration In A Monopolistically Competitive Industry. International Journal of Industrial Organization 1: 63-78
10. Gallini N, Winter R (1983) On Vertical Control in Monopolistic Competition. International Journal of Industrial Organization 1: 275-286
11. Kaufmann P, Dant R (1996) Multi-Unit Franchising: Growth and Management Issues. Journal of Business Venturing 11: 343-358
12. Kaufmann P, Lafontaine F (1994) Costs of Control: The Source of Economic Rents for Mc Donald's Franchisees. Journal of Law and Economics 37:417-453
13. Krueger A (1991) Ownership, Agency and Wages: an Examination of Franchising in the Fast Food Industry. Quaterly Journal of Economics February:75-100
14. Lafontaine F (1992) Agency Theory and Franchising: Some Empirical Results. Rand Journal of Economics 23:263-283
15. Lafontaine F (1993) Contractual Arrangements as Signaling Devices : Evidence from Franchising. Journal of Law, Economics and Organization 9: 256-289
16. Lafontaine F, Shaw K (1999) The Dynamics of Franchise Contracting : Evidence from Panel Data. Journal of Political Economy 107:1041-1080
17. Lafontaine F, Slade M (1997) Retail Contracting: Theory and Practice. Journal of Industrial Economics 45:1-25
18. Marvel H, Mc Cafferty S (1996) Comparing Vertical Restraints. Journal of Economics and Business 48:473-486
19. Masten S, Saussier S (2000) Econometrics of Contracts : An Assessment of Developments in Empirical Literature on Contracting . Revue d'Economie Industrielle 92:215-236
20. Matheweson F, Winter R (1985a) The Economics of Franchise Contracts. Journal of Law and Economics 28:503-526
21. Matheweson F, Winter R (1985b) Competition Policy and Vertical Exchange. University of Toronto Press
22. Matheweson F, Winter R (1998) The Law And Economics of Resale Price Maintenance. Review of Industrial Organization 84:13-57
23. Mathewson F , Winter R (1983a) The Economics of Vertical Restraints in Distribution. In: Stiglitz J, Mathewson GF (eds) New Developments in the Analysis of Market Structure, pp 211-239
24. Mathewson F , Winter R (1983b) Vertical Integration by Contractual Restraints in Spatial Markets. Journal of Business 56:497-517
25. Mathewson F , Winter R (1984) An Economic Theory of Vertical Restraints. Rand Journal of Economic 15:27-38
26. Minkler A (1990) An Empirical Analysis of a Firm's Decision to Franchise. Economics Letters 34:77-82
27. Norton S (1988) An Empirical Look at Franchising as an Organisational Form. Journal of Business 61:197-218
28. Rey P, Caballero-Sanz F (1996) The Policy Implications of Economic Analysis of Vertical Restaints. Economic Papers. European Commission, 119, November

29.Rey P, Tirole J (1986a) The Logic of Vertical Restraints. American Economic Review 76: 921-939
30.Rey P, Tirole J (1986b) Vertical Restraints from a Principal-Agent Viewpoint. In: Pellegrini L, Reddy SK (eds) Marketing Channels, Relationships and Performance. Lexington Books, pp 3-30
31.Salanie B (1994) Théorie des Contrats. Economica
32.Salanie B (1999) Développements Récents en Econométrie des Contrats. Revue Economique 50:611-620
33.Shepard A (1993) Contractual Form, Retail Price, and Asset Characteristics in Gasoline Retailing. Rand Journal Of Economics 24:58-77
34.Slade M (1996) Multitask Agency and Contract Choice: an Empirical Exploration. International Economic Review 37:465-486
35.Spengler J (1950) Vertical Integration And Antitrust Policy. Journal of Political Economy 58:347-352
36.Spiegel Y, Yehezkel Y (2001) Price And Non-Price Restraints when Retailers are Vertically Differentiated , EARIE 2002
37.Telser L (1960) Why Should Manufacturers Want Fair Trade ? Journal of Law and Economics 3: 86-105
38.Tirole J (1988) The Theory of Industrial Organization. Cambridge, MIT Press
39.Williams D (1999) Why Do Entrepreneurs Become Franchisees ? An Empirical Analysis of Organizational Choice. Journal of Business Venturing 14: 103-124

Part C:

Contract Design and Compensation

The Use of Up-front Fees, Royalties and Franchisor Sales to Franchisees in Business Format Franchising*

Luis Vázquez

Universidad de Salamanca
Department of Economics and Business
Campus Miguel de Unamuno, s./n. Salamanca, Spain, E-37005
lvazquez@usal.es

Abstract. This article provides evidence on the determinants of compensation provisions included in franchise contracts. The results support for both the optimal allocation of risk and double-sided moral hazard explanations for franchise contracts. The results also reveal that the value of both the initial and ongoing services provided by franchisors to franchisees strongly affects the compensation arrangements, which implies that a capital goal of these arrangements is to recover the costs of the services offered by franchisors.

1 Introduction

The conventional franchise contract is an arrangement whereby the franchisee compensates the franchisor for the right to use the latter's trademark in a certain location for a determined time period. The franchise contract includes various compensation provisions. These are usually made up of three parts. The franchisee pays an initial franchise fee and an ongoing royalty (usually a percentage of sales), and purchases inputs from the franchisor at prices greater than marginal costs. Most of the empirical franchising literature on contract design has focused on the pecuniary aspects of the contracts, dealing with royalty rates and initial franchise fees.[1]

The contribution of this work is threefold. First, it provides a comprehensive explanation for compensation provisions in franchise contracts drawing on the agency theory. The economic literature has studied mainly two of these compensa-

* I thank numerous workshop participants for their comments and suggestions. The usual disclaimers apply. The study received financial support from the MCYT, a research agency of the Spanish Government, through grants SEC2001-1756 and SEC2002-04471-C02-02.

[1] For example, see Lafontaine (1992), Sen (1993), Rao and Srinivasan (1995), Wimmer and Garen (1997), Lafontaine and Shaw (1999) and Brickley (2002).

tion arrangements—the royalty rate and the up-front franchise fee. This work expands the analysis to another important source of revenues for the franchisors, the sales of inputs to franchisees at prices greater than marginal costs. The results provide support for both the optimal allocation of risk and double-sided moral hazard explanations for franchise contracts. It was found that, as the amount of risk rises, the initial franchise fee decreases and both royalty rate and franchisor sales to franchisees increase. It was also observed that the more important the franchisee effort and the harder it is to monitor this effort, the higher the up-front fee and the lower both the royalty rate and the franchisor sales to franchisees. Moreover, I find that the more important the franchisor effort and the harder it is to monitor this effort, the lower the initial franchise fee and the greater both the royalty rate and the franchisor sales to franchisee.

Second, the results reveal that the value of both initial and ongoing services provided by franchisors to franchisees strongly affects the compensation arrangements studied. On the one hand, the more valuable the continuous services provided by franchisors, the greater both the royalty rate and the magnitude of franchisor sales to franchisees. On the other hand, the value of the franchisor's initial services alone explain 67% of the variation in the up-front fee, which implies that the main goal of the initial franchise fee is to recover the franchisor costs in locating, selecting and training new franchisees.

Third, it utilizes a data source that includes a broad variety of information about a representative sample of franchise networks. The high level of data disaggregation—all variables used are disaggregated at chain level—improves the estimation of the factors the theory considers affect the compensation arrangements.

The article is organized as follows. In the next section, I present the theoretical determinants of the compensation arrangements used in franchise contracts and derive testable implications from the theory. Section 3 contains a description of the data used in the empirical analyses. Section 4 presents the methodology used and discusses the empirical results, while Section 5 summarizes and concludes.

2 Determinants of Compensation Arrangements

In business format franchising, there are several sources of revenue for franchisors. The economic literature has focused mainly on two of these sources—the royalty rate and the up-front franchise fee. The compensation obtained via royalties and up-front fees is especially important for the franchisor since these instruments make up over 50% of the franchisor's total profit (Stern and El-Ansary 1988).

But franchisors also have another important source of revenue. It is the wholesale price they can charge for goods transferred to the franchisees. Franchisors can require franchisees to purchase some inputs from them. When franchisees operate under a fixed-proportion technology, franchisor sales to franchisees at prices greater than marginal costs are equivalent to royalties on sales. Consequently, such an instrument should also be a substitute for the royalty rate and the up-front franchise fee. Although these purchases—voluntary or required—are valued at less than 10% of the franchisees' sales in most business format franchise sectors (Lafontaine 1992), they produce about 50% of the franchisor's total profit (Stern and El-Ansary 1988). Unfortunately, no article in the literature has studied the value of franchisor sales to franchisees as a dependent variable when researching compensation arrangements in business format franchising.

Factors that have been used in the franchising literature to explain the extent of both royalty rates and initial franchise fees include inefficient risk allocation, franchisee's and franchisor's moral hazard, and the value of the services provided by the franchisors.

2.1 Inefficient Risk Allocation

Agency theory has emphasized that increases in the risk aversion of the agents in relation to that of the principal and in exogenous uncertainty make powerful incentives more costly.[2] Therefore, assuming that the franchisor is less risk averse than the franchisees,[3] it was hypothesized that:

Hypothesis 1a: Both the royalty rate and franchisor sales to franchisee will increase as the amount of risk rises.

Hypothesis 1b: The initial franchise fee decreases as the amount of risk increases.

2.2 Franchisee Moral Hazard

In the conventional agency model, optimal incentive intensity increases with the marginal productivity of agent effort. Moreover, the principal may spend resources to estimate agents' efforts directly or motivate them by linking their pay to the outcomes obtained. I therefore expect that:

Hypothesis 2a: Both the royalty rate and franchisor sales to franchisee will be lower the greater the franchisee effort and the harder it is to monitor this effort.

Hypothesis 2b: The initial franchise fee will be higher the greater the franchisee effort and the harder it is to monitor this effort.

---

[2] See, for example, Lafontaine and Slade (2001).

[3] Although Martin (1988) makes the opposite assumption, most of the literature (i.e., Brickley and Dark 1987; Lafontaine 1992; Norton 1988) assumes that franchisors are less risk averse than franchisees. Moreover, the majority of franchisors in my sample are relatively large corporations and most franchisees are family-owned firms often ill diversified. It may then be inferred that franchisees are relatively more risk-averse than franchisors.

2.3 Franchisor Moral Hazard

The effort exerted by the franchisor is very important for the success of a franchise chain. Franchisees expect their franchisors to exert effort towards maintaining the value of the trademark under which they operate, as well as screening and policing other franchisees in the chain. Given that this behavior is not easily assessed by the franchisees, there is moral hazard on both sides, the franchisee's and the franchisor's.

In this context of double-sided moral hazard, Rubin (1978) stated that sharing occurs as a result of both parties' need for incentives. Lal (1990) developed this argument formally. In his model, the royalty rate is the element of the contract that gives the franchisor an ongoing interest in the success of the franchisees. Hence, I conjecture that:

Hypothesis 3a: Both the royalty rate and franchisor sales to franchisee will be larger the greater the franchisor effort and the harder it is to monitor this effort.

Hypothesis 3b: The up-front franchise fee will be lower the greater the franchisor effort and the harder it is to monitor this effort.

2.4 Value of Services Provided by Franchisors

Franchisors provide both initial and continuous services to franchisees. Initial services such as those related to locating, selecting and training are available to the new franchisees before their stores are operational. But franchisees also use other continuous services provided by the franchisor after their businesses become operational, such as ongoing training and marketing campaigns. I therefore expect that:

Hypothesis 4a: The initial franchise fee and both the royalty rate and franchisor sales to franchisee will be higher the more valuable the services provided by the franchisor after the outlet becomes operational.

Hypothesis 4b: The initial franchise fee and both the royalty rate and franchisor sales to franchisee will be higher the more valuable the services provided by the franchisor before the outlet becomes operational.

3 The Data

The empirical setting for testing the aforementioned hypotheses is the franchise sector in Spain. The data set was collected in 2001 and stems from two sources: the Spanish Register of Franchisors[4] and the questionnaires completed by a sample of franchisors.

[4] Spanish Royal Decree no. 2,485/1998 requires firms wishing to franchise in Spain to be entered in the Register of Franchisors. The data each franchisor must facilitate to this Register include, among others, the up-front fee and the royalty rates, the length of the

The complete population of franchise chains operating in Spain at the end of 2000 was obtained from the Register of Franchisors. After various preliminary steps in questionnaire development, including in-depth interviews with franchisors, the final version of the questionnaire was pretested with 15 franchisors. Questionnaires were sent to all members of the population—619 franchise chains—and a supplemental telephone survey was carried out asking that the questionnaires be completed. Finally, 145 usable responses were obtained. table 1 contains the number of chains in each of the business format franchising sectors.

Table 1. Distribution of Sample Chains by Sector

Sector	Number	Sample %
Adventure	1	0.69
Automobile services	6	4.13
Beauty and personal hygiene	4	2.75
Cafés & ice-cream	4	2.75
Ceramic surfaces	1	0.69
Cleaning-interior restoration	1	0.69
Clothing-fashion	16	11.03
Computers	4	2.75
Consulting firms	6	4.13
Cosmetics	5	3.45
Drugstore	3	2.06
Dry-cleaning	6	4.13
Food and bakery	3	2.06
Furniture and decoration	4	2.75
Hairdressers	1	0.69
Herbalist's	2	1.38
Jewelry and costume jewelry	3	2.06
Leisure	2	1.38
Lingerie and notions	3	2.06
Office-stationer's	2	1.38
Personalized editions	3	2.06
Photography	1	0.69

contract, the average investment per outlet, the date of creation of the franchisor, the date when the franchisor began to franchise, and the number of company-owned and franchised outlets in Spain.

Printing and signs	2	1.38
Real estate agencies	5	3.45
Restaurants	19	13.10
Specialized products	3	2.06
Specialized services	7	4.83
Specialized shops	6	4.13
Sports	2	1.38
Teaching	6	4.13
Telephone stores	2	1.38
Textiles	2	1.38
Transport services	3	2.06
Travel	4	2.75
Vending	3	2.06
Total	145	

NOTE.—The sample consists of 145 business format franchising networks from 2000.

To test for a potential response bias in the sample of franchise chains, the sectors represented in the sample were compared to the population. The sample and population did not appear to differ by sectors. To further test for non-response bias, early-returned questionnaires were compared to late returned questionnaires concerning several variables: respondent position, company size and sector. Analyses indicated that no significant mean differences existed between early and late respondents. Thus, there was no evidence of obvious response bias in the sample.

3.1 Dependent Variables

The empirical analysis includes regressions that use the total percentage of sales paid by franchisee to franchisor, including advertising fees.[5] In most of the sample chains, franchisors charge all franchisees a single percentage. When franchisors vary the royalties across franchisees by charging a sliding rate based on the level of sales, the average between the maximun and minimum royalties applied by each chain was calculated, assuming that this average royalty represents the mean

---

[5] As in other studies (for example, Lafontaine 1992; Sen 1993; Lafontaine and Shaw 1999; Brickley 2002), I use the sum of the two kinds of variable fees as the effective royalty rate because franchisees have few ways of knowing whether their payments are used for advertising.

franchisee.[6] When the chains use a fixed-rent contract, the royalty rate is treated as zero.[7]

Similarly, most of the firms in the sample charge a single initial franchise fee to all franchisees. For the remaining firms, the average between the maximun and minimum up-front fees applied by each chain was calculated, assuming that this average up-front fee represents the mean franchisee.[8]

The third dependent variable was calculated, for each chain, as the percentage of the sales of inputs from franchisor to franchisees on franchisee sales in the period 1998-2000.

3.2 Independent Variables

Given the difficulty of measuring the inefficient risk allocation, the franchisee's and franchisor's moral hazard, and the value of the services provided by franchisors, I have used many variables to proxy for these factors.

Inefficient Risk Allocation. Two proxies were used for the risk borne by franchisees. First, the variation in sales per outlet in each chain in the period 1998-2000. Other works have used a similar variable in order to estimate the risk borne by franchisees, but they used sectoral data.[9] It was assumed that the more volatile the sales per outlet in a chain, the greater the risk borne by their franchisees.

Second, the average proportion of outlets discontinued annually in each chain in the period 1998-2000. For each year, this proportion was calculated as the ratio between the discontinued outlets in each network and the number of outlets of this network at the beginning of that year.[10] It was assumed that the higher the proportion of discontinued outlets in each chain, the greater the risk borne by their franchisees.

Franchisee Moral Hazard. In order to measure the franchisee moral hazard, I estimated the importance of the franchisee effort and the costs of monitoring such effort by the franchisor.

The importance of the franchisee effort was proxied by the average number of employees per outlet in each chain in the period 1998-2000. It was assumed that when this number rises, the franchisee has more responsibility. In other words, given that humans shirk, monitoring costs in which franchisees incur will rise with the increasing labor intensity of their outlets.[11]

---

[6] Similar results were obtained when these chains were excluded from the sample.

[7] The removal of these chains from the sample does not qualitatively affect the results.

[8] Similar results hold when these chains are excluded.

[9] See, for instance, Martin (1988), Norton (1988) and Lafontaine (1992).

[10] A similar variable was used by Lafontaine (1992), but her data were measured at sectoral level. A sectoral measure might not be representative of each franchise chain in that sector. For example, the proportion of outlets discontinued by Burger King cannot be a reliable indicator for somebody considering taking up a franchise in a small fast-food chain.

[11] One way of reducing the higher agency costs associated with labor intensity is to hire an agent that monitors, but that agent has an incentive to shirk as a monitor unless his wealth

The cost of monitoring franchisee behavior was estimated through the number of Spanish regions in which each franchisor had established stores at the end of 2000. This proxy variable estimates the costs of sending a franchisor employee to each outlet to verify the accomplishment of franchisee obligations.

Franchisor Moral Hazard. To measure franchisor moral hazard, I estimated the importance of the franchisor's effort and how easy it is for the franchisees to control franchisor moral hazard.

The importance of franchisor effort is measured by the value of the trade name of each chain, proxied by the number of outlets in each franchise network at the end of 2000.

In order to measure how easy it is for the franchisees to control franchisor moral hazard, a dummy was used which takes a value of 1 if there is a franchisee council in the chain and 0 otherwise. Many chains have councils of franchisees elected by their peers who meet regularly with managers of the franchisor. Their main functions are (*a*) to represent franchisees with regard to the franchisor when discussing everything from functional strategies to specific challenges facing the organization, and (*b*) to ensure that franchisors apply control mechanisms in a fair, non-discriminating way.[12]

Value of the Services Provided by Franchisors. I estimated the value of franchisor services before and after the outlets were operational through three proxies. In order to proxy the value of the initial services, the average franchisor costs in locating, selecting and training new franchisees was used.[13] To measure the value of the continuous services, I took the percentages of chain sales spent by each franchisor on advertising and training franchisees'employees in the period 1998-2000.

Control Variables. I used a dummy variable indicating whether or not each chain pertains to the retail sector. It was expected that networks operating in the retail sector would use franchisor sales to franchisees as substitutes for royalty rates more frequently than chains operating in the non-retail sector.[14] The age of each chain in 2000 was also used as a control variable. Finally, I also used, for each chain, the average profit margin in franchisor sales to franchisees.

Descriptive statistics of the sample chains are shown in table 2.

---

is significantly affected by his performance. The typical restriction of ownership to managers who monitor local outlets is a typical feature of franchise relationships (Norton 1988).

[12] These councils also provide legal assistance to franchisees in their conflicts and allow them to achieve scale economies in the acquisition of some inputs.

[13] Similar variables are used by Dnes (1992), Sen (1993) and Bercovitz (2000).

[14] Compensation arrangements used by non-retail chains are limited to up-front fees and royalties, so these chains can not use the franchisor sales to franchisees.

Table 2. Descriptive Statistics

Variable	Mean	Standard Deviation	Minimum	Maximum	N
Initial franchise fee (000 €)	17.73	23.46	0.00	192.32	145
Royalty rate (%)	3.64	3.89	0.00	16.00	145
Franchisor sales to franchisees (%)	8.24	19.26	0.00	38.42	145
Variation of sales	0.16	0.04	0.05	0.29	145
Average discontinued (%)	4.12	1.35	0.00	12.14	145
Average number of employees	6.28	3.29	2.13	21.30	145
Geographical dispersion	7.29	3.16	1.00	17.00	145
Network size	34.62	32.11	1.00	541.00	145
Franchise council	0.14	0.35	0.00	1.00	145
Franchisor set up expenses (000 €)	12.38	9.54	4.04	116.45	145
Advertising expenses (%)	3.12	2.24	0.00	8.16	145
Training expenses (%)	1.11	0.87	0.00	3.46	145
Retail sector	0.37	0.48	0.00	1.00	145
Network age	8.92	7.86	1.00	24.00	145
Avg. profit margin in franchisor sales to franchisees (%)	52.14	22.36	11.26	126.28	145

NOTE.—The sample consists of 145 business format franchising networks from 2000.

4 Methodology and Results

Given the nature of the three dependent variables, a Tobit regression model was used to consider the lower-limit censoring. The models were also estimated using ordinary least squares and similar results were found. Tables 3 and 4 show the results obtained.

Table 3. Tobit Regressions Explaining Initial Franchise Fee, Royalty Rate and Franchisor Sales to Franchisees

	Dependent variables						
	Initial franchise fee			Royalty rate		Franchisor sales to franchisees	
Independent variables	(1)	(2)	(3)	(4)	(5)	(6)	(7)
Variation of sales		-0.141		-0.076		-0.095	
		(0.46)		(0.65)		(1.06)	
Average discontinued		-2.124	-2.414	0.116	0.071	0.423	0.361
		(2.94)**	(3.09)**	(2.36)*	(2.95)**	(1.86)+	(2.33)*
Avg. number of employees		1.841	1.887	-0.073	-0.090	-0.553	-0.518
		(3.61)**	(3.94)**	(3.41)**	(3.81)**	(3.11)**	(3.48)**
Geographical dispersion		0.191	0.179	-0.049	-0.052	-0.284	-0.308
		(2.07)*	(2.33)*	(3.14)**	(3.63)**	(1.91)+	(2.16)*
Network size		-0.128	-0.134	0.017	0.018	0.310	
		(2.11)*	(2.21)*	(1.86)+	(1.98)+	(0.24)	
Franchise council		2.692	2.513	-0.003		-0.032	
		(2.29)*	(2.97)**	(0.56)		(0.59)	
Franchisor set up expenses	0.646	0.586	0.616	0.088		-0.813	
	(6.79)**	(5.64)**	(6.48)**	(0.41)		(0.77)	
Advertising expenses		-1.84		0.385	0.362	3.254	3.120
		(0.45)		(4.39)**	(4.84)**	(3.18)**	(3.84)**
Training expenses		-5.162		0.729	0.685	1.156	1.182
		(1.01)		(4.17)**	(4.26)**	(3.28)**	(3.58)**
Retail sector		1.954		-0.823	-1.112	6.481	6.849
		(0.54)		(3.42)**	(3.76)**	(5.84)**	(6.19)**
Network age		0.287		0.001		0.710	
		(0.17)		(0.68)		(0.44)	
Avg. profit margin in franchisor sales to franchisees		0.038		-0.052	-0.051	0.047	0.050
		(0.23)		(4.16)**	(4.53)**	(3.84)**	(4.05)**
Constant	10.231	22.468	11.246	4.581	5.047	-2.519	-1.057
	(8.66)**	(3.143)**	(4.418)**	(2.93)**	(4.49)**	(3.39)**	(4.20)**
N	145	145	145	145	145	145	145

NOTES.—Absolute value of t statistics in parentheses. Significance levels: ** $P< .01$; * $P< .05$; + $P< .10$.

Table 4. OLS Regressions Explaining Initial Franchise Fee, Royalty Rate and Franchisor Sales to Franchisees

	Dependent variables						
	Initial franchise fee			Royalty rate		Franchisor sales to franchisees	
Independent variables	(1)	(2)	(3)	(4)	(5)	(6)	(7)
Variation of sales		-0.124		-0.013		-0.131	
		(0.69)		(0.51)		(0.18)	
Average discontinued		-2.134	-2.198	0.087	0.084	0.435	0.406
		(2.89)**	(3.23)**	(2.34)*	(2.84)**	(1.95)+	(2.08)*
Avg. number of employees		1.643	1.852	-0.103	-0.112	-0.581	-0.542
		(3.42)**	(3.74)**	(3.48)**	(3.45)**	(3.36)**	(3.32)**
Geographical dispersion		0.196	0.178	-0.061	-0.054	-0.351	-0.384
		(1.87)+	(2.26)*	(2.83)**	(2.91)**	(1.82)+	(1.96)+
Network size		-0.162	-0.142	0.031	0.025	0.221	
		(2.18)*	(2.31)*	(1.92)+	(1.94)+	(0.96)	
Franchise council		2.416	2.681	-0.001		-0.023	
		(2.18)*	(2.31)*	(0.85)		(0.48)	
Franchisor set up expenses	0.689	0.638	0.669	0.120		-1.025	
	(8.62)**	(6.74)**	(7.19)**	(0.81)		(0.42)	
Advertising expenses		-2.104		0.398	0.426	3.016	2.843
		(0.46)		(3.75)**	(3.86)**	(3.14)**	(3.46)**
Training expenses		-6.215		0.812	0.746	1.305	1.411
		(1.08)		(3.49)**	(3.68)**	(2.99)**	(3.16)**
Retail sector		2.329		-0.963	-1.027	5.819	6.527
		(0.41)		(3.04)**	(3.23)**	(5.64)**	(5.47)**
Network age		0.216		0.001		0.802	
		(0.85)		(1.01)		(0.63)	
Avg. profit margin in franchisor sales to franchisees		0.025		-0.049	-0.052	0.057	0.055
		(0.23)		(3.74)**	(3.91)**	(3.46)**	(3.68)**
Constant	9.200	22.841	10.116	0.021	1.748	-2.447	-0.081
	(9.65)**	(3.398)**	(5.68)**	(3.41)**	(3.18)**	(3.94)**	(4.53)**
N	145	145	145	145	145	145	145
R^2	0.67	0.83	0.80	0.14	0.13	0.12	0.10

NOTES.—Absolute value of *t* statistics in parentheses. Significance levels: ** P< .01; * P< .05; + P< .10.

The empirical evidence obtained on hypotheses *1a* and *1b* relating to risk allocation presents some ambiguity. On the one hand, the parameters estimated for the average proportion of discontinued outlets apparently support the hypotheses. On the other hand, however, the results are not those predicted for sales variation.

The coefficients estimated for the average proportion of discontinued outlets in each chain strongly support hypotheses *1a* and *1b*. This variable is positively and significantly related to both the royalty rate and the level of franchisor sales to franchisees, and negatively and significantly related to the initial franchise fee. Hence, it appears that when exogenous risk rises, the intensity of incentives decreases.[15]

However, the results of the variation of sales are never significantly different from zero, which may imply that this variable is not a good indicator of the exogenous risk. This evidence suggests that sales variability may be proxying for monitoring costs instead of exogenous risk, probably because the cost of observing franchisees' effort is higher in volatile environments.

The results observed also support hypotheses *2a* and *2b* relating to franchisee moral hazard. The parameters estimated for the proxies of (*a*) the importance of the franchisee effort, and (*b*) the costs of monitoring such effort by franchisors, show the predicted signs and are significant.

In relation to the effect of the importance of franchisee effort on compensation arrangements, the coefficients estimated for the average number of employees per outlet support hypotheses *2a* and *2b*. As predicted, that variable is negatively and significantly related to both the level of the royalty rate and the magnitude of franchisor sales to franchisees, and positively and significantly related to the initial franchise fee. Therefore, it appears that the franchisee is given stronger incentives as the relative importance of his/her effort increases.[16] With respect to the costs of franchisors' monitoring franchisees' behavior, the parameters estimated for geographical dispersion have the predicted signs and are significant, which supports the notion that increases in this variable raise the costs of monitoring franchisees behavior.

I also found partial support for hypotheses *3a* and *3b* relating to franchisor moral hazard. Most of the coefficients estimated for the proxies of (*a*) the importance of the franchisor effort, and (*b*) the costs of monitoring such effort by franchisees, show the predicted signs and are significant.

In relation to the effect of the importance of franchisor effort on compensation provisions, the parameters estimated for network size partially support hypotheses *3a* and *3b*. As predicted, this variable is negatively and significantly related to the up-front fee and positively related to both the level of the royalty rate and the level of franchisor sales to franchisees. These results may indicate that the compensation arrangements are chosen to give incentives to the franchisors.

---

[15] Lafontaine (1992) uses a similar variable to proxy exogenous risk, but she does not observe a significant effect on both royalty rate and franchise fee. Different results may be due to the different levels of aggregation of the data used. While the data utilized by Lafontaine are aggregated at the sectoral level, the data used in this study are aggregated at chain level.

[16] The empirical literature supports the hypothesis that the marginal product of the franchisee's effort affects the intensity of incentives at outlet level (see, for example, Lafontaine 1992; Sen 1993; Rao and Srinivasan 1995; Wimmer and Garen 1997; Bercovitz 2000).

With respect to the costs of franchiseesmonitoring franchisors' behavior, also consistent with hypotheses *3a* and *3b*, all parameters estimated for the franchise council have the predicted signs and one of them is significant. These results may indicate that the use of franchise councils allows franchisees to control franchisor moral hazard.

The parameters estimated for both advertising and training expenses partially support hypotheses *4a* and *4b*. As predicted, these variables are positively and significantly related to both the level of the royalty rate and the magnitude of franchisor sales to franchisees, which may hint that the more valuable the continuous services offered by franchisors, the greater the continuous compensations received from franchisees. But results also show that there is no significant relationship between the magnitude of the initial franchise fee and the advertising and training expenses.

Related to hypothesis *4b*, I find the coefficient of franchisor set-up expenses is positively and significantly related to the up-front fee. This result implies that the initial franchise fee may, indeed, enable the franchisor to recoup the costs derived from the openings of new franchisees. As Table IV shows in equation 1, franchisor set-up expenses alone explain 67% of the variation in the initial franchisee fee, so it seems that the main purpose of the initial franchise fee is to recoup those franchisor costs in locating, selecting and training new franchisees. However, franchisor set-up expenses are not significantly related to either the level of the royalty rate or the magnitude of franchisor sales to franchisees. Thus findings appear to show that franchisors recoup the costs of the initial services via up-front fees, and the costs of continuous services through royalties or input sales to franchisees.

Finally, a significantly greater use of franchisor sales to franchisees in chains belonging to the retail sector was observed, where the substitution of the franchisor inputs is more difficult than in other chains pertaining to other non-retail sectors, such as those related to business services. I also found the coefficients estimated for network age are never significantly different from zero. Last, I observed that the average profit margin in franchisor sales to franchisees is negatively and significantly related to the royalty rate, and positively and significantly related to the magnitude of the franchisor sales to franchisees.

5 Conclusions

This work extends the empirical literature on incentive contracts by providing evidence on the determinants of compensation arrangements in franchise contracts. The results support both the optimal allocation of risk and the double-sided moral hazard explanations for those compensation arrangements. Many of the findings obtained are consistent with those of the earlier literature.[17]

[17] See, for instance, Lafontaine (1992), Sen (1993), Wimmer and Garen (1997) and Lafontaine and Shaw (1999).

To complete the findings obtained in this work, future research in franchising literature should analyze the choice of compensation arrangements in a richer contractual setting, studying the interaction between these kinds of arrangements and other non-pecuniary clauses used in franchise contracts.

References

1. Arora A, Gambardella A (1990) Complementarity and External Linkages: the Strategies of the Large Firms in Biotechnology. Journal of Industrial Economics 38: 361-379
2. Arruñada B, Garicano L, Vázquez L. Contractual Allocation of Decision Rights and Incentives: The Case of Automobile Distribution. Journal of Law, Economics, and Organization 17: 256-283
3. Athey S, Stern S (1998) An Empirical Framework for Testing Theories about Complementarity in Organizational Design. Working paper. National Bureau of Economic Research, 1998
4. Bercovitz JEL (2000) An Analysis of the Contract Provisions in Business-Format Franchise Agreements. Working paper, Duke University, 2000
5. Bhattacharyya S, Lafontaine F (1995) Double-Sided Moral Hazard and the Nature of Share Contracts. Rand Journal of Economics 26: 761-781
6. Brickley JA (1999) Incentive Conflicts and Contractual Restraints. Journal of Law and Economics 37: 745-774
7. Brickley JA (2002) Royalty Rates and Upfront Fees in Share Contracts: Evidence From Franchising. Journal of Law, Economics, and Organization 18: 511-535
8. Brickley JA, Dark FH (1987) The Choice of Organizational Form: The Case of Franchising. Journal of Financial Economics 18: 401-420
9. Dnes AW (1992) Unfair' Contractual Practices and Hostages in Franchise Contracts. Journal of Institutional and Theoretical Economics 148: 484-504
10. Ichiniowski C, Shaw K, Prennushi G (1997) The Effects of Human Resource Management Practices on Productivity. American Economic Review 87: 291-313
11. Kaufmann PJ, Lafontaine F (1994) Costs of Control: The Source of Economic Rents for McDonald's Franchisees. Journal of Law and Economics 37: 417-453
12. Lafontaine F (1992) Agency Theory and Franchising: Some Empirical Results. Rand Journal Economics 23: 263-283
13. Lafontaine F, Shaw K (1999) The Dynamics of Franchise Contracting: Evidence from Panel Data. Journal of Political Economy 107: 1041-1080
14. Lafontaine F, Slade ME (2001) Incentive Contracting and the Franchise Decision. In Advances in Business Applications of Game Theory. Edited by K Chatterjee, W Samuelson. Dordrecht: Kluwer Academic Press, 2001
15. Lal R (1990) Improving Channel Coordination through Franchising. Marketing Science 9: 299-318
16. Martin RE (1988) Franchising and Risk Management. American Economic Review 78: 954-968
17. Michael SC, Moore HJ (1995) Returns to Franchising. Journal of Corporate Finance 2: 133-155
18. Norton S (1988) An Empirical Look at Franchising as an Organizational Form. Journal of Business 61: 197-217
19. Rao RC, Srinivasan S (1995) Why Are Royalty Rates Higher in Services-type Franchises? Journal of Economics and Management Strategy 4: 7-31

20.Rubin PH (1978) The Theory of the Firm and the Structure of Franchise Contracts. Journal of Law and Economics 21: 223-233.
21.Scott FA (1995) Franchising vs. Company Ownership as a Decision Variable of the Firm. Review of Industrial Organization 10: 69-81
22.Sen KC (1993) The Use of Initial Fees and Royalties in Business Format Franchising. Managerial and Decision Economics 14: 175-190
23.Stern LW, El-Ansary AI (1988) Marketing Channels. Englewood Cliffs, NJ: Prentice-Hall
24.Wimmer BS, Garen, JE (1997) Moral Hazard, Asset Specificity, Implicit Bonding and Compensation: The Case of Franchising. Economic Inquiry 35: 544-554

Contract Design and Range of Services in Franchising: An Empirical Contribution to the Effect of Incentives and Reputation

Thomas Ehrmann

Center for Entrepreneurship, University of Muenster
Leonardo-Campus 18, 48149 Muenster, Germany
www.ug.uni-muenster.de

Abstract. A major problem in franchise systems is the effect of contract design and range of services on success. This study interprets the consequences of contract design in franchise chains in terms of sales. Therefore, the royalty rate dependent on sales and the initial lump sum fee will be investigated. Furthermore, the impact of the franchisor's activities and policies on the sales volume of the franchisee will be studied. The following hypotheses reflect the impact of incentives and reputation on success:

- the higher the fixed fee the higher the revenue of a franchisee
- the lower the royalty rate, the higher the revenue of a franchisee, the higher the degree of freedom for individual franchisees, the higher the revenue of a franchisee
- the higher the initial investment, the higher the revenue of a franchisee

These hypotheses were tested using a questionnaire sent to a representative sample of franchise systems operating in Germany . The OLS-regression results offer strong support to the tested hypotheses. The results show that high fixed fees combined with low variable fees and a certain degree of freedom for franchisees are positive indicators for a high individual revenue for a franchisee.

1 Introduction

A major problem in franchise systems is the effect of contract design and range of services on success. The signaling literature discusses ways by which little-known franchisors use these to attract potential franchisees. Equally important is how franchisees select their franchisors. In real life, franchisors as well as franchisees differ in terms of quality. It is in both parties' interest to find an optimal stable matching that brings together pairs of franchisors and franchisees that correspond in terms of their respective qualities. A solution to this matching problem must overcome problems of observability: neither can the franchisor observe the quality of its future franchisees directly, nor is it possible for franchisees to observe the quality of little-known franchise systems. Therefore, the main challenge for franchisors is to design contracts that differentiate themselves from franchise systems of lower quality. Furthermore, they have to attract those franchisees who correspond to their level of quality. Sales per franchisee (dependent variable) will serve as a proxy for successful systems as it simultaneously represents both successes of the franchisor and of the franchisee. Royalty fees and support services from the franchise system to franchisees will serve as independent variables.

In a recent study Brickley (2002) pointed to the gap of empirical evidence on royalties in franchise contracts. Prior work of Lafontaine (1992, 1993) tested a two-sided moral-hazard-model. Two important streams in the theoretical literature are, on the one side, work on signaling theory (Gallini and Lutz 1992; Brickley 2002; Lafontaine 1993; Dant and Kaufmann 2003), and incentive mechanisms and reputation on the other (Lafontaine 1992, 1993). The present study presents an explorative contribution towards an integrated empirical analysis of these two approaches.

The study interprets the consequences of contract design in franchise chains in terms of sales (see Fritz (1995) for further evidence on firm success). Therefore, the royalty rate dependent on sales and the initial lump sum fee will be investigated. Furthermore, the impact of the franchisor's activities and policies on the sales volume of the franchisee will be studied. (Sales per franchisee will serve as a proxy for successful matching as it simultaneously represents both successes of the franchisor and of the franchisee.) First, some results from the theoretical literature will be reviewed and empirical implications derived (2.). Second, hypotheses are generated and tested on a German data set. The data is presented following the literature review (3.) and prior to the empirical results (4.). The paper will be closed by a summary and an outlook (5.).

2 Signaling, Reputation and Entrepreneurial Freedom: Theoretical Foundations and Empirical Implications

2.1 Theoretical Foundations

Manufacturers (as principals) have multiple possibilities regarding the organizational form of their distribution system. The extreme positions are a manufacturer-owned distribution system, on the one hand, and retailing through independent entities, on the other. Franchising is a hybrid form of retailing combining a contractual relationship of the manufacturer with independent retailers. The choice between a manufacturer-owned and independent retail system is determined by its contractual adequacy of the respective solutions. Assuming that the agent's effort as well as the observability of output data (e.g. sales) plays a key role in choosing the contractual regime (Lafontaine and Slade 1998), the following holds: With rising importance of the agent's effort vertical integration becomes more interesting relative to franchising if output is more easily observed (vice versa). If output data (e.g. sales) are more easily detected than the input (i. e. effort) then franchising becomes more interesting (Lafontaine and Slade 1998).

From a contract theory perspective, franchising is seen as a solution to the one-sided incentive problem referring to the agent not performing in a way which is in the best interest of the manufacturer. With risk-neutral franchisees and non-credible capital constraints a solution to the one-sided incentive problem implies no royalty fees (Kreps 1990). The relative importance of the franchisor for sales in the system is not relevant for an explanation of the royalty fee being dependent on sales.

An extended analysis considers the double-moral-hazard which integrates the incentive problems of both the franchisor and the franchisees. (The following is based on the model of Bhattacharyya and Lafontaine 1995).[1] The model assumes that franchisor and franchisees influence the demand for the product by their respective efforts:

$$U = g(a, A) + \varepsilon \;,$$

with a, A representing the level of effort chosen by the franchisee and franchisor respectively; g (a, A) represents the effort-output function. ε is a random variable with an expected value of zero that cannot be observed by the contracting parties. The effort of franchisor and franchisee enhances sales with:

$$\partial g / \partial a > 0, \partial g / \partial A > 0 \text{ and } \partial^2 g / \partial a^2 < 0,\; \partial^2 g / \partial A^2 < 0 .$$

Maximizing the franchisor's expected profit (where *f* is the royalty fee, *F* the initial lump sum fee, and *C* the cost):

$$\Pi^{FG} = f \cdot g(a, A) + F - C^{FG}(A),$$

subject to the franchisee's profit being at least his reservation profit Π_0^{FN} :

$$\Pi^{FN} = (1 - f) \cdot g(a^*, A^*) - F - C^{FN}(a^*) \geq \Pi_0^{FN} .$$

In the optimum marginal profits are equal to marginal costs:

$$f \cdot \frac{\partial g(a^*, A^*)}{\partial A^*} = C'^{FG}(A^*)$$

$$(1 - f) \cdot \frac{\partial g(a^*, A^*)}{\partial a^*} = C'^{FN}(a^*).$$

The franchisees participation constraint is just fulfilled. For a detailed analyses of the optimal contract the production function has to be specified (Bhattacharyya and Lafontaine 1995). It is assumed that the effort-output relation can be represented by a neoclassical production function (Cobb-Douglas):

[1] We refer to the simplified presentation proposed by Hempelmann 2001.

$$g(a, A) = K \cdot a^{\gamma} \cdot A^{\alpha} ,$$

where γ and α are the sales elasticity with respect to the effort of franchisee and franchisor respectively. $K > 0$ is a parameter to represent the sales potential in the market.

The cost functions are specified by:

$$C^{FG}(A) = \frac{A^n}{n} mit\, n \geq 1 \text{ and } C^{FN}(a) = \frac{a^m}{m} mit\, m \geq 1 .$$

The cost elasticities indicate by how much (in percentage) costs of effort rise with the effort level. The optimal running royalty fee is then given by:

$$f^* = [1 + \sqrt{\frac{\gamma(n-a)}{\alpha(m-\gamma)}}]^{-1} .$$

The royalty fee is equal for all franchisees that exhibit the same cost function with respect to its power (Bhattacharyya and Lafontaine 1995; Hempelmann 2000). The royalty fee is independent of the market size (*K*) but dependent on the effort levels of the contracting parties.

Depending on the activities and the business framework in which *f* and *F* are paid, their values will vary accordingly (Brickley 2002 and Lafontaine 1992). Correspondingly these variables can have differing effects on the success of the franchisee. In the model of Bhattacharyya and Lafontaine, *(1-f)* and *f* stand for the activities of franchisee and franchisor respectively. Depending on the relative importance of *f* for the generation of sales, *f* will be influenced in favor of the franchisor or the franchisee.

F should take a level to extract all of the downstream rents from the franchisees; where a running royalty fee is assumed (Lafontaine 1992; Dnes 1992; Dnes 1996; Klein 1995). *F* should correspond to the net present value of the franchisee's future profits (for every given level of sales and royalty fees (Lafontaine 1992). In other words: *F* should be correlated positively to the total value of the franchise system. This total value represents the characteristics of the local market, the value of the brand, the number of franchisees as well as the market power of the system. *f* on the other side, stands for the activities, e. g. marketing effort etc., that can be influenced by franchisors and franchisees to ascertain the market success. The question which arises is about what kinds of effects result from which part of the fees.

From the above reasoning it follows that *F* and *f* should be correlated negatively when no rent remains with the franchisee (Lafontaine 1992; Ehrmann 2002). The effect of different levels of *f* and *F* on the matching of franchisors and franchisees is ambiguous. This question is particularly interesting for potential franchisees who are keen on buying into a system without being able to measure their future entrepreneurial success ex ante (Klein 1995; Kaufmann and Lafontaine 1994a). From this point of view the two parts of the fee structure are particularly important.

2.2 Empirical Implications

General Reasoning. When selecting each other, franchisors and franchisees do not observe the other parties' qualities. What are observable are *f* and *F*. Furthermore, sales of franchisees already in the system and sales of the overall system can be observed. Also observable is the level of effort by the franchisor supporting franchisees, more or less, and the level of the franchisor leaving the franchisees different degrees of entrepreneurial freedom.

Then the following holds: good but little-known systems have to differentiate from less attractive systems. To signalize their respective quality, they should offer a contract $V = V(f,F)$ that low quality franchisors cannot copy. The quality of good franchisors and franchisees will then be observable by higher sales than in comparable but low quality systems.

Empirical implications. In order for a franchise system to be successful, incentives and reputation are important. By combining incentive and reputation arguments, further hypotheses regarding the effect of different fee structures on the success of franchisees can be formulated. The chances for success of a franchisee should be reflected by the total value of the franchise system, measured by the brand value or market power. A high value should correspond to a high initial lump sum fee. At the same time a high initial lump sum fee should represent a self-selection criterion for good franchisees who expect to recoup the outlay in the future (Sen 1993). Following this reasoning the following hypotheses should hold:

> *H1: The higher the initial lump sum fee, the higher the franchisee's sales level.*

Given that the initial lump sum fee valued by the market is a prerequisite for the franchisee's success, the level of the royalty fee is important for the achieved sales volume. Lower running fees allow ceteris paribus franchisees to offer lower prices to customers than higher taxed franchisees can offer. Higher royalty fees are then a reason for lower sales. Good franchisees should also offer other services (marketing) at low prices. Thereby good franchisees have good incentives for profit- making. Thus, the following statement should hold:

> *H2: The lower the royalty fee, the higher the franchisee's sales level.*

Furthermore, the assumption is that good franchise systems equally guarantee the success of the franchisor by selecting good franchisees because they offer good franchisees opportunities for success. Services that are delivered by the system should relate positively to the sales volume of franchisee:

H3: The higher the sum of delivered services, the higher the franchisee's sales volume.

A classical task of franchise systems is the central administration of business planning which is a part of the support services that are well suited to be centralized. Therefore:

H4: Business planning activities should have a positive effect on the franchisee's sales volume.

From the reputation and incentive reasoning it follows, (as opposed to the signaling theory) that franchisors attribute high importance to the selection of good franchisees. Given the relevance of cooperation and socially compatible groups (Boyer and Orleans 1992), trust in the qualities of franchisees should be very important. This may imply that these franchisees are entrepreneurial and able to make decisions on their own. Besides tasks that are suitable for central planning, some may only be executed effectively on site. It may be that a higher degree of organization, i.e. more policies and manuals, affects franchisee's sales negatively. Therefore:

H5: The lower the degree of organization, the higher the sales by franchisees.

3 The Data

The underlying data of the study were provided by the Peckert-Group. The data was initially collected for the "Jahrbuch Franchise und Lizenz 2002" (FAZ-Verlag) that gives an overview of 500 franchise systems out of the 1240 that were initially addressed. The franchise systems that were included in the study (Table 1) were extracted from the initial sample according to the variables studied here.

Table 1. Descriptive Statistics

Variable	Mean	Standard Deviation	n*
Requirements total invest	178,17	316,30	55
Age of franchise system	8,8841	8,1863	69
Partner outlets D 2001	46,04	112,50	70
Total sales D 2001	94031905,41	375566172,84	37
Gross sales T €	659,08	974,13	78

Table 1. Continued

Industry	n	%
Retail	21	32,3%
General services	13	20,0%
Gastronomy	9	13,8%
Construction	8	12,3%
Other	6	9,2%
Travel / Leisure	3	4,6%
Services B2B	3	4,6%
Services B2C	1	1,5%
Environmental services	1	1,5%
Real Estate	0	0,0%
Sum	65	100,0%

* Differing n reflect data availability for differing variables.

The distribution of the systems on different industries is typical for franchise systems. Through the focus on the retailing and services industries franchise systems are generally open for lateral entry.

4 Empirical Results

For the falsification of the above stated hypotheses regarding signaling, on the one hand, and incentives and reputation, on the other, the following model was tested by multiple linear regressions[2]:

$$U = \alpha_0 + \alpha_1 EG + \alpha_2 LG + \alpha_3 SL + \alpha_4 KPLA + \alpha_5 ORG + \alpha_6 INVEST + \alpha_7 ALT$$

The degree of organization was established using responses on a five-point scale (high-low) regarding the standardization of procedures through the franchisor. The sum of all services was identified by summing up (unweighted) all services offered by the franchisor.

[2] U = sales by a franchisee; EG = initial fees; LG = royalty rate; SL = sum of services; KPLA = business planning instruments; ORG = degree of organization; INVEST = requirements on the initial investment by franchisees; ALT = age of the system.

Table 2. Sales, Contract Design and Range of Services in Franchise Systems

Coefficients(a)	Non-standardized coefficients		Standardized coefficients		
Model*	B	Standard error	Beta	T	Sign.
(Intercept)	2662,022	683,517		3,895	,000
Initial fees	45,337	9,735	,457	4,657	,000
Royalty rate (%/sales)	-105,321	31,667	-,321	-3,326	,001
Sum of services (sum of general, building, development)	-79,065	29,935	-,519	-2,641	,010
Business planning instruments (cf. annex)	155,871	69,077	,453	2,256	,027
Degree of organization	-411,151	171,642	-,244	-2,395	,019

(a) Dependent variable: Gross sales T € * R-Square= 0,35, F = 7,758, Sign. at 0,1% level

Descriptive Statistics	Mean	Standard deviation	N
Gross sales T €	659,08	974,13	78
Initial fees	13,45	9,83	78
Royalty rate (%/sales)	5,14	2,97	78
Sum of services (Sum of General, Building, Development)	21,3846	6,3985	78
Business planning instruments (cf. annex)	7,9744	2,8283	78
Degree of organization	3,95	,58	78

The coefficients confirm the hypotheses resulting from the incentives and reputation arguments. Given that theoretical arguments suggest that f and F should be negatively correlated (Lafontaine 1992) the correlations were checked (cf. appendix). As can be seen in Table 6 multicollinearity can be excluded. The results indicate that good franchise systems are looking for very active and entrepreneurial franchisees. An interesting result is that both support services (exceeding business planning in its classical-centralized form) and a high degree of organization affect sales negatively. One could object that the results are biased towards "old" systems that do not have to signal their quality by the contract $V(f, F)$ as "new" systems have to.

In order to check this argument, a further model was tested which included age as an independent variable. Should the coefficient of the variable age be positive and significant there would be an indication for such a bias. Table 3 shows that there is a positive sign attached to the variable age. However, the correlation is weak and not significant. Consequently, there is no case for a bias in the data.

Table 3. Sales, Contract Design, Range of Services and System Age

Coefficients(a)	Non-standardized coefficients		Standardized coefficients		
Model*	B	Standard error	Beta	T	Sign.
(Intercept)	3019,303	727,978		4,148	,000
Initial fees	53,197	10,413	,524	5,109	,000
Royalty rate (%/sales)	-155,326	41,033	-,398	-3,785	,000
Sum of services (sum of general, building, development)	-84,025	34,348	-,537	-2,446	,017
Business planning instruments (cf. annex)	137,847	80,439	,380	1,714	,092
Degree of organization	-418,045	179,359	-,242	-2,331	,023
Age of franchise system	7,604	12,612	,061	,603	,549

(a) Dependent variable: Gross sales T € * R-Square= 0,414, F = 7,239, Sign. at 0,1% level

Descriptive Statistics	Mean	Standard deviation	N
Gross sales T €	710,96	1023,54	69
Initial fees	13,49	10,08	69
Royalty rate (%/sales)	4,90	2,62	69
Sum of services (Sum of General, Building, Development)	21,3478	6,5436	69
Business planning instruments (cf. annex)	8,1304	2,8228	69
Degree of organization	3,97	,59	69
Age of franchise system	8,8841	8,1863	69

The algebraic sign of the variable initial lump sum fee indicates that franchisees have a good idea about their own skills as well as one concerning the market value of the franchise system. The royalty fee variable indicates that incentive and price effects dominate signaling effects. The negative effects of a higher royalty fee on the franchisees sales illustrate the costs of such a kind of signaling. It seems to be the case that signaling of good quality to the franchisees could be achieved more cost efficiently (licensing etc.) than by increasing the running royalty fee. The negative (algebraic) sign of the coefficient degree of organization indicates that successful franchise systems do not have detailed schedules for the franchisee's activities.

In this context it seems appropriate to segment the franchise system of the sample along industries in which different prerequisites exist with regard to the franchisee skills. The simplest way of segmentation was to classify all retailing companies (a third of the overall sample) as being of the category "weak entrepreneurial skill set needed" while putting all other companies in the category "high entrepreneurial skill set needed". Table 4 represents the regression results for the latter category. In comparison to Table 2, which contains all companies, the negative impact of the degree of organization is much higher where a high entrepreneurial skill set is needed. Apparently, the entrepreneurial skills needed to succeed differ across industries. Equivalently, the results suggest that entrepreneurial minded franchisees must not be restricted too much in their freedom. Again, the importance of a successful matching between franchisors and franchisees is must be emphasized.

Table 4. Sales and Organizational Freedom in High Entrepreneurial Skill Set Needed-Industries (without retailing)

Coefficients(a)	Non-standardized coefficients		Standardized coefficients		
Model	B	Standard error	Beta	T	Sign.
(Intercept)	3599,568	966,216		3,725	,001
Initial fees	53,096	12,640	,509	4,201	,000
Royalty rate (%/sales)	-95,442	46,804	-,254	-2,039	,048
Sum of services (sum of general, building, development)	-98,405	42,563	-,514	-2,312	,026
Business planning instruments (cf. annex)	182,649	96,452	,411	1,894	,066
Degree of organization	-634,655	259,733	-,328	-2,443	,019

(a) Dependent variable: Gross sales T €

In another model the influence of the franchisee's total investments on sales was tested.

Table 5. Sales, Contract Design and Total Investment Requirements

Coefficients(a)	Non-standardized coefficients		Standardized coefficients		
Model	B	Standard error	Beta	T	Sign.
(Intercept)	3813,171	923,442		4,129	,000
Initial fees	45,259	12,046	,425	3,757	,000
Royalty rate (%/sales)	-77,270	43,069	-,204	-1,794	,079
Sum of services (sum of general, building, development)	-86,185	40,174	-,501	-2,145	,037
Business planning instruments (cf. annex)	159,937	90,225	,419	1,773	,083
Degree of organization	-728,209	244,643	-,349	-2,977	,005
Requirements total investments	,910	,419	,253	2,174	,035

(a) Dependent variable: Gross sales T € * R-Square= 0,455, F = 6,672, Sign. at 0,1% level

Table 5. Continued

Descriptive Statistics	Mean	Standard deviation	N
Gross sales T €	751,08	1136,02	55
Initial fees	14,28	10,68	55
Royalty rate (%/sales)	4,91	3,00	55
Sum of services (Sum of General, Building, Development)	22,2000	6,6092	55
Business planning instruments (cf. annex)	8,3455	2,9766	55
Degree of organization	4,00	,54	55
Requirements total investments	178,17	316,30	55

The positive effect of the total investment on sales is significant at the 5%-level. This is equivalent to the high importance of the franchisor's reputation. Some franchise systems explicitly expect some form of "submission" of their franchisees. The computer training firm New Horizons (at a franchise conference on 9/7/2001) made clear that "Honda and ego are to be restarted after work" (for theoretical counter examples see Boyer and Orleans 1992). Such systems are not interested in entrepreneurial minded franchisees and base their long-term competitive advantage on the skills of the franchisor. In such a setting the role of the local entrepreneurial activity is ranked very low. The study's findings indicate that such a strategy could be misleading in a knowledge intensive services industry.

5 Conclusion

The influence of contract design and the range of services offered by franchisors was at the heart of this paper. A data set on German franchise systems generated initial empirical results concerning the relation between the levels of the running royalty fee and initial lump sum fee, on the one hand, and the degree of organization and sales, on the other. Furthermore, the effects of initial investments and the degree of entrepreneurial freedom on sales were investigated. The advantage of a study on franchise systems is the simultaneous consideration of the interest of franchisor and franchisees for the variables F and f.

This essay points to the optimal system choice for founders who are interested in a franchise outlet. The study's franchise systems confirm the reputation and incentive arguments. A lower running royalty rate and a higher initial lump sum fee go along with lower sales by the franchisee. The latter relationship points to well-established systems in the market. The sum of the franchisors support services (see Table 4) has a rather negative effect on sales, while business planning instruments have a positive effect on sales (at a 10% significance level).[3] Good franchisors should therefore allow more entrepreneurial freedom for their franchisees while assuming key centrally planned tasks.

[3] Due to a low variety of franchise systems in Germany that are able or willing to answer questionnaire mailings it seems rather difficult to extend this study.

References

1. Albach H (1980) Vertrauen in der ökonomischen Theorie. Journal of Institutional and Theoretical Economics 136:2-11
2. Bhattacharyya FS, Lafontaine F (1995) Double-sided Moral Hazard and the Nature of Share Contracts. Rand Journal of Economics 26:761-781
3. Boeckenholt I, Wiens R (2001) Führung einer Franchise-Organisation am Beispiel des Mischsystems der Blume 2000 GmbH & Co. KG. Ahlert D (Ed.) Handbuch Franchising und Cooperation. Neuwied, pp 175 -184
4. Bohnet I, Frey BS (1997) Rent Leaving, in: Journal of Institutional and Theoretical Economics 153:711-721
5. Boyer R, Orleans A (1992) How Do Conventions Evolve? Journal of Evolutionary Economics (2):165-177
6. Brickley J (2002) Royalty Rates and Upfront Fees in Share Contracts: Evidence from Franchising. Journal of Law, Economics and Organization (18):511-535
7. Buerhle T, Posselt T (2003) Die Auswahl produktiver Mitglieder in Franchisesystemen. Zeitschrift für betriebswirtschaftliche Forschung, (55)
8. Dant R, Kaufmann P (2003) Structural and Strategic Dynamics in Franchising. Journal of Retailing (79):63-79
9. Deutscher Franchiseverband (1992) Europäischer Verhaltenskodex für Franchising. Code of honour for Members of the German Franchise Association
10. Dnes AW (1992) 'Unfair' Contractual Practices and Hostages in Franchise Contracts. Journal of Institutional and Theoretical Economics 148:484-504
11. Dnes AW (1996) The Economic Analysis of Franchise Contracts. Journal of Institutional and Theoretical Economics 152:297-324
12. Ehrmann T (2002) Reale Franchisesysteme, begrenzter Opportunismus und kooperative Elemente. Zeitschrift fuer Betriebswirtschaft 72(11):1133 – 1153
13. Erdmann G, Kiewitt A, Peckert F (2002) Franchise und Lizenz 2002. FAZ-Verlag
14. Fehr E, Schmidt KM (1999) A Theory of Fairness, Competition and Cooperation. Quarterly Journal of Economics: 817-868
15. Fehr E, Klein A, Schmidt KM (2001) Fairness, Incentives and Contractual Incompleteness. IfER-Working Paper (2), Zurich
16. Frey BS, Frost J, Osterloh M (1999) Was kann das Unternehmen besser als der Markt? Zeitschrift fuer Betriebswirtschaft 69:1245-1262
17. Fritz W (1995) Marketingmanagement und Unternehmenserfolg. Stuttgart
18. Gallini NT, Lutz NA (1992) Dual Distribution and Royalty Fees in Franchising. Journal of Law, Economics and Organization 8:471-501
19. Hempelmann B (2000) Optimales Franchising - Eine ökonomische Analyse der Vertragsgestaltung in Franchise-Beziehungen. Heidelberg
20. Hempelmann B (2001) Ökonomische Analyse der Vertragsbeziehungen im Franchising. WiSt (2):75-78
21. Kaufmann PJ, Lafontaine F (1994a) Costs of Control - The Source of Economic Rents for Mc Donald's Franchisees. Journal of Law and Economics 37:417-453
22. Kaufmann PJ, Lafontaine F (1994b) The Evolution of Ownership Patterns in Franchise Systems. Journal of Retailing 70:97-113
23. Klein B (1995) The Economics of Franchise contracts. Journal of Corporate Finance (2): 9-37
24. Kreps D (1990) A Course in Microeconomic Theory. Princeton University Press
25. Lafontaine F (1992) Agency Theory and Franchising - Some Empirical Results. Rand Journal of Economics 23:263-283

26.Lafontaine F (1993) Contractual Arrangements as Signaling Devices - Evidence from Franchising. Journal of Law, Economics and Organisation (9):256-289
27.Lafontaine F, Shaw KL (1999) The Dynamics of Franchise Contracting - Evidence from Panel Data. Journal of Political Economy 107:1041-1080
28.Lafontaine F, Slade M (1998) Incentive Contracting and the Franchise Decision, Mimeo, University of Michigan Business School
29.Minkler AP (1990) An Empirical Analysis of a Firm's Decision to Franchise. Economics Letters (34):77-82
30.Posselt T (1999) Das Design vertraglicher Vertriebsbeziehungen am Beispiel Franchising. Zeitschrift fuer Betriebswirtschaft 69:347-375
31.Roth A (1999) The Redesign of the Matching Market for American Physicians - Some Engineering Aspects of Economic Design. American Review 89 (4):748-778
32.Schlueter H (2000) Die Zufriedenheit von Franchisenehmern. Working paper Internationales Centrum für Franchising und Kooperation, University of Muenster
33.Sen KC (1993) The Use of Initial Fees and Royalties in Business-format Franchising. Managerial and Decision Economics (14):175-190
34.Sydow J (1998) Franchise Systems as Strategic Networks, Working Paper, FU Berlin
35.Williamson O (1985) The Economic Institutions of Capitalism
36.Windsperger J (2001) Ownership Rights in Franchising Firms, GEABA Discussion Paper, No. 01-24

Appendix

As business building instruments the following subset of support services was considered:

Group: General
- enterprise resource planning system
- Research & Development
- Market analyses
- QM-systems
- Collective purchase

Group: "Building up of the company"
- investment planning
- human resource management

Group: „Development of the company“
- innovation management
- intercompany comparison
- budgeting / controlling
- consulting
- marketing consulting

The sum of positive responses was added (unweighted).

Table 6. Correlations

		initial fee	royalty rate (%) sales	royalty rate €/monthly	sum of services	business planning in-struments	age of franchise system	degree of organiza-tion
initial fee	correlation	1	-,009	,073	-,019	,017	,002	,102
	significance (two-tailed)	.	,921	,653	,770	,800	,975	,124
	N	230	130	40	230	230	201	229
royalty rate (%) sales	correlation	-,009	1	-,466	-,043	-,079	-,123	-,111
	significance (2-tailed)	,921	.	,244	,585	,313	,133	,155
	N	130	167	8	167	167	150	167
royalty rate €/monthly	correlation	,073	-,466	1	,272(*)	,236	,366(*)	,208
	significance (2-tailed)	,653	,244	.	,045	,083	,011	,127
	N	40	8	55	55	55	47	55
sum of services	correlation	-,019	-,043	,272(*)	1	,920(**)	,033	,348(**)
	significance (2-tailed)	,770	,585	,045	.	,000	,575	,000
	N	230	167	55	364	364	300	340
business planning in-struments	correlation	,017	-,079	,236	,920(**)	1	,018	,347(**)
	significance (2-tailed)	,800	,313	,083	,000	.	,758	,000
	N	230	167	55	364	364	300	340
age of franchise system	correlation	,002	-,123	,366(*)	,033	,018	1	-,053
	significance (2-tailed)	,975	,133	,011	,575	,758	.	,360
	N	201	150	47	300	300	300	300
degree of organization	correlation	,102	-,111	,208	,348(**)	,347(**)	-,053	1
	significance (2-tailed)	,124	,155	,127	,000	,000	,360	.
	N	229	167	55	340	340	300	340

Franchising Public Services
An Analysis of the Duration of Passenger Rail Franchises in Great Britain

Anne Yvrande-Billon

ATOM, University of Paris I Panthéon-Sorbonne,
106-112 Boulevard de l'Hôpital, 75013 Paris, France
yvrande@univ-paris1.fr

Abstract. For two decades, the procurement of public utilities has been engaged in a process of intensive reform. One type of organizational change that has been massively introduced is the use of franchise agreements for the provision of public services. This is the choice adopted by the reformers of the British railways, who decided to franchise the passenger rail service. But, whereas the theory on utilities restructuring recommends turning to long-term contracting, the British policy makers have chosen to rely on short-term franchise agreements.

Our objective in this paper is to examine the relevance of these contractual choices. Referring to Transaction Cost Economics, we investigate the determinants of franchise contracts duration. The results of our econometric tests show that the British reformers' contractual choices are not consistent with the theoretical propositions. The new organizational mode of the British railways tends to increase the potential for opportunism and therefore the transaction costs.

1 Introduction

Private companies are not the only entities to use franchising system for the provision of goods or services. In many countries and various sectors, public authorities have also massively turned to this mode of organization for the procurement of public services, such as, for instance, urban transport, water supply or waste collection (Littlechild 2002; Guasch et al. 2002). In such cases, local or national governments behave as franchisors, i.e. grant the right to deliver a public service for a limited length of time and under certain conditions to private franchisees. In the worldwide context of utilities reforms, franchising public services is seen as a 'tool of government' to allow private sector participation while retaining some degree of control. It is also a means to introduce competition at least for the market (Demsetz 1968) and therefore to improve the performances of network industries.

However, many questions arise about the efficiency of this form of governance for providing public services (Williamson 1976; Goldberg 1976; Priest 1993). One particular and important issue regards the duration of the franchise agreements public authorities sign with their private franchisees. Indeed, the franchise term affects, amongst other things, the quality and price of the service offered and the incentives to invest. As put by Baldwin and Cave (1999, p 272), 'where large sunk investments are involved in operation, a long–term franchise may be necessary to combat incentive to under-investment […] and may encourage service innovation […]'. As we will develop later on, this argument is based on a Transaction Cost Economics reasoning according to which the length of contracts must be chosen in accordance with the characteristics of the transactions the contracts monitor. In order to realize transaction cost economies, franchise contracts, like all contracts, must indeed be designed carefully, particularly considering the level of specificity of the assets involved in the transactions at stake (Joskow 1987; Brickley et al. 2002).

Our objective in this article is to assess the transactional efficiency of the contractual choices made by the reformers of the British railways, who recently introduced a franchising system for the provision of passenger service and decided to rely on short-term agreements. In other words, we aim at investigating whether the British authorities' decision to use short-term franchise contracts for the procurement of passenger rail transport matches a transaction cost minimizing logic.

Consequently, the contributions of the paper are twofold. First, it enriches the analysis of the new British railways structure by referring to an original theoretical background, namely Transaction Cost Economics, while a large body of the literature regarding the British railway reform is made of monographs and provides few theoretical hypotheses. Second, our work is one of the only two empirical studies[1] regarding the determinants of franchise contract duration in the British railways. It relies on original data, collected for the purpose of the study and coming from various sources including regulatory reports, specialised industry publications and interviews of the actors of the new system.

The remainder of the paper is organized as follows. Section 2 presents our theoretical framework. Section 3 contains an analysis of the duration of franchise contracts chosen by the reformers of the British railways and provides an estimation of the specificity of rail assets. Section 4 presents our econometric results. We show that the contractual choices made by the British railway reformers do not rely on transaction cost minimizing principles and therefore are inefficient.

2 The Theoretical Determinants of Contract Duration

The duration of contracts has been the subject of many empirical works in Transaction Cost Economics (TCE) (Masten and Saussier 2002). From this theoretical perspective, it is considered to be a key dimension of the contractual design, which must be chosen cautiously. In order to economize transaction costs, the length of a contractual agreement must indeed be determined according to the characteristics of the transactions the agreement supports. More precisely, transac-

[1] To our knowledge, only Affuso and Newbery (2002) have dealt with this topic.

tion costs are assumed to be minimized if contract duration is positively correlated with the level of asset specificity (Masten 1986; Joskow 1987; Crocker and Masten 1988). This assumption is based on the following argument.

The specialization of a durable asset to a particular user or more accurately the high costs of making it available to others generates a quasi rent which corresponds to the difference between the value of the asset in its intended use and its value in its next best use (Klein et al. 1978; Crocker and Masten 1991). Given that agents are inclined to opportunistic behaviours according to TCE (Williamson 1975), the distribution of the quasi rent resulting from relationship-specific investments is a source of conflicts between trading partners. Each of them will indeed try and expropriate the rents accruing to specific assets through hold up activities and *ex post* strategic bargaining. Therefore, if on the one hand relationship-specific investments enhance the value of exchange by engendering quasi-rents, they, on the other hand, may also cause resources to be wasted in order to influence the distribution of gains from trade.

This is why, when exchange involves significant investments in relationship-specific capital, an exchange relationship that relies on repeated bargaining is unattractive (Joskow 1987). To secure the value of such investments, that is, to safeguard the quasi rent they engender, long term contracting is advocated. According to TCE reasoning, the duration of contractual agreements is thus supposed to increase with the value of relationship-specific investments at stake. Indeed, if this 'alignment' principle is respected, that is to say, if the duration of contracts is adapted to the features of the transactions - more accurately to the degree to which specific assets are involved - , then transaction costs are minimized. Consequently, a firm has better performances if the contractual agreements it has signed with its trading partners match the characteristics of the firms transactions.

3 Contract Duration and Asset Specificity in the New British Railways System

3.1 The Length of Franchise Agreements

Following the 1993 Railway Act, the British railways have been completely reorganized. There is now an extensive literature describing the complex structure that emerged after the reform (Harris and Goodward 1997; Freeman and Shaw 2000). In a nutshell, all the segments of the industry (infrastructure, rolling stock ownership, operation) have been privatized and disintegrated vertically and sometimes horizontally. Thus, the passenger rail business has been divided into 25 local monopoly franchises awarded for a fixed term to private bidders, the Train Operating Companies (TOCs), who own virtually no assets since trains are leased from the rolling stock companies (the ROSCOs) and stations, track and signalling belong to the infrastructure monopoly (Railtrack).

In the reformers' mind, since franchises merely consisted of a commitment to run a minimum level of services and were not investment franchises, their term could be relatively short. As operating franchisees, the operators would only take the revenue and operational risks but would not bear the large and sunk costs associated with investments in rail assets. Therefore, long term franchise agreements were considered as useless and even more inefficient since they would hinder competition.

To obtain a compromise between the proposition of the Treasury, who wanted the shortest possible terms to stimulate competition, and the suggestions of the potential franchisees, who wanted the maximum, it was decided that the standard duration would be 7 years (Wolmar 2000). And indeed the duration of the franchises awarded to the Train Operating Companies (TOCs) is very homogeneous (Table 1) and very short in comparison with the physical lifetime of trains (30 years approximately). 17 franchise agreements out of 25 cover a period of between 84 and 90 months. A very particular contract lasts for 60 months[2]. The remaining agreements, which have a term of between 120 and 180 months, are those for the operators required to replace and/or refurbish at least part of their rolling stock fleet. Part 4 of the franchise agreements makes the lengthening of contract duration dependent upon the realization of massive investments in rolling stock. In fact, as explained above, the operating franchisees are not required to invest directly. An investment for a TOC consists in ordering new trains to a rolling stock company who then leases them to the TOC for the entire duration of its franchise.

Table 1. Distribution of Contractual Length

Contract Duration (in months)	Number of observations
60	1
84<-<87	13
90	4
120	2
180	5

Source: OPRAF Annual Report (1996/97)

Thus, the reformers did take into account in their contractual choices the fact that some franchisees might have to make, or more accurately to order, massive investments in rolling stock renewal and refurbishment. The more sizable the investment in rolling stock needed on one particular franchise sector, the longer the franchise agreement granted to the franchisee by the public authorities was. But, as we intend to show, they did not take into consideration the nature of the existing fleet and its low level of remarketability.

[2] The franchise granted for the island of Wight.

3.2 The Specificity of the Rolling Stock

3.2.1 The Degree of Interoperability of British Trains

The rolling stock involved in the procurement of passenger rail services in Britain, are specific assets.

First, as in all other countries, passenger trains are durable assets[3] that are physically specific since their value depreciates in alternative uses, even freight transportation.

Moreover, the British fleet inherited by the new operators is made up of trains that have various technical characteristics, matching the heterogeneity or the absence of standardisation of the infrastructure interface. During the British Rail (BR) era, the design of the trains was dominated by a 'made-to-measure' logic. The network was a patchwork of different systems inherited from the private companies of the nineteenth and early twentieth centuries. The regional organization coincided with regional political interests; and it combined with the powerful influence of engineers in each region, reinforcing the heterogeneity of the system. As a result, BR's industrial strategy was based on the design of trains for specific tracks. Not only was the equipment designed for specific purposes, e.g., long distance passengers transportation as opposed to suburban services, but it was also adapted to tracks and to their specific power supply system, i.e. diesel or electricity and, in the later case, using a third rail or a catenary system.

Therefore, most of the trains inherited by the franchise operators on privatisation had been designed to circulate on parts of the network. They cannot operate on all tracks, i.e. they are not fully interchangeable.

Table 2 presents an approximation of the degree of interoperability of each type of train composing the British fleet in 1996. To create this indicator of redeployability of the British trains, we have estimated the proportion of the network on which each type of train can operate. Thus, for instance, electric locomotives can only run on 9% of the network (corresponding to the proportion of the long distance network that is electrified), whereas diesel multiple units (DMUs) can be used on 62% of the tracks (i.e. the proportion of the network which is not electrified).

[3] Their physical lifetime is in average 30 years.

Table 2. Distribution of the Fleet in 1996 and Interoperability of Each Type of Train

Type of train[a]	Distribution[b]	Degree of interoperability
Electric Locomotives	2%	9%
DC EMUs	31%	14%
Diesel Locomotives	3%	15%
AC EMUs	20%	24%
Dual EMUs	5%	38%
DMUs	16%	62%

Sources: British Railway Guidebook 1997; Railtrack Network Management Statement 1998; National Audit Office 1998.
[a]*DC EMUs* Direct Current Electric Multiple Units, *AC EMUs* Alternative Current Electric Multiple Units, *Dual EMUs* Dual Current Electric Multiple Units, *DMUs* Diesel Multiple Units.
[b]Carriages do not appear in this table. That is why the total of column 2 is not equal to 100%.

According to these estimations, EMUs dual (i.e. electric multiple units which are compatible with both the overhead-powered and the third-rail systems used in different parts of the country) and DMUs (i.e. diesel multiple units) are the more interoperable types of trains, while locomotives and EMUs DC (electric multiple units compatible with third rail system) are the less interchangeable rolling stock. In other words, some types of trains are more specific than others. The technical characteristics of some rolling stock constrain the geographical zone on which they can be used. Thus, paradoxically for mobile assets like trains, the physical specificity of the rolling stock combines with a site specificity which is all the more significant since these assets are durable and since British trains are not interoperable on foreign rail networks.

Furthermore, because the size and the composition of the fleet leased by each operator are different, the level of specificity of their assets is not the same.

3.2.2 A Measurement of the Rolling Stock Specificity

To measure the degree of specificity of the rolling stock, we have used the data on the size and the composition of each TOC's fleet published in the *British Railways Guidebooks* (1997) and we have taken up the indicators of interoperability of each type of trains that were built.

The level of redeployability of the fleet leased by TOC x is then :

$$REDEP^{x} = \frac{\sum_i R_i \times N_i^x}{\sum_i N_i^x}$$

where:

i = type of train = {electric locomotive, DC EMUs, diesel locomotives, AC EMUs, dual EMUs, DMUs},

R_i = degree of interoperability of train i (see table 2),

N_i^x = number of type i trains leased by TOC x,

$\sum_i N_i^x$ = size of the fleet operated by TOC x.

The resulting ratio varies between 0 and 1. The closer to 1 this indicator, the less specific the rolling stock, and the closer to 0, the more specific the rolling stock.

The degrees of redeployability we obtain with this measure are very heterogeneous, depending on the operating company and the type of service (regional, intercity, commuter).

Table 3. Statistics on REDEP

Average Value	0,32
Standard Deviation	0,19
Minimum	0,10
Maximum	0,62
Average Value (Intercity)	0,18
Average Value (Commuter)	0,30
Average Value (Regional)	0,48

Theoretically, this variability in the characteristics of the rail transactions might translate into a variability in the contractual practices. According to TCE hypotheses, a transaction involving redeployable assets can efficiently be governed by short term market-type contracts. Alternatively, a transaction requiring durable specialized assets implies the need for an extended contractual arrangement, protecting the value of the relationship-specific investments. We might then observe that the duration of franchise agreements changes according to the degree of specificity of the assets needed to provide the service. More accurately, TOCs operating rolling stock of very little redeployability should have longer contracts than companies using more interoperable trains.

4 The Logic Behind the Reformers' Contractual Choices

4.1 A Proposition

Comparing the length of each franchise agreement with the degree of specificity of each transaction, it appears that the duration of contracts chosen by public authorities is relatively independent of the level of redeployability of the fleet. The resulting misalignment is summarized in figure 1 which shows the lack of correspondence between the specificity of the investments considered and the duration of contracts.

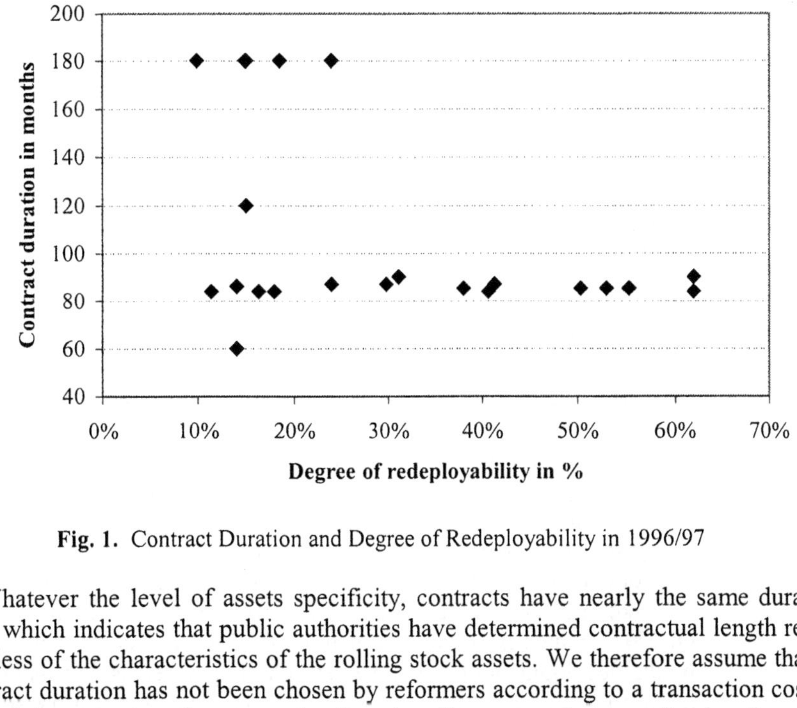

Fig. 1. Contract Duration and Degree of Redeployability in 1996/97

Whatever the level of assets specificity, contracts have nearly the same duration, which indicates that public authorities have determined contractual length regardless of the characteristics of the rolling stock assets. We therefore assume that contract duration has not been chosen by reformers according to a transaction cost minimizing criterion. Consequently, there is a discrepancy between the duration of the contracts imposed by the reform and the initial characteristics of the transactions they are supposed to monitor. We argue that the problem with these contractual choices is that, even though the franchisees do not have to realize investments, they indirectly bear the residual-value risks of the rolling stock, through the lease rentals they pay to their lessors (the ROSCOs) (Ljungqvist and Holt 1998; Prideaux 2000). And, due to the low level of redeployability of certain types of trains, this risk (that is, for the ROSCOs, the risk of not being able to relet the assets at the end of the initial lease and/or at the leasing fee which covers the investment cost and generate profit) might be high and encourage opportunistic behaviors[4]. In other words, this new system induces transaction costs that could have been avoided if contracts had been signed differently.

Our objective in the next section is to test econometrically this proposition, that is to say to analyse the determinants of contract duration and investigate whether the contractual choices of the reformers are consistent with transaction cost predictions.

4.2 The Determinants of Franchise Contracts Duration

4.2.1 *Explanatory Variables*

As already mentioned, the contractual design of the new structure has been imposed by reformers. Our aim is thus to analyse the determinants of the regulators' choices. The question we would like to answer is then the following : on which basis was the contractual length determined ?

To investigate our proposition, the determinants of franchise contracts duration we choose are the following.

- The contractual commitments to invest. As already mentioned, some franchise agreements require train operating companies to invest in new rolling stock, or, more accurately, to order new trains to the rolling stock companies and lease them for the entire duration of their franchise. We hypothesize that the length of franchise contracts might depend on whether the contract incorporates obligations to invest in new rolling stock (DUMINV=1) or not (DUMINV=0). More precisely, we assume that the higher the amount of investments in rolling stock renewal and refurbishment imposed on the franchisees by the regulator, related to the number of passenger-kilometres carried (INVREL), the longer the franchise contract.
- The level of asset specificity. We suggest that the more redeployable the fleet operated by a TOC[5] (REDEP>0,5), the shorter its franchise contract. To take into account the size of the fleet, we also create a variable QRENT[6], which is our approximation of the level of quasi-rent generated by the development of specific assets. Our hypothesis is thus that contract duration is positively related to QRENT. The less standard the specification of a fleet, the less 'liquid' it will be in terms of the lessor's ability to

[4] For the lessors, opportunism would consist in excessive leasing fees, whereas for the franchisees, it could take the form of strategic bargaining at contract renewal (Office of the Rail Regulator 1998).

[5] i.e. the less specific its assets.

[6] *QRENT=(1-REDEP)*FLEET*, where *FLEET* is the number of trains operated, i.e. the size of the fleet.

release it on a different route to a potentially different operator in the future, and the higher the potential for opportunism (Berdugo 1998). Therefore, the more route or operator-specific features a fleet has, the more concerned the regulator should have been about the length of contractual agreement granted to the TOC operating this fleet.

Table 4 provides a description of the different variables. The expected signs of the variablesare summarized in table 5.

Table 4. Sample Statistics

Variables	Observations	Mean	Standard Deviation	Minimum	Maximum
DURATION[a]	25	106,68	39,03	60	180
DUMINV	25	0,56	0,51	0	1
INVREL[b]	25	0,57	0,08	0	0,29
REDEP	25	0,32	0,19	0,09	0,62
QRENT	25	304,87	309,22	10,32	1141,74

[a]In months.
[b]In £/passenger-kilometre.

Table 5. Expected Signs

Dependent Variable: DURATION	
Independent Variables	Expected Sign
DUMINV	+
INVREL	+
REDEP	-
QRENT	+

4.2.2 Estimation Results

OLS regressions give the following estimates:

Table 6. Correlation Matrix

	DURATION	DUMINV	INVREL	REDEP	QRENT
DURATION	1	-	-	-	-
DUMINV	0,51	1	-	-	-
INVREL	0,87	0,61	1	-	-
REDEP	-0,43	-0,18	-0,31	1	-
QRENT	0,26	0,27	0,09	-0,49	1

Table 7. The Determinants of Contract Duration

Independent variables	DURATION (1)	DURATION (2)	DURATION (3)	DURATION (4)
DUMINV	34,49 (2,62)***	36,56 (2,52)***		
INVREL			378,87 (8,10)***	396,33 (9)***
REDEP	-72,07 (-2,05)**		-36,48 (-1,74)*	
QRENT		0,02 $(0,72)^{ns}$		0,02 (1,94)*
Constant	110,35 (6,95)***	81 (6,98)***	96,82 (11,10)***	77,07 (16,77)***
Adjusted R^2	0,32	0,21	0,77	0,78
Observations	25	25	25	25

t-ratios in parentheses.
*** indicates significance beyond the 1% level, ** indicates significance beyond the 5% level, * indicates significance beyond the 10% level.

These results confirm the importance of the variables DUMINV and INVREL in the choice of contract duration. The fact that some franchisees have to invest, as well as the relative amount of investment they are required to realize (indirectly), are the first criteria on which the reformers have relied to determine the length of franchise agreements. However, INVREL gives more satisfactory estimations than the dummy variable DUMINV.

On the other hand, our results also suggest that the degree of specificity of rolling stock assets and the level of quasi rent they generate are not the most significant determinants of contract duration. As already illustrated in figure 1, contract duration depends little on asset specificity. Thus, if we refer to estimation (3), the duration of the franchises requiring very specific rolling stock (REDEP=0,1 for instance) is only 18 months longer than the duration of the franchises of the companies operating more redeployable trains (REDEP=0,6). In the same way, according to estimation (4), transactions that generate an important quasi-rent

(QRENT=1000) are governed by contracts that are about 20 months longer than the contracts supporting transactions which involve a small quasi-rent (QRENT=10). In a TCE syntax, one would say that there is a misalignment between the franchise length and the characteristics of the transactions they monitor.

This discrepancy is supposed to have implications on the financial performances of the operators since their transaction costs are not minimized. Indeed, in a situation of misalignment between the duration of the contracts and the characteristics of the transactions at stake, TCE assumes that transaction costs are not minimized and therefore that profits are not maximised (Williamson 1985). The Williamson's misalignment hypothesis suggests that proper alignment of governance structures enhances performances (Riordan and Williamson 1985). Therefore, franchisees whose contractual arrangements are aligned to the attributes of the assets they operate will outperform operators whose contracts do not match the features of rolling stock.

5 Conclusion

Our analysis shows that the contractual duration imposed by the reformers of the British railways does not match the degree of specificity of rolling stock assets. In other words, the new organizational structure of railways in Great Britain relies on contractual arrangements that do not minimize transaction costs and which therefore are not efficient. Given the high level of specificity of rolling stock assets, the use of short-term operating franchise agreements for the provision of passenger rail services creates opportunities of rent expropriation, both for the franchisees and their suppliers. This proposition, which is often developed by observers of the British rail reform, is corroborated by an econometric test relying on an original measure of the specificity of rails assets. We point out that the reformers have taken into account the size of the investments needed by the franchisees in their contractual choices, but have not considered the nature of the existing and future assets. For this reason, we conclude that the franchise contracts imposed by the British policy makers are not cost minimizing governance structures.

In fact, the inefficiency of the contractual arrangements is inferred rather than demonstrated. Our results reveal that the authorities' choices have been little influenced by transaction cost minimizing considerations. But, they do not show that these contractual choices effectively impact on the performances of the operators. Our analysis of the determinants of contract duration is just a preliminary step, even though crucial, to assess the efficiency of the contractual choices. The consequences of these choices on the performances of the rail industry still have to be estimated.

References

1. Affuso L, Newbery DMG. (2002) The Impact of Structural and Contractual Arrangements on a Vertically Separated Railway. The Economic and Social Review 33(1):83-92
2. Baldwin R, Cave M (1999) Franchising and its Limitations. In: Baldwin R, Cave M (eds) Understanding Regulation. Oxford University Press, Oxford, pp 257-285
3. Berdugo P (1998) New Train Procurement – Commercial Considerations of the Operating Leasing Company. European Railway Review 4 (November):59-66
4. Brickley JA, Misra S, Van Horn RL (2002) Contract Duration: Evidence from Franchise Contracts. University of Rochester, Working Paper
5. British Railways Guidebooks (1997) Platform 5 Publishing Ltd., Sheffield, UK
6. Crocker KJ, Masten SE (1988) Mitigating Contractual Hazards: Unilateral Options and Contract Length. Rand Journal of Economics 19(3):327-343
7. Crocker KJ, Masten SE (1991) Pretia ex Machina ?: Prices and Process in Long Term Contracts. Journal of Law and Economics 34:64-69
8. Demsetz H (1968) Why Regulate Utilities?. Journal of Law and Economics 11(April):55-66
9. Freeman R, Shaw J (2000) British Railway Privatisation. McGraw-Hill, Maidenhead
10. Goldberg VP (1976) Regulation and Administered Contracts. Bell Journal of Econom ics 10(2):426-448
11. Guasch JL, Laffont JJ, Straub S (2002) Renegotiation of Concession Contracts in Latin America. USC Center for Law, Economics and Organization Research Paper No. C02-22
12. Harris NG, Goodward E (1997) The Privatisation of British Railways. The Railway Consultancy Press, London
13. Klein B, Crawford RA, Alchian AA (1978) Vertical Integration, Appropriable Rents, and the Competitive Contracting Process. Journal of Law and Economics 21(2):297-326
14. Littlechild SC (2002) Competitive Bidding for a Long-Term Electricity Distribution Contract. Review of Network Economics 1(1):1-38
15. Ljungqvist A, Holt D (1998) Should the ROSCOs be Regulated?. OXERA Publications, Oxford
16. Masten SE (1986) Institutional Choice and the Organization of Production: The Make or Buy Decision. Journal of Institutional and Theoretical Economics 142:493-509
17. Masten SE, Saussier S (2002) Econometrics of Contracts: An Assessment of Developments in the Empirical Literature on Contracting. In: Brousseau E, Glachant JM (eds) The Economics of Contracts. Cambridge University Press, Cambridge, pp 273-292
18. National Audit Office (1998) Privatisation of the Rolling Stock Leasing Companies Report by the Comptroller and Auditor General, HC 576 Session 1997-98, The Stationery Office, London
19. Office of the Rail Regulator (1998) Review of the Rolling Stock Market. ORR Publica tions, London
20. Prideaux J (2000) Trains: The Rolling-Stock Companies. In Freeman R, Shaw J (eds.) British Railway Privatisation. McGraw-Hill, Maidenhead, pp 97-117
21. Railtrack (1998) Network Management Statement for Great Britain
22. Priest GL (1993) The Origins of Utility Regulation and the 'Theories of Regulation' Debate. Journal of Law and Economics 36(1):289-323
23. Riordan MH, Williamson OE (1985) Asset Specificity and Economic Organization. In ternational Journal of Industrial Organization 3:365-378
24. Williamson OE (1975) Markets and Hierarchies-Analysis and Antitrust Implications. The Free Press, New York

25. Williamson OE (1976) Franchise Bidding for Natural Monopolies-in General and with Respect to CATV. Bell Journal of Economics 7(1):73-104
26. Williamson OE (1985) The Economic Institutions of Capitalism. The Free Press, New York
27. Wolmar C (2000) Creating the Passenger Rail Franchises. In Freeman R, Shaw J (eds.) British Railway Privatisation. McGraw-Hill, Maidenhead, pp 119-145

Part D:

Knowledge and Strategic Management Issues

Understanding Exploration and Exploitation in Franchising and Other Forms of Commercial Cooperation

Evelien Croonen

University of Groningen
Faculty of Management and Organization,
P.O. Box 800
9700 AV Groningen
The Netherlands
e.p.m.croonen@bdk.rug.nl

Abstract. The objective of this paper is to present and illustrate a framework for understanding how and why franchise partners and partners in other forms of commercial cooperation deal with the paradox of exploration and exploitation in their relationships through time. Two levels of analysis are distinguished: the level of strategic characteristics of the franchise system and the level of relationships between the franchisor and the franchisees that are part of the franchise system. For the level of the system, it is argued that franchise systems, as any other organizational form, have to balance exploration and exploitation in order to survive and prosper in their environment. The following five strategic characteristics of franchise systems reflect the franchisor's exploration and exploitation objectives: the positioning of the franchise system, the "hardness" of the franchise system, the system's entrepreneurial orientation, the degree of strategic participation of franchisees in the system and growth objectives for the system. On the relationship level, the franchise relationship between the franchisor and its franchisees is considered a specific form of strategic alliance. The following variables are distinguished for understanding both franchise partner's response strategies towards each other: the degree of strategic compatibility between the franchise partners (depending on the above five system's characteristics), the degree of operational compatibility, the evaluation of available alternatives, and switching costs. Both franchise partners' response strategies can vary according to two dimensions: constructive versus destructive and active versus passive.

Acknowledgements. The author would like to thank Prof. Dr. D. Jacobs, Prof. Dr. Mr. E.M. Kneppers-Heijnert and Dr. M.J. Brand for their helpful comments and suggestions.

1 Introduction

The objective of this paper is to present and illustrate a framework for understanding how and why franchise partners and partners in other forms of commercial cooperation deal with the paradox of exploration and exploitation in their relationships through time. As pointed out by Tuunanen and Hyrsky (2001), franchisors and franchisees have to deal with several ambiguities and contradictions in their relationships. This paper focuses on ambiguities and contradictions in franchise relationships that relate to March's paradox of exploration and exploitation (March 1991).

Although different forms of commercial cooperation can be distinguished, one common characteristic of commercial cooperation is that the business owners participating in the cooperation remain independent business owners. They run their businesses at their own risks and retain the rights to the establishment's earnings (Rubin 1978). The forms of commercial cooperation vary from loose to tight. For example, some looser forms only focus on joint purchasing, while other forms not only purchase together but also have a joint marketing strategy. In the tightest form of commercial cooperation, business format franchising, a franchisor provides a proven method of operating (the "business format") and support to its franchisees. In business format franchising the business format is central: the franchisee is an independent business owner that becomes part of a "franchise system" with a certain uniform identity towards customers. This franchise system consists of the franchisor, its franchised units, and sometimes also the franchisor-owned units that all operate under the same business format (also see Fig. 1).

Ideally, all these units of the franchise system operate under the same business format with a uniform presentation towards customers. This sharing of a common identity sends a message to customers, so customers know what to expect when they visit a unit of a certain system. For example, customers generally know what to expect when visiting a McDonald's restaurant (Kneppers-Heijnert 1988). This relates to another important aspect of business format franchising. The franchisor supervises the use of the business format by the franchisees in the system in order to enhance this uniform presentation towards customers and to preserve a uniform quality of the provided goods and/or services to customers (Kneppers-Heijnert 1988).

The framework in this paper focuses on business format franchising and franchise-related forms of commercial cooperation because these entail closer relationships between the partners, which are more interesting from a strategic point of view. The illustrations in this paper are based on a Dutch drugstore system (the DA-system) that through time has become a tight form of cooperation. In 1942, the DA-system started as a loose form of cooperation between five druggists that wanted to purchase together. Through time, the group of DA-druggists became larger and larger, and their cooperation became tighter. Before 1992, the druggists from the DA-system operated under the DA-name, they jointly purchased goods and did some promotion activities together with the support of a central organization (the Druggists Association). However, after a process of complex changes at this central organization, in 1992, a new organization called Dynaretail BV which would perform the retailing and supporting activities for the DA-participants in a more centralized and structured manner. In short, from 1992 Dynaretail wanted to make some changes to the DA-system, which would result in several destructive response strategies of the DA-participants (and about 100 of 1000 DA-druggists stepping out of the DA-system). The illustrations in this paper are based on this change process that occurred in the beginning of the 90's. Currently, Dynaretail no longer exists because in 2000 Dynaretail BV merged with the wholesaler Dynadro BV to become the new organization Dynadro BV. Since 2000, the new Dynadro BV has been the central organization that administers the DA-system.

Although this paper takes into account other forms of commercial cooperation that do not classify themselves as franchising (such as the DA-system), for the sake of readability the term "franchisor" is used to indicate the organization that administers a certain business format and the term "franchisee" is used to indicate business owners that are part of the system operating under the business format.

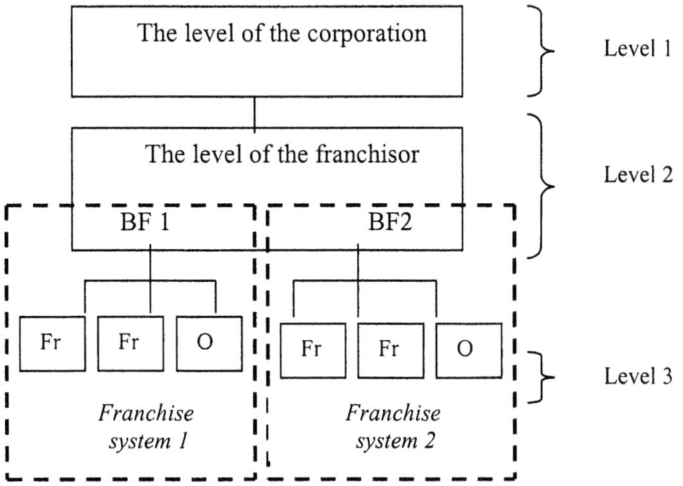

Fig. 1. Different Levels of Analysis in Franchising

Three possible levels of analysis can be distinguished in franchising:

- Level 1 is the level of the corporation. This level is distinguished because a franchisor can in itself be part of a larger corporation. Level 1 is not explicitly taken into account in this paper, but it is recognized that it is part of the context of franchise relationships and can therefore influence strategic interactions between the franchisor and its franchisees in the franchise system.
- Level 2 is the level of the franchisor. A franchisor can administer one or more different business formats. These are the BFs in Fig.1. As argued

earlier, around each business format there is a "franchise system" (indicated by the dashed lines in Fig. 1) that consists of the franchisor, its franchised units, and sometimes also the franchisor's company-owned units. In Fig.1 the franchised units are indicated with FR, and O indicates the company-owned units in the system. Fig. 1 shows a franchisor that administers two franchise systems. The framework presented in this paper distinguishes five strategic characteristics of franchise systems. These characteristics are discussed in section 3.

- Level 3 is the level of the franchisees that are part of the franchise system. The framework presented in this paper focuses on the relationships between the franchisor (level 2) and the franchisees (level 3) within a franchise system. On this relationship level, the framework includes the response strategies of both franchise partners that are influenced by the strategic compatibility, operational compatibility, availability and attractiveness of alternatives, and the costs of switching to these alternatives. These variables are discussed in section 3.

In summary, the framework presented in this paper focuses on the level of the franchise system. First, the framework distinguishes five strategic characteristics of franchise systems. Second, the framework focuses on the relationships between the franchisor that administers the system and the franchisees that are part of this system.

This paper aims to overcome several limitations of franchising research by viewing franchise relationships as a specific form of alliance in which *both* franchisor and franchisee are "intelligent" partners that interact and adjust to each other through time. The franchise relationship is still too often seen as a static, top-down relationship in which the focus is on efficiency-aspects, such as monitoring and control of franchisees. However, it is argued here that franchise systems and the relationships within them have to deal with March's (1991) paradox of exploitation and exploration in organizational adaptation. According to March, exploitation includes aspects such as refinement, choice, production, efficiency, selection, implementation, and execution. Exploration includes issues such as search, variation, risk-taking, experimentation, play, flexibility, discovery, and innovation. March argues that firms must try to find an appropriate balance between exploitation and exploration in order to survive and prosper in their environment. However, there has been little attention to the way franchise partners in franchise systems deal with this paradox of exploitation and exploration.

In summary, the framework presented in this paper distinguishes five strategic characteristics of franchise systems that reflect different types of exploration and exploitation. These are the positioning of the system in the market, the degree of "hardness" of the system, the system's entrepreneurial orientation, the room for strategic participation of franchisees in the system and the system's growth objectives. These characteristics influence the degree of strategic compatibility between franchise partners: the franchisor of a certain franchise system and a specific franchisee that is part of this system. Next to this strategic compatibility, the partners' operational compatibility, available alternatives and switching costs influence both franchise partners' response strategies towards each other in the relationship.

2 Theoretical Backgrounds

For some researchers (and also some practitioners), franchising at the level of the franchisee is the anti-thesis of strategy and entrepreneurship because the franchisee operates under the established business format of its franchisor and has little influence on strategic decision-making with respect to the franchise system. This idea has often led to too simplifying assumptions in franchising research. The framework discussed in this paper aims to provide a less simplistic understanding of franchise relationships as a specific form of alliance. This section briefly discusses the three most important limitations of current alliance and franchising research.

The first limitation of current alliance and franchise research refers to the use of single-faceted perspectives instead of multi-faceted perspectives. Osborn and Hagedoorn (1997) point out that several perspectives have been adopted to understand the formation, evolution, operation and outcomes of different forms of alliances. Each of these perspectives has its own strengths and limitations. Franchise relationships are often studied from a resource-based or an agency perspective (cf. Carney and Gedajlovic 1991). From a resource-based perspective, the franchisee is seen as a source of capital and labor for the franchisor. From an agency perspective, franchising reduces agency costs because the franchisee owns specific assets (for example, store equipment that is specific to the business format) and will therefore be motivated to perform effectively within the franchise system. So, the franchise literature largely focuses on March's "exploitative" aspects such as efficiency, monitoring and control of franchisees, and not on March's "explorative" aspects such as innovation, play and search within the franchise system (March 1991). However, according to many authors, in today's environment of rapid technological and market changes, shortening product life cycles and changing customer tastes, the strategic management of innovation has become more important (Stanworth et al. 1996). Moreover, Jacobs (1999) points out that the traditional forms of innovation -product innovation and process innovation- have become more and more intertwined and have gained new meanings. So, product innovation not only refers to new products; it also concerns new business concepts or formats (like McDonald's or Benetton). It was already argued that the business format or shared identity is central to business format franchise relationships. However, such a standardized and uniform identity may seem inappropriate in the current environment with rapid technological and market changes, shortening product (and concept!) life cycles, and changing customers' tastes. Therefore, it is surprising that only few researchers explicitly refer to this paradox of exploitation *and* exploration in franchise systems. In section 3, it is argued that franchisors and franchisees have to deal with different types of exploration *and* exploitation in the franchise system. By studying both explorative and exploitative aspects a multifaceted perspective of franchise relationships is adopted.

The second limitation of alliance and franchise research refers to the assumption of alliance and franchise relationships as static relationships instead of dynamic relationships. Next to a focus on "exploitative" aspects of franchise relationships, the use of certain perspectives has probably also caused a focus on "static" aspects of franchising. In alliance research in general, there is also lack of research in the "dynamics" or processes of alliances (Ring and Van de Ven 1994). However, processes in alliances influence the partner's perceptions of the alliance and their motivation to continue or terminate the relationship over time. Also, with respect to franchise relationships, Elango and Fried (1997) acknowledge that there is lack of research in the "dynamics" of franchise relationships. Franchising researchers often focus on one important governance decision for franchisors: the share of company-owned and franchised units in their franchise systems. However, there has been little attention for the way franchise partners interact and respond to each other in a dynamic environment. Through time the needs and offers of the franchise partners can change and may change the partner's motivations to continue or to break up the franchising relationship, which is reflected in their response strategies towards each other.

The third and final limitation of franchise research refers to the assumption of the franchise relationship as a top-down relationship instead of a two-sided relationship. As already argued, for some people (both researchers and practitioners), franchising is the antithesis of entrepreneurship and strategic thinking. Some authors even refer to the franchisee as a "strategic non-entity" because the franchisee has no influence on strategic planning and decision-making within the franchise system (e.g. English 1993). In the literature, the franchise relationship is often viewed as a top-down relationship in which the franchisor has all the influence. Therefore, Elango and Fried (1997) propose to view the franchisee more as an "intelligent player" with its own specific contributions and needs in the franchising relationship. Also, Hoy and Shane (1998), Bradach (1998) and Sorenson and Sørensen (2001) argue that many franchisors rely on franchisee experimentation to generate the innovations that keep their organizations healthy and competitive. Or put differently, also the franchisee can contribute to renewal or exploration in the franchise system.

3 A Framework for Understanding Exploration and Exploitation in Franchise Relationships

In order to gain a better understanding of how franchise partners deal with the paradox of exploitation and exploration in franchise relationships, a general framework for understanding the dynamics of strategic alliances was first developed. Fig. 2 presents this framework between partner X and partner Y from the perspective of X. This model was developed based on a literature review of alliance and franchising research and exploratory interviews with franchisors and franchisees in different branches of industry (and especially the Dutch drugstore sector).

Nooteboom's model (1999) of strategic alliances served as an initial starting point for developing the framework presented in this paper. Nooteboom's model is a very general model for alliances, and it was adapted to franchise relationships between the franchisor and its franchisees. It synthesizes a resource-based perspective, a transaction cost perspective, a game perspective, a social exchange perspective and a perspective of learning and knowledge. It offers a more integrated perspective on franchise relationships and takes into account the growing importance of learning, trust and building competencies in the rapidly changing business environment. Another strength of the model is that both partners in the alliance are viewed as "intelligent" partners that can influence the development of the alliance. So, the model pays attention to the influencing role franchisees can play in franchise relationships and franchise systems. Finally, the model takes a dynamic perspective because it takes into account issues of learning en the possibilities of partner's response strategies towards each other.

The framework presented in this paper includes the following variables from the perspective of partner X (see Fig. 2): strategic compatibility with partner Y in the eyes of X, operational compatibility with Y in the eyes of X, available alternatives for Y in the eyes of X, and X's perception of costs of switching to these alternatives. These variables influence the response strategies of X with respect to Y. The model can be reversed in the sense that Y will also evaluate the strategic and operational compatibility, will perceive certain switching costs, and therefore will adopt a certain response strategy towards partner X.

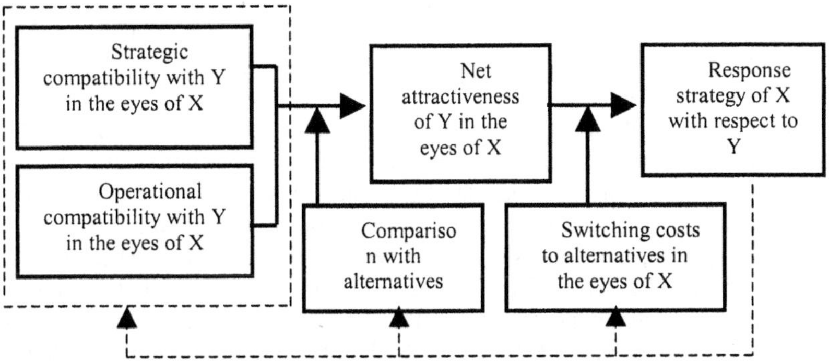

Fig. 2. A Framework for Understanding the Dynamics of Alliances in General

Authors often distinguish two factors that determine the evolution or dynamics of cooperative relationships or alliances: the "strategic compatibility" of the partners and the "operational compatibility" of the partners (for example Niederkofler 1991, Medcof 1997, Doz and Hamel 1998). However, strategic and operational compatibility are defined in different ways. According to Niederkofler "strategic compatibility" refers to the question: "Should we cooperate?" With respect to strategic compatibility, Koza and Lewin (1998 and 2000) bring all alliance objectives back to two basic logics (or "strategic intents") for entering into alliances: an "exploitation" intent and an "exploration intent" (they do this based on March 1991). They argue that, for most types of alliances, an asymmetry or incompatibility of strategic intents of the partners may lead to certain response strategies of the partners in the relationship.

Although Koza and Lewin (1998 and 2000) distinguish between an "exploration intent" and "exploitation intent" of strategic alliances in general, only few researchers have studied the paradox of exploitation and exploration for franchise relationships as specific alliance form. Exceptions are Winter and Szulanski (2001) and Sorenson and Sørensen (2001). These authors have directly referred to this paradox by acknowledging that franchise systems must try to balance exploration and exploitation. Sorenson and Sørensen (2001) argue that franchised units and company-owned units offer different benefits for systems concerning their exploitation and exploration objectives. For a large part, they base their arguments on Bradach (1998) who has studied the benefits of the "plural form" for franchisors. This "plural form" refers to a franchise system in which both company-owned and franchised units are present. According to Bradach (1998) the plural form provides a context for franchisors in which both self-correction or control (exploitation) and self-renewal or innovation (exploration) are supported. Both Bradach and Sorenson and Sørensen argue that company-owned units enhance exploitation, while franchised units enhance exploration (although Bradach does not explicitly refer to these terms). According to them, company managers are monitored more extensively, and their evaluations are often based on observable outcomes such as unit sales. This encourages "exploitative" behavior (improvement of existing routines) of company managers. On the other hand, franchisee behavior is monitored less stringently and less systematically, which encourages "explorative" behavior of franchisees. However, the authors do not consider differences between different types of franchisees, while franchisees in a franchise system can differ in their exploration intents.

March's definition of exploitation and exploration is narrowed down by relating this paradox to he central element of franchise relationships: the system's business format with a certain identity towards customers. The framework in this paper distinguishes different types of exploration and exploitation within the franchise system, and this is mainly based on Bradach's (1998) paradox of self-correction and self-renewal in franchise systems. He argues that franchisors face four primary challenges in the management of their franchise systems: maintaining uniformity of the shared identity across the units of the system, allowing for local responsiveness by units of the system, making adaptations to the identity for the system as a whole, and adding units to the system. These challenges were used as an initial starting point for the development of the five system characteristics of the framework. Some adaptations have been made to Bradach's challenges, and two characteristics have been added: the positioning of the system in the market and the room for strategic participation of franchisees. In the remainder of this section, these adaptations are discussed and the meaning of each of the following five characteristics 1) the positioning of the system 2) the degree of hardness of the system, 3) the system's entrepreneurial orientation, 4) the room for strategic participation of franchisees, 5) growth objectives of the system. These five characteristics are presented in Fig. 3. Note that these characteristics are on the level of a specific franchise system because one franchisor can administer different franchise systems that differ with respect to these characteristics. It is argued that these five strategic characteristics influence both franchise partner's perceptions of strategic compatibility and therefore their response strategies (exit, voice, loyalty and neglect) towards each other in the relationship.

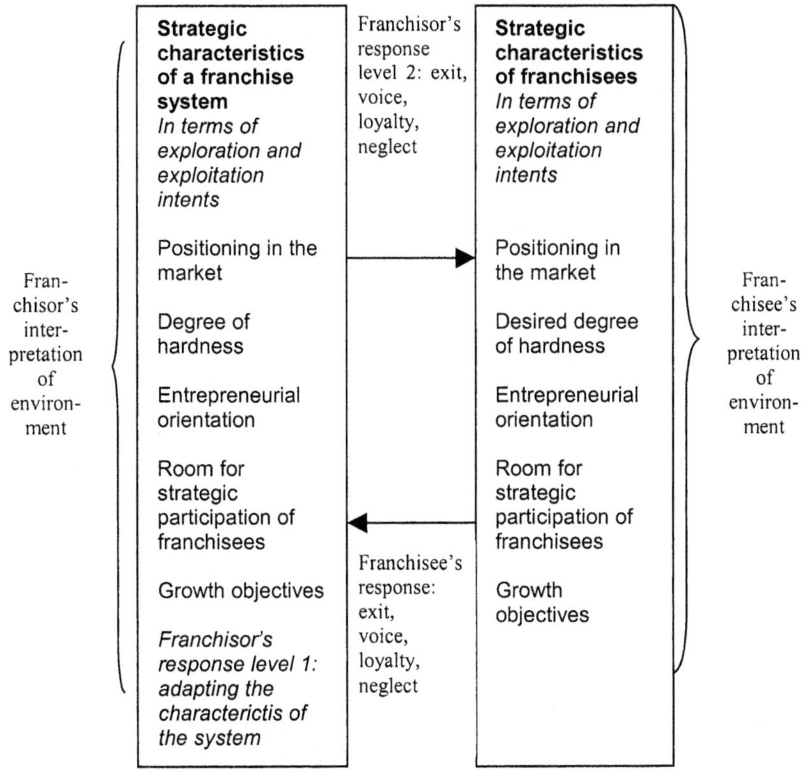

Fig. 3. Five Strategic Characteristics that Influence the Degree of Strategic Compatibility of the Franchisor and Its Franchisees

3.1 Strategic Compatibility Between the Franchise Partners

As argued above, the strategic compatibility between the franchise partners is influenced by five characteristics. The first characteristic is the positioning of the system towards customers and competitors in the market. Sullivan and Adcock (2002) distinguish two forms of positioning for single retail stores or a group of stores (like a franchise system). An important strategic decision for organizations is whether to position themselves as a high-quality, high-price company (high in the market) or to have a "pile it high, sell it cheap" positioning with relatively lower quality and lower prices (low in the market). These two forms each have their own characteristics concerning different aspects of the business format, such as the composition of the assortment, the degree of service, price level, store interior, store exterior, and promotion activities. This relates to Porter's (1980) distinction between cost leadership (competing on low cost and price) and differentiation (adding extra value to products and services). The term "differentiation" encompasses various dimensions firms can compete on. Firms must try to find out what dimensions are important for their customers and compete accordingly. Usually, customers do not buy products based on only one dimension, and firms must combine several dimensions in order to attract customers. The business format reflects those dimensions, and units from the franchise system in turn reflect these dimensions in their shared identity.

DA-illustration for positioning of the system

In the beginning of the 90's, Dynaretail (the central organization for the DA-system) perceived a lot of competition from large discounting drugstore chains. Customer research had shown that customers perceived DA's identity as expensive. Dynaretail wanted to give the DA-system a less expensive identity. So, Dynaretail advised the DA-participants to adapt their assortment, store interior and exterior, and Dynaretail introduced price promotion activities. However, several DA-participants did not agree with this change in positioning. For example, through time the DA-druggists had exchanged low-margin product groups (like diapers and baby food) in their assortment for high margin product groups (like perfumes), and Dynaretail wanted to re-introduce these product groups in the assortment of the DA-participants. Another example was the change from carpet to tiled pavements in the stores. The discounting chains all used these tiled pavements, and Dynaretail thought it would help in giving the DA-stores a cheaper presentation towards customers. However, several DA-druggists resisted because they felt it did not fit in their drugstore. Moreover, it would take investments to renovate their stores.

The second system characteristic that influences strategic compatibility between the franchise partners refers to the degree of hardness of the franchise system. It has already been argued that the business format is the central element of a franchise system. The challenge of maintaining uniformity therefore means preserving the shared identity of the units belonging to a certain franchise system. In business format franchising this means that every aspect of a unit's operation should be uniform. Although, ideally, the business format is uniform across all units of a franchise system, the system's units operate in diverse local markets with different environmental circumstances. For example, different units may face different customer tastes, or competitive circumstances demanding different strategies (competition by means of price or service/differentiation). So, although they are part of a shared identity, units need to respond locally in order to survive in their local circumstances. Bradach (1998) points out that finding a balance between maintaining uniformity and adapting locally is an important management challenge for franchisors. In general, this is a well-known paradox in the franchising literature (cf. Kaufmann and Eroglu 1998, Dant and Gundlach 1998,

Stanworth et al.1996). In the framework presented in this paper, part of the strategic compatibility in the eyes of franchisees is defined as the difference between the franchisee's intention to adapt the business format to its own local circumstances (in whatever way), and its perceived room for doing this. In some cases strategic incompatibility between the franchise partners can arise, resulting in specific response strategies of the partners.

DA-illustration for degree of hardness of the system

Dynaretail thought the drugstores of the DA-system were too diverse and therefore did not have a uniform identity towards customers. Before the change process in the beginning of the 90's, the DA-participantss had few obligations. In order to emphasize its renewed positioning, Dynaretail wanted to increase the uniformity of the DA-drugstores towards customers. At that time, an important change for the DA-participants was the introduction of "shelf designs" in which the composition of a large part of the assortment was prescribed. Dynaretail had developed these shelf designs in cooperation with its suppliers. Because of their large group of druggists, Dynaretail could give its suppliers guarantees that it would purchase a certain quantity of goods, and thanks to these guarantees Dynaretail could negotiate attractive purchasing prices. The goods of this basic assortment were obligatory for the DA-participants and were automatically sent to the DA-participants, which led many of them to feel as though they had lost their autonomy.

The third system characteristic that influences strategic compatibility between the franchise partners refers to entrepreneurial orientation. A strength of Bradach's research is that he acknowledges that threats and opportunities can arise locally or for the system as a whole. According to Bradach (1998), threats or opportunities sometimes arise for a system as a whole that need to be translated into changes in the business format for the whole franchise system. These changes constitute, for example, the introduction of a new product group in the assortment or new procedures. So, when threats and opportunities arise, franchisors and franchisees need to decide how to react to these. Moreover, franchisors may differ in their ideas about upgrading the business format for the system as a whole. Falbe et al. (1998) refer to this by the term "entrepreneurial orientation" of a franchise system, and distinguish four dimensions of entrepreneurial orientation: the propensity to undertake risk, proactiveness, competitive aggressiveness, and the capacity for adaptation and renewal of the system.

Some franchisors may have a higher entrepreneurial orientation, while others are more "conservative" and will adapt their system less quickly when threats or opportunities arise. This can be a source of strategic incompatibility in the eyes of the franchise partners, and therefore it can cause specific response strategies.

DA-illustration for entrepreneurial orientation

Dynaretail's customer research showed that the customers often saw the DA-stores as "dusty" and "not active". According to Dynaretail, DA-participants were not very entrepreneurial in their markets (in terms of taking risks or experimenting), Dynaretail thought that increasing competition required DA-participants to be more active in their promotions and to adapt their stores to the changing circumstances. According to

Dynaretail, one cause for this lack of entrepreneurial orientation was the fact that the druggists saw themselves as "semi-doctors" who regarded the use of price promotions as embarrassing. In addition, according to several DA-participants these price promotions resulted in lower margins, which resulted in a lot of resistance. However, Dynaretail argued that the lower prices resulted in more customers and an overall profit for the DA-participants that stayed the same or even grew.

The fourth system characteristic that influences the franchise partners' degree of strategic compatibility is based on Weima (1974). Bradach (1998) does not explicitly take into account the degree of involving franchisees in decisions about the system. Bradach briefly mentions this but he does not refer to it as a specific management challenge for franchisors. In a harder system franchisees have little room for local exploration, but they can be involved in the franchisor's decision-making concerning the franchise system by means of franchisee associations or working groups of franchisees. According to Weima (1974), franchisees in the United States have put pressure on their franchisors by means of individual or collective actions (for example in undertaking a lawsuit against the franchisor). Furthermore, Weima points out that franchisees who felt uncomfortable with the influence of the franchisor have united in associations for franchisees of the same system or associations for franchisees in general. At the time of Weima's book, franchisees were not organized very much on the system level, but rather on the national level. Nowadays, these system-level associations are more common. With respect to the degree of strategic participation of franchisees in a certain system the following aspects are important: the existence of an association of franchisees for the system, the existence of other working groups of franchisees in the system, the role and influence of these association and other groups within the system.

DA-illustration for the degree of strategic participation of franchisees

In an attempt to convince the DA participants of the need for the change process and to increase the bonding with them, Dynaretail established three "boards of participants": the assortment board, the operations board, and the board for formula management. In this way Dynaretail at least had contact with 54 DA-participants, who they tried to convince of the need for change. According to the former formula manager, who was in charge of the change process, this has taken Dynaretail many years due to too little knowledge at the level of the druggists, and their denial of the need for change. Furthermore, according to him, the other DA-participants put pressure on these druggists not to agree with Dynaretail. On the other hand, several DA-participants felt that these boards did not really have influence and that the members of these boards only acted in their own interests.

The fifth system characteristic distinguished in this framework consists of the system's growth objectives. According to Bradach (1998) it is very difficult to boost the sales of existing units beyond a certain threshold. Therefore, franchisors rely heavily on growth by means of adding new units to the system. The fast-food systems that Bradach (1998) studied often used existing franchisees to add a large number of units to the system. This is called "multi-unit franchising". For the franchisor the "economics" are the same as for adding new franchisees: for each new unit the franchisor receives franchise fees and royalties. One important advantage of multi-unit franchising is the smaller risk that the franchisee is a "problematic franchisee" because the franchisor already has a relationship with the franchisee. Or in other words, problems and risks of franchisee selection become smaller in multi-unit franchising, and this results in lower transaction costs.

Next to the franchisor, franchisees can also have growth objectives, and may want to purchase additional units. In Bradach's research (1998) most franchisees of American fast-food chains were motivated to grow by means of adding additional units because the possibility of growth by means of their existing units was limited. However, some franchisors do not prefer franchisees to purchase additional units, while others stimulate it. Some franchisees in the system might have growth objectives while others do not. A difference in growth objectives can cause strategic incompatibility between a franchisor and a franchisee and can therefore result in destructive response strategies.

DA-illustration for growth objectives

The DA-system had many stores, but some stores were too small to meet the increased requirements (delivery of goods, promotion activities, etc). Before the change process, the stores had an average floor area of 117 m², with most stores having a floor area between 51 and 150 m². According to Dynaretail, the average floor area needed to increase and some druggists were asked to relocate to locations with a larger floor area or to expand their current locations. Dynaretail thought it could be more powerful with a smaller group of larger participants than with a large group of smaller participants. This also led to some destructive responses because this different format required investments from the DA-druggists.

3.2 Operational Compatibility of the Franchise Partners

With respect to operational compatibility in an alliance, the question is "Can we make it work?" (Niederkofler 1991). Operational compatibility addresses the ways and means in which the relationship can be implemented in a mutually beneficial way. Medcof (1997) distinguishes four factors (the four C's) which influence the operational fit between two alliance partners: capability, compatibility, commitment and control. These factors have been adapted based on a literature review and exploratory interviews, which have resulted in two factors that influence the operational compatibility of partner Y with X in the eyes of X in the framework: capability of Y in the eyes of X and solidarity of Y in the eyes of X.

The first factor is partner Y's capability of carrying out its role in the alliance in the eyes of X. For the franchisees these capabilities refer to the franchisor's capabilities in the management of the franchise system. The important capabilities of the franchisor are, support, automation, logistics, communication, and the provision of information, and the ability to protect the business format.

Secondly, the framework focuses on "solidarity". This consists of the following two elements. First, the degree of "trust" of partner X towards Y. This means that partner X believes that his partner Y is likely to cooperate even if he is not coerced into doing so and has no direct material interest (Nooteboom 1999). The second element of solidarity refers to what Ring and Van de Ven (1994) call "fair dealing". This does not require inputs or outcomes to be equally divided between the partners, but it means that partner X perceives receiving benefits that are proportional to its investments in the relationship with Y.

DA-illustration with respect to operational compatibility

One druggist implicitly referred to the fair dealing principle: "Ideally, in cooperation 1 and 1 is 3. But what is even more important is that 3 divided by 2 is 1,5! This is where the problems start. Entrepreneurs and central organizations start cooperating because each of them has certain competencies, and together they have more than they would have had separately. However, sometimes they can get into a fight because one partner may find its tasks more important than the tasks of its partner and wants a larger share of the benefits. But I think the central organization and its participants need each other, so each should get 1,5".

3.3 The Availability of Alternatives

The availability of alternatives is part of an often-used construct in the alliance literature, namely dependence. Emerson (1962) defines dependence as being a function of, 1) the attractiveness of the present relationship, and 2) the availability of alternatives. The attractiveness of the present relationship is reflected in the sum of strategic and operational compatibility in our framework. The higher the strategic and operational compatibility in the eyes of the partners, the more it is expected that they are inclined to continue and cooperate in the relationship. However, the availability and attractiveness of alternatives is also important in understanding the behaviors of alliance partners. A partner in an unattractive relationship will probably sooner switch to an alternative when there is an attractive alternative available. So, in summary, the net attractiveness of the current relationship with Y from the perspective of X depends on three factors: the attractiveness of the current relationship with Y in the eyes of X, the availability of alternatives for Y in the eyes of X, and the attractiveness of these alternatives in the eyes of X.

In the eyes of the franchisor, alternatives for a specific franchisee are either another franchisee or a company-owned unit. For the franchisee alternatives are: becoming a franchisee of another system (in the same or a different industry sector), starting a new business without being part of a franchise system or becoming a salaried employee.

DA-illustration with respect to alternatives

Of course, competitors knew about the changes in the DA-system in the beginning of the 90's and the discontent of several DA-participants. A lot of DA-participants received offers by other systems for selling their stores. Additionally, several other wholesalers started their own systems during the 90's. These forms had relatively few obligations for its participants, which attracted many DA-druggists.

3.4 Switching Costs of the Partners

In the case of problems or changes in the relationship, partners must decide what response strategies to adopt towards each other. However, in this decision they will also take into account the costs of switching to the next best alternative (Nooteboom 1999). Or in other words, they will take into account certain "barriers" for exiting the relationship. First, switching costs of the franchise partners towards each other increase with their investments in specific assets. For example, with respect to franchisees, Dnes (1992) argues that franchisees have to deal with greater asset specificity than completely independent business owners. At the start of the relationship franchisees often pay a lump sum and invest in equipping their businesses. The business format entails certain distinguishable (and therefore specific) assets in which the franchisee must invest by virtue of the franchise contract. These assets are then specific to the business format and are therefore useless in other situations (Dnes 1992). Therefore, these specific investments contribute to the franchisee's switching costs unless the franchisee can sell the specific investments back to the franchisor or to a new franchisee.

Furthermore, the perceived switching costs of the franchise partners increase with "hostages" and guarantees provided in the relationship. Hostages only have value to the giver and not to the keeper, so that the keeper is not tempted to keep the hostage even if the agreement is honored. According to Nooteboom (1999), hostages can take the form of people, information, knowledge or technology. An example of a hostage provided to the franchisee by the franchisor may be knowledge of the contents of the business format (often established in a manual with detailed procedures etc.). Also, guarantees can take several forms, for example a minimum duration of the relationship or a minimum volume of transactions. These guarantees, often provided in the contract, make sure that franchisees can recoup their specific investments. The duration of the franchise relationship is established in the contract and also provides a guarantee for both partners to recoup their investments. Another guarantee is, for example, the exclusive territory in which the franchisee is allowed to operate without the interference of franchisees from the same system or of the franchisor itself.

Finally, another variable that influences each franchise partner's switching costs is its income resulting from the relationship as a percentage of its total income. In most cases, the franchisee owns one or more units of one system and has relationships with only one franchisor; in this case the franchisee's income from the relationship equals its total income. However, in some cases franchisees have relationships with different franchisors, which means that their total income is spread across different franchisors.

3.5 Response Strategies of the Partners

The franchisor can respond on two levels; these are called these level 1 and level 2 (see Fig. 3). On level 1, the franchisor can respond by adapting one or more strategic characteristics of the system (for example the positioning or the hardness) or starting a new system or quitting with a system. However, as mentioned above, some decisions may be made on the level of the corporation, and the franchisor itself may then have little influence on decision-making. For example, the decision to start with another system can be taken at the level of the corporation. In order not to complicate things further, these decisions are considered part of the context and the framework focuses on how franchisors and franchisees on the relationship level deal with each other given these decisions.

On the relationship level, both franchisor and franchisee can adopt specific response strategies towards each other. For the franchisor this is a level 2 response (see Fig. 3), and for the franchisee this is the only level to respond to the franchisor. In the literature these strategies are often based on the work of Hirschman (1970), who made a distinction between two general options for dealing with problematic situations in firms, organizations and states: "exit" or "voice". The exit-option refers to ending the relationship, while the voice-option refers to actively expressing and discussing one's problems with the intent of trying to improve conditions. Hirschman argues that the presence of "loyalty" makes exit less likely. Loyalty refers to remaining silent and confident that the problematic conditions will get better by "giving things some time". Based on research on customer relationships, Ping (1993) adds a fourth option for dealing with relationship problems: neglect, which means passively allowing the relationship to deteriorate by "letting things fall apart". In a research on employer-employee relationships, Hagedoorn et al. (1999) argue that the category of voice responses is often considered too homogeneous and needs to be differentiated further. Therefore, they distinguish between a considerate voice and an aggressive voice strategy. The considerate voice strategy consists of attempts to solve the problem concerning one's own concerns as well as those of the other partner. The aggressive voice strategy is more destructive than the considerate voice strategy, but less destructive than the exit option. Using this strategy the partner wants to win, without considerations for the concerns of the other partner. This strategy can be seen as a "cry for attention" between a destructive and constructive response strategy. In summary, this results in the following five response strategies that (franchise) partners in a relationship can adopt: considerate voice, loyalty, neglect, aggressive voice and exit (see Fig.4).

It is emphasized here that partners in a relationship can perceive response strategies differently from how the other partner intended it. For example, partner X intends to actively construct the relationship, while his partner Y may perceive X's response strategy as a destructive strategy and react accordingly. Another important issue is that response strategies can go through certain phases. For example, in a relationship one partner may start with a constructive response, but it may find out that this does not work and turn to a more destructive response.

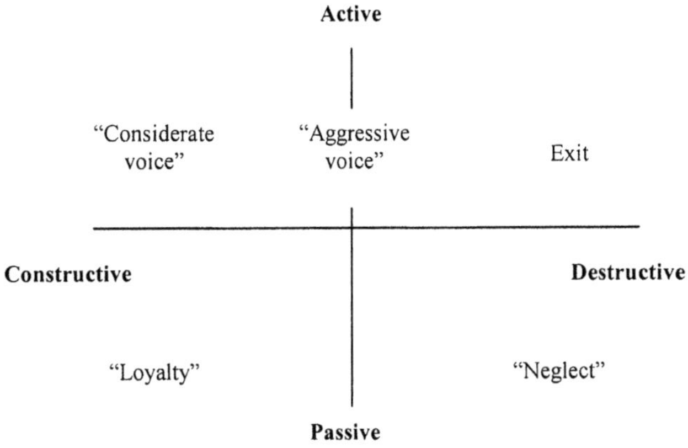

Fig. 4. Possible Response Strategies of Both Partners in the Relationship

DA-illustration for response strategies

The former formula manager of Dynaretail estimated the druggist's response strategies to the change process of the beginning of the 90's as follows:

- *"Considerate voice". This group consisted of 15 % of the DA participants, and they mainly took part in one of the three boards.*
- *"Loyalty". About 40% of the druggists have used this strategy; they were just waiting to see and assumed that things would turn out the right way.*
- *"Neglect". About 25 % of the druggists acted like this. At that time a lot of older druggists were part of this group. They were on the verge of retirement, and were unwilling to change their stores.*
- *"Aggressive voice". About 10% of the DA-druggists used this response strategy but did not leave the relationship in the end.*
- *"Exit" The most extreme form of active and destructive behavior is to leave the relationship. About 10% of the druggists actually did this as a response to the change process.*

4 Summary and Conclusions

This paper has presented a theoretical framework for understanding how franchise partners and partners in franchise-like forms of cooperation deal with the paradox of exploration and exploitation in their relationships through time. The framework fits into the increasing stream of research on dynamic phenomena, such as organizational learning, competitive interaction, innovation, strategic change and development. As was pointed out in this paper, in franchising research there is still a lack of research on franchising and franchise relationships as a dynamic phenomenon. As mentioned in section 2 of this paper, the theoretical relevance of the paper is threefold: First, the framework aims to provide a multifaceted understanding of franchise relationships by focusing on both exploitative *and* explorative aspects of franchise systems and relationships. Second, the framework considers alliances and franchise relationships as dynamic relationships instead of static relationships. Third, franchisors and franchisees are both seen as "intelligent players" that can contribute to exploration in the franchise system and that can adopt their own response strategies.

Further to the above theoretical relevance, the framework has a high practical and managerial relevance. First, it was already pointed out in this paper that in recent years the strategic management of innovation has become more important. This is not only true for the traditional forms of innovation, but also for new business formats or franchise systems. So, for franchisors the strategic management of innovation of their franchise systems has become more important. Or in other words, March's well-known paradox of exploration and exploitation has also become more visible for franchisors. In this paper, this paradox was explicitly translated to franchise systems in order to describe how franchisors in practice deal with this paradox. The framework described in this paper shows five strategic characteristics of franchise systems that franchisors should consider in the management of their systems.

Secondly, for franchisors it is important to be aware of the connection between the level of the franchise system and the level of the relationships with franchisees. It was argued that changes in the system characteristics can result in changes in the franchisees' perceptions of strategic compatibility, which in turn may result in specific response strategies adopted by the franchisee. So, when a franchisor introduces changes in the system characteristics it is possible that franchisees will adopt certain response strategies. For franchisors it is important to understand why franchisees adopt certain response strategies in the relationship. Especially franchisee's response strategies of aggressive voice, neglect and exit should be understood and managed well by the franchisor. If not managed well by the franchisor, franchisees adopting these strategies can harm the franchise system and/or franchisees can delay important change processes in franchise systems. As was pointed out in this paper, the factors that influence the franchisees' response strategies are the strategic compatibility, operational compatibility, the availability of alternatives and switching costs. These factors give the franchisor (or consultants) the opportunity to analyze and manage its franchise relationships with franchisees. On the other hand, for the franchisee these factors can also help in analyzing their own position in the relationship with the franchisor and to, therefore, react accordingly.

Third, the framework has a high practical relevance because according to Leunissen (1998), in recent years many looser forms of commercial cooperation have become tighter with more obligations on participants. The DA-illustration showed how Dynaretail wanted to introduce more obligations for its participants and how and why the DA participants responded to these changes. It is very likely that other initially looser forms of cooperation will have to deal with these problems when/if they want to tighten the cooperation with their participants.

The view of franchising as a more "dynamic" phenomenon also involves some requirements with respect to methodology. According to Langley (1999), research on dynamic phenomena has been approached in two ways. Some researchers have used coarse-grained research strategies in order to test a-priori formulated theories, while others have used fine-grained qualitative research strategies in an attempt to build theory. The current franchising literature is often based on coarse-grained approaches (Elango and Fried 1997). However, a lot of literature – including the franchising literature- calls for more in-depth process research that helps to understand organizational phenomena at more than a superficial level and over time. Fine grained case studies that include both the level of the franchise system and the franchise relationships within it can contribute highly to the understanding of how and why franchise partners and partners in franchise-like forms of cooperation deal with the paradox of exploration and exploitation.

References

1. Bradach, JL (1998) Franchise Organizations. Harvard Business School Press, Boston
2. Carney M, Gedajlovic E (1991) Vertical Integration in Franchise Systems: Agency Theory and Resource Explanations, Strategic Management Journal 12::607-629
3. Caves RE, Murphy WF (1976) Franchising: Firms, Markets and Intangible Assets. Southern Economic Journal 42:572-586
4. Dant RP, Gundlach GT (1998) The Challenge of Autonomy and Dependence in Franchised Channels of Distribution. Journal of Business Venturing 14, pp. 35-67
5. Dnes, AW (1992) "Unfair" Contractual Practices and Hostages in Franchise Contracts. Journal of Institutional and Theoretical Economics 148 (3):484-504
6. Doz YL, Hamel G (1998) Alliance Advantage: the Art of Creating Value through Partnering, Boston: Harvard Business School Press
7. Elango B.Fried VH (1997) Franchising research: a Literature Review and Synthesis. Journal of Small Business Management 35 (3):68-81
8. Emerson RM (1962) Power-Dependence Relations. American Sociological Review 27 February:31-41
9. English W (1993) Franchising, by its Proper Name is Wholesaling!, Journal of Marketing Channels 2 (3):1-26
10. Hagedoorn M.van Yperen NW van de Vliert E Buunk BP (1999) Employees' Reactions to Problematic Events: a Circumplex Structure of Five Categories of Responses, and the Role of Job Satisfaction. Journal of Organizational Behavior 20:309-321
11. Hirschman AO (1970) Voice and Loyalty: Responses to Decline in Firms, Organizations and States. Harvard University Press, Cambridge, MA
12. Hoy F. Shane S (1998) Franchising as an Entrepreneurial Venture Form. Journal of Business Venturing 13:91-94
13. Jacobs D (1999), Het Kennisoffensief: Slim Concurreren in de Kenniseconomie. Samson, Deventer/Alphen aan den Rijn
14. Kneppers-Heijnert EM (1988) Een economische en juridische analyse van franchising tegen de achtergrond van een property rights- en transactiekostenbenadering (proefschrift RuG), Van Denderen, Groningen
15. Koza MP Lewin AY (1998) The Co-evolution of Strategic Alliances. Organization Science 9 (3):255-264

16.Koza MP Lewin AY (2000) Managing Partnerships and Strategic Alliances: Raising the Odds of Success, European Management Journal 16 (2):146-151
17.Langley A. (1999) Strategies for Theorizing from Process Data. Academy of Management Review 24 (4): 691-710
18.Leunissen PJJ (1998) Feiten over franchising, Hoofdbedrijfsschap Detailhandel
19.March JG (1991) Exploration and Exploitation in Organizational Learning. Organization Science 2 (1):71-87
20.Medcof JW (1997) Why Too Many Alliances End in Divorce. Long Range Planning 30 (5):718-732
21.Niederkofler M (1991) The Evolution of Strategic Alliances: Opportunities for Managerial Influence. Journal of Business Venturing 6:237-257
22.Nooteboom B (1999) Inter-firm Alliances: Analysis and Design. Routledge, London
23.Osborn RN Hagedoorn J (1997) The Institutionalization and Evolutionary Dynamics of Inter-Organizational Alliances and Networks. Academy of Management Journal 40(2):261-278
24.Ping, RA (1993) The Effect of Satisfaction and Structural Constraints on Retailer Exiting, Voice, Loyalty, Opportunism, and Neglect. Journal of Retailing 69 (3):320-352
25.Porter ME (1980) Competitive Strategy. Free Press, New York
26.Ring PS van de Ven AH (1994) Developmental Processes of Cooperative Inter-organizational Relationships. Academy of Management Review 19(1):90-118
27.Rubin PH (1978) The Theory of the Firm and the Structure of the Franchise Contract. The Journal of Law and Economics:223-233
28.Sorenson O. Sørensen JB (2001) Research Note: Finding the Right Mix: Franchising, Organizational Learning, and Chain Performance. Strategic Management Journal 22:713-724
29.Stanworth J Price S, Purdy D Zafiris N Gandolfo A (1996) Business Format Franchising: Innovation and Creativity or Replication and Conformity?, Franchising Research: An International Journal 1(2):29-39
30.Sullivan M. Adcock D (2002) Retail Marketing. Thomson, London:
31.Tuunanen M. Hyrsky K (2001), Entrepreneurial Paradoxes in Business Format Franchising: an Empirical Survey of Finnish Franchisees. International Small Business Journal 19 (4):47-62
32.Vrolijk H (2002) Efficiënte contracten? Institutioneel-economische beschouwingen over franchising (Proefschrift KuN)
33.Weima W (1974) Franchising als samenwerkingsvorm tussen ondernemingen, Stenfert Kroese BV, Leiden
33.Winter SG Szulanski G (2001) Replication as Strategy. Organization Science 12(6):730-743

The Importance of Time Management for the Performance of Franchising Networks

Rozenn Perrigot, Gérard Cliquet

CREREG UMR CNRS 6585, Center for Research on Economics and Management, Institute of Management of Rennes (IGR-IAE), University of Rennes 1,
11 rue Jean Macé CS, 70803 Rennes Cedex 7, France
rozenn.perrigot@wanadoo.fr

Abstract. Network performance is very important, both for the franchisor who wants to promote his network and for the prospective franchisee who wants to invest in a store operated under a performing national or international brand name. Nevertheless, this network performance often presents some difficulties in being evaluated. Time management can appear consequently a good measure of the performance. This paper presents the importance of time management for the performance of franchising network, at both levels: for the franchisor and the franchisee. Some periods, such as network or store survival, must be maximized, whereas others, such as durations before internationalization, must be minimized. The difficulties linked to longitudinal studies are also reminded and a particularly adequate methodology is recommended: the survival analysis.

1 Introduction

Retailing and service stores are increasingly more organized within networks in an increasing number of sectors and countries. Through the network organization, they can expand better and react to competitors. In this environment, characterized by wide competition, the notion of network performance is very important, both for the franchisor who wants to promote his network and for the prospective franchisees who want to invest in a store operated under a performing national or international brand name. Nevertheless, this network performance often presents a few difficulties which need to be evaluated. On the one hand, at the practitioner level, do all franchisees mention the true results? Or, do all franchisors declare the true possible results when they try to attract new franchisees? It must not be forgotten that the franchisee remains an independent retailer, and sometimes, he need only show the results that he wants. Moreover, showing a good performance is in the franchisor's interest in order to attract and recruit new franchisees. On the other hand, at the researcher level, the performance does not present one best way to be evaluated. Indeed, several criteria can reflect network performance: productivity, effectiveness, efficiency, etc. The problem raised by these measures is the data availability, objectiveness and reliability. In order to overcome this difficulty, a performance criterion appears very interesting: the notion of time management. In fact, for instance, anyone can observe, measure and understand the survival period of a network or a store, the duration before internationalization or before franchising. Time management remains a difficult task for the practitioners. Perhaps this comes from the fact that it can be influenced not only by controllable factors but also by environmental ones. However, it constitutes an important element of the performance and must be taken into account by the franchising actors.

For example, many consulting guides try to present the best options to ensure a good retail survival. For instance, 50 strategies, tips and secrets for a retail survival can be found on the internet (retail survival guide on internet). It deals with daily valuable tips to help a store to stay competitive such as: "The purpose of a sign is service to the customer. Are you giving your customers the service they demand?" "Don't lie. Write facts, not fiction. 'Amazing' is overused." This every day advice is helpful but are there further determinants of survival? The concept of survival is central to the franchising topics and can be studied in various ways: survival of a network, survival of a store within a network, survival of a contract between franchisor and franchisees, i.e. franchisee turnover, etc (Perrigot et al. 2004).

The term "survival" implies, of course, the notion of time, of duration. Time, like location, is really a main task for the retailers. A good location is very important but a good management of time is also essential. Some relevant durations can be therefore analyzed: the durations before internationalization, before franchising, before location, before franchisee choice, etc.

This paper tries to expose the importance of time management for the performance of franchising networks, both at the franchisor and the franchisees levels. Section 2 presents some measures of network performance and the possible use of time such as a performance criterion, in terms of maximizing the survival or minimizing some durations in the network development process. Several kinds of survivals and period durations are proposed in section 3. Some are established from the franchising literature and others are given in order to be studied in future research. The difficulties linked to longitudinal studies are reviewed in section 4. Then, in section 5, the conclusion gives the managerial implications of these kinds of research, indicates the limitations of this paper and provides some tracks for future research.

2 Network Performance

2.1 Network Performance Measure

Performance is the main task, or one of the main tasks, for the franchisors and the franchisees. Indeed, without performing, it is not possible and/or not interesting to stay as a network operator or as a network member. Performance is also an important concept in the franchising research papers. For instance, nearly every year since the creation of the International Society Of Franchising, in 1986, papers with the word "performance" in the title have been on the program of its annual conference (ISOF website).

Measuring this concept of performance is not always easy. Indeed, in this aim, researchers need several indicators. It can deal, for instance, with sales in the case of retail sector, occupation rates in the case of the hotel industry, number of meals served in the case of restaurant or fast-food industries, etc. However, the network operators do not always diffuse publicly these data. Some of these indicators are given in Franchise Directories such as the ACFCI Bulletin of retail and service networks of independents or the French Federation of Franchising directories in France, or Franchise 500-Entrepreneur Magazine in the United States of America. But, in general, the list of networks is not exhaustive and along the itemized networks, the information diffused is not always complete. Additionally, even contacted directly or during a personal meeting or interview, many network operators do not agree with giving precise performance data. One reason seems to be the fear that the competitors have these data at their disposal. This is particularly accentuated when we want to improve the validity of the research adding input data. Improving performance evaluation by the use of input data, such as the value of the products sold, the number of employees, etc. becomes consequently more difficult.

Performance does not have a unique meaning. When we talk about network performance, we can refer to productivity, effectiveness, efficiency and so on. These main features of performance are now exposed.

2.2 Productivity

Retail and service productivity has been considered as an important topic for firms and networks (Bucklin 1978; Ingene 1984). There is still no single widely accepted definition and measurement methodology for retail productivity (Donthu and Yoo 1998). In fact, the concept of productivity is fundamentally a physical concept which compares produced units to a production factor (De La Villarmois 1999). Productivity is a ratio of output to any input factor, both measured in specific units (Bloom 1972). Productivity can be influenced by controllable factors or not, environmental ones like competition intensity, market environmental characteristics, consumer socio-economic and demographic characteristics, etc. or internal ones like size, management form, marketing mix, etc. (Lusch and Moon 1984).

Productivity is actually the combination of efficiency and effectiveness. Indeed, increasing productivity assumes increasing simultaneously effectiveness and efficiency (Ingene 1984). We shall briefly define these two concepts. On the one hand, effectiveness focuses on outputs relative to a particular objective (Thomas *et al.* 1998). Effectiveness means that things are well done (Drucker 1966). It is defined as a way of using resources in order to maximize return on capital investment (Achabal et al. 1984), in a long-term perspective. On the other hand, efficiency focuses on the relationships between inputs and outputs. In an organization, efficiency describes the optimization of the resources used to obtain a result. Efficiency, also referred to return productivity, means that good things are done (Drucker 1966). In the particular case of the Data Envelopment Analysis method, efficiency deals with the resource allocation optimization among alternative uses. Two equivalent orientations can express this optimization (Parsons 1992):

- the *output orientation* concerns the production of the maximum quantity of outputs for any given amount of inputs;

- the *input orientation* deals with the use of the minimum quantity of inputs for any given amount of outputs.

2.3 Time Management and the Concept of Survival

The conceptualizations of performance, presented above, require precise financial, economic, etc. data that all the network actors are not ready to diffuse. One way to overcome these problems of data availability is by working on other conceptualizations of performance. For instance, performance can be measured through network survival which is closely related to the notion of time management. In fact, some time durations must be maximized whereas others must be minimized in order to increase the network or store performance.

On the one hand, the periods which must be maximized for increasing performance deal with the concept of survival. In a general perspective, if "something" survives, it means that this "thing" performs. In franchising management, this "thing" can refer to a network, a store within a network, a franchising contract between the franchisor and his franchisees. The longer the network life, the store life or the relationship are, the more 'performing' the franchising system is. For instance, the network survival implies the competitiveness, the good resource allocation optimization, the good consideration of its social, legal, economic, political environments, etc. Consequently, it becomes decisive for the managers, franchisor or franchisees or better for both of them, to manage the determinants of this survival well in order to maximize it.

In order to illustrate what we have just mentioned, we can remember that survival is not live mortality. This organizational longevity considered as such a performance criterion, Carroll and Hannan (2000) explained:

> "We believe that, when properly formulated, organizational mortality is potentially valuable as a performance indicator. [...] proper formulation means thinking in terms of firm-specific instantaneous rates of failure. Such rates have a number of attractive features as performance measures. First, mortality can be measured with a minimum of ambiguity and noise. Second, hazard function models – the usual modeling framework for investigating organizational mortality – provide for precise comparability across firms, industries, and sectors [...]. Third, variations in firm-specific mortality are

> likely greater than variations in financial accounting measures, meaning that this outcome might prove more helpful in reconciling theories with the real world. Fourth, organizational mortality is one performance standard that it is difficult to envision becoming run-down over-time."

On the other hand, for survival implying the notion of time, there are some periods which must be minimized in order to increase performance, development, speed expansion, etc. This deals with various aspects, such as durations before franchising, franchising internationalization, site selection (store location choice), the franchisee choice by the franchisor, multi-store openings in the case of multi-unit franchise, etc. Even if the managerial choices require, of course, some precautions and preliminary considerations, the shorter these periods are, the better the network development is. It remains therefore important for both franchisor and franchisees, to shorten these periods in order to facilitate the development.

We expose more in detail these two kinds of durations that must draw franchisor and franchisees attention. The first ones must be extended as much as possible whereas the second ones, becoming shorter, will favor the network development.

3 Time Management Illustrations

Among the research papers dealing with the importance of time management, the concept of survival is perhaps the most studied in the franchising arena. For illustration, Shane (1996; 1998a), Shane and Spell (1998b), Shane and Foo (1999) have worked on survival, mortality and success. Stanworth et al. (1998) have studied the failure rates. Bates (1995a; 1995b; 1998) has analyzed the rates of survival. And Falbe and Welsh (1998) have focused on the perception of the franchisors regarding franchisee success and failure, etc. We now indicate some time periods which are important to take into account for franchising practitioners and also franchising researchers.

We first expose the survival theme, related to a maximization of a time period and then present the various durations to be minimized.

3.1 Durations to Maximize Network

Network survival can reflect network performance. Indeed, if the network is able to survive, it means that it can react to the environment and its competitors, that the network outputs are sufficient compared to the inputs, etc. Some factors can influence the network survival and must be taken into account by the franchisor to ensure perenniality. This deals for instance with the network size. Some research papers have revealed size such as one of the network survival determinants (Shane and Foo 1999; Perrigot and Cliquet 2003). It is shown that the larger the network, the longer the life time it has. Age also appears as one of the variables favoring the network survival (Shane and Foo 1999). Greater age will decrease the probability of failure. Managerial form seems to be a survival determinant as well. Plural form networks present a propensity for having a better survival time than predominantly franchised networks or predominantly company-owned networks (Perrigot 2002). Some other variables can be also considered: nationality (Perrigot and Cliquet 2003), external certification (Shane and Foo 1999), etc.

Store Survival

The survival time of a retailing or service store is important to maximize. The question is "which factors cause one store to survive whereas another one to fail?" Some controllable variables can be envisaged. Star and Massel (1981) pointed out the kind of business: "rates of survival are highest for corporations, intermediate for partnerships, and lowest for proprietorships", the store size: "the larger the size of the retail business, the higher the rate of survival", the store location: "the greater the degree of urbanization, the lower the rate of retail business survival". The number of employees, number of days or hours open per week, etc. can also be relevant. Some other variables are not controllable: number of competitors, economic situation of the region, currency value of the products sold at retail: "retailers dealing in "big ticket" products have a higher rate of survival than retailers dealing in "small ticket" products" (Star and Massel 1981), etc. This can be interesting to observe the store durations within the same network (Dekimpe and Morrison 1991). For instance, the units can be grouped according to their managerial form and one research question can consist in knowing if company-owned units present a propensity to having a longer survival time than franchised units within the same network.

Franchisee Turnover (Duration of the Franchisee/Franchisor Relationship)

Franchising contract stops are interesting to study in franchising research. Indeed, some franchisees can choose to stop or not renew their contract. This can also stem from the franchisor: he can prefer not to renew the contract with a franchisee who, for instance, does not respect the brand concept and/or breaks the homogeneity in the brand image. Consequently, two kinds of variables can explain this contract stop, and by extension, the franchisee turnover. The first ones concern the franchisee himself: his age, his financial situation, his business income, his personal situation, his point of view about the future of his town, etc. The second ones deal with the franchisor himself: his financial situation (he can want to buy the franchised unit to transform it into a company-owned unit and keep the profit for himself (Oxenfeldt and Kelly 1968-69)), his wish for concept respect (Manolis et al. 1995), his managerial strategy, etc.

3.2 Durations to Minimize

Even each franchisor and/or franchisee decision requires precautions and exhaustive preliminary considerations in this competitive context, it is often a good option to be like "the first one" and appear like the pioneer (Carpenter and Nakamoto 1988; 1989; Robinson and Fornell 1985; Robinson 1988). It is said that market pioneers generally have substantially higher market shares than late entrants. In the franchising arena, the pioneer advantage can be illustrated through the first system to franchise its concept, the first franchise system to internationalize, the first one to integrate a new franchisee, etc.

Duration before Internationalization through Franchising

The internationalization is now a very important process. Many networks such as Mango, Mercure, MacDonalds, etc. are global players in the sense that their brand and their concept are present in various countries. Nevertheless, among the networks, there are still differences in the time periods before internationalization. Using the literature of the competitive theory of the firm, Huszagh et al. (1992) found that age (time in operation), size (number of units), and, to a lesser extent, equity capital and headquarters location, are significant factors differentiating between domestic and international franchisors. The resource-based explanation of international franchising suggests that before deciding to internationalize, firms must gain a sufficient amount of resources such as financial capital, brand name recognition, and managerial and routine-processing know-how. As the franchising firm grows, it develops additional franchised units, which allow it to acquire the resources necessary for expanding overseas. As such, the franchising firm's size, age, rate of growth were often used as measures of the amount of resources the franchising firm possesses. The more resources the franchising firm has, the more likely it will seek international expansion.

Duration/Experience before Franchising

Which factors can influence the duration before franchising? First of all, the concept must be well managed. The know-how must be excellent before deciding to franchise a store concept. It seems that this experience allows the creation of a perennial franchised network. This experience can be reflected by different variables, such as age (number of years since the first store opening), size (number of stores already opened), human resources management (number of employees), etc.

Duration before Site Selection (Store Location Choice)

Location speed is important for network development and success (Lafontaine, 1992). Which environmental variables: number of inhabitants in the town, number of competitors in the town, available store area, etc. can explain these differences of time periods? The theme of spatial strategies, with commercial location decisions (Ghosh and McLafferty 1987; Cliquet 2002) and the necessity of territorial coverage (Cliquet 1998; 2002), is central for each network. Indeed, like time, location is one of the keys of business success. The choice of the company-owned store location and the time necessary to open it are determinants for the results of the store, and by extension the results of the network even if "multi-unit site selection models have long ignored the impact of time delays in store openings" (Kaufmann et al. 2000).

Duration before the Franchisee Choice by the Franchisor

The time before the franchising contract is signed by both the franchisor and the franchisee can vary in length. Which variables could explain the differences between the time periods before that the franchisor chooses a franchisee? Several variables can explain this heterogeneity in time. They can be divided into two groups. The first ones deal with the franchisee himself: his know-how in the activity sector, his competencies, his money, his personal investment in the business, etc. The second ones concern the environment. Location is an important criterion in accepting a new franchisee and so in opening a new store. Potential of customers, competitors, etc. could be some other explanations.

Duration before Multi-store Openings in the Case of Multi-unit Franchise

Multi-unit franchise is increasingly more used in the network development. Indeed, for the franchisor, it seems easier to give the opportunity to an already well-known franchisee than to a new franchisee to open a new store. The franchisor is sure that the routine, the know-how, the concept, the brand image are already well managed. In many sectors, and particularly in the hotel industry, the same franchisee can possess several units. The different time periods between two store openings in the case of multi-unit franchise are interesting to study (Kaufmann and Dant 1996). But, what determines the time period between the opening, by the same franchisee, of the nth store and the $(n+1)^{th}$ store? The number of units already possessed, the distance between the two stores, etc. could be analyzed.

4 Some Difficulties in the Longitudinal Studies

Longitudinal studies are particularly interesting in franchising research. Even if they do not always require financial, economic data, they are costly in collecting and recording the data over a long period of time. Nevertheless, they offer more insights than cross-sectional studies.

In these longitudinal studies, additionally to the fact that it is not always easy to have access to the entire data, one other constraint can appear, the censorship. Indeed, in many fields and mainly in management sciences, data are often constituted by duration period: survival, period before a particular event, etc. Here, the term "event" can be understood as "a change in state as defined by one or more qualitative variables within some observation period and within the relevant state space" (Blossfeld et al. 1989). This consists in "some form of change in state" (Melnyk et al. 1995). According to Allison (1984), qualitative changes can be identified as events if there is a "relatively sharp disjunction between what precedes and what follows" the change over a period of time. For instance, an event can be a store/network opening, a store/network failure, the penetration of a new country, etc. Sometimes, the duration is censored: it has not been completely observed. The censorship refers to an incomplete survival time (Li 1995-1996) such as the lack of initial date (left censorship), the lack of ending date of the event (right censorship) or the loss of the unit studied: its disappearance of the sample during the period of observation (right censorship). The term "censored" means that the exact length of the duration is ignored because the initial event date of this duration and/or the final event date is/are unknown or outside the observation window.

A particular methodology seems adequate to study longitudinal data in which censorship occurs. It deals with the survival analysis methodology. Indeed, survival analysis can be used for each problem involving events (Melnyk et al. 1995). There are four characteristics associated to data for which survival analysis is particularly well adapted. First, dependent variables vary over time. Second, dependent variables are not supposed to be normally and independently distributed or identically distributed. Third, censorship is not a problem. Fourth, data collection is longitudinal. This technique, still little used in franchising research, is very helpful in these longitudinal studies (Perrigot et al. 2004).

5 Conclusion

There is no gap between the franchisor and franchisee notions of time management. Indeed, if a franchisor manages his network in a good way, it will increase the performance of his franchisees, and reciprocally, if a franchisee well manages his store, it will increase the performance of the network itself. Both of them have the same aim: the good performance of their own business, and thus the good performance of the network. "Timing management" is an expression often heard in the franchising practitioner's environment. But, it usually concerns a preoccupation with a short-time perspective. It seems interesting to work on the factors that influence this notion of timing. With these studies, the variables explaining the survival or the relative short period before an event, consequently the business success, emerge and appear very important for the manager.

On the one hand, a focus on the concept of survival allows the managers to take into account the explanatory variables of survival. For example, if it is shown that size reduces the probability of failure, the manager will have to focus on its business development in size in order to ensure its business long term survival. These comments concern the franchisor, the franchisees, the store managers, etc. As far as contract durations are concerned, the features characterizing a long time contract could be well analyzed by practitioners before signing the contract. This could ensure a long-term relationship and all the advantages linked to it. On the other hand, if we focus on time durations before franchising, before internationalizing, before choosing a location or a franchisee, or before opening a new store in the case of multi-unit franchise, the aim will be to make this period as short as possible. The emergence of the variables explaining these durations will allow the manager to consider these characteristics carefully.

The purpose of this paper was to present the importance of time management for the performance of franchising networks, for both franchisors and franchisees. The brief presentation of traditional performance conceptualizations has shown that working on time management could be a good alternative - with some periods to be maximized and other ones to be minimized - in order to increase network performance. Some non-exhaustive ideas have also been given for future research. To conclude, the concept of time is very important in the franchising context and must be studied in detail.

References

1. Achabal DD, Heineke JM, Mc Intyre SH (1984) Issues and Perspectives on Retail Productivity. Journal of Retailing, 60(3):107-127
2. Allison P (1984) Event History Analysis: Regression and Longitudinal Data. Beverly Hills: Sage Publications
3. Bates T (1995a) A Comparison of Franchise and Independent Small Business Survival Rates. Small Business Economics 7(5):377-388
4. Bates T (1995b) Analysis of Survival Rates Among Franchise and Independent Small Business Startups. Journal of Small Business Management 33(2):23-36
5. Bates T (1998) Survival Patterns Among Newcomers to Franchising. Journal of Business Venturing 13(2):113-130
6. Bloom GF (1972) Productivity In The Food Industry: Problems and Potential. Cambridge, MA: MIT Press
7. Blossfeld HP, Hamerle A, Mayer KU (1989) Event History Analysis. Lawrence Erlbaum, Hillsdale, NJ
8. Bucklin LP (1978) Productivity In Marketing. Chicago: AMA
9. Carpenter GS, Nakamoto K (1988) Market Pioneering, Learning, and Preference. Advances in Consumer Research 15:275-279
10. Carpenter GS, Nakamoto K (1989) Consumer Preference Formation and Pioneering Advantage. Journal of Marketing Research 26:285-298
11. Carroll GR, Hannan MT (2000) The Demography of Corporations and Industries. Princeton University Press, Princeton, New Jersey
12. Cliquet G (1998) Integration and Territory Coverage of the Hypermarket Industry in France: a Relative Entropy Measure. The International Review of Retail, Distribution and Consumer Research 8(2):205-224
13. Cliquet G (2002) Les réseaux mixtes franchises/succursalisme: apports de la littérature et implications pour le marketing des réseaux de points de vente. Recherche et Applications en Marketing 17(1):57-73
14. Dekimpe MG and Morrison DG (1991) A Modeling Framework for Analyzing Retail Store Durations. Journal of Retailing 67(1):68-92
15. De La Villarmois O (1999) Evaluer la performance des réseaux bancaires: La méthode DEA. Décisions Marketing 16:39-51
16. Donthu N, Yoo B (1998) Retail Productivity Assessment Using Data Envelopment Analysis. Journal of Retailing 74(1):89-105
17. Drucker P (1966) The Effective Executive. NY, Harper and Row

18.Falbe CM, Welsh DH (1998) NAFTA And Franchising: A Comparison of Franchisor Perceptions of Characteristics Associated With Franchisee Success and Failure In Canada, Mexico, and The United States. Journal of Business Venturing. 13:151-171

19.Ghosh A, McLafferty S (1987) Location Strategies for Retail and Service Firms. Lexington, MA: D.C. Heath

20.Huszagh SM, Huszagh FW, McIntyre F (1992) International Franchising in the Context of Competitive Strategy and the Theory of the Firm. International Marketing Review 9:5-18

21.Ingene CA. (1984) Productivity and Functional Shifting in Spatial Retailing: Private and Social Perspectives. Journal of Retailing 60(3):15-36

22.ISOF website, *http://www.huizenga.nova.edu/business/internationalSocietyFranchising_Research Papers.cfm*

23.Kaufmann PJ, Dant R (1996) Multi-unit franchising: Growth and management issues. Journal of Business Venturing 11(5):343-358

24.Kaufmann PJ, Donthu N, Brooks CM (2000) Multi-Unit Retail Site Selection Processes: Incorporating Opening Delays and Unidentified Competition. Journal of Retailing 76(1):113-127

25.Lafontaine F (1992) How and Why Do Franchisors Do What They Do; A Survey Report, in Franchising Passport for Growth and World Opportunity. Kaufmann PJ ed., Proceedings of the Society of Franchising, Lincoln, NE: International Center for Franchise Studies, University of Nebraska

26.Li S (1995-1996) Survival analysis. Marketing Research 7(4):17-23

27.Lusch RF, Moon SY (1984) An Exploratory Analysis of the Correlates of Labor Productivity in Retailing. Journal of Retailing 60(3):37-61

28.Manolis C, Dahlstrom R, Nygaard A (1995) A Preliminary Investigation of Ownership Conversions in Franchised Distribution Systems. Journal of Applied Business Research 11(2):1-8

29.Melnyk SA, Pagell M, Jorae G, Sharpe AS (1995) Applying Survival Analysis to Operations Management: Analyzing the Differences in Donor Classes in the Blood Donation Process. Journal of Operations Management 13:339-356

30.Oxenfeldt AR, Kelly AO (1968-69) Will Successful Franchise Systems Eventually Become Wholly-Owned Chains?, Journal of Retailing, 44:69-83

31.Parsons L (1992) Productivity Versus Relative Efficiency in Marketing: Past and Future? In: Lilien G, Laurent G, Pras B (Eds.), Research Traditions in Marketing. Kluwer, Amsterdam, pp 169-196

32.Perrigot R (2002) La pluralité des formes statutaires au sein d'un réseau de points de vente: une application à la survie des chaînes de pizzas en France entre 1987 et 2001. Sciences de Gestion et Pratiques Managériales, V. Giard Ed., Economica.

33.Perrigot R, Cliquet G (2003) Survival Analysis Along a Hotel Chain Classification in France. Influence of Network Managerial Form and Nationality on the Fall in the Classification, International Franchising in Developed Markets: Western and Northern Europe, edited by Dianne Welsh and Ilan Alon.

34.Perrigot R, Cliquet G, Mesbah M (2004) Possible Applications of Survival Analysis in Franchising Research International Review of Retail, Distribution and Consumer Research 14(1):129-143

35.Retail survival guide on internet, *http://www.insigniasystems.com/isig/pdfs/RetailSurvivalGuide.pdf*

36.Robinson WT, Fornell C (1985) Sources of Market Pioneer Advantages in Consumer Goods Industries. Journal of Marketing Research 22:305-317

37.Robinson WT (1988) Sources of Market Pioneer Advantages: The Case of Industrial Goods Industries. Journal of Marketing Research 25:87-94

38.Shane S (1996) Hybrid Organizational Arrangements and their Implications for Firm Growth and Survival: A Study of New Franchisors. The Academy of Management Journal 39(1):216-234

39.Shane S (1998a) Making New Franchise Systems Work, Strategic Management Journal 19:697-707

40.Shane S, Spell C (1998b) Factors for New Franchise Success. Sloan Management Review 39(3):43-50

41.Shane S, Foo MD (1999) New Firm Survival: Institutional Explanations for New Franchisor Mortality. Management Science, 45(2):142-159

42.Stanworth J, Purdy D, Price S, Zafiris N (1998) Franchise Versus Conventional Small Business Failure Rates in the US and UK: More Similarities than Differences. International Small Business Journal 16(3):56-69

43.Star AD, Massel MD (1981) Survival Rates for Retailers. Journal of Retailing 5:87-99.

44.Thomas RR, Barr RS, Cron WL, Slocum Jr JW (1998) A Process for Evaluating Retail Store Efficiency: A Restricted DEA Approach. International Journal of Research in Marketing 15:487-503

Relocate, Render and Renovate: A Framework for Marketing Implementation across Franchise Networks

Mukul P. Gupta

Marketing Area, Management Development Institute,
Mehrauli Road, Sukhrali, Gurgaon 122001, India
mukul@mdi.ac.in

Abstract. Marketing organizations must establish processes to manage firm-customer connectivity across boundaries of their franchisees. Franchisees are selected based on their competencies in the specialized and task-dependent forms of activity domains designed and prescribed for them by the marketing strategists at the firm. Franchisees may excel at their domains but that may not necessarily result in optimal firm-customer connectivity since the strength of the connectivity is only as much as the strength of the weakest link. To address this challenge, an integrative framework is developed that identifies and integrates the value of different approaches to managing marketing channels that are often presented as incompatible in the literature. The framework describes three progressively complex types of peripheries: course, concept and conduct. Each increasingly complex periphery requires a more complex process to facilitate communication and innovation across specialized forms of marketing channels. The framework categorizes types of peripheries, gauges their complexity and then describes the processes involved in managing the firm-customer connectivity across each of them. The examples from gasoline, mobile telephony, health care, credit cards, fast food, school education, and automobile industry from the Indian market are presented to illustrate the conceptual strength of this framework [1].

1 Introduction

Individual consumers and organizational customers are all aware that literally thousands of goods and services are available through a very large number of diverse channel outlets. They might not however be aware of the fact that the networks that connect them to the marketing firms can be amazingly complex. Usually a combination of institutions specializing in manufacturing, owning & operating connectivity infrastructure, physical redistribution and many other areas

[1] The motivation for articulating these thoughts in this format came from an unpublished paper of Paul R. Carlile of Sloan School of Management, MIT.

join forces in marketing system arrangements to make possible a marketing exchange.

This paper suggests that the concern for implementation of firm's marketing strategy across franchise networks has arisen because the nature and dynamics of market conditions and the strategic responses have out-stripped both our theoretical and managerial frameworks, creating a disparity between what we expect from strategic initiatives and what they ultimately deliver. A primary reason for this divide is that there are several approaches to designing and managing networks that connect firms and their customers. These approaches offer varying and sometimes incompatible views (Dant, Kaufmann and Paswan 1992; Dant, Paswan and Stanworth 1996). There are mechanistic perspectives that focus on flows of physical possession, payments, servicing and the like. These structural views confine themselves to functional limitations of capture, store and transfer (Coughlan, Anderson, Stern and El-Ansary 2001). The advances in theory building in this school of thought have started to consider borrowing understanding from 'fluid-dynamics' from the physical sciences (Coughlan et. al. 2001). More cultural approaches emphasize the requirements of social interactions and building relationships (Stanworth and Curran 1999). These approaches, typified by the CRM buzz, limit themselves to an interactive process of translate, internalize and share. There are yet another sets of approaches that call attention to the 'political and power bases' in networks heavily borrowing from the political science and international relations thought (Hunt and Nevin 1974). All of these approaches serve a useful purpose in providing insights into the way that the firm-customer connectivity works. Yet none of them completes the picture. Any insights into the processes necessary to deliver more effective connectivity initiatives will remain under-specified without a way to integrate the values of these different approaches. Consequently, the frustration with the inadequate ability of firms to connect with the customer through the implementation process of marketing strategy will continue to grow (Tikoo 1996; Shane and Spell 1998; Fein and Jap 1999).

The purpose of this paper is to provide an integrated framework to understand these different approaches and their collective value by focussing on the challenge of managing across firm-franchisee peripheries. The framework describes three progressively complex types of peripheries – *course, concept* and *conduct* – each managed by a different process – *relocate, render* and *renovate.* The value of this framework is that it categorizes the relative complexity of different types of peripheries, and addresses the process of managing relationships with the franchisee across these peripheries.

Complex peripheral problems are especially acute in the early stages of new franchise system development. The following description offers a glimpse into the challenge at this initial stage and provides an introduction to one of the cases that is used throughout in the paper to illustrate the conceptual and practical value of the framework. Other cases are discussed subsequently for illustrating the usefulness of the framework, albeit briefly for reasons of limits on space.

Local Loop, the last link of the Telecom Network, is also called a bottleneck facility in regulatory jargon. The Local Loop i.e., the 'last mile' of the Telecom Network provides the vital link between the customer and the Local exchange.

This vital link has traditionally been a pair of copper wire connecting the Customer Premises Equipment (CPE) to the Main Distribution Frame (MDF) of the Local exchange. The deployment of Access Network based on copper requires long roll out period and huge initial investments. The wire connection therefore leaves the telephone equipment at a fixed location in the customer's premises. For this reason, basic services are also called the fixed line services.

In mobile services, the CPE connects to the local exchange through wireless. The honeycomb-cell like design enables the CPE to connect to the nearest equipment. The CPE is free to be in motion and the connection is automatically routed to the next best equipment depending on the motion of the CPE. Thus the customer receives nearly seamless connectivity (depending on technology) and is free to be mobile. Hence the name.

The Local Loop is the most capital-intensive element of the Telecom Network. Therefore telecom engineers and planners have been searching for an alternative to copper based Local Loop since decades, to find a more cost-effective alternative, preferably based on Wireless technology, to cut down the Network Roll out time as well as cost. A number of alternatives to copper based Local Loop have emerged under the generic name of 'Wireless in Local Loop (WLL)'. WLL Systems are applications of cellular technology (either Micro or Macro) to connect a fixed telephone set to the exchange through an open interface. Such Systems employing different Access technologies (CDMA/ GSM/ DECT /PHS etc.) & operating in different frequency bands are increasingly becoming available and are likely to play an important role in increasing the level of coverage and competition in the last mile. The proper term to use for WLL, which has received wide acceptance, is Wireless Access, which is defined as "End User Radio Access Connection(s) to Core Networks. Core Networks include for example, PSTN, ISDN, PLMN, PSDN, Internet, WAN/LAN, CATV, etc. Wireless Access may be considered from a number of perspectives, such as:

1. *Fixed Wireless Access*: Wireless Access application in which location of the end-user termination and the Network Access point to be connected to the end-user are fixed.
2. *Mobile Wireless Access*: Wireless Access System in which the location of end-user termination is Mobile.
3. *Nomadic Wireless Access*: Wireless Access Application in which the location of end user termination may be in different places but it must be stationary while in use.

The telecom industry in India has been categorized into Basic services (conventionally meaning the fixed landline systems) and Mobile services. The Government has issued licenses for basic services and mobile services separately. The Basic Service License stipulates WLL as the preferred method for providing Basic Service. All the Licensees of Basic Services have deployed WLL Systems as Fixed Wireless Access (FWA) Systems in conformance with the stipulation in their License Agreement. The government owned telecom companies (MTNL/ BSNL) have introduced the WLL with Limited Mobility later. MTNL has introduced Wireless in Local Loop (WLL) with Limited Mobility based on CDMA (IS-

95) technology in 1999. The Mobile handset offered by MTNL to the subscribers is identical to a cellular handset. BSNL has also followed suit.

The question that the market regulator and all the players face is about mobility. Limited mobility, say within 500 meters (later relaxed) as stipulated in the basic licenses while providing flexibility to the customer and saving the huge investments in local loop does not make the service truly mobile. Once this mobility is not restricted, the differentiation in fixed and mobile service really vanishes.

Reliance Infocom (RIL – a division of the Reliance Industries Limited, the largest private company in India) holds a license for basic telephony. RIL announced a WLL service using CDMA2000 technology offering (un) limited mobility. RIL has set up its own infrastructure comprising of 60000 kms. of optical fiber network. The RIL offer comes in conflict with the other mobile telephone service providers once the mobility goes unlimited. RIL faces significant challenges in the early stages of the launch of their CDMA/WLL based basic telephone services to the consumer. The technology provides mobility to the consumer. The quality of voice is superior; most consumers don't need unlimited geographical mobility. Yet, the consumer is familiar with either fixed line systems or GSM mobile systems. GSM Mobile is considered an expensive yet fully mobile system as against fixed line being an inexpensive but totally fixed system except for some within the premises or within the room flexibility through the use of cordless CPEs. WLL phones are somewhere in between where limited mobility say within a range of a few hundred meters is possible. These phones represent a conflict in the minds of the potential consumers both in terms of extent of mobility and pricing. Similar conflict exists even in the minds of franchisees and even the sales force of the company. The competitors both mobile operators and basic operators are aghast with the offer and the regulator is besieged with the issue.

There are clearly two groups spearheading the new RIL business:

1. *The Marketing Group* – handling the development of the marketing program and its implementation,

2. *The Franchise Network* – connecting with the consumer for and behalf of the company to sell phone connections and in turn meet their own business goals.

Since long, the dominant object or method used by organizations has been the training and communications effort (Anderson, Day and Kasturi Rangan 1997) by marketing groups to franchise groups. This has covered the areas of the overall marketing process that the company had drawn up and is to be followed by all the groups (*course*); the business definition and drivers (*concept*); and the linkages between the two groups and the customers that determine the outcome of the process (*conduct*).

Each of the three components, *course, concept* and *conduct*, that make up the complete marketing system functionally by integrating the two participating groups don't create a seamless system. Rather, there are peripheries that need to be overcome. These peripheries have varying levels of complexity.

2 Peripheries and Complexity

Peripheries are inescapable because of the hierarchical and functional specialization of the two groups. Additionally, since all inputs to the marketing system cannot be known in advance, these peripheries are dynamic and the collective capabilities of the two groups would produce the final marketing results based on ongoing inputs from these groups that keep changing throughout the process. For example, if the marketing group proposes to offer SMS text messages on WLL system, it will have to assess the impact of providing this service as a part of the consumer offer. The franchise group will have to assess the role of this development and see how it fits with market expectations specially in light of the competitive reactions from GSM mobile phones and fixed landline phones. The dynamic nature of the different requirements between and dependencies among the two groups brings into focus the complexity of relationships at the periphery.

To talk meaningfully about the complexity at periphery and the challenge of managing relationships across them, it is useful to identify two properties of a periphery – *variance* and *reliance.*

Variance at the periphery arises from variation in the type of skills and backgrounds or amount of experience between individuals or groups. If there is no variance between individuals or groups then the periphery is not a consequential one. At a conceptual level, variance between A and B is not simply (A-B) rather that the variances between A and B arise from the fact that they occupy different "thought worlds" (Dougherty 1992). Using a more geometric expression we could say that the variance between A and B arise because they occupy different positions relative to each other—they specialize in different problem-solving domains. For example, the marketing group specializes in seeking small opportunity windows in competitive market and tries to muster all their capabilities to design and offer a profitable offer to the consumer. The franchisee is interested in selling a connection to the consumer whose operational or performance parameters are not understood by him. When work domain is localized around different problems, this specialization, even if it is very small, creates variance that generates a potential periphery. Going back to the geometric expression, the farther apart the relative positions of A and B, the greater the variance.

At RIL the *variance* arises from variation in formal education, training, past experience and types of methods used by the marketing group and franchisee group. The most common way to conceptualize these sources of variance is to frame them in terms of specialization (Weber 1947). However, it should be recognized that this specialization goes deeper than just an individual's role; it extends to the different problems or tasks that each is responsible for and requires specialization in. The marketing group offers a distinctive phone system, compared to its competitors and develops the most innovative and efficient marketing plan. The franchisee group adequately takes the market offer to the consumer.

The second property of a periphery is *reliance*. Reliance is a relation that exists between individuals or groups. If there is no reliance between individuals or groups that are different then there is no consequential periphery. In the geometric example, if A and B rely on each other, they constrain or have consequences for the other's movement. For example, the reliance between marketing and franchisee group comes with the recognition that SMS enabled telecom service will create the need for SMS enabled handsets, making them look similar to GSM mobile handsets and thus trigger a new set of market expectations. This will in turn fetch reaction from the mobile telephony operators. But franchisee has not known any marketing plan where he sells specific CPEs provided by the marketing group and doesn't have the freedom to sell any CPEs of his choice. It could be a marketing opportunity as well as a competitive or regulatory threat. Clearly, *reliance* across these different positions (i.e., specialized domains) are not always simple, neutral relations, but generate consequences and sometimes conflicts. Overall, the more *variance* and *reliance* there is at a given periphery the more challenging and complex it is to cross.

In organizational theory literature there are two dominant expressions of the idea of *reliance*, one direct and the other more indirect. The direct expression comes from Emerson's (1962) use of the word dependence to explain power relations, which was then built upon by Pfeffer and Salancik (1974) in the resource dependency model. Here the variances in resources accumulated by various groups and the dependencies among those groups determine the current status of power relations. The indirect conceptualization stems from Thompson's (1967) discussion of interdependence (i.e., serial, pooled and reciprocal) as a way to describe increasingly complex ways of organizing for a task. As used here, *reliance* implies that the relations across elements in the system are well defined, that is, that the variances and dependencies in the system are known. The similarity between Emerson and Thompson is that they describe situations where the *variances* and *reliance* that exist, are either known in advance or are stable. Their conceptualization of *reliance* is limited when applied to situations where conditions are less stable.

The varying conditions from stable to more fluid impact how we describe the complexity of the relations at a periphery. When *variance* and *reliance* are known and the conditions surrounding them are stable, managing the periphery is straightforward. However, when new *variance* and *reliance* arise, managing the periphery becomes progressively more challenging. For example, if a previous design is re-used in a new phone service redesign, there is a significant amount of previous knowledge and experience that makes managing the peripheries across marketing and selling much easier. Using a new phone design generates considerable novelty about what variances and reliance are relevant, and how they will be recognized and dealt with between the groups. Like most new product/market development firms, the marketing group at RIL needs to put in their latest approach into the product to remain competitive. This newness generates novelty in the amount of variance between groups, but also increases the novelty of what reliance is consequential at the periphery.

These varying conditions of a periphery can be scaled along a vector, starting with known and moving outwards to increasing novelty. Fig.1 represents these variable conditions along with the properties of variance and reliance. The shape of this triangle represents a way to gauge the complexity of a given periphery between two specialized entities—called here Group A and Group B. Although there is an analytic separation between variance and reliance above, at any periphery both properties have to exist. Starting at the origin variances and reliance are known, thus the complexity of the periphery between Group A and Group B is minimal. However, as novelty increases the amount of variance or "gap" at the periphery grows, so closing the gap takes progressively more time and resources. Fig.1 then offers a way to gauge the complexity of managing marketing implementation across a periphery. For example, when Group A and Group B are specialized in different domains and rely on each other in completing a task, the periphery is complex. However, even under these complex circumstances, if Group A and Group B have previously accumulated shared experience in working together at the periphery and the periphery remains stable, then managing the variances and dependencies will be much less challenging than when novelty is present.

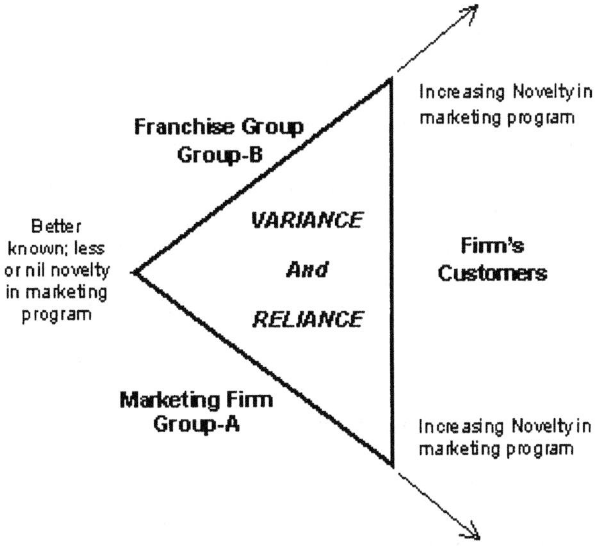

Fig. 1. Connectivity Gap: Increasing Complexity at Peripheries

The hierarchical nature of managing has a positive effect when the conditions of its process are stable, similar to what was faced in the past. However, when novelty increases, the hierarchy of managing has negative effects (Hardagon and Sutton 1997), because what is known or used before may not take into consideration the novelties present in the next cycle. Given the tremendous time pressures under which individuals must take action, their familiarity with what they have done in the past can make individuals wrongly recognize what is novel as something that is already known (i.e., competency traps; Barnett and Hansen 1996). Without the recognition of novelty (new variances and reliance that have arisen), the gap at the periphery cannot be effectively managed. This is why the role a group currently performs in the marketing process is such a problematic anchor point when novelty arises (Carlile 2002).

3 Building the Integrative Framework

There is a way to link the discussion of periphery complexity (Fig. 1) to the *course*, *concept* and *conduct* approaches to peripheries. This effort leads to the development of a framework that represents this increasing complexity and integrates the various literatures on marketing implementation across franchise networks.

3.1 Course Periphery: Mode of Implementation

Franchisees are expected to adopt and follow the marketing process as designed by the marketing group. In case of RIL, the company decided to bundle the phone connection with the CPE (phone instrument) and collect the price through monthly installments. This was a new course of doing business in this industry not seen by the market nor handled by the franchisee firms earlier. This called for customer credit rating, documentation, risk management and new forms of customer contact programs. RIL and its franchisees needed to understand the new mode of marketing implementation and specify variances and reliance. The periphery is "unproblematic;" if they could do so and the primary concern becomes "*relocating*" or transferring the new mode of marketing from marketing group to franchisee group.

3.2 Concept Periphery: Meaning of Implementation

A Concept approach to crossing a periphery recognizes that problems of interpretation exist because the contexts in which people develop their capabilities are different or as novelty increases, interpretative or conceptual variances as to what a marketing method, measurement or outcome means arise at a periphery. RIL franchisee may fail to see how the concept of recovering price through installments helps his business. This concept needs to be *rendered* to the franchisee, its meaning clearly explained.

3.3 Conduct Periphery: Manner of Implementation

Manners of implementation adopted by different groups that are dependent on each other often generate sub-optimal consequences. RIL was seeking intensive distribution reach. It therefore relied on a large number of franchisees. The franchisees came with large variance in their previous experience, background and capabilities including laundry shops, small provision stores, and each with a unique manner of doing business and interacting with their customers. Given the novelty that naturally arises in product development settings, negative consequences between groups are a natural outgrowth of developing new marketing plans and products. This is why the manner of implementation itself must be recognized as problematic; that is, it can be barrier as well as a source of innovation. To understand the problematic nature of manner of implementation, it must be understood as localized, embedded and invested in the tasks, methods and outcomes of a specific practice. Manner is costly to develop (i.e., education, training, experience) and to change, so it should be seen as "at stake" for the individuals in a given practice (Bourdieu and Wacquant 1992). This explains why accommodating the manner of another group is not a neutral or cost-free effort. The cost for any group dealing with increasing novelty at a periphery is not just the *cost of learning* about what is new. It is also the *costs of adjusting* or *renovating* their "current" ways of doing things to accommodate the manner developed by another group to collaborate at a periphery. By characterizing manner-in-practice, one could see better why and how individuals are inclined to take action along a path dependent trajectory, given that they have acquired their manner using the tools and methods to solve problems in their specialized domain or practice (Bourdieu 1980).

In the early phase of launch of RIL service, the marketing group wanted to place their newest service into the hands of their customers free from any usage charge for few months. The problem, however, was that the free trial offer for few months for all the customers signing up for the service came with little customer support. The franchisees had therefore to face unhappy, 'non-paying for the time being' customers whose bad mouthing on account of poor marketing experience jeopardized future sales.

The practical challenge in dealing with and resolving the consequences at a *conduct* periphery is for each side to represent, specify, negotiate, compromise and renovate their current manner to accommodate the novelty present at the periphery. This *conduct* approach is not simply a process of just adding or combining manner, nor is it one of jettisoning the old manner and bringing in all new. Here a complex periphery process has to be developed where current and more novel forms of manner can be represented, learned about, and then jointly *renovated.* Through such a process, a composition of known and more novel variances and reliance are collectively *renovated* resolving the negative consequences at the periphery. As compared to a *course* periphery or a *concept* periphery and their associated hurdles (i.e., costs of *relocating* and *rendering*), crossing a *conduct* periphery entails the additional *costs of renovating* manner to manage marketing implementation across that periphery.

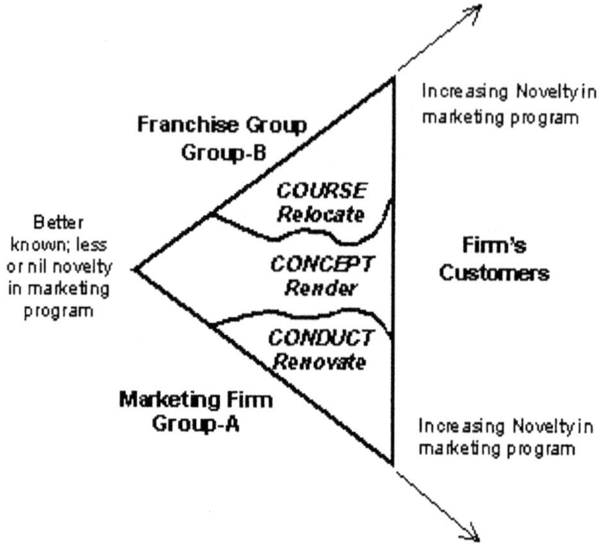

Fig. 2. Integrated/ 3-R Framework for Marketing Implementation Across Peripheries of Franchise Networks

3.4 Integrative -"3-R" - Framework

The purpose of this review and framework development has been to clarify the different approaches to implementation of marketing programs and peripheries that can be identified (see Table 1 for summary). In Fig. 2 each type of implementation periphery is used to categorize the complexity of the periphery framework described earlier. This framework recognizes the importance of three periphery processes - *relocating*, *rendering* and *renovating* - the 3-R framework.

`The tip of the triangle represents those unique situations where the mode of implementation is shared and sufficient, so marketing plan can be efficiently relocated across the periphery. As novelty begins to increase a course approach can still be effective if the consequential or requisite variances and reliance are clarified at the periphery (i.e., the concept of requisite variety; Shannon and Weaver 1949; Ashby 1956; Weick 1979). As novelty increases and the gap grows, new variances and reliance arise that have to be identified and their meaning understood. This is a concept periphery and in some cases new agreements can be created to resolve these consequences. However, as novelty continues to increase and the gap gets larger, a conduct periphery is faced. To address this larger gap, current manner needs to be changed to accommodate the creation of new manner that addresses the novelty present and the negative consequences that have been identified.

Table 1. Three-C Approach to Peripheries

	Course Approach	Concept Approach	Conduct Approach
Hypotheses	The marketing process is shared and understood.	The franchiser and franchisee have different concepts of marketing processes, their goals, roles and domains.	The results achieved by franchiser or franchisee are not neutral or indifferent to another's conduct of marketing process.
	Variances and reliance are clear and stable at the periphery.	Variances, reliance and interdependencies are not clear at the periphery.	Negative consequences for either have to be resolved at the periphery.
Resolutions	Intensive and extensive communication and relocation of marketing process know how.	Rendering goals, roles and domains into a congruous marketing process.	Current and more novel manner of marketing process must be jointly renovated to manage the periphery.
	Communication is understood and know how on mode of marketing process is received.	Create common meaning and agreements on variance and reliance in goals, roles and domains.	Distinctly defined manner, goals, roles and domains at the periphery. The definition process is kept dynamic.
Vulnerability	Ability to comprehend communication and acquire know how may be limited.	The real concept of goals, roles and domains of franchisers and franchisees are hard to surface – they are tacit.	Clash in manner of marketing process at the Periphery can create sub-system optimality but system sub-optimality.
	Communication and transfer of know-how are necessary, but not always sufficient	Variances at the periphery in the understanding of goals, roles and domains often generate negative consequences.	Individuals limit representing, negotiating and renovating the manner of marketing process at the periphery.

Fig. 2 should not be read as a formal hierarchy in the sense that to get to a *conduct* periphery one has to go through the first two. Its purpose is to categorize and gauge the size of the gap—the complexity of a periphery faced—to clarify the types of processes necessary to manage implementation across it. At a *conduct* periphery Fig. 2 suggests that all the three periphery processes need to be used to manage implementation across the periphery. At a *concept* periphery *relocation* and *rendering* processes are required; and at a *course* periphery a *relocation* process is required. The question that remains, however, is what are the requirements involved in such periphery processes? That would essentially be a matter of further research.

4 Empirical Cases in Support of the Framework

The data on RIL case was collected over four months immediately following the launch of their 'Dhirubhai Ambani Pioneer Offer' and included eleven interviews. These included two senior RIL marketing officials, three franchisees, two customers, one marketing official from competing public Telephony Company, another from a private mobile telephony company and two customers in waiting. Although the case data was collected somewhat opportunistically, large amount of information was available from media reports during the period. The reactions from the interviews could be summarized as follows:

1. *Marketing Group*: Great marketing program where customer is sure winner and competitors will have a tough time.
2. *Franchisee Group*: Such a lot of noises, high customer curiosity, if one has some money to invest, why not make a buck. But RIL is an arrogant company.
3. *Customer*: How is such a low cost service possible? RIL may be taking us for a ride and may increase prices later.
4. *Competitors*: RIL has cheated the government and flouted the rules. We must all get together and take up the challenge on all fronts- regulator, government, and customers.

All the three peripheries between RIL and its franchisees showed strong complexities. RIL did not succeed in relocating the marketing process to its franchisees, could not render to them the meaning of their plan and could do little with the renovation of the manner of implementation followed by its franchisees. RIL announced in April 2003 that they are scrapping their franchisees and will put up a new system in place; surely, a case of poor marketing implementation on account of insufficient periphery management.

Other examples from Indian businesses illustrate the utility of the framework as well.

4.1 Case of Gasoline Retailing

Retail gasoline distribution in India typically continues in the hands of public companies, the leaders being Indian Oil (IOC) and Bharat Petroleum (BP). With selective deregulation and decontrol, the competition in domestic LPG and lubricants has already intensified while the same is likely in gasoline retailing soon. To connect better and with more customers through their franchisees, IOC planned small convenience stores alongside their gasoline stations. BP decided to address the issue by promising better product by launching the 'Pure for Sure' campaign. Gasoline stations had typically made money in the past through adulteration or shorter dispensing or even both. Customer care was unknown due to lack of accountability. BP was trying to address the basic concern of the customer while IOC was trying to offer assorted added convenience. Both were redesigned market offers needing new implementation. Both had new course, concept and conduct peripheries. IOC tied up with suppliers for merchandise, provided layouts for stores, created self-service transactions and implemented the program. It succeeded in relocating the new mode of business to its franchisees, succeeded in rendering to them the meaning of new program and did not let the manner of its franchisees come in way. BP plan created high complexity in concept and conduct peripheries for its franchisees and failed to render the new meaning or renovate their manner. The franchisees did not see how they would gain by selling pure gasoline over their usual malpractice or by being more concerned about the customer. They had not done that ever in the past. The results are there to be noticed - IOC succeeded in increasing customer footfalls while BP continues with its old ways.

4.2 Case of Fast Food Chains

Taking the example from fast-food chains, KFC (Kentucky Fried Chicken) came to India a few years back. Their marketing program was totally new for the market. They succeeded in managing all the peripheries with their franchisees and soon had a chain of establishments going around. They had recreated the same mode, meaning and manner for their franchisees as anywhere else in the world. However, the Indian market had its nuances. The franchisees noticed it earlier and wanted KFC to modify its meaning and manner to suit local conditions. Whether the franchisees failed or KFC failed is immaterial. The complexity in concept and conduct peripheries kept increasing and no rendering or renovation took place. KFC had to close down and is struggling with just one outlet today. On the other hand, McDonalds did not commit the same mistakes. While they also started off much like KFC, they did succeed in rendering and renovation. They modified the menu (course relocated), modified their positioning from a fast-food joint to family hangouts (concept rendered), and altered the manner of serving the customer from just 'self service' to also 'take sit-down orders' (conduct renovated). McDonalds is on a fast track growth in India. Pizza Hut and Domino's are trying to do much the same and are seeing healthy growth in their business.

4.3 Case of Automobiles

In case of automobiles, Hero Honda and Bajaj are the two largest players in the two-wheeler market. Bajaj is an older company with large portfolio of scooters and motorbikes. Hero Honda is a late entrant with only motorbikes. Their products, prices and other policies are competitive and analogous. Hero Honda has replicated the distribution system of Bajaj. Yet Bajaj is beginning to trail behind Hero Honda. The reasons are obvious. The peripheries have emerged between the companies and their franchisees due to changes in market place. Consumers prefer motorbikes to scooters now. More consumers now buy automobiles through consumer financing rather than savings. Consumers commute longer distances on two wheelers for work. Two wheelers are bought more for work than for family transportation. Younger people are buying two wheelers. These changes create course, concept and conduct peripheries together. Hero Honda is able to relocate, render and renovate the implementation of the marketing programs in line with these changes, something that Bajaj seems to have either ignored for long or have failed at it. Bajaj and its franchisees are often mired in their internal problems of domains; roles and goals while Hero Honda franchisees deliver a near seamless connectivity between the customer and the company.

4.4 Case of Health Care Business

In case of health care, Apollo hospitals is trying to set up a chain of franchisee clinics supplying simple diagnostic services, health-checks and non-expert consultations. This creates a doorstep service and builds reference pool of customers for their bigger hospitals. They are trying to rely on first-generation entrepreneurs as their franchisees. The simplicity of services enables the franchisee to face lesser complexity in course, concept or conduct and there is enough time available for incremental relocation, rendering or renovation as may be needed. The business is looking up. Max Health care is trying to franchise existing unorganized single outlet diagnostic labs for a similar business. These labs have thrived following their own business model and face severe complexity in course, concept and conduct with the business model of Max Health care. The relocation, rendering and renovating tasks are difficult and expensive. The results are a much slower and expensive growth.

4.5 Case of Credit Cards Marketing

Similar experience is available from the credit cards industry. The largest card issuer in the world GE tied up with State Bank of India, the largest Bank in India to launch their card. As against this Standard Chartered Bank which has a very small presence in India has actually sold the maximum cards. GE-SBI had a great marketing program but its implementation ran in trouble with its franchisees as can be explained by the 3-C-3-R model. The success of Standard Chartered is exactly for the reasons opposite to that of the poor performance of GE-SBI.

4.6 Case of School Education

In case of school education, there is a big brand called DPS (Delhi Public School). Today they are into franchising their product and process across different cities and even in some countries in the Middle East. Not all of their schools are equally successful. Examining each franchisee school on this model explains the variation in their performance.

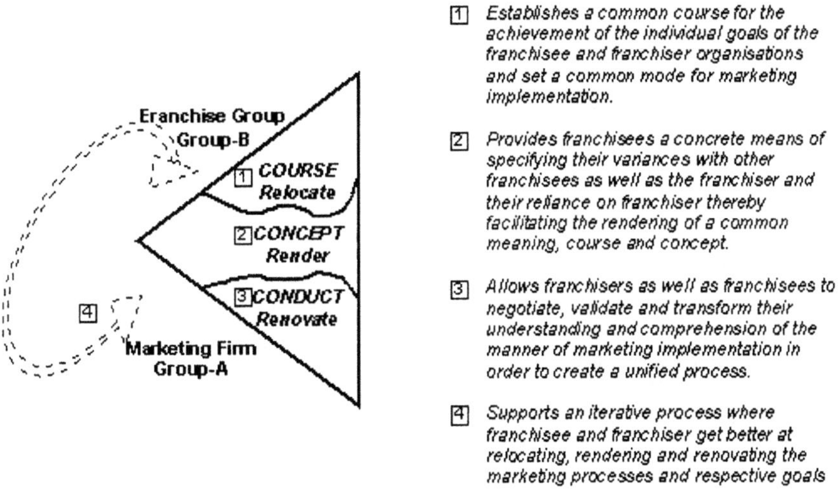

Fig. 3. "3-R" Framework and the Characteristics of Marketing Implementation

5 Discussion and Implications

The cases above indicate that effective marketing implementation across different periphery of franchisees requires the development of a common mode of marketing (see Fig. 3). This mode needs to be relocated from marketing firm to the franchise system. McDonalds could do it but RIL could not.

There has to be a common meaning to the concept of business. This meaning needs to be rendered to the franchise system by the marketing firm. IOC succeeded in it while HP could not. The manner of implementation has to be congruous. RIL failed in it.

There is another ingredient to successful implementation – renovation. Renovation is not lateral or one sided. The franchisees need to renovate so also the marketing firm needs to renovate as per the context of business. McDonalds in India is an excellent example of renovation while KFC failed due to lack of renovation.

This paper has described three different types of peripheries and developed an integrative framework to resolve many of the incompatibilities among the different approaches to managing marketing implementation across franchise systems. Describing the properties of a periphery in terms of variance and reliance, and the conditions present at a periphery from known to increasing novelty, provides a way to categorize and gauge the complexity of a periphery. The framework also outlines the characteristics of the periphery processes required for each type of periphery. Finally, the framework provides an integrative way to assess the value and costs associated with each approach to managing implementation across a periphery. The cases helped demonstrate the usefulness of the framework by describing "typical" successes and failures as a match and mismatch between the type of periphery and the type of periphery approach or process used to manage the periphery. The fact that most marketing successes occurs at the peripheries (Leonard-Barton 1992) reminds us that managing implementation across the various types of peripheries in distribution systems is what lies at the source of competitive advantage.

References

1. Anderson E, Day GS, Kasturi Rangan V (1997) Strategic Channel Design. Sloan Management Review. 38(4):59-69
2. Ashby R (1956) Introduction to Cybernetics. London: Chapman and Hall
3. Bourdieu P (1980) The Logic of Practice. Cambridge, UK: Cambridge University Press
4. Bourdieu P, Wacquant L (1992) An Invitation to Reflexive Sociology. Chicago: University of Chicago Press
5. Carlile P (2002) A Pragmatic View of Knowledge and Boundaries: Periphery Objects in New Product Development. Organization Science 13(4)
6. Coughlan AT, Anderson E, Stern LW, El-Ansary AI (2001) Marketing Channels. 6 ed. New Jersey: Prentice Hall
7. Dant RP, Paswan AK, Stanworth J (1996) Ownership Redirection Trends in Franchising. International Journal of Entrepreneurial Behavior and Research. 2(3):48-67
8. Dant RP, Kaufmann PJ, Paswan AK (1992) Ownership Redirection in Franchised Channels. Journal of Public Policy and Marketing. 11:33-44
9. Dougherty D (1992) Interpretive Barriers to Successful Product Innovation in Large Firms. Organization Science 3:179-202
10. Emerson R (1962) Power-reliance relations. American Sociological Review 27:31-40
11. Fein AJ, Jap SD (1999) Managing Consolidation in the Distribution Channel. Sloan Management Review 41(1):61-72
12. Hargadon A, Sutton R (1997) Technology Brokering and Innovation in a Product Development Firm. Administrative Science Quarterly 42:716-749
13. Hunt SD, Nevin JR (1974) Power in a Channel of Distribution: Sources and Consequences. Journal of Marketing Research 11(May):186-193
14. Leonard-Barton D (1992) Core Capabilities and Core Rigidities: A Paradox in Managing New Product Development. Strategic Management Journal 13:111-126
15. Pfeffer J, Salancik G (1974) Organizational Decision Making as a Political Process: The Case of a University Budget. Administrative Science Quarterly 19:135-51
16. Shane S, Spell C (1998) Factors for New Franchise Success. Sloan Management Review 39(3):43-50.

17.Shannon C, Weaver W (1949) The Mathematical Theory of Communications. Urbana, IL: University of Illinois Press
18.Stanworth J, Curran J (1999) Colas, Burgers, Shakes and Shirkers: Towards a Sociological Model of Franchising in the Market Economy. Journal of Business Venturing. 14(4):323-344
19.Thompson J (1967) Organizations in Action. New York: McGraw-Hill
20.Tikoo S(1996) Assessing the Franchise Option. Business Horizons. May-June:78-82
21.Weber M (1924/1947) The Theory of Social and Economic Organization. A. H. Henderson and T. Parsons (eds.), Glencoe, IL: Free Press
22.Weick K (1979) The Social Psychology of Organizing. Reading MA: Addison-Wesley

Part E:

International Market Entry Through Franchising

Franchising and the Choice of International Entry Mode

Krista Duniach-Smith

Université Montpellier I,
Faculté d'Administration et Gestion, Avenue de la Mer, BP 9640
34054 Montpellier, France

Abstract. In this study, international entry mode choice is examined in a franchise setting. As in the traditional entry mode and international franchising literatures, it is suggested that both organizational and environmental determinants influence the franchisor's choice of entry mode (direct franchising, foreign direct investment, area development agreement, joint venture and master franchising). Expert opinion is used to identify the most influential determinants of entry mode choice by international franchisors. However, the results of the Delphi panel - composed of 35 international franchising experts - show that international franchising mode of entry determinants differ somewhat from those identified for entry mode choice in general. The findings also suggest that a specific conceptual framework is needed to explain entry mode choice by international franchisors and provide valuable insight into organizing future research in this area.

Acknowledgements. The author would like to thank the anonymous reviewer and Dr. Y. Chirouze for their insightful comments and suggestions on an earlier version of this paper, as well as all international franchising experts who so kindly agreed to participate in this study.

1 Introduction

The rapid growth of franchising during the twentieth century has made it one of the most important distribution channels in modern business. Furthermore, franchising is recognized throughout the world as a possible entry mode choice for firms seeking international expansion. Many authors have underlined the growing trend towards international franchising and have estimated that a majority of franchisors will soon have international operations.

Most recent studies on international franchising, using resource-based and agency theory, focus primarily on explaining the decision to internationalize in franchise systems or why franchisors internationalize. The international development of franchising firms has been attributed to a number of factors, both environmental and organizational (Alon 1999). However, very few studies have attempted to explain how these firms enter into foreign markets. This question seems to be of utmost importance to franchisors and may prove to be one of the major barriers to the internationalization of franchise systems around the globe.

Franchisors use various methods of development for international expansion: direct franchising, foreign direct investment, joint ventures, area development agreements and master franchising. Nevertheless, very little is actually known concerning the choice between these different entry modes. Although the importance of entry mode choice has been underlined in the past, there has not been a comprehensive framework allowing for a better understanding of entry mode choice by international franchisors. The purpose of this paper is to review existing literature on international franchising and entry mode choice and to respond to the question "Which factors influence the choice of international entry mode by franchisors?". Thus, the aim of this research is to provide answers to this critical question in the internationalization process of franchising firms.

To respond to this question, the Delphi method, one of the most well-established means of collecting expert opinion, has been used. More precisely, the electronic Delphi, a recent variation of the method, was implemented. The results contribute to identifying both environmental and organizational factors that influence international entry mode choice by franchisors. In addition, the findings make it possible to evaluate the relevant importance of each factor in the decision process.

2 Theoretical Framework

Very few studies have focused on analyzing the choice of mode of entry in a franchise setting. In this section, two different streams of research, international franchising literature and entry mode literature, will be examined before developing a model pertaining to international franchising entry mode choice.

2.1 International Franchising Literature

Most research in the field of franchising has focused on explaining the use of franchising networks in a strictly national context by using both resource-based and agency theories (Allix-Desfautaux 1994, 1998). It seems, however, that increasingly more franchisors are engaging in the internationalization process. While it is difficult to evaluate the actual extent of international franchising, the following figures published by the World Franchise Council (2002) underscore the importance of franchising in Europe (Table 1).

Although franchising has become a major growth strategy in Europe, its development remains rather heterogeneous (Fédération Française de la Franchise 2001). However, in major franchising countries, such as the United States and France, it has been estimated that between one-third and one-half of all franchising firms have or will soon have international operations (Direction du Commerce Extérieur 1998, Fédération Française de la Franchise 2001). Although many authors have underlined the natural tendency of franchising networks to develop internationally (Ferrier 1988), relatively few conceptual and empirical studies have actually concentrated on international franchising (Huszagh et al. 1992: Shane 1996;Fladmoe-Lindquist and Jacque 1995; Alon 1999).

Table 1. Franchising in Europe (2001)

Country	Number of franchisors	Number of franchisees
Great Britain	665	35,600
France	653	32,240
Germany (including all forms of associated commerce)	1125	-
Italy	536	28,127
Greece	400	-
Holland	380	14,250
Sweden	350	18,000
Austria	280	3,865
Belgium	170	3,500
Switzerland	150	-
Finland	122	4,171
Slovenia	94	980

For some authors, international franchising appears to be the most logical strategy for franchisors who have succeeded in their domestic market (Huszagh et al. 1992). From this point of view, international franchising is simply the extension of a domestic franchising concept outside of the franchisor's national boundaries, a form of cooperation between two partners from different cultural backgrounds (Allix-Desfautaux 1994).

Others define international franchising as "a foreign market entry mode that involves a relationship between the entrant (the franchisor) and a host country entity, in which the former transfers, under contract, a business package (or format), which it has developed and owns, to the latter" (Burton and Cross 1995 in Alon 1999). Considered as an international entry mode, franchising has often been compared to other modes of entry such as licensing or foreign direct investment (Root 1994; Shane 1996). However, international franchising can greatly differ from these other modes of entry in many ways (Fladmoe-Lindquist and Jacque 1995: Alon 1999) and is perceived by many firms as an alternative means of developing foreign markets (Allix-Desfautaux 1994). Although the characteristics of international franchising can most certainly differ according to the method chosen by the franchisor (direct franchising, joint-venture, master franchising), it is important to consider international franchising as a full-fledged international mode of entry rather than a temporary business strategy (Shane 1996; Allix-Desfautaux 1994).

Two different yet complementary streams of literature can be identified in international franchising. The first approach is rather descriptive in nature and focuses essentially on the strategic behavior of international franchisors (Walker and Etzel 1973; Hackett 1976), the numerous barriers to the internationalization of franchise systems (Aydin and Kacker 1990), and the differences between domestic and international franchisors (Aydin and Kacker 1990; Huszagh et al. 1992). These first studies have helped better our understanding of the international franchising, but do not sufficiently explain why or how franchisors internationalize.

More recently, a conceptual approach to international franchising has been adopted. Given the important advancements in internationalization research and franchising research, several authors have attempted to transpose existing theories to the field of international franchising (Eroglu 1992, McIntyre and Huszagh 1995). Some researchers have studied the internationalization of franchising firms and have proposed various models pertaining to the process. Welch (1989), for example, explained the diffusion of franchise system use throughout the world, while McIntyre and Huszagh (1995) identified the different phases of the internationalization process much as other authors have done for export activities. Fladmoe-Lindquist (1996) further developed this research by proposing a typology of international franchisors.

Perhaps the most comprehensive research in international franchising is that which focuses on explaining why franchisors internationalize and on identifying those factors which influence the intention to internationalize. This stream of literature comprises what certain researchers refer to as international franchising theory or the paradigm of international franchising (Eroglu 1992; Shane 1996, Alon 1999). Eroglu (1992) proposed the following conceptual model to explain international franchising.

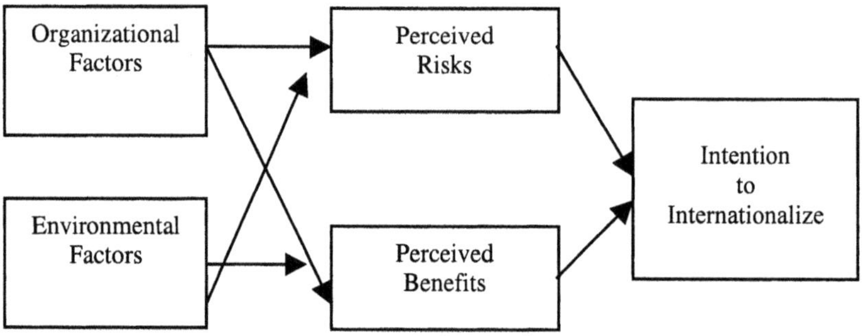

Fig. 1. Conceptual Model of the Internationalization Process of Franchise Systems

This model has been further developed by several empirical studies. Some authors have primarily focused on environmental factors (such as the economic situation, country risk and cultural distance) influencing the internationalization process (Bosereewong 1994; Alon 1999). By integrating both resource-based and agency theory into this framework, other researchers have underscored the importance of organizational factors (such as size, age, growth, price bonding and dispersion) (Shane 1996; Alon 1999). Although these studies greatly contribute to a better understanding of the internationalization process of franchising firms, they do not directly explain entry mode choice by international franchisors.

2.2 Entry Mode Literature

Entry mode choice is considered by many as one of the most important decisions in international marketing (Erramilli and Rao 1993; Root 1994; Contractor and Kundu 1998). Anderson and Gatignon (1986, p 2) define "mode of entry" as the "institutional arrangement" chosen by the firm for the foreign market. These institutional arrangements are numerous, ranging from indirect exporting to wholly-owned subsidiaries. Several authors have suggested clustering entry modes according to the entrant's level of control and level of resource commitment. Within these clusters, international franchising is described as a medium-control mode allowing balanced interests between partners (Anderson and Gatignon 1986) or as an entry mode requiring little investment, yet allowing for little control (De Leersynder 1986).

Prior explanations for entry mode choice draw from several different theoretical backgrounds: the Scandinavian stages model of entry (Johanson and Vahlne 1990), transaction-cost economics (Anderson and Gatignon 1986; Erramilli and Rao 1993), and the eclectic paradigm (Dunning 1988; Hill et al. 1990).

The first school of thought views internationalization as being inherently risky and thus advocates gradual involvement in foreign markets (Johanson and Vahlne 1990). When first entering into a foreign market, firms will tend to prefer low resource commitment modes such as exporting or licensing. As market knowledge and international experience increase, the firm will assume a higher level of resource commitment with higher levels of risk, control and profit return (Pan and Tse 2000). According to this perspective, international entry modes can be viewed as a continuum of incremental involvement in international markets.

The second school of thought uses transaction-cost analysis to explain entry mode choice (Anderson and Gatignon 1986; Erramilli and Rao 1993). This theoretical view holds that firms will internalize (or integrate) those activities that they can perform at a lower cost, but will subcontract those activities externally if potential partners have a cost advantage. From this perspective, market failure (characterized essentially by asset specificity, bounded rationality, uncertainty and opportunism) is the primary antecedent to the firm's decision to integrate international activities (Erramilli and Rao 1993). Thus, Anderson and Gatignon (1986) postulate that, in choosing entry modes, firms make trade-offs between control (benefit of integration) and cost of resource commitments (cost of integration).

The third school of thought is founded on Dunning's eclectic paradigm of international production and underlines the importance of country-specific factors in entry mode choice (Dunning 1988; Hill et al. 1990; Agarwal and Ramaswami 1992). This paradigm identifies three groups of factors influencing choice of entry mode: ownership-specific factors, location-specific factors and internalization factors. According to this model, foreign direct investment will be preferred to shared-control modes of entry when all three of these advantages are reunited (Hill et al. 1990).

Recently, several new approaches have been added to this theoretical framework. Shane (1994, 1996) and Fladmoe-Lindquist and Jacque (1995) have used agency theory to show that licensing and franchising can be considered as effective alternatives to foreign direct investment. Other researchers have suggested integrating institutional theory to the existing framework to improve entry mode choice explanations (Davis et al. 2000; Brouthers 2002). Pan and Tse (2000) have proposed a hierarchical model of entry mode choice identifying two different levels in the decision process. Several researchers have previously suggested that integrating different perspectives into the entry mode framework enhances our understanding of international entry mode choice (Kogut and Singh 1988; Brouthers 2002). In all of these streams of literature, researchers have attempted to identify the determining factors of international entry mode choice (Tables 2 and 3).

Table 2. Organizational Factors Influencing Entry Mode Choice

Factors	Author(s)
Control	Anderson and Gatignon (1986), Hill et al. (1990), Fladmoe-Lindquist and Jacque (1995), Buckley and Casson (1998), Contractor and Kundu (1998), Brouthers (2002)
National culture	Kogut and Singh (1988), Erramilli and Rao (1993), Shane (1994), Hennart and Larimo (1998), Makino and Neupert (2000), Almor (2001)
Level of investment	Hill, Hwang and Kim (1990), Erramilli and Rao (1993), Chang (1995), Ekeledo and Sivakumar (1998), Brouthers (2002), Lu (2002)
Asset specificity	Anderson and Gatignon (1986), Hill et al. (1990), Erramilli and Rao (1993), Fladmoe-Lindquist and Jacque (1995), Ekeledo and Sivakumar (1998),Lu (2002)
Experience	Anderson and Gatignon (1986), Anderson and Coughlan (1987), Dunning (1988), Kogut and Singh (1988), Agarwal and Ramswami (1992), Erramilli and Rao (1993), Fladmoe-Lindquist and Jacque (1995), Hennart and Larimo (1998), Ekeledo and Sivakumar (1998), Buckley and Casson (1998), Contractor and Kundu (1998), Davis et al. (2000),Almor (2001)
Firm size	Gatignon and Anderson (1988), Agarwal and Ramaswami (1992), Erramilli and Rao (1993), Hennart and Larimo (1998), Buckley and Casson (1998), Ekeledo and Sivakumar (1998), Almor (2001)
Product differentiation	Anderson and Coughlan (1987), Agarwal and Ramswami (1992), Erramilli and Rao (1993)
Strategic behavior	Kogut and Singh (1988), Dunning (1988), Hill et al. (1990), Contractor and Kundu (1998), Davis et al. (2000)
Advertising	Gatignon and Anderson (1988), Davis et al. (2000), Pan and Tse (2000)

Research and Development	Kogut and Singh (1988), Gatignon and Anderson (1988), Buckley and Casson (1998), Hennart and Larimo (1998), Davis et al. (2000)
Transaction costs	Anderson and Gatignon (1986), Gatignon and Anderson (1988), Erramilli and Rao (1993)
Internationalization rate	Contractor and Kundu (1998), Almor (2001)
Importance of ownership	Kogut and Singh (1988), Argarwal and Ramaswami (1992)
Product category	Anderson and Gatignon (1986), Erramilli and Rao (1993)
Brand image	Anderson and Gatignon (1986), Anderson and Coughlan (1987), Ekeledo and Sivakumar (1998)
Logistic capacity	Buckley and Casson (1998), Davis et al. (2000)
Recruiting, negotiating with partners	Contractor and Kundu (1998), Brouthers (2002)
Service level	Anderson and Coughlan (1987), Erramilli and Rao (1993), Ekeledo and Sivakumar (1998)
Isomorphism	Davis et al. (2000), Lu (2002)

Further to these organizational variables, Table 3 summarizes the entry mode literature pertaining to environmental determinants of international entry mode choice.

Table 3. Environmental factors influencing entry mode choice

Factors	Author(s)
Political and legal environment	Anderson and Coughlan (1987), Dunning (1988), Buckley and Casson (1998), Ekeledo and Sivakumar (1998), Davis et al. (2000), Brouthers (2002)
Country risk	Anderson and Gatignon (1986), Gatignon and Anderson (1988), Hill et al. (1990), Agarwal and Ramaswami (1992), Erramilli and Rao (1993), Fladmoe-Lindquist and Jacque (1995), Contractor and Kundu (1998), Ekeledo and Sivakumar (1998), Pan and Tse (2000), Davis et al. (2000), Almor (2001), Brouthers (2002)
Cultural distance	Anderson and Gatignon (1986), Anderson and Coughlan (1987), Kogut and Singh (1988), Johanson and Vahlne (1990), Erramilli and Rao (1993), Shane (1994), Fladmoe-Lindquist and Jacque (1995), Barkema and Vermeulen (1997), Ekeledo and Sivakumar (1998), Buckley and Casson (1998), Hennart and Larimo (1998), Davis et al. (2000), Pan and Tse (2000)
Geographical distance	Root (1994), Fladmoe-Lindquist and Jacque (1995)

Level of economic development	Contractor and Kundu (1998), Ekeledo and Sivakumar (1998)
Penetration by foreign firms	Anderson and Gatignon (1986), Ekeledo and Sivakumar (1998), Contractor and Kundu (1998)
Location	Anderson and Coughlan (1987), Dunning (1988), Hill et al. (1990), Buckley and Casson (1998), Pan and Tse (2000)
Competition	Anderson and Coughlan (1987), Dunning (1988), Hill et al. (1990), Ekeledo and Sivakumar (1998), Buckley and Casson (1998)
Market potential (size)	Agarwal and Ramaswami (1992), Buckley and Casson (1998), Ekeledo and Sivakumar (1998)
Market demand	Hill et al. (1990), Buckley and Casson (1998)
Growth rate	Hennart and Larimo (1998), Brouthers (2002)
Marketing infrastructure	Ekeledo and Sivakumar (1998)

2.3 Entry Mode Choice in International Franchising

Although entry mode literature is abundant in economics and management, few researchers have studied international franchising in this context or attempted to explain how franchising firms enter into foreign markets. Motivation for internationalization have been examined by numerous researchers (Shane 1996; Alon 1999). However, very little is actually known concerning the choice between different franchising modes of entry.

Franchisors may use various methods of development for international expansion. Although master franchising seems to be the entry mode that is most often associated with international franchising in the literature (Nègre 2000; Alon 2000; Ferrier 1988), several other entry modes are available to international franchisors. These firms may enter into foreign markets not only by using master franchising, but also by direct franchising or area development agreements, by setting up a local subsidiary or by entering into joint-venture agreements with local partners (Konigsberg 1996).

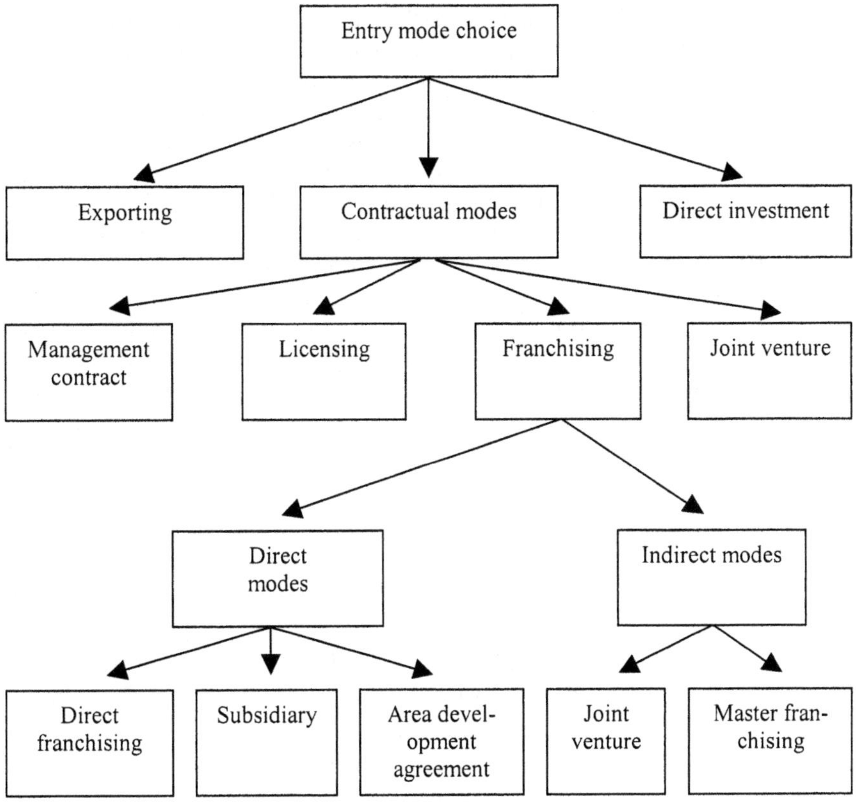

Fig. 2. International Franchising Entry Mode Choices

Direct entry modes are arrangements that allow for a direct relationship between the franchisor and foreign franchisees. In the case of direct franchising, the franchisor manages foreign franchisees from the home country. The franchisor may also choose to establish a subsidiary in the host country in order to develop and control the local network. Although area development agreements are sometimes considered as a type of master franchise agreement (Alon 2000), the developer is not a sub-franchisor, but rather a franchisee who owns all outlets in the zone and who interacts directly with the franchisor (Nègre 2000).

In indirect modes of entry, an intermediary in the host country intervenes in the relationship between the franchisor and foreign franchisees. Some franchisors choose to enter into joint venture agreements with local partners. The joint venture entity manages the local network on behalf of the international franchisor. Master franchising may also be chosen. According to Alon (2000, p 3) "master international franchising refers to the contractual agreement between the franchisor and an independently owned sub-franchisor to develop a specified number of franchises in a given country in exchange for the exclusive right to use the business format for a specified amount of time". Thus, master franchising allows the franchisor to entrust the development and supervision of the franchise system to a third party who will act as the franchisor in the foreign market.

While most studies in this area have focused on only one mode of entry, primarily on master franchising (Alon 2000; Nègre 2000), others have concentrated on the choice between international franchising and foreign direct investment, or franchised units versus company-owned units in foreign markets (Shane 1994; Fladmoe-Lindquist and Jacque 1995). A comprehensive approach, including both direct and indirect modes, has been chosen for this study and is used for model development.

Although international entry mode choice in a franchise setting is a complex decision determined by numerous variables, the model developed in this paper is illustrated in figure 3.

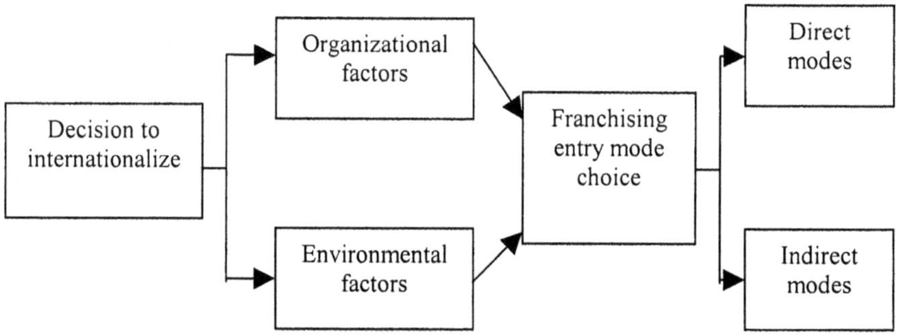

Fig. 3. Model of International Franchising Entry Mode Choice

As with all entry modes, international franchising alternatives most likely depend on both organizational and environmental conditions (Tables 2 and 3). These determinants may also coincide with those factors influencing the franchisor's decision to internationalize (Bosereewong 1994; Shane 1996; Alon 1999). However, it is possible that the relative importance of each determinant be altered in a franchising setting.

Thus, the general research proposition developed in this paper is that the factors influencing international franchising mode of entry will differ from those influencing entry mode choice in general. It is believed that the specific nature of international franchising modes of entry calls for an adaptation of the conceptual framework found in the traditional entry mode literature.

As suggested by Pan and Tse (2000), entry mode choice must be considered as a hierarchical decision process. In the case of franchising, a firm will first choose whether to use international franchising and then choose the type of agreement that is to be implemented in the foreign market. The factors influencing the choice of international franchising compared to other modes of entry (such as exporting, licensing or foreign direct investment) may not necessarily be as important when choosing a precise franchising mode of entry (direct franchising, area development agreement, joint venture, subsidiary or master franchising). Some determinants, such as size and age, have been shown to influence both general entry mode choice and the franchisor's decision to internationalize (Erramilli and Rao 1993; Alon 1999). However, once the franchisor has decided to expand abroad, these factors may play a less important role in determining international strategy. On the other hand, some franchise-specific variables, such as the importance of franchising in the host country or the proportion of franchisor-owned units in the network, may influence the choice between international franchising modes of entry. Furthermore, while most general entry mode determinants will surely intervene somewhat in deciding franchising modes of entry, it is possible that the intensity of each determinant will be altered in an international franchise setting.

3 Methods and Results

Given the fact that relatively few studies have been conducted in the past concerning entry mode choice in a franchise setting, an exploratory approach has been adopted to analyze this important aspect of international franchising. In this section, the research design and findings will be presented and then discussed.

3.1 Research Design

The Delphi technique was employed to respond to the previously established research question. This technique is one of the most well established means of collecting expert opinion and of gaining consensus among experts on various critical factors under consideration (Dalkey and Helmer 1962; Linstone and Turoff 1975). This iterative technique allows the researcher to incorporate subjective data into the evaluation of complex research problems, which is important in exploratory studies. The Delphi method has proven to be a useful research tool providing valuable insight in social sciences.

This Delphi study was conducted by e-mail over a five-month period. After identifying international franchising experts in various journals and professional associations (all national franchise associations, various franchising directories, *Franchising World* and *Franchise International* professional journals, numerous research journals and several universities), an invitation to participate in the study was sent to over a hundred prospective panel members. An important well-diversified expert panel was established and an overall response rate of 26 percent was obtained. Thirty-five international franchising experts participated in this three-round iterative process aimed at identifying and evaluating determining factors of international entry mode choice by franchisors. These experts come from various professional backgrounds (executives of several franchising associations, franchise and export directors in international franchising firms, university researchers, and franchising consultants and attorneys) and represent all regions of the world (Table 4).

Table 4. Profil of Expert Panel

Region	Number of experts	Profession	Number of experts
Europe	23	International franchising executives	12
North America	7	Franchising association executives	9
Asia-Pacific	2	Franchising consultants	7
Middle East	1	University researchers	4
South America	1	Franchising attorneys and legal consultants	3
Africa	1		

The expert panel members were asked to respond to the following question: Which factors influence the choice of international entry mode for franchisors? For this question, several environmental and organizational factors were listed and each expert was asked to evaluate the different variables on a 4-point Likert-type scale anchored unimportant to very important (1 = unimportant, 2 = slight important, 3 = important, and 4 = very important). Furthermore, all experts had the possibility to identify additional items in the first round.

For the round two questionnaire, a statistical summary of first round results was sent to all experts along with the questionnaire, including the additional items suggested by panel members. For each environmental and organizational variable, statistical information pertaining to the group's first round responses, as well as to each expert's previous response, was given. The experts were then asked to reaffirm or modify responses in the light of the statistical data provided. For responses deviating from the group's central response, panel members were invited to explain their opinions. A response rate of 89 percent was obtained for this round of the study.

In the third round, a revised statistical summary taking into account previous modifications was sent to all experts. Panel members were asked once again to confirm or modify responses. Very few modifications between rounds two and three occurred and a response rate of 100 percent was obtained for the final round.

For data analysis, several statistical measures were used. As with nearly all Delphi studies, mean and median panel scores were calculated for each item to reveal central group responses. Items were then ranked according to mean scores; in the case of the same mean score occuring for two items, the median was used for ranking purposes. Standard deviation, inter-quartile range and coefficient of variation were used as a measure of dispersion, thus evaluating the degree of consensus between experts. As researchers have previously stated (Bosereewong 1994), a reduction in standard deviation and in coefficient of variation over the different Delphi rounds represents an increasing consensus among panel members.

3.2 Findings

One drawback of the Delphi technique is that it is impossible to foresee the number of rounds necessary for achieving optimal results. The Delphi process can stop when the researcher observes an important decrease in standard deviation (which represents dispersion and dissension within the group) between the different rounds and when few modifications are made by panel members (Dalkey and Helmer 1962). For the purposes of this study, three rounds were believed to be sufficient because (1) most panel members did not wish to modify third round results, (2) standard deviation was minimal and decreasing, and (3) consensus was achieved for nearly all items.

Table 5. Variation of Average Standard Deviation over the Three Delphi Rounds

	Round I Standard deviation	Round II Standard deviation	Round III Standard deviation
Environmental factors	0.76	0.66	0.64
Organizational factors	0.71	0.66	0.65

After receiving third round questionnaires with modified responses from all experts composing the panel, statistical analysis was used to evaluate the data obtained during the Delphi process. Tables 6 and 7 represent the results of the final round of the study pertaining to environmental and organization determinants of international entry mode choice by franchisors. Taking into consideration the mean score for each variable, these factors have been ranked from most important determinant (4) to least important determinant (1) according to the experts' opinions.

Table 6. Environmental Determinants of Entry Mode Choice by Franchisors

Environmental factors	Mean score	Standard deviation	Coefficient of variation
Financial situation of local partners	3.63	0.55	0.15
Economic risk	3.48	0.50	0.14
Brand protection conditions	3.47	0.50	0.14
Local regulations	3.42	0.55	0.16
Market size	3.23	0.55	0.17
Political risk	3.23	0.61	0.19
Competitive situation	3.19	0.74	0.23
Level of economic development	3.06	0.50	0.16

Cultural differences	3.03	0.78	0.26
Sources of supply	3.00	0.62	0.21
Conditions of out-going money transfer	2.97	0.75	0.25
Tax system	2.81	0.59	0.21
Geographical/physical distance	2.74	0.72	0.26
Franchisor's national culture	2.65	0.74	0.28
Penetration rate of foreign firms	2.48	0.67	0.27
Marketing infrastructure	2.48	0.76	0.30
Importance of franchising in the host country	2.42	0.71	0.29

The financial situation of (potential) local partners, economic risk, brand protection conditions, local regulations and market size are considered to be the five most important environmental determinants of entry mode choice by international franchising members (Table 6). Although no factor was considered to be unimportant in the decision process, the importance of franchising in the host country, marketing infrastructure, the penetration rate of foreign firms in the host country, the franchisor's national culture and geographical distance are all thought to be only slightly important in influencing the franchisor's entry mode choice.

As with the environmental determinants, financial considerations are ranked as being very important among the organizational factors affecting franchisor's choice of entry mode (Table 7). According to the experts participating in this study, the franchisor's financial resources, executive attitudes and orientations, recruiting and training franchisees, the franchisor's human resources and brand image are the five most important organizational determinants of entry mode choice. Other factors, such as the proportion of company-owned units, the age of the franchise system, experience of local (potential) franchisees, the search for scale economies and the size of the franchise system, seem to be of minor importance, although previous research has found some of these variables to be important in explaining why franchisors decide to internationalize (Alon 1999).

Table 7. Organizational Determinants of Entry Mode Choice by Franchisors

Organizational factors	Mean score	Standard deviation	Coefficient of variation
Franchisor's financial resources	3.58	0.55	0.15
Executive attitudes and orientations	3.45	0.66	0.19
Recruiting and training franchisees	3.40	0.70	0.21
Franchisor's human resources	3.23	0.55	0.17
Brand image	3.16	0.72	0.23
Franchisor's international experience	3.16	0.72	0.23
Need for control	3.13	0.75	0.24
Type of products and services sold	3.08	0.57	0.18
Degree of standardization of the franchise	3.06	0.76	0.25
Franchisor's logistic capacity	3.03	0.74	0.24
Brand and trade name recognition	3.03	0.82	0.27
Geographic dispersion of units	2.84	0.57	0.20
Price bonding ratio (entry fees / royalties)	2.84	0.72	0.25
Franchisor's internationalization rate	2.68	0.53	0.20
Network mode of coordination	2.67	0.47	0.18
Size of the franchise system	2.65	0.54	0.20
Search for scale economies	2.65	0.60	0.23
Experience of local franchisees	2.57	0.67	0.26
Age of the franchise system	2.29	0.58	0.25
Proportion of company-owned units	2.29	0.68	0.30

3.3 Summary of Results and Discussion

The Delphi technique used for this study has shed a considerable amount of light on entry mode choice in a franchise setting. The research approach employed is exploratory in nature, but the research proposition previously developed was confronted contested by expert opinion. Furthermore, descriptive statistical analysis was used to evaluate the relative importance of each entry mode determinant in the entry mode decision process.

The research proposition pertaining to the importance of various environmental and organizational determinants of international franchising entry mode choice seems to be confirmed by the data obtained in this study. Some of the variables that were found to be very important in previous international franchising or entry mode studies were observed to be of lesser importance by the international franchising experts comprising the Delphi panel. Table 8 summarizes the principal determinants of international franchising entry mode choice, as judged by the group of international franchising experts.

Table 8. Principal Determinants of International Franchising Entry Mode Choice

Environmental factors	Organizational factors
- Financial situation of local partners	- Franchisor's financial resources
- Economic risk	- Executive attitudes and orientations
- Brand protection conditions	- Recruiting and training franchisees
- Local regulations	- Brand image
- Market size	- Franchisor's international experience
- Political risk	- Need for control
- Competitive situation	- Type of products and services sold
- Level of economic development	- Degree of standardization of the franchise
- Cultural differences	- Franchisor's logistical capacity
- Sources of supply	- Brand and trade name recognition

These most important factors differ from those found in previous studies, whether they be in the field of entry mode choice in general or in the field of international franchising. Among the organizational factors, for example, Alon (1999) has found both resourced-based factors (such as age and size) and agency related factors (such as price bonding and geographical dispersion) to be important determinants of the franchisor's decision to internationalize. These factors do not rank within the top ten determinants of franchising entry mode choice and thus seem to be of lesser importance once the franchisor has decided to internationalize. Interestingly, agency related factors score slightly higher than resource-based factors, suggesting that agency theory may provide better explanation of entry mode choice by franchisors than resource-based theory. However, the capital-scarcity construct cannot be ignored because the franchisor's financial resources are believed to be the most critical factor influencing entry mode choice.

For environmental factors, the same type of observations can be made. Although some determinants such as country risk, competitive situation, and institutional environment were found to be important in the decision process as in previous studies (Anderson and Gatignon 1986, Davis et al. 2000), other factors, such as cultural distance and franchisor's national culture, were surprisingly viewed as being of lesser importance by the experts surveyed in this study. It is thus possible that franchising, as a business concept, reduces to some extent the effects of culture. Or, it may also be that franchisors do not sufficiently take into account the importance of cultural differences when entering into foreign markets. This could account for some of the failures of international franchising firms in distant markets. Concerning the entry mode literature, the results of this study do not show one stream of literature as explaining franchising entry mode choice better than another. Location-specific variables (such as country risk and level of economic development) suggested by the eclectic paradigm appear to be as important as transaction cost variables (such as brand image, important in determining asset specificity).

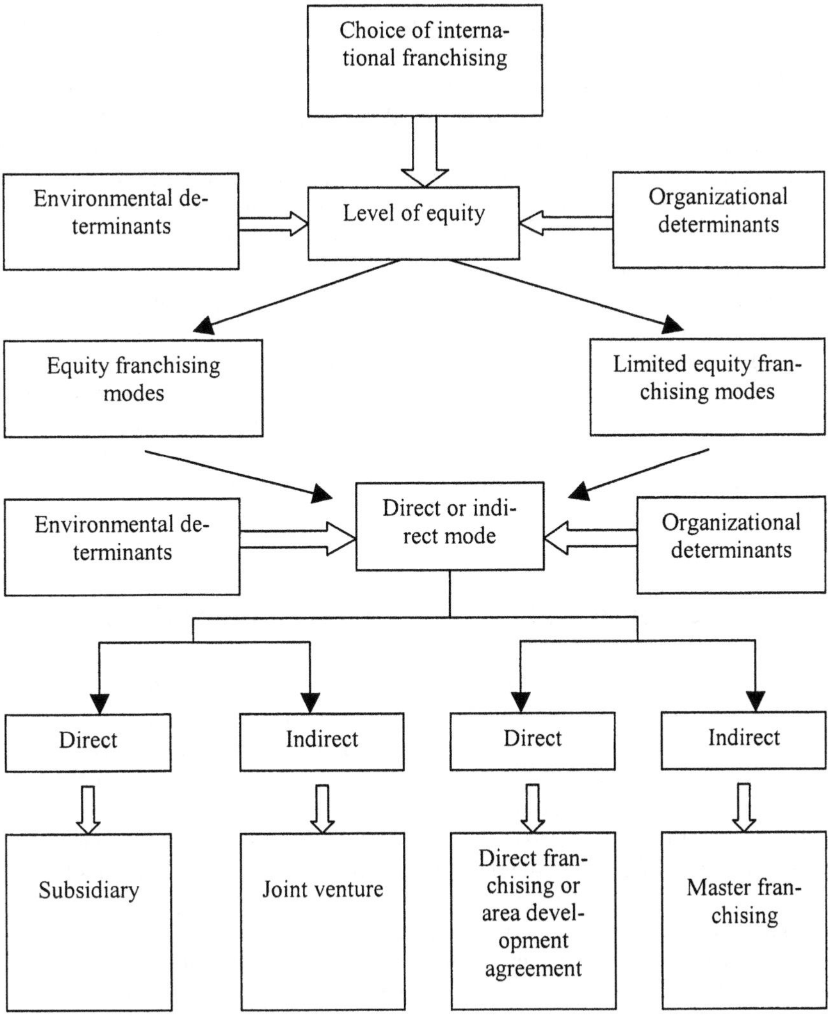

Fig. 4. Modified Hierarchical Model of International Franchising Entry Mode Choice

Thus, for some determinants, the effects on international franchising entry mode choice do differ from those suggested by the traditional entry mode literature. Furthermore, in terms of importance, some franchise-specific variables were not confirmed by the expert panel. Two franchise-specific variables, the importance of franchising in the host country and the proportion of company-owned units in the franchise system, were found to be the least important factors influencing entry mode choice.

The findings observed in this study also suggest that the hierarchical model of entry modes proposed by Pan and Tse (2000) applies somewhat to the case of international franchising (Figure 4). However, rather than first choosing between direct and indirect modes of entry, it seems that international franchisors first choose between equity and non-equity (or limited-equity) franchising options. Financial determinants appear to be of utmost importance in the decision process. It is possible that the franchisor's financial resources and the financial situation of prospective partners influence the choice between equity (subsidiary or joint venture) and non-equity modes of entry (master franchising or area development agreements), while other factors such as market conditions, executive attitudes and international experience apply secondly to the choice between specific equity or non-equity, direct or indirect modes of entry. The findings of this study suggest that the determinants of the first-level decision differ from the determinants of the second-level decision in the hierarchical process of international franchising entry mode choice.

4 Conclusion and Implications for Future Studies

In this study, a conceptual framework for explaining entry mode choice in a franchise setting was developed. The Delphi technique was used to test this framework by a group of prominent international franchising experts. Both environmental and organization determinants of entry mode choice were identified and the importance of each determinant in the decision process was evaluated in comparison to others. Furthermore, some clarifications were made concerning the various modes of entry available to franchising firms seeking international expansion.

The findings of this study may be of interest to both researchers and franchising professionals alike. From a theoretical point of view, this paper provides valuable insight into the choice of various international franchising techniques by using a conceptual framework drawn from both the entry-mode and franchising literature. It presents certain methodological interests as well. It explores and tests recent variations of a research method aimed at obtaining expert opinion on complex business problems. Finally, this study will be useful for franchisors seeking international expansion by guiding them in their choice of different international franchising modes of entry. Although the results of this research must be confirmed by future empirical studies, they suggest the hierarchical nature of the entry mode decision process, identifying the factors influencing each level of entry mode choice.

This may prove to be valuable to franchisors who are reluctant to enter foreign markets because of the complexity of entry mode choice. Given these important implications, future studies and more empirical research are needed in order to contribute to a better understanding of entry mode choice by international franchisors.

In spite of the interesting approach used to analyze this important international franchising problem, there are some limitations to this study. First, as with all Delphi studies, the quality of the results obtained depends essentially on the choice of experts. Although it was important for the purposes of this research to have a well-diversified panel of experts, some differences of opinion may be related to national and professional backgrounds. However, given the reputation and experience of the selected experts, the risk of obtaining biased information was kept at a minimum. Second, although previous studies have shown that differences exist between franchisors in the retailing and services sectors, and even within each business category, a global approach was adopted for this study. It may be interesting in future studies to isolate specific industries in order to validate the determinants identified by this research. Third, some interesting questions, directly related to entry mode choice by international franchisors, have not been addressed in this paper. It would be interesting, for example, to collect expert opinion pertaining to the benefits and risks of each different entry mode or to forecast the relative importance of each entry mode in time. Future research will focus on these questions.

Future direction for upcoming investigations can be oriented in several directions. First of all, the hierarchical model of international franchising entry mode choice is still in an exploratory phase. It is thus necessary to further develop and empirically test the model that was put forth by the present study. Secondly, it is important to adopt not only a descriptive and prescriptive approach in future studies, but also a prospective one. This is why upcoming studies will take into consideration the evolution of international franchising entry modes over time, allowing franchisors to anticipate entry mode strategies in an ever-changing international environment. Finally, several experts in the Delphi panel underscored the growing importance of new technologies on entry mode choice in franchising networks. Future research will focus on the consequences of multi-channel strategies (franchising and Internet) and of communication via Internet on international franchising and on entry mode choice.

References

1. Agarwal S, Ramaswami SN (1992) Choice of Foreign Market Entry Mode : Impact of Ownership, Location and Internalization Factors. Journal of International Business Studies, First Quarter:1-27
2. Allix-Desfautaux C (1998) Le choix de la franchise, Revue Française de Gestion, mars-avril-mail, 59-65
3. Allix-Desfautaux C (1994) La franchise internationale: un mode de développement à part entière? Annales du management, 12ème journées nationales des IAE :527-546

4. Almor T (2002) Towards a Contingency View of Market Entry Strategies: Contextual and Strategic Factors. Journal of Euromarketing 10(1):5-25
5. Alon I (2000) The Organizational Determinants of Master International Franchising. Journal of Business and Entrepreneurship 12 (2):1-18
6. Alon I (1999) The Internationalization of U.S. Franchising Systems. New York: Garland Publishing Inc.
7. Alon I (1999b) Organizational Determinants of International Franchising in the Hotel Sector, Journal of Global Business 10(18):55-62
8. Alon I, McKee DL (1999) The Internationalization of Professional Business Service Franchises. Journal of Consumer Marketing 16(1):74-85
9. Anderson E, Coughlan AT (1987) International Market Entry and Expansion Via Independent or Integrated Channels of Distribution. Journal of Marketing 51:71-82
10. Anderson E, Gatignon H (1986) Modes of Foreign Entry: A Transaction Cost Analysis and Propositions. Journal of International Business Studies, Fall:1-26
11. Aydin N, Kacker M (1990) International Outlook of US-based Franchisers. International Marketing Review 7(2):43-53
12. Barkema HG, Vermeulen F (1997) What Differences in the Cultural Backgrounds of Partners are Detrimental for International Joint Ventures? Journal of International Business Studies, 28:845-863
13. Bosereewong V (1994) Identification of Environmental Factors that Influence the Choice of Franchising Methods of U.S. Restaurant Companies in Pan Pacific Region, PhD dissertation, Virginia Polytechnic Institute
14. Brouthers KD (2002) Institutional, Cultural and Transaction Cost Influences on Entry Mode Choice and Performance. Journal of International Business Studies 33(2):203-221
15. Buckley PJ, Casson MC (1998) Analyzing Foreign Market Entry Strategies: Extending the Internalization Approach. Journal of International Business Studies 29(3):539-562
16. Chang S (1995) International Expansion Strategy of Japanese Firms: Capability Building Through Sequential Entry. Academy of Management Journal 38(2):383-407
17. Contractor FJ, Kundu SK (1998) Modal Choice in a World of Alliances: Analyzing Organizational Forms in the International Hotel Sector. Journal of International Business Studies, 29(2):325-358
18. Dalkey N, Helmer O (1962) An Experimental Application of the Delphi Method to the Use of Experts. Management Science 9(3):458-467
19. Davis PS, Desai AB, Francis JD (2000) Mode of International Entry: An Isomorphism Perspective. Journal of International Business Studies 31 (2):239-258
20. De Leersnyder (1986) Marketing international, Paris: Dalloz
21. Direction du Commerce Intérieur (1998) Groupe de réflexion sur l'évolution du droit de la franchise: rapport de synthèse, Paris: DCI, 25 pp
22. Dunning JH (1988) The Eclectic Paradigm of International Production: A Restatement and Some Possible Extensions. Journal of International Business Studies, Spring:1-31
23. Ekeledo I, Sivakumar K (1998) Foreign Market Entry Mode Choice of Service Firms: A Contingency Perspective. Journal of the Academy of Marketing Science 26 (4):274-292
24. Eroglu S (1992) The Internationalization Process of Franchise Systems: A Conceptual Model. International Marketing Review 9(5):19-30
25. Erramilli MK, Rao CP (1993) Service Firms' International Entry-Mode Choice: A Modified Transaction-Cost Analysis Approach. Journal of Marketing 57:19-38
26. Fédération Française de la Franchise (2001), www.franchise-fff.com
27. Ferrier D (1988) La franchise internationale. Journal du droit international 3 :625-662
28. Fladmoe-Lindquist K (1996) International Franchising: Capabilities and Developments. Journal of Business Venturing 11(6):419-438

29.Fladmoe-Lindquist K, Jacque LL (1995) Control Modes in International Service Operations: The Propensity to Franchise. Management Science 41(7):1238-1249
30.Hackett DW (1976) The International Expansion of US Franchise Systems: Status and Strategies. Journal of International Business Studies, Spring:65-75
31.Hennart J-F, Larimo J (1998) The Impact of Culture on the Strategy of Multinational Enterprises: Does National Origin Affect Ownership Decisions?, Journal of International Business Studies 29(3): 515-538
32.Hill CWL, Hwang P, Kim WC (1990) An Eclectic Theory of the Choice of International Entry Mode. Strategic Management Journal 11:117-128
33.Huszagh SM, Huszagh FW, McIntyre FS (1992) International Franchising in the Context of Competitive Strategy and the Theory of the Firm. International Marketing Review 9(5):5-18
34.Johanson J, Vahlne J-E (1990) The Mechanism of Internationalization, International Marketing Review 7:11-24
35.Justis RT, Judd R (1986) Master Franchising: A New Look. Journal of Small Business Management July:16-21
36.Kogut B, Singh H (1988) The Effect of National Culture on the Choice of Entry Mode. Journal of International Business Studies 19(3): 411-432
37.Konigsberg AS (1996) International Franchising. New York: Juris Publishing Inc.
38.Linstone HA, Turoff (1975) The Delphi Method: Techniques and Applications. Reading: Addison-Wesley
39.Lu JW (2002) Intra- and Inter-Organizational Imitative Behavior: Institutional Influences on Japanese Firms' Entry Mode Choice. Journal of International Business Studies 33(1):19-37
40.Makino S, Neupert KE (2000) National Culture, Transaction Costs, and the Choice Between Joint Venture and Wholly Owned Subsidiary. Journal of International Business Studies 31(4):705-713
41.McIntyre FS, Huszagh SM (1995) Internationalization of Franchise Systems. Journal of International Marketing 3(4):39-56.
42.Nègre C (2000) Master franchise, épiphénomène et transitoirité, Paris: Fédération Française de la Franchise
43.Nègre C (1997) Master franchise, stratégie d'alliance, Paris: Fédération Française de la Franchise
44.Pan Y, Tse DK (2000) The Hierarchical Model of Market Entry Modes. Journal of International Business Studies 31(4):535-554
45.Root FR (1994) Entry Strategy for International Markets. Lexington :Lexington Books
46.Shane SA (1996) Why Franchise Companies Expand Overseas. Journal of Business Venturing 11:73-88
47.Shane SA (1994) The Effect of National Culture on the Choice Between Licensing and Direct Foreign Investment. Strategic Management Journal 15:627-642
48.Walker BJ, Etzel MJ (1973) The Internationalization of US Franchise Systems: Progress and Procedures. Journal of Marketing 37:38-46
49.Welch LS (1989) Diffusion of Franchise System Use in International Operations. International Marketing Review 6:7-19

The Choice of Foreign Entry Mode by the Franchiser: Case Studies of Lithuanian Franchisers Entering Latvia

Regina Jarmalaite, Irina Sekundo

Stockholm School of Economics in Riga
Strelnieku 4a, LV-1010 Riga, Latvia
r_jarmalaite@hotmail.com
irina.sekundo@parex.lv

Abstract. This paper is the first attempt in the Baltic market to explain the strategic motives behind and to find reasons for decision-making factors related to the expansion of franchise companies internationally via either ownership or contractual entry modes. On the basis of two case studies concerning Lithuanian franchisers that have entered the Latvian market in order to create a franchising network, motivating factors and their influences on a franchise's choice of entry mode have been explored. Twelve factors have been identified and critically evaluated, and five propositions that reflect the decision-making considerations for Lithuanian franchisers concerning the choice of entry mode to Latvia have been put forward. The findings of this paper are expected to help future Baltic franchisers in choosing the best mode within which to enter the foreign market.

1 Introduction

Throughout the United States and Western Europe - the countries of the world that are called mature in their economic development - the concept of franchising is an integral part of the entrepreneurial environment. Nevertheless, the Baltic countries have proven to portray rather undeveloped local company franchising practices.

Several factors that would foster the growth of the franchise business in the Baltics have already been explored by Brennere and Petrova (2002) in their research, which focuses on the situation in the Baltic country of Latvia. Taking a step forward in this research, a fundamentally different perspective was explored: international expansion of companies that have already been operating as franchisers in the domestic market and which in the near or far future are also planning to operate as franchisers in the foreign market. In this paper, the Lithuanian franchisers' choices of entry mode into the Latvian market have been investigated.

The strategic motives, choices, and development of the company as it acts in the domestic market as a franchiser via different modes for entering the foreign market are regarded by new entrants into the foreign market as extremely important. Moreover, such a topic is of greatest importance to entrepreneurs in the Baltics, countries which have fast developing economies (GDP increase in 2000 – 6,0%, 2001- 7,0%, 2002-6,2%)[1] which, due to the scarcity of investment resources, must take very cautious steps when dealing with foreign development. Thus, the analyzed topic is a source considered valuable by the SME, a franchise management that pursues a possible foreign market entry strategy into Latvia. Even though this paper does not provide a general recipe for an entrance strategy, the research it supplies sets guidelines for the SME – franchisers that may be contemplating the growth they could achieve in other countries' markets.

The primary aim of this research is to recognize and to evaluate the critical motives behind the choice of entry mode of Lithuanian franchisers entering the Latvian market. Critical motives behind the choice of entry mode can furthermore be understood as the issues considered by the franchiser before and during its entrance phase into the foreign market. In this research, an attempt to answer the following questions has been made: What are the factors influencing the choice of a franchiser when selecting the mode of entry into a foreign market? How have the aforementioned factors influenced the choice of entry mode in the case of Lithuanian franchisers entering Latvia?

Three different ways in which a company can start an international business have been recognized: the contractual entry mode (the formation of franchising relationships, management contracts, joint ventures and licensing), the ownership entry mode (the direct investment of one's own capital to build up a branch in a foreign country) (Root 1994; Shane 1996), and exporting (Konigsberg 1996). However, our research very early on had been limited to only two entry modes: contractual (franchising) and ownership (equity), because these two modes relate to long-lasting relationship formations in the foreign market, whereas export is a more case-wide occurrence.

The structure of this paper is as follows. Examination of the theoretical framework necessary for analysis is represented in the section 2. Further on, the methodological approach chosen for the study is revealed. Next, empirical data is explored in section 4, which consists of two case company discussions. After initially presenting the general background of the companies, the factors influencing the choice of entry mode into the foreign market have been examined explicitly. Finally, in the last section, the interpretation of research findings and the discussion of critical motives for the choice of entry mode have been revealed in a broader context.

2 Theoretical Background

In the prior researches only few authors examine foreign entry mode in a franchise setting. This section unfolds literature on franchising and internalization, focusing on reasons for choice of foreign entry mode.

[1] Data is provided by respective Central Statistical Bureaus in the Baltic Countries.

2.1 Franchising and Internationalization

Franchising has been regarded as a form of entrepreneurial activity in which an agreement has been defined that "the owner of protected trademark grants to another person or firm, for some consideration the right to operate under this trademark for the purpose of producing or distributing a product or service" (Caves and Murphy 1976, p 572). Apart from the trademark that creates value for the franchiser, a competitive uniqueness also exists in the business methods, procedures and services offered to customers (Contractor and Kundu 1998, p 29). It has been regarded as common business practice that the first steps in franchising a business are taken in the domestic market, the closest region around the recognizable brand outlet (Huszagh et al. 1992). However, domestic market utilization, if the brand loyalty and service or product quality are well worked out, has proven to be a fast process. Once the benefits of the domestic market have been utilized, it is expected that a successful entrepreneur would attempt to enter the foreign market in order to open up a franchising network there.

International franchisees are mainly regarded as market seekers who exploit their firm-specific capabilities overseas (Pak 2002, p 28). Indeed franchising is one of the fastest ways to expand in foreign countries by using the least amount of capital expenditures and management time. The majority of time and effort should be spent on the screening of possible partners (Brouthers 2002), agreement formation, and franchisee staff training (Anderson and Gatignon 1986). It then becomes the responsibility of the franchiser to secure its competitiveness in the market, which requires even less effort if the brand name is already known. It would then seem obvious that franchisers should enter a new market, without hesitation, through a franchising agreement; however, there are still some that choose another mode.

Two different foreign market entry modes for franchisers have been categorized as contractual and ownership modes. The *Contractual entry* mode is when the owner of the service concept (principal) enters into a contract with an unrelated party (agent) to use a specifically formatted business service concept to sell services or goods under the principal's trademark. However, the principal does not invest funds of its own in the local service unit, as the agent takes responsibility for the construction, maintenance, and management of the local operation (Fladmoe-Lindquist and Jacque 1995, p 1238). This international expansion occurs either via direct franchising, subsidiary, area development agreement, joint venture, or master franchisers (Zietlow and Hennart 1996, as cited by Pak 2002). The *Ownership entry mode* is a mode directed to a foreign market when a parent company either entirely owns or manages the foreign unit or relies on some type of joint venture agreement (Fladmoe-Lindquist and Jacque 1995, p 1238). This entry mode involves a franchise setting up its own outlet or joint venture formation with a local company, a merger, by acquisition of a local firm, or through direct foreign investment.

The franchiser's strategy concerning the future and the strategic importance of the foreign market have been recognized as the main criterion regarding which entry mode a franchiser will choose (Pak 2002, p 34). It has been assumed that those who choose the contractual mode seek a fast way of increasing revenues and decreasing costs. When an independent entrepreneur operates the outlet, management and supervision costs are reduced. Pak (2002) regards such an approach as static since "it focuses on the exploitation of franchiser's current positions and emphasizes the benefit of being a franchiser that enables to minimize the investment requirements and to access foreign markets easily". The companies entering the foreign market through ownership mode, on the contrary, are regarded as dynamic as they seem to possess more knowledge regarding the specifics of the local market orientation strategy. They list experience and adaptations in local conditions as primary goals; only after these goals are achieved do they make the decision to open a franchise network. According to Dunning (1993), the importance of foreign locations as a source of a firm's valuable new ideas and/or strategic assets needs to be especially stressed. Thus, the equity type entry companies are recognized as keener on learning because they realize that knowledge of local specifics can give them a competitive edge and can increase their ability to exploit foreign market opportunities.

The reasoning and approaches behind the two different entry modes suggest that companies which invest their own capital into foreign branches more critically assess the local market conditions than those who enter via franchising mode. This could possibly lead to a less effective market potential recognition by franchising mode entrants.

2.2 Reasons for Choice of Entry Modes

As it has been recognized by Contractor and Kundu (1998), the decision of a franchiser concerning the foreign entry mode to choose can be based on three general criteria: firm and industry specific factors, country characteristics and firm strategic intent and preferences. Evaluation of each of these criteria would then lead the franchiser to the best-fit entry mode.

2.2.1 Firm and Industry Specific Factors

Firm and industry specific factors are those which, firstly, differentiate the company from its competitors, and, secondly, clarify the power distribution in the exact industry from other industries. Primarily, these factors are advantages regarding the company's resource, capabilities, and the ability to cope with tension and form alliances, a successful combination of which can result in the company's internationalization (Shane 1996). However, not all of these advantages are mobile; often a sophisticated adaptation to the local market must be made in order to make these advantages usable abroad. Many previous pieces of research (Anderson and Gatignon 1986; Agarwal and Ramaswami 1992; Erramilli and Rao 1993) have identified firm- and industry-specific factors that have impacted the choice of an entry mode. The firm-specific factors are the size of the company, product specifics, and international experience. The industry-specific factor is, in this case, the distribution of rivalry power in the particular industry.

The first firm specific factor - the size of the company - represents the amount of resources the company has at its disposal and the capabilities it has developed, which are considered to be the knowledge resources of the company (Erramilli and Rao 1993). Firms with greater resource availability have a greater possibility to perform an ownership mode entry into the foreign market (Brouthers and Nakos 2002, p 49).

Secondly, ownership of a unique product or advantages of production or service creation technology makes the company search for the balance between the possibility to maximize its profits and the need to protect its unique advantage from the competitors (Brouthers and Nakos 2002, p 50). Companies that have differentiated products, or unique products, prefer equity modes of entry because, firstly, "the unique nature of their technology makes *a priori* evaluation of market benefits difficult" (Klein et al. 1990). This means that if such a company chose a contractual mode of entry, it would be hard for potential partners to appropriately evaluate the differentiated or unique technology, thus assigning a lower value than can be achieved by more direct exploitation (John and Weitz 1988). Secondly, if the company has once exploited the benefits of a differentiated product in its home country, it will have the advantage of replicating this success abroad due to its developed marketing and delivery system.

As for the third firm specific factor, two contrasting views regarding the impact of the company's international experience for decision-making exist. The traditional view is that, gradually, while growing in size, companies change their organizational choice and channels of distribution from contractual licensing and distribution to the company's own operations (Johnson and Vahlne 1977, p 18).

The opposite view expressed by Fladmoe - Lindquist and Jacque (1995, p 1240) in service industry analysis, is that "as a service firm gains international experience, it develops a knowledge base about management of global business, thereby becoming more confident about engagement in long term international franchising." In their early stages, novice international firms have a tendency to rely on their contractual relationship, letting the internal and market risks of foreign entity be monitored by a local partner (Root 1994). Commonly, contractual mode is chosen by service industries, while ownership mode is chosen by production industries that open their own production outlet in a foreign country and afterwards create a network of franchised sales offices in this country.

Finally, with regard to industry specific factors, the theory (Buckley and Casson 1998) suggests that those companies which operate in intensively competitive industries would choose the ownership mode of entry, which allows for fast reaction and the possibility of forming a stable relationship with other key players. Forming such a relationship would be harder for franchisees, as they are perceived as less reliable partners (Fladmoe - Lindquist and Jacque 1995, p 1241).

2.2.2 Country Characteristics

A major advantage of international expansion is a wider market for the firm's product or service (Dunning 1993). According to Ramcharran (2000) firms entering foreign markets can be confronted with unstable political, economic, foreign exchange, and/or social environments. Contractor and Kundu (1998) identify three factors that affect the propensity of a company to choose a franchising entry mode: country risk, the cultural distance between the firm's nation and the host nation, and the host country's openness to global business. These factors will now be analyzed in greater detail.

The country risk refers to economic and political uncertainty in the country where the business should be situated. This does not mean the turmoil in the country but rather the level of environmental uncertainty in the country which is politically stable (Contractor and Kundu 1998, p 33). Of course, political elections, membership of political or economic blocks, such as NATO, EU, NAFTA, development of new enterprise operation regulatory systems, rise or fall of foreign investments in the country, and other significant issues as well relate to the company entry mode choice.

Successful operations abroad require an understanding of foreign work ethics, mental sets, and cultural traditions. The agency's theory suggests that an "adverse selection" problem exists when recruiting employees in culturally different settings leading to high costs of maintaining agency relationships. It is more likely that, if the cultural difference between the home and host nation is large, the contractual mode of entry will be chosen.

The countries that have an open door policy to international operations and foreign investors entering their country are expected to have a greater number of ownership mode entry cases (Dunning and McQueen 1981, p 204).

2.2.3 Firm Strategic Intent and Preferences

Company, industry, and country specifics cannot be sufficient grounds for choice of entry mode; only in combination with firm strategy specifics can the entry mode be determined. Firstly, the decision to move into the foreign market is very dependent on the company's strategies concerning its preferences for further development (Walker and Etzel 1973; Hackett 1976). Secondly, only after evaluating its future vision and goals, can the company make a decision regarding which mode of entry to choose. Six different criteria for entry mode choice will be looked at. These criteria are, perceived strategic importance of control over quality, brand, investment in training, foreign applicants, a wish to quickly penetrate the foreign market, the level of motivation to learn overseas, and the level of alertness to the rival firm's activities.

In previous research, two contradicting views dominated concerning the strategic importance of control over quality in relation to the choice of entry modes. Firstly, Contractor and Kundu (1998) consider that franchising a business can be a problem because the franchisee might not maintain the original quality of services, or it might decide to shrink its operations. As in the modern market the quality of a service or product is crucial, the franchising mode would be preferred only if regular and direct quality control over the franchisee could be maintained. Otherwise, the ownership mode would be more appropriate.

The second view states that there is a trade-off between providing the agent with sufficient incentives to work hard and the appropriate risk of sharing and/or preventing free-riding on the brand reputation of the principal (Lafontaine and Oxeley 2001, p 11). A "moral hazard" problem may form here involving the possible shirking by employees and, consequently, a high cost of monitoring abroad, as opposed to self-interested dedication on part of the franchisee. This means that the franchisers that perceive control as an important tool would choose to enter a foreign country via the contractual mode.

For a franchisee, the importance and strategic perception of brand is dual. On one hand, the brand already has an acquired value. On the other hand, the franchisee is legally independent from the franchiser. Thus, if any problems occur, the franchisee bears the losses, which, in the case of the franchisee's risk, can result in an additional risk to the franchiser and a shrinking of the brand's value. Nevertheless, the franchise unit and the principal company are indivisible parts, and failures from any side would dramatically affect the brand name, and thus both parties. Therefore, it is expected that companies with better reputations and greater assets would not prefer franchising as the means for going international. Moreover, it is expected that companies willing to penetrate the foreign market quickly would choose franchising entry mode, as it requires small capital investments and is usually faster than equity unit opening (Buckley and Casson 1998).

By going international, the company also acquires know-how and knowledge because it benefits from international comparative advantages (Pak 2002, p 30). The foreign market is a priceless source for new ideas and strategic knowledge. Organizational learning, both inside and outside the company, is central to understanding the underlying strategic intention of a company (Ingram and Braum 1997). Personal work experience, which can be gained only through personal participation in the operation of a company in the foreign market, is most valuable. This is a portrait of the equity mode entry into the foreign market.

Thorough examination of market conditions in advance and proof of high alertness to the competitive power of rivals results in the ability to exercise more authority in the foreign market, as is characterized by the equity entry mode. This allows the company to maintain hands-on management and to react quickly to any competitive challenges. In addition, being aware of rivalry reduces the risk of investment; therefore, the company would be able to invest in the foreign country without fear of losing a major portion of its investment. Franchising is less appropriate when considering a turbulent competitive situation.

Based on the previous theoretical framework analysis, the following structure of decision-making factors was created. This structure should ease the perception of reasoning for choice of foreign entry modes by Lithuanian franchiser companies (see table 1).

The pluses in the table indicate the compliance with the statements expressed in the theoretical framework, whereas the minuses indicate the disagreement with these statements. If there is both plus and minus, this means that contradicting views exist in the theory about the effect of either criteria, in this case as is expressed as a normative statement.

Table 1. Criteria for Choice of Entry Modes.

CRITERION	OWNERSHIP	CONTRACTUAL
FIRM AND INDUSTRY SPECIFIC FACTORS		
Big size of the company	+	-
High product differentiation specifics	+	-
Industry specifics – highly powerful key parties	+	-
Has international experience	+/-	+/-
COUNTRY SPECIFIC FACTORS		
High country risk	-	+
High cultural distance	-	+
Host country open to global business	+	-
FIRM STRATEGIC INTENT AND PREFERENCES		
High perceived strategic importance of control over quality	+/-	+/-
Strategic perception of high importance of brand to franchiser	+	+/-
Wish to quickly penetrate foreign market	-	+
High level of motivation to learn abroad	+	-
High level of alertness to rival firm's activities	+	-

3 Methodology

After the theoretical description of motives for entry mode have been discussed in theory, this section will provide a description of the actual methods used to find answers to the research questions. In the methodology section, the choice of research strategy, selection of case companies, data generation, constraints, and limitations will be described.

Taking exploratory objectives and the scope of the research into consideration, a qualitative research approach was chosen. Firstly, the pilot study, in which top management representatives of the companies were interviewed on the semi-structured interview basis, was conducted. Then two case studies of Lithuanian capital based franchising companies *Kemi* and *Pizza Jazz* were tackled. In addition, the study also involved an in-depth contemplation of Lithuanian SME's involvement in franchising. A simultaneous investigation and analysis of such information lends insight into understanding the reasons why these companies preferred either contractual or ownership entry mode.

In regard to the initial interest of local SME development only Lithuanian capital companies-franchisers have been chosen for the scope of research. An initial list of 5 franchising companies was drawn, consisting of *Kemi*, *Pizza Jazz, Sarma Ltd., Senuku Prekybos Centras Ltd.* and *Presto Prekyba Ltd.* Of this sample, only those companies that had expanded their operations overseas have been taken into account. Therefore, the number of sample companies decreased to three (*Pizza Jazz, Kemi* and *Senukai*). Consequently, *Senukai* was rejected as a case study since it had operated for only a few months in Latvian market. Thus, the final case study sample companies decided upon were *Kemi* and *Pizza Jazz*.

Whereas the case study allows the examination of a phenomenon within its real life context (Yin 1994, pp 6-13), there are certain limitations for generating data. The basis for this research is the primary data obtained during interviews with the top management of the companies and legal and industrial experts, as well as the secondary data acquired from databases and media. Subsequently, the chain of evidence has been set up and analyzed according to the suggestion proposed by numerous researchers in this field, as was previously described in the theoretical background.

Regarding constraints and delimitations, firstly, the franchiser-franchisee relationship within Lithuania was not looked at, as such information has only an indirect impact on the franchiser's intentions to expand over the borders. Secondly, when looking at *Kemi*, an analysis of wholesale business, as is the second part of its entrepreneurial activity, was not made. This is because *Kemi* has been involved in franchising relationships within Lithuania only as an automobile service division. In its strategic plans, only these service divisions will be franchised in Latvia.

Moreover, the franchising entry mode was chosen to represent the contractual entry modes into the foreign market, and the equity mode was chosen to represent the ownership entry modes into the foreign market. The reasoning for such choices was dictated by the sample of the case study companies that entered the Latvian market exactly through these two modes. For this reason, a decision not to elaborate on other ways of ownership and contractual entry modes was taken.

4 Empirical Part

Given the nature of study, this section reveals the actual case study companies with regard to firm and industry specific factors, country characteristics, firm strategic intent and preferences. At the beginning of each case study, the basic facts of the company are presented. Afterwards, the situation regarding each of the decision-making factors in the sequence of their appearance in the theoretical background section is shortly presented for both companies.

4.1 Case Study – Kemi Entering Latvia

Kemi is an establisher of automobile service centers as well as a wholesaler of car components. Founded in 1988, it currently has 22 outlets of its own equity and of franchise type in Lithuania, and two equity-based outlets in Riga, Latvia. They entered the franchising business in 1995 and are cooperating with 10 franchisee companies in Lithuania within the automobile service centers' business scope. Since 1999, the Latvian outlet of *Kemi* has grown 250% in turnover (State Enterprise Register. *Lursoft Database*), and is planning to grow even more with the opening of a third outlet in the near future.

4.1.1 Firm and Industry Specific Factors

At the moment *Kemi* decided to enter the Latvian market, it had already established six franchisees in Lithuania. Franchising fees had been providing *Kemi* with valuable income that resulted in an availability of capital resources if the company decided to make some investments needed for expansion.

The products and services provided by *Kemi* could not be considered unique; the car repair services they provide are rather similar to those provided in other car repair centers.

Possible barriers of entry in the car repair business were not substantial in 1998: no minimum size requirements existed, and customers were not loyal to any particular brand. As for the rivalry power, at the time *Kemi* entered Latvia there was an intense competition between numerous alternative car repair services, which also created a strong bargaining power of buyers. Furthermore, as *Kemi* purchases goods from a very wide range of suppliers, the bargaining power of suppliers was weak. Since the target group of *Kemi* mostly owns rather new cars which are not likely to be left without regular repairs or repairs of which would be done without specialist help, threat of substitutes was low.

Therefore, risks exerted on *Kemi* by interested parties were rather high, as competitive firms could easily challenge the market share of *Kemi* if they took one strategic move to attract the clients of *Kemi*. There was obviously a need for Latvia to choose a hands-on approach in order to protect itself against competition, which, moreover, could have been increased because of low entry barriers in the market.

The Latvian market was *Kemi's* first attempt to expand its operations to a foreign market and to serve unfamiliar customers. In contrast to the theory presented that a novice company in a foreign country would enter though the contractual mode, *Kemi* initially entered the Latvian market with its own capital investment.

4.1.2 Country Characteristics

In order to proficiently examine the country-related risk, an examination of macroeconomic variables, with the assistance of PEST (Johnson and Scholes 1999, p 104), ie Political, Economical Social and Technological environment analysis, was made. The results of the examination have shown that Latvia, as a country of choice of entry for the Lithuanian franchiser, has not signaled huge potential risks. Moreover, the business in the chosen country was expected to show a rather stable and positive development of the company.

Lithuania and Latvia have been neighboring countries and have always held a rather similar cultural background, perception, language, history, and mentality. At the same time, there was an economic proximity between the consumers of both countries: a similar number of privately owned passenger cars, similar average car age, the same development phase, close personal income per head and propensity to spend on car repairs.

In 1998, when *Kemi* was considering an entry into the Latvian market, the companies providing repair services for *Audi, BMW, Volkswagen, Volvo* were already operating there. Their existence in the Latvian market indicated not only the country's openness to foreign brands, but also a customer readiness to pay for quality and to trust in foreign businesses.

4.1.3 Firm Strategic Intent and Preferences

According to the company CEO, the only possible approach for *Kemi* was to open its own branch in Latvia from which the franchising network could develop in the future. In this way, the future franchisees' quality could be controlled better. With regard to the agency's theory, *Kemi* should have chosen the contractual mode of entry, as the monitoring quality would have cost less. This means that the franchisee with the residual claims to the profits of its company would be willing to maximize the residual value. However, *Kemi* had another motive for ignoring the importance of the problem of moral hazard, i.e. a Lithuanian was chosen to be the director of *Kemi Baltija*[2].

Kemi started to work in the car repair industry in 1988. By the time it entered Latvia in 1998, it already had a strong brand name and developed customer loyalty in the local market. *Kemi* registered its trademark in 1998 with the date of expiration in 2008, thus protecting its intellectual property. Hence, it was obvious to *Kemi* that, as a brand, it had the major value.

Kemi entered the Latvian market via equity mode with the future goal to develop a strong franchising network. It chose the building of a long-lasting relationship with the consumers rather than quick penetration. The view expressed by *Kemi* management has been that it is important to maintain quality. A year for market examination is not that much of a sacrifice when compared to 10 years of successful business.

Kemi realized that knowledge of the foreign market could not only positively affect its Latvian operations, but could also improve its overall business concept with the know-how and local expertise gained in Latvia. *Kemi* had recognized that before being able to sell franchises in local market, it first had to learn the needs the market possessed and adapt the company's image to the local culture.

Before entry into Latvia, the company had thoroughly scrutinized the entire car repair services market. This resulted in an awareness of local market conditions and built credibility in the actions to be pursued in future. Therefore, the company was prepared to face the competition and to continue operation in the Latvian market.

---

[2] The subsidiary of Kemi Ltd in Latvia has been named Kemi Baltija Ltd.

4.2 Case Study – *Pizza Jazz* Entering Latvia

The history of Pizza Jazz dates back to 1993, when two Lithuanian entrepreneurs established the *Pizza Jazz* trademark (hereinafter referred to as *Pizza Jazz*). *Pizza Jazz* had already developed a franchise concept in 1997, and it is now in control of 5 investment-based restaurants in Lithuania and 5 franchises. Since the Spring of 2000, the Latvian franchise *Pizza Jazz* has grown more than twice in sales. Also, international franchising to Belarus, Ukraine, and the Kaliningrad region has been considered as an option for future development.

4.2.1 Firm and Industry Specific Factors

At the moment of entering the Latvian market (Spring, 2000), *Pizza Jazz* did not have extensive financial resources in its possession. According to the management, they possessed enough capital potential to pursue no more than an expansion of one or two outlets in a year, and only if they remained inside the country. Thus, opening two outlets simultaneously in a foreign country was a serious challenge.

Industry experts revealed that, in 2000, the pizza and other fast food restaurant markets in Latvia were rather developed (*Dienas Bizness Homepage*). Even if technological procedures and food ingredients could create distinct characteristics the product *per se* could not be too different from its original.

Analysis of the industry specifics using Porter's 5 Forces model (Porter 1980, p 4) has shown that, in the restaurant business, the existence of regulations which might differ significantly from the domestic ones created high barriers of entry for foreign companies willing to enter the Latvian market. For restaurants serving pizza and other similar products, the customers were fragmented and had different tastes for the products/services supplied in the market. Thus, no buyer could possess any particular influence on the product or the price. As there have been numerous food product suppliers in both Latvia and Lithuania, the supplier's power was found to be rather low. The center of Riga abounds with small restaurants, the majority being cheaper or in the same price range as *Pizza Jazz,* which means that the threat of substitutes to the pizza restaurant industry is strong. Before *Pizza Jazz* entered Latvia, there were already two competitive pizzerias operating, both of them having more than one outlet and supplying rather similar products. Furthermore, as the switching costs for consumers between the competitors were very low, the rivalry power in the market was moderately high. Therefore, the pizza restaurant industry in Latvia could be assessed as highly competitive with strong rivalry forces acting in the market.

The company did not have any international franchising practice until the year 2000 (the year of entrance to Latvian market), but the first franchise experience within Lithuania was successful enough for the company to apply a similar strategy in Latvia.

4.2.2 Country Characteristics

With regard to the threats of the foreign country, Latvia had not signaled a high level of risks for the Lithuanian franchiser. However, major attention had to be paid to Latvia's accession and adoption of legislation concerning the European Union. Such changes in macroeconomic variables would alter the stance of competitiveness of the company as well as industry growth or decay.

Lithuanians and Latvians have a very similar pattern of food consumption. Both nationalities are big meat lovers who have gone through the same development phases in the recent years so that they are equally familiar with pizza and other fast food products.

In 2000, when *Pizza Jazz* entered the Latvian market, many foreign brands were already known in the restaurant business. Thus, a conclusion about the existence of very many foreign culture restaurants in this market could be made, and the risk of entering the foreign market would be considered low.

4.2.3 Firm Strategic Intent and Preferences

On a monthly basis, *Pizza Jazz* has been assessing the quality of dishes and the technological preparation in Lithuanian outlets, and it has planned to do the same in Latvia. Therefore, an evaluation of *Pizza Jazz* as a company with high strategic importance of control over quality was made. In regard to the "moral hazard" problem, *Pizza Jazz* has chosen the advisable strategy for entering the foreign market following the franchise format. Therefore, the residual claims for the franchisee would be the motivational factor to act in compliance with the franchiser's practices and advice.

The *Pizza Jazz* trademark was registered in 1999 with an expiration date of 2008 (Register of Trademarks of the Republic of Lithuania, The State Patent Bureau of the Republic of Lithuania Database). As explained by the company's management, brand awareness and customer loyalty are the major strategies for future growth in *Pizza Jazz*'s pan-Baltic environment.

Pizza Jazz has had a clear vision of using franchising as a possibility for quickly penetrating the new market. Company management has revealed that it would not commit to using many resources for the proper screening of employees and for dealing with numerous administrative issues before starting up a company in a foreign environment. Certainly, this aspect is one of the major motives utilized by franchising, as such proceedings take much less time when locals deal with them than they would for foreigners, due to a lack of awareness in regard to how to tackle local bureaucracy.

The possibility of an easy and cost efficient move to the foreign market appeared as an attractive option to the management of *Pizza Jazz,* whose plan to promote its own brand and increase its profits was the major issue anyway. The company was not concerned with gaining new knowledge from foreign sources, but was simply interested in international development. The management was aware that the Latvian representative would do the work in Latvia and that the management would only have to take care of monitoring the franchisee without staking serious involvement in the actual business process.

According to the company CEO, *Pizza Jazz* did not explore the market conditions in Riga at that time. Thus, it was completely unaware of the practices in the Latvian pizza restaurant business as well as in rival forces. Moreover, *Pizza Jazz* was not prepared to risk investing money in a foreign country, as it had spotted much more potential that could be utilized in the local market.

5 Interpretations of Research Findings

The analysis of empirical data in the two case study companies has revealed several contradictions concerning the theoretically proposed reasoning in favor of entry mode choices into the foreign market and the practically encountered flow of reasoning made by *Pizza Jazz* and *Kemi*. **Table 2** summarizes the findings of empirical data as it does or does not conform to the criteria presented in theory. Plusses in the table indicate conformity with statements expressed in the left column and the hyphens indicate that the case study companies' criteria do not match these statements. From the evidence attained regarding real cases, several propositions concerning the factors influencing the franchiser's choice of entry mode into the foreign market will be presented.

Proposition 1. The franchiser, which has enough resources, a high level of motivation to learn abroad, an alertness to the rival firm's activities, but is not striving for fast penetration into the market chooses the ownership mode of entry into a foreign country.

The resources the company possesses are one of the major factors that determine the choice of entry mode; this has also been confirmed by the case study companies. However, a clear link also existed between how a company perceives the value of its brand and how much attention and resources it is ready to devote to exercising control over a foreign unit, be it a franchisee or equity-owned outlet. *Kemi*, the company that has chosen the equity entry mode, undertook serious research and analysis of rival companies in the Latvian car repair service industry before entering the country. This company did not rush to open as many outlets as possible. Instead, it wanted to retain hands-on management and control over its outlet operations, at least in the first years after entry, so to be able to react quickly to all turbulences, and thus reduce the risks of losing initial investments.

Table 2. Criteria for Choice of Entry Mode into the Latvian Market as Made by the Case Study Companies

CRITERION	KEMI	PIZZA JAZZ
FIRM AND INDUSTRY SPECIFIC FACTORS		
Big size of the company	+	-
High product differentiation specifics	-	-
Industry specifics – highly powerful key parties	+	+
Has international experience	-	-
COUNTRY SPECIFIC FACTORS		
High country risk	-	-
Large cultural distance	-	-
Host country's openness to global business	+	+
FIRM STRATEGIC INTENT AND PREFERENCES		
Highly perceived strategic importance of control over quality	+	+/-
High importance of brand and strategic perception to franchiser	+	+
Wish to quickly penetrate foreign market	-	+
High level of motivation to learn abroad	+	-
High level of alertness to rival firm's activities	+	-

Pizza Jazz, on the contrary, only had to decide whether they were willing to turn their future strategy in the proposed direction. Research and main supply chain contacting arrangements were done by the prospective franchisee. *Pizza Jazz* only took part in the screening process and initial arrangements. From the moment the outlet was opened, the majority of business problems were handled by the agent, and only regular controls to ensure proper compliance with quality requirements were required from the *Pizza Jazz* management. As a result, *Pizza Jazz* has entered the Latvian market, and done so quickly and resource efficiently.

Proposition 2. For a franchiser entering a culturally similar market with a low degree of country risk, previous international experience does not influence the choice of entry mode.

The two companies, *Pizza Jazz* and *Kemi* chose Latvia as their first foreign market. Neither of these companies had ever before tried going into a foreign, unknown market where the preferences of consumers, the market forces, governmental regulations, and conditions for opening outlets were different from those in their previous host environments. For their first challenge, both companies chose exactly the same foreign market, one which was closest to their own in all respects: geographically, culturally, historically, economically and politically. In such a way, the risks of losing initial investments were reduced, and entry into the foreign market via equity was less risky. This contradicts the view expressed by Root (1994), and proves that novice international firms may decide to commit significant resources to their first international venture, *if* the market they enter is culturally close and has a low degree of risk.

Proposition 3. A franchiser, when choosing an entry mode into a foreign market where highly powerful players exist, does not necessarily choose to enter via equity mode.

The two case studies have revealed that the foreign market can be entered via equity mode and via franchising mode regardless of the fact that pressure from key players in the market is perceived as strong. *Pizza Jazz* was very much affected by both substitute and buyer power; the firm had to monitor its competitors and to be prepared for the sudden strategic moves the competitors may have made. Although the management of the company knew of the situation, the franchising mode was chosen, and *Pizza Jazz* managed to plan its strategy so that it was able to monitor the franchisees to create a stable relationship with the local market players. This example of *Pizza Jazz* contradicts the theoretical understanding of how the existence of powerful players in the market would affect the choice of entry mode for franchisers into the foreign market. The following conclusion can be made, that the existence of powerful players and high competitive forces in the potential market are not obstacles regarding a company's decision to choose the franchising mode.

Proposition 4. For a franchiser who plans entering the foreign market, the absence of differentiation specifics in regards to products or services is not an obstacle that restricts the franchiser from choosing the equity mode of entry.

Observations revealed that a company planning to enter a foreign country with low differentiation specifics of its products/services does not perceive the previous factor as a determinant for choosing a franchising mode. Even though the services and products of *Kemi* are not unique, the company has seized the market with the "quality" image and with certain additional services offered to the customer. These features have endowed *Kemi* with a strong position in the market, and have thus left product differentiation specifics aside from the decisive role regarding the choice of entry mode into a new market. In contrast to the theory that, in general, the choice of equity mode is made with regard to high product differentiation specifics, *Kemi* has captured a niche in Latvian market. Considering these arguments, the franchiser could utilize an equity-based expansion to the foreign market without offering significantly specific products or services.

Proposition 5. For a franchiser, the perceived importance of brand and control over quality are not crucial factors that determine the choice between the contractual and equity modes of entry into foreign country.

The case studies have disclosed that two aspects exist that are indivisible from the franchising *per se,* but are not perceived as factors of key significance for making a decision regarding an entry strategy. Evidently, *Kemi* and *Pizza Jazz* have indicated that the importance of brand and control over quality are the most critically important factors for franchisers to consider. Their reasoning lies in the very roots of the following franchising concept: brand awareness makes this format attractive for expansion. In order to sustain the brand's value, it is necessary that a company performs adequate control measures. Yet, *Kemi* and *Pizza Jazz* point out that, when considering a firm's strategic intent and preference determinants, these two factors are exceptionally vital for both companies. Subsequently, by using the strategic values of the company to ensure the brand's value and control, the company has already taken care of the measures needed to sustain its franchise scheme of development and growth. However, neither of the companies identifies these motives as having made a significant contribution to the decision of entry mode that has been taken. Therefore, a conclusion can be made that, while the perceived importance of brand and control over quality are significant, they are not the decisive factors regarding the choice of entry mode.

6 Conclusion

The goal of this research was, first of all, to recognize and evaluate what factors influence the choice of entry mode into the foreign market as made by Lithuanian franchise companies. The conclusion drawn was that there is no single most important factor, but that several combinations of factors can affect a franchiser's choice of entry mode.

The most important factors influencing a decision regarding entry mode selection coincide with the correlation described in theory. For equity-owned unit expansion, the company size, its willingness to learn abroad, and its awareness of the competition in the corresponding industry in foreign market were the main reasons for choosing this mode of entry. A company preferring the contractual mode is driven by the desire to penetrate the new market quickly and the inability to devote large resources and to make significant investments in the foreign outlet.

Additionally, it was revealed in this paper that Lithuanian franchisers who wish to expand over the border tend to prefer Latvia as their best option. Both case companies have chosen their first international expansion location to be in Latvia, mostly because of positive country-specific factors, i.e. low risk, cultural proximity, and the country's openness to foreign businesses. At the same time the two companies have picked different entry modes, which is a clear indication that the choice of entry mode is not affected by pre-existing international business experience.

It is also important for a company to be aware of which rival powers exist in the foreign market, independently of what mode it wishes to pursue. However, existence of highly powerful players in the market does not necessarily restrain a company from entering the market via franchising.

Furthermore, it is argued that the discoveries made through this research are reciprocal and can be used by Latvian franchisers who decide to enter Lithuania in order to establish a franchise network there. Certain aspects that have been left out from the scope and scale of this research could be the subject of further studies. As this paper covers only the relationships between Lithuanian and Latvian businesses, the analysis of other culturally close countries would be valuable in order to confirm the propositions expressed in this paper. For instance, Estonian and Finnish markets, which are culturally close but different in their economic development, would be interesting target markets for further research concerning this topic.

Moreover, a quantitative research project might be suggested in order to test the presented propositions and to compare the results of Lithuanian cases to cases in other countries. Yet, the scarcity of such cases in developing economies would not present a clear-cut judgment of how Lithuanian franchisers' motives for entering the foreign market differ from franchisers' motives in relation to other emerging markets.

To conclude, it is expected in the future that Baltic franchisers will expand internationally. Franchising networks will become a significant part of the Baltic countries' economic growth.

References

1. Agarwal S, Ramaswami SN (1992) Choice of Foreign Market Entry Mode: Impact of Ownership, Location and Internalization Factors. Journal of International Business Studies First Quarter:1-27
2. Anderson E, Gatignon H (1986) Modes of Foreign Entry: A Transaction Cost Analysis and Propositions. Journal of International Business Studies Fall:1-26
3. Brennere J, Petrova A (2002) Critical Aspects for Franchise Business Development in Latvia. Bachelor thesis, Stockholm School of Economics in Riga
4. Brouthers KD (2002) Institutional, Cultural and Transaction Cost Influences on Entry Mode Choice and Performance. Journal of International Business Studies 33(2):203-221
5. Brouthers KD, Nakos G (2002) Entry Mode Choice of SMEs in Central and Eastern Europe. Entrepreneurship Theory and Practice 27(1):47-63. Retrieved December 17, 2002, from EBSCO on-line database on the World Wide Web: http://search.epnet.com
6. Buckley PJ, Casson MC (1998) Analyzing Foreign Market Entry Strategies: Extending the Internalization Approach. Journal of International Business Studies 29(3):539-562
7. Caves RE, Murphy II WF (1976) Franchising: Firms, Markets and Intangible Assets. Southern Economic Journal 42(4):572-587. Retrieved December 17, 2002, from EBSCO on-line database on the World Wide Web: http://search.epnet.com
8. Contractor FJ, Kundu SK (1998) Franchising Versus Company Run Operations: Modal Choice in the Global Hotel Sector. Journal of International Marketing 6(2):28-53. Retrieved December 13, 2002, from EBSCO on-line database on the World Wide Web: http://search.epnet.com
9. Dienas Bizness Archive. Dienas Bizness Homepage. Retrieved September 3, 2003, from the World Wide Web: www.db.lv
10. Dunning JH (1993) Multinational Enterprises and the Global Economy. Addison-Wesley Publishing, New York

11.Dunning JH, McQueen M (1981) The Eclectic Theory of International Production: A Case Study of International Hotel Industry. Managerial and Decision Economics 2(4):197-210. Retrieved December 18, 2002, from EBSCO on-line database on the World Wide Web: http://search.epnet.com
12.Erramilli MK, Rao CP (1993) Service Firms' International Entry-Mode Choice: A Modified Transaction-Cost Analysis Approach. Journal of Marketing 57:19-38
13.Fladmoe – Lindquist K, Jacque LL (1995) Control modes in International service Operations: The Propensity to Franchise. Management Science 41(7):1238-1249. Retrieved December 27, 2002, from EBSCO on-line database on the World Wide Web: http://search.epnet.com
14.Hackett DW (1976) The International Expansion of US Franchise Systems: Status and Strategies. Journal of International Business Studies Spring: 65-75
15.Huszagh SM, Huszagh FW, McIntyre FS (1992) International Franchising in the Context of Competitive Strategy and the Theory of the Firm. International Marketing Review 9(5):5-18
16.Ingram P, Baum JA (1997) Opportunity and Constraint: Organizations' learning from the operating and competitive experience of industries. Strategic Management Journal 18 (summer special issue):75-98
17.Johnson G, Scholes K (1999) Exploring Corporate Strategy. Prentice Hall Europe, Hemel Hempstead
18.Johanson J, Vahlne JE (1977) The Internationalization Process of the Firm-A Model of Knowledge Development and Increasing Foreign Market Commitments. Journal of International Business Studies 8(1):5-22. Retrieved December 5, 2002, from Journal of International Business Studies on-line database on the World Wide Web: http://copenhagen.jibs.net
19.John G, Weitz BA (1988) Forward integration into distribution: Empirical test of transaction analysis. Journal of Law, Economics and Organization 4(2):337-355. Retrieved December 17, 2002, from EBSCO on-line database on the World Wide Web: http://search.epnet.com
20.Klein S, Frazier GL, Roth VJ (1990) A transaction cost analysis model of channel integration in international markets. Journal of Marketing Research 27:196–208
21.Konigsberg AS (1996) International Franchising. Juris Publishing Inc., New York
22.Lafontaine F, Oxley J (2001) International Franchising: Evidence form US and Canadian Franchisers in Mexico. NBER Working Paper w8179. Retrieved December 15, 2002, from NBER on-line database on the World Wide Web: http://papers.nber.org
23.Pak YS (2002) The Effect of Strategic Motives of the Choice of Entry Modes: an Empirical Test of International Franchisers. Multinational Business Review 10(1):28-36. Retrieved December 17, 2002, from EBSCO on-line database on the World Wide Web: http://search.epnet.com
24.Porter ME (1980) Competitive Strategy. Techniques for analyzing Industries and Competitors. The Free Press, New York
25.Ramcharran H (2000) Foreign direct investments in central and eastern Europe: An analysis of regulatory and country risk factors. American Business Review 18:1–8
26.Register of Trademarks of the Republic of Lithuania. The State Patent Bureau of the Republic of Lithuania Database. Retrieved November 11, 2002, from the World Wide Web: www.vpb.lt/db/rezult2-n.php
27.Root FR (1994) Entry Strategy for International Markets. Lexington Books, Lexington
28.Shane SA (1996) Why Franchise Companies Expand Overseas. Journal of Business Venturing 11:73-88
29.State Enterprise Register. Lursoft Database. Retrieved October 24, 2002, from the World Wide Web: www.lursoft.lv

30.Statistical Yearbook of Latvia 1999 (1999). Riga, Latvia: Central Statistical Bureau of Latvia.
31.Statistical Yearbook of Latvia 2002 (2002). Riga, Latvia: Central Statistical Bureau of Latvia.
32.Statistical Yearbook of Lithuania 2002 (2002). Vilnius, Lithuania: Department of Statistics to the Government of the Republic of Lithuania.
33.Walker BJ, Etzel MJ (1973) The Internationalization of U.S. Franchise Systems: Progress and Procedures. Journal of Marketing 37:38-46
34.Yin RK (1994) Case Study Research. Design and Methods. Thousand Oaks, California

Part F:

Country Studies

Exploring the Anatomy of Franchising: A Cross-National Examination of US and Finnish Franchise Contract Provisions

Mika Tuunanen

School of Business & Economics, University of Jyväskylä
P.O. Box 35, FIN-40351 Jyväskylä, Finland
mptuunan@econ.jyu.fi

Abstract. The present study focuses on describing and comparing the provisions of the franchise contracts and pre-sale disclosures to prospective franchisees in the USA and Finland. A fact that makes the investigation especially interesting is that no franchising specific legislation exists in Finland. Whereas in the USA franchisors are by a directive of the Federal Trade Commission required to publicly disclose key information on their franchise systems. The information is of paramount importance for potential franchisees who need to analyze franchise offering(s) before their buying decision. Two separate samples were developed for the study. The member franchisors of the *International Franchise Association* and franchisors listed in *Entrepreneur Magazine's* "Franchise 500" were sampled for the US data and in Finland the member franchisors of the *Finnish Franchising Association* were surveyed. The obtained data sets from the two countries were combined and then analyzed statistically to reveal differences and similarities between franchise contract characteristics. It was found that significant differences in franchise contract provisions occur and they have concrete consequences on franchisees' business operations.

Acknowledgements. The author is grateful to professor Robert T. Justis for providing the US data for the study. The author is also indebted to professors Andrew Terry and William S. Vincent for their valuable comments for the final manuscript.

1 Introduction

In the past, franchise contracts and legislation have been investigated rather intensely in the fields of law and economics. Actually, Elango and Fried (1994) proposed this orientation as one of the three main streams of franchising research by calling it "Franchising and society". The applied perspective has been utility of franchising to society. Generally explored questions have been "should franchising be allowed" and "whether the social benefits of franchising outweigh the cost society incurs because of it". (Elango and Fried 1994, pp 69-70). Although there are several recognized beneficial social impacts of franchising, at the same time there is also a concern that certain clauses of franchise agreements may restrain trade and free competition (Scherer and Ross 1990). Included in this concern are the questions about potential franchisee abuse by franchisor, franchisor's ability to terminate the contract, and pre-sale disclosure issues (see e.g. Brickley, Dark and Weisbach; Castrogiovanni et al. 1993; Hadfield 1990; Stadfeild 1992).

However, the present study takes an approach that is more managerially than public policy oriented. The question whether some contractual provisions are detrimental or not, will not be discussed. The purpose is to describe the variety of the contractual provisions in a cross-national context. This information serves both the future franchise owners and franchisors and particularly those that are seeking to internationalize their franchises. The franchise contract is the foundation for franchise relationship and that is why extended knowledge on the topic is pertinent and requisite.

The present study aims to find out whether there are differences in US and Finnish franchise contracts and, if so, how they differ. To be able to answer the research question, selected *Uniform Franchise Offering Circular* (UFOC) items concerning contractual provisions of the franchise agreements are utilized. Relevant issues in regards to pre-sale disclosure are also investigated.

The paper is organized as follows: an introduction section provides a brief overview of the two countries involved in the study to give an outline of the cultural[1] and other differences between the US and Finland. The current state of franchising in the USA is then concisely outlined with the state of Finnish franchising dealt with more thoroughly. The background to the study is laid down with a description of the research design. Finally, the focal results of the cross-national analysis are presented and discussed along with implications and propositions for future research endeavors.

1.1 USA versus Finland in a Nut Shell

To describe the characteristics of the two very different markets where the sampled franchisors operate, Table 1 presents some facts concerning the demographics, economy and legislation of the USA and Finland. The population of the USA is 55 times bigger than the population in Finland. Furthermore, the USA is 27 times greater than Finland by the geographic area. Despite these enormous differences in size of the markets both countries represent highly competitive industrialized western economies.

In the context of the analysis the dissimilar legal systems have an important role to play. The civil law system prevails in Finland as in all EU countries with

[1] The author holds a view that cross-national explorations are inevitably also cross-cultural investigations since e.g. national legislation and socio-economic systems are cultural products. Webster's Dictionary (1993) defines culture as "the total pattern of human behavior and its products, embodied in thought, speech, action, and artifacts and dependent upon man's capacity for learning and transmitting knowledge to succeeding generations through the use of tools, language and abstract thought". Referring to Hofstede's (1980) cultural dimensions it can be postulated that culturally the USA and Finland are unlike.

the exception of Great Britain and Ireland. On the contrary, the common law system of the US and its federal and state constitutions, plus a mix of federal and state legislation have shaped a complex and unique juridical entity that influences how contracts are drafted in the USA. The respective systems are in fact significantly different.

Table 1. Facts about the USA and Finland

ITEM	USA	FINLAND
Population (millions; estimates for year 2002)	289.95	5.20
Geographic area (square kilometers)	9,363,520	338,145
Gross Domestic Product in 2001 (millions USD)	10,143,200	120,900
GDP per capita in 2000 (USD)	36,517	22,156
Global Competitiveness in year 2002: (Year 2001 rankings given in the brackets)		
Overall Ranking	1 (2)	2 (1)
Growth Competitiveness Index Ranking	1 (2)	2 (1)
Micro Economic Competitiveness Index Ranking	1 (2)	2 (1)
Entrepreneurial activity	High	Low
Legal system	Common law	Civil law
Attorneys per capita	High	Moderate

Sources: Statistics Finland; U.S. Census Bureau;
Reynolds et al. 1999; World Economic Forum 2003.

1.2 Franchising in the USA

According to Justis, Tuunanen, Chen and Castrogiovanni (2003) franchising presently accounts for more than 40% of all retail sales and some one sixth of the GDP of the USA. It is estimated that there are more than 3,000 franchise organizations and over 600,000 franchise outlets in the North-American markets. Franchising grosses more than $1000 billions, i.e. one trillion USD, in annual sales and employs some eight million people, i.e. one out of sixteen workers. The majority, roughly 70% of the total sales derive from Trade Name and Product Distribution Franchising (Dandridge and Falbe 1994). Some five percent of the eight million North-American small businesses are franchised. Today, franchising is utilized in more than 75 different trades, and is available to virtually all business enterprise. The enormous success of franchising in the USA, which has resulted in a slower growth pace in saturated domestic markets, has led to a global expansion of North-American franchise systems.

1.3 Franchising in Finland

Finnish franchising culture can be considered rather adolescent (see e.g. Koiranen and Hyrsky 1996; Tuunanen and Koiranen 1998). Among the currently operating franchisors the median year for starting franchising is 1995. Despite the recent strong growth, franchising is still a poorly recognized method of conducting business. For more than a decade, franchising has annually shown two-digit growth figures measured by the numbers of franchisors, franchised outlets, employees and sales. However, the penetration of Finnish franchising is still running behind the European averages (Koiranen 1998; Tuunanen 2003).

In Finland, as well as in all EU countries, only Business Format Franchising is regarded as franchising, whereas in the USA Product Distribution and Trade Name Franchising is also regarded as franchising. The following description defines (Business Format) franchising:

> *"Franchising is a relationship which involves a contractual and long-term collaboration between two independent firms, a franchisor and a franchisee, in which the franchisor grants for payment a right to the franchisee to make use of the franchisor's business format in a pre-described and controlled manner at a certain location or area for a certain period of time."* (Tuunanen 2002a, p 32)

According to the 2002 franchising statistics[2], the total number of the franchises operating in the Finnish market is 164 (Tuunanen 2002a). A majority of the franchises are homegrown and have purely domestic origin while slightly more than a quarter have foreign ancestry. International franchises operating in Finland have mainly European roots. They originate from North-Europe (i.e. Scandinavia or Nordic countries) or West-Europe. A little less than one third (n=13) of the foreign-based franchises are from North America. More than a quarter (28% or 46 franchises) of the total number of franchises are members of the national franchise association, the *Finnish Franchising Association* (FFA). The FFA was established in 1988, and so far it is the only organization that promotes franchising nationally. The FFA is a member of the *European Franchise Federation* (EFF) and the *World Franchise Council.*

The total number of franchised outlets is presently some 5,750. Two out of three outlets (68% or 3,900) are owned and managed by a franchisee. The number of franchisees is some 3,400; hence nearly 500 stores are governed by multiple-unit franchisees. Franchising employs directly 38,000 people. The gross annual sales of franchising in 2001 were €3.54 billion (equivalent to some USD 3.25 billions)[3] that accounting for some 2.2% of the gross domestic product. Only 1.5% of all active enterprises in the Finnish market are franchised.

---

[2] The formal Finnish Franchising Statistics 1999–2002 have been collected in an annual study "Franchising in Finland" by the University of Jyväskylä. The study has been carried out with the financial support of the Finnish Franchising Association. The facts and figures of Finnish franchising presented in this section of the paper are gathered in that study. (cf. Tuunanen 2002a; Tuunanen 2003).

[3] the applied currency rate is from March 2002

Finland can expect franchising to continue to develop since an overwhelming majority of the franchises are in the growth phase of their lifecycle. A quarter are in early stage of the life cycle while one fifth are mature. Very few franchises are exiting the markets. Three out of four franchisors aim to grow in the future. Every seventh Finnish franchisor will seek growth in international markets in the near future while every fifth homegrown franchises has already internationalized.

2 Background to the Study

2.1 Two Different Juridical Starting Points

The present study is a cross-national investigation on the differences in provisions of the franchise agreements between Finland and the USA. The study was conducted in collaboration between the *University of Jyväskylä* and *Louisiana State University*. It was carried out at the end of 2001 in the USA and in spring 2002 in Finland (see Justis et al. 2003). The nature of the study is exploratory since no previous academic research on the topic in a cross-cultural setting was found.

This paper concentrates on describing the stipulations, franchisee obligations and other characteristics of the franchise contracts and pre-sale disclosures for nascent franchisees in the two countries. In Finland this information is scarce and typically not available to the public since the franchise contracts are strictly confidential and, in a franchise relationship, no information about the contract may be given to a third party. Therefore, the results of the survey are of predominant importance for potential franchisees who need to analyze a franchise offering or evaluate the pros and cons of various franchise offerings prior to making a buying decision. According to Tuunanen (2002b), there should be adequate, reliable and relevant information available for the decision making process of buying a franchise, since this is vital for the future satisfaction of the franchisee. Sufficient and correct information is a corner stone of a thoroughly considered and well-informed decision to establish a franchised business (see also Hing 1995).

The fact that makes this study particularly interesting is that no franchising specific legislation exists in Finland. Thus, franchisors are not required by the law to reveal information on their operations. In the United States, on the other hand franchisors are by the federal law forced to publicly disclose key information relating to their franchise systems. A standard form for disclosure, accepted in every state, is called the *Uniform Franchise Offering Circular* (UFOC). It is administered by the *North American Securities Administrators Association* (NASAA), and enforced by the *Federal Trade Commission* (FTC). In 1993, the NASAA developed a newly designed UFOC format including 23 items.

Table 2. UFOC Table of Contents

ITEM	TOPIC
1	The Franchisor, its Predecessors, and Affiliates
2	Business Experience
3	Litigation
4	Bankruptcy
5	Initial Franchise Fee
6	Other Fees
7	Initial Investment
8	Restrictions on Sources of Products and Services
9	Franchisee's Obligations
10	Financing
11	Franchisor's Obligations
12	Territory
13	Trademarks
14	Patents, Copyrights, and Proprietary Information
15	Obligations to Participate in the Actual Operation of the Franchise Business
16	Restrictions on What the Franchisee May Sell
17	Renewal, Termination, Transfer and Dispute Resolution
18	Public Figures
19	Earnings Claims
20	List of Outlets
21	Financial Statements
22	Contracts
23	Receipt

The contents of the UFOC are detailed in Table 2.[4] The document is supposed to be in plain English, free of legalese and technical language. The document serves two primary functions: to prevent fraud or misrepresentation of material facts, and to present relevant facts to prospective franchisees. (Justis et al. 1991; Justis and Judd 1998; Justis and Vincent 2001). Moreover, the uniform standard of the disclosure enables comparisons between various franchise offerings.

As a member of the *European Franchise Federation* (EFF), the FFA applies the *European Code of Ethics for Franchising* (EFF 2002). The Code of Ethics prohibits member franchisors from giving misleading or subjective information to franchisees. Moreover, franchisors should give franchisees all possible written material concerning the franchise relationship well before signing the franchise

---

[4] For a detailed UFOC contents, see http://www.nasaa.org/nasaa/scripts/fu_display_list.asp?ptid=34
To compare with Federal Trade Commission "Franchise Rule" 16 C.F.R. part 436, see http://www.ftc.gov/bcp/franchise/16cfr436.htm
The Franchise Rule is added to in 15 states. The content of the Franchise Rule is substantially similar to the UFOC.

contract. Franchisors should also choose and accept as franchisees only persons who have the skills, the education, personal traits and financial qualifications required in running a franchise outlet in that particular franchise. However, it is important to take into account that the law does not enforce the Code. Instead, it is meant to promote good franchising practice. In addition, in Finland it binds only the member franchises of the FFA and more than two thirds of the franchises do not belong to the FFA. This implies that in Finland a prospective franchisee might be in a weaker position regarding the quantity and quality of information accessible for his or her disposal. As a result, franchisee dissatisfaction may arise and lead to friction between the parties.

For comparison, the IFA's *Code of Ethics* (IFA 2002) intends to establish a framework for the implementation of the best practices for the franchisor and franchisee co-operation. It also represents the ideals for the franchise relationships and core values that are the basis for the resolution of the challenges that may arise between the parties. The Code provides five core values: (1) trust, truth and honesty, (2) mutual respect and reward, (3) open and frequent communication, (4) obedience to the law and (5) conflict resolution. Adherence to the values is expected to result in healthy, productive and mutually beneficial franchise relationships. The IFA's *Code of Ethics* is one integral component of its self-regulation program, which covers the IFA *Ombudsman* and revisions to the IFA bylaws.

Differences between the Code of Ethics of the EFF's and the IFA's Code of Ethics are evident. While the European Code offers straightforward and detailed instructions and guidelines concerning mainly franchisors' actions, such as presale disclosure, franchisee recruiting and the minimum contents of the franchise contract, the American Code deals with the moral nature of the interdependent relationship between the parties. In general, the differences between the respective codes may reflect the dissimilarities of the franchise specific regulations.

Justification for this cross-cultural analysis stems principally from the two distinct starting points: in the United States franchising is regulated by the federal and state specific legislation, while, on the contrary, in Finland as well as in other EU countries, franchising specific legislation is virtually non-existent[5]. In this sense, the current elaboration makes an interesting comparison between intensively regulated versus loosely regulated conditions. These different conditions are likely to have an effect on the contractual practices. The findings of the study are relevant for those who work or will operate in international franchise business.

2.2 Franchise Contract from the Franchisor's Viewpoint

The franchise contract has at least two substantial purposes for the franchisor. First, it primarily protects the franchisor's knowledge assets. The know-how refers to the non-contractible, intangible and tacit system-specific assets that are accu-

[5] France and Spain are exceptions from this. Their franchise laws govern also franchising disclosure. For specified information on EU Competition rules for supply and distribution agreements, see http://europa.eu.int/comm/competition/publications/rules_en.pdf

mulated in the franchisor's brand name capital.[6] Second, the contract also delineates the property rights, i.e. decision and ownership rights. "Decision rights" include the right to utilize the asset and the right to change its substance, whereas "ownership rights" cover the right to appropriate the returns from assets (residual income claim).

According to Windsperger (2002, p 25), the dependence of the decision rights on the knowledge assets can be postulated as follows: decision rights have to be allocated according to the distribution of knowledge assets between the franchisor (system specific, brand name capital) and the franchisee (outlet specific and local market know-how).

In the franchise channels strategic decision-making is virtually centralized to the franchisor while operative decisions (e.g. marketing: product, price, promotion, service; procurement and human resource decisions) are decentralized through co-ordination and delegation to the franchisees. The ownership rights include residual income rights (franchisee's payments to the franchisor: initial fee, royalties, advertising fees, and other fees) and complementary ownership surrogates (e.g. tying arrangements, exclusive dealing clauses, resale price maintenance, lease control, option rights at the end of the contract period such as buy back arrangement, approval and termination rights). The ownership surrogates stimulate the incentive effect of undiluted residual income rights and compensate for the attenuated ownership rights. When the franchisor's incentive to invest in intangible knowledge assets is higher, the fees are higher and ownership surrogates compensate the more the diluted residual income rights. While the franchisee's incentive to invest in intangible knowledge assets is higher when the fees are lower and the more ownership surrogates (such as exclusive territory, exclusive customer clauses, alienation rights, option rights) are included in the franchise contract. (see Windsperger 2002)

The higher the portion of the franchisor's intangible knowledge assets relative to the franchisee, the more residual decision rights must be transferred to the franchisor. The co-location of knowledge assets and decision and ownership rights as well as the complementary relationship between decision and ownership rights are key drivers of an effective institutional structure. This means that both the franchisor and franchisees are motivated to utilize the knowledge assets to maximize the residual income stream because of ex post surplus (Windsperger 2002, p 27).

The franchise contract is the core of the interdependent franchise relationship. It defines the roles of the parties and expresses their rights and obligations. The contract also organizes the exchange process and provides a strategic outfit for the network. By investigating the franchise contracts the structure ("anatomy") of the franchise arrangement ("collaborative organisms") can be understood.

---

[6] This is supported by Spinelli (1994). He provides a formula for prospective franchisee to evaluate a franchise option versus a stand-alone business: Franchise fee + Present Value of Royalty = Present Value of the increased net income from the value of the franchise trademark. Franchise decision is economically justified if the right-hand side of the equation is greater than the left-hand side.

3 Methodology

3.1 The Samples and Methods

Two samples were created for the study. The member franchisors of the IFA and franchisors listed in *Entrepreneur Magazine's* "Franchise 500" were randomly sampled to compile the US data. Five hundred letters requesting the franchisor's current UFOC documents for the study, were mailed. After a two-week period a follow-up reminder was sent. In total, 114 franchisors agreed to submit their UFOCs yielding a response rate of 23%. The data were composed by reviewing systematically selected items of the UFOCs. The data were statistically coded and saved into SPSS software. The representativeness of the US sample could not be tested statistically. The size of the sample (n=114) is approximately 15% of the IFA franchisor members but less than 10% of the registered franchisors in the USA.

For the Finnish sample, a mailed questionnaire closely based on the earlier collected US data was designed and sent to all 45 member franchisors of the FFA. The questionnaire included in total 44 questions pertaining to franchise contract characteristics and provisions for pre-sale disclosure for nascent franchisees. The informants were requested to carefully review their franchise contracts to be able to respond exactly to inquiries concerning characteristics of the agreement. There were no open-ended questions. More than half of the questions, twenty-three, were dichotomized including options "Yes" or "No". Thirty usable responses were received and hence, the response rate was 67%. The data was saved to the same data set with the US data. The data was analyzed by utilizing descriptive statistics, T-tests, Mann-Whitney U-tests, and Binominal tests.

Although the Finnish sample is rather small, only thirty franchisors, it represents 18% of the present population of the franchises (N=164). The representativeness of the sample was examined statistically by using a data set containing descriptive information (such as the year the business was founded, the year franchising was started, the total number of outlets, the number of company-owned and franchisee-owned outlets, and the number of the franchise owners in the chain) for every known franchise operating in the Finnish market. No bias was found and, accordingly, it can be stated that the sample is representative. However, it should be taken into account that the surveyed franchises are members of the FFA. Therefore, it can be assumed that member franchises' commitment to the Ethical Code guides their actions towards potential franchisees. If this postulate holds, the results may not be generalizable in this particular sense.

3.2 Representation of the Samples

A detailed description of the samples is presented in Table 3. Despite the origin, the average ages of the sampled franchisor companies were found to be similar.

However, a significant difference was found regarding the time elapsed from the company start-up to initiating franchise operations. It appeared that many of the sampled US companies started with franchising as a strategy whereas among Finnish companies franchising seemed to be more of an evolution or adaptation. On the average, the studied US franchisors launched franchise operations four times sooner than their Finnish counterparts. Hence, the US franchisors had two and a half times longer experience in franchising than the sampled Finnish firms. These differences clearly emphasize the developing nature of the Finnish franchising culture.

The longer franchising tenure and the enormous size difference of the national markets of the two countries may explain the findings regarding the average size of the franchises (see Table 1). The average investigated US franchise chain turned out to be ten times larger than a respective average Finnish franchise measured by the number of outlets. For instance, there are only a few Finnish franchises that have close to two hundred outlets in their channel of distribution. Furthermore, the findings indicate that Finnish franchisors' have a much lower proportion of franchisee owned outlets than their US peers.

Table 3. Description of the Samples

ITEM		USA (n=114)	FINLAND (n=30)	Sig.
The year when the company was established	1969 or prior	28.1%	23.3%	
	1970 – 1989	53.5%	40.0%	
	1990 or later	18.4%	36.7%	
The average age of the companies (Md)		25 yrs 7 months (20.5)	28 yrs (18.0)	.663 (.262)
The year when franchising was started	1969 or prior	21.4%	0%	
	1970 – 1989	48.2%	23.3%	
	1990 or later	30.4%	76.7%	
The average tenure in franchising (Md)		20 yrs 8 months (17.0)	7 yrs 10 months (7.5)	.000 (.000)
Time elapsed from the start-up to launching the franchise operations	Up to 5 years	74.1%	43.3%	
	6 – 19	20.5%	20.0%	
	20 or more	5.4%	36.6%	
The average period in years (Md)		4 yrs 9 months (1.5)	20 yrs 2 months (10.5)	.005 (.000)

Number of outlets in a franchise	< 50	21.5%	73.4%	
	50 – 200	27.1%	20.0%	
	> 200	51.4%	6.6%	
				.000
The average number of outlets (Md)		679.14 (211.0)	63.17 (28.5)	(.000)
Number of company-owned outlets	< 50	74.5%	90.1%	
	50 – 200	17.0%	6.6%	
	> 200	8.5%	3.3%	
The average number of c-o outlets (Md)		100.96 (7.0)	27.00 (4.5)	.213 (.433)
Number of franchisee-owned outlets	< 50	25.0%	80.1%	
	50 – 200	27.7%	13.3%	
	> 200	47.3%	6.6%	
The average number of f-o outlets (Md)		517.82 (178.5)	36.17 (10.5)	.000 (.000)
Proportion of the f-o outlets from the total amount of outlets		79.8%	57.3%	[.000]

Sig.: T-test (Mann-Whitney U-test) [Binominal test]

The businesses of the respondents are broken down in Table 4. Some striking differences between the countries were recorded. The Finnish sample seemed to be skewed compared to the US sample, because of the greater representation of retail, quick service restaurants and business service franchisors.

Table 4. Distribution of the Industries of the Franchisors

BUSINESS	USA % (n=114)	FINLAND % (n=30)
Automotive	6.1%	6.7%
Business services	7.0%	20.0%
Children's products & services	0.9%	0%
Computer businesses	1.8%	3.3%
Food/Quick service restaurants	35.0%	20.0%
Food/Full-Service restaurants	2.6%	3.3%
Food/Retail sales	3.5%	0%
Health care businesses	1.8%	0%
Home-Improvement products & services	0.9%	0%
Maintenance services	1.8%	0%
Personal-Care businesses	5.3%	3.3%
Pets	0.9%	3.3%
Recreation	12.3%	0%
Retail	6.1%	33.4%
Service businesses	14.0%	6.7%
Total	100.0%	100.0%

4 Findings

The collected data was grouped, analyzed and reported under four categories: 1) "Franchisor's background", 2) "Franchise contract governance", 3) "Obligations concerning franchisees' business operations", and 4) "Financial aspects of starting and running a franchised outlet".

4.1 Franchisor's Background

The UFOC form requires that a franchisor disclose the owners, predecessors and affiliates of the company. Moreover, the franchisor's litigation and bankruptcy history must be disclosed. No such requirements bind franchisors in Finland, but it would be beneficial for a nascent franchisee to acquire this kind of information before entering into franchise relationship. It appeared that in majority of the cases in both countries, present owners of the franchisor companies were also the initial founders. Nevertheless, in Finland the ownership of the companies had changed significantly more frequently at some phase after the business start-up (see Table 5).

Paradoxically, and in spite of the franchising legislation, it emerged that the researched US franchisors had been involved four times more often than their Finnish colleagues in a legal dispute during the past seven years. Of course, the length of the franchising experience and the size of the chain may increase the likelihood of being involved in some type of litigation. Also, different law systems, legislation and cultural factors may affect this. It turned out that the US franchisor companies' managers and officers had been involved in a bankruptcy ten times more often than in the Finnish sample.

Table 5. Franchisor's Background

ITEM		USA (n=114)	FINLAND (n=30)	Sig.
Franchisor is the initial founder of the company	Yes	99.1%	80.0%	.000
	No	0.9%	20.0%	
Involvement in a litigation during the past 7 years	Yes	79.8%	20.0%	.000
	No	20.2%	80.0%	
Involvement in a bankruptcy during the past 7 years	Yes	32.5%	3.3%	.000
	No	67.5%	96.7%	

Sig.: Binominal test

4.2 Franchise Contract Governance

There are many obligations that a franchisor and a franchisee agree to (cf. Leblebici and Shalley 1996). Table 6 portrays the term of the contract, renewal term, and transfer and termination of the contract in both samples.

Franchise agreements were typically fixed-term contracts among the franchises in both countries, although the US contracts were found to be more than twice as long as the Finnish ones (see Brickley et al. 2003). In a similar vein, among the US franchisors the average renewal term of the franchise contracts was also significantly longer than in Finland. A franchisor has a right to refuse to renew the franchise contract under certain circumstances, yet the results indicate that this occurs rarely.

Sometimes, the contracting parties may wish to conclude the franchise relationship before the end of the term. Theoretically, either party may be eligible to terminate the franchise contract. The results indicate that Finnish franchisors allow franchisees to terminate the contract significantly more often than their US counterparts. The findings showed that sampled US and Finnish franchisors prefer to hold the right to end the contract. Rather surprisingly, it emerged that relatively more terminations by the studied franchisors happened in Finland than in the US (see Table 6).

At times a franchisee desires to sell or transfer the franchise to another party during the contract period. When this happens, it is essential for both a franchisor and a franchisee to find a competent successor to take over the business. If no skilled successor is found, the franchisor may be willing to acquire the franchisee's outlet. Nevertheless, re-acquirements are exceptions, and judging from the results they arise infrequently. Furthermore, a transfer fee is often involved under which a franchisee has to pay a fee to a franchisor when the latter approves the transfer. However, in Finland a majority (70%) of the studied franchisors indicated that they do not charge transfer fees at all while in the US more or less an equal proportion of the franchisors charge a fixed fee for the transfer. The analysis also showed that considerably more transfers take place in the US.

Table 6. Franchise Contract Governance

ITEM		USA (n=114)	FINLAND (n=30)	Sig.
Term of the initial contract	NA	2.6%	0%	
	For time being	0%	3.3%	
	Varies	4.3%	0%	
	Fixed term:			
	1 – 5 yrs	12.3%	83.5%	
	6 – 10 yrs	36.9%	9.9%	
	11 – 20 yrs	43.9%	3.3%	
The average term of the initial contract (Md)		13 yrs 4 months (10.0)	5 yrs (5.0)	.000 (.000)
Renewal term of the contract	NA	11.4%	3.3%	
	For time being	0%	13.3%	
	Varies	3.5%	0%	
	Fixed term:			
	0 – 5 yrs	27.2%	66.8%	
	6 – 10 yrs	39.5%	13.3%	
	11 – 20 yrs	17.5%	3.3%	
	> 20 yrs	0.9%	0%	
The average term of the renewed contract (Md)		9 yrs 11 months (10.0)	4 yrs 2 months (3.0)	.000 (.000)
Franchisee has a right to terminate the contract	Yes	54.0%	83.3%	[.000]
	No	46.0%	16.7%	
Franchisor has a right to terminate the contract	Yes	99.1%	93.3%	[.011]
	No	0.9%	6.3%	
Payments related to contract transfer	NA	4.4%	3.3%	
	No amount	13.2%	70.0%	
	Fixed sum	69.2%	6.7%	
	Fixed-%	8.8%	6.7%	
	$ or € range	4.4%	13.3%	

In year 2000: Contract transfers % (n/Franchisees' outlets)	5.17% (3,574/69,084)	2.69% (29/1,080)	-
Contract terminations by franchisors % (n/Franchisees' outlets)	1.91% (1,322/69,084)	5.00% (54/1,080)	-
Refused renewals by franchisors % (n/Franchisees' outlets)	0.19% (128/69,084)	0.19% (2/1,080)	-
Re-acquirements by franchisors % (n/Franchisees' outlets)	1.19% (823/69,084)	1.38% (15/1,080)	-

Sig.: T-test (Mann-Whitney U-test) [Binominal test]

4.3 Obligations Concerning Franchisees' Business Operations

In Table 7 the following contractual items are presented: territorial rights, limitations on purchase and sale of goods or services, requirements to participate in actual business operations, and the covenant not to compete.

A territory specifies the area in which a franchisee may operate. If the territorial right is granted as exclusive, it means that a franchisor will not open company owned or new franchised outlets within the specified territory. It was found that the majority of the sampled franchisors in both countries grant territorial rights or guarantees to their franchisees and at the same time, specify the territory. While three out of four North-American franchisors granted territorial rights to franchisees, the corresponding result in Finland was significantly higher. A territory can be defined in several complementary ways, e.g. mile radius, region, population, etc. and indeed, a lot of variation was found among the surveyed franchises.

Most franchisors require their franchisees to purchase goods or equipment solely from approved suppliers (Inaba 1980). By demanding this franchisors want to ensure proper quality of the products and concentrate the purchasing power of the chain, i.e. gain economies of scale. An equal amount, more than 70% of the subjects were found to follow this in both countries. Further, almost all the franchisors, which responded, limited the goods or services their franchisees were allowed to sell. In this way franchisees can pursue uniformity and support the brand (Mathewson and Winter 1985; Kaufmann and Eroglu 1999). Interestingly, in the Finnish sample the clause concerning limitations of sales was used significantly more often than among the investigated US franchises. Nearly every examined franchisor in both countries demanded their franchisees to adhere to the registered trademarks used in that franchise. Nevertheless, the US franchisors seemed to be even more demanding than the respective Finnish franchisors.

In addition to the territorial rights and limitations in relation to purchasing and selling, franchisors frequently require franchisees to actually participate in and operate the franchised business. However, this practice may vary from franchise to franchise. Many of the sampled franchisors required the franchisees to operate the franchised business and be involved in the outlet's day-to-day operations. Nonetheless, the Finnish franchisors seemed to be much stricter in this sense than the US as well as in relation to the requirement that a franchisee has to be the full-time operator of a franchised outlet (see Table 7).

An integral part of the franchise agreement for a franchisor and a franchisee is the covenant not to compete. It usually concerns two separate periods of time: the time of the contract term and time after expiration of the contract. The covenant not to compete means that the franchisee may not without the franchisor's written approval engage in a similar or comparable business at the time of the contract or for a reasonable period of time after the contract has expired. Under EU legislation, the maximum time for the covenant not to compete is one year. To be enforceable the covenant must be limited to competing products and must be restricted to the business premises and the area specified in the franchise contract. A further condition is that the covenant is fundamental for protecting the know-how invested in the franchisor's business format (Commission Regulation EC No 2790/1999; Tommila and Elo 2001). Nearly every respondent - all Finnish franchisors and nine out of ten US franchisors - reported using the covenant during the time of the contract. Eight out of ten sampled US and Finnish franchisors employed it also after the contract had expired.

A franchisor may also require that a franchisee use proprietary software updated on a regular basis. Similarly, minimum requirements can be set for the franchisee's computer hardware. In addition, the franchisee may need to equip the computer with a data connection to facilitate adequate and on-line information exchange and communication with the franchisor. It should be noted that in addition to versatile and effective communication purposes, on-line connections (e.g. online cash register) can be used for monitoring a franchisee's business transactions. Regarding these issues Finnish franchisors seem to be technologically more advanced than their researched US peers (see Table 7). In every explored item (proprietary software, periodic upgrades, computer requirements, data connections) the differences were statistically significant and in the same direction, i.e. favoring the Finns.

Table 7. Obligations Concerning Franchisees' Business Operations

ITEM		USA (n=114)	FINLAND (n=30)	Sig.
Territorial rights	Yes	73.7%	90.0%	.000
	No	26.3%	10.0%	
Type of the territory	Address	8.8%	6.7%	
	Mile radius	23.7%	6.7%	
	Region	30.6%	60.0%	
	Population	16.7%	3.3%	
	Other	0%	13.3%	
	NA	20.2%	10.0%	
Purchases from approved suppliers	Yes	71.1%	76.7%	.094
	No	28.9%	23.3%	
Restrictions on sales	Yes	92.9%	100.0%	.000
	No	7.1%	0%	
Adherence to specified trademarks	Yes	100.0%	90.0%	.000
	No	0%	10.0%	
Participation in actual business operation	Yes	62.3%	93.3%	.000
	No	37.7%	6.7%	
Franchisee must be a full-time operator	Yes	19.3%	86.7%	.000
	No	80.7%	13.3%	
Covenant not to compete during the term of the contract	Yes	89.4%	100.0%	.000
	No	10.6%	0%	
Covenant not to compete after expiration of the contract term	Yes	81.4%	83.3%	.341
	No	18.6%	16.7%	
Proprietary software	Yes	62.3%	76.7%	.000
	No	37.7%	23.3%	
Periodic upgrade of software	Yes	45.6%	70.0%	.000
	No	54.4%	30.0%	
Minimum requirements for the computer	Yes	34.2%	80.0%	.000
	No	65.8%	20.0%	
Modem or other data connection	Yes	33.3%	86.7%	.000
	No	66.7%	13.3%	

Sig.: Binominal test

4.4 Financial Aspects of Starting and Running a Franchised Outlet

Starting a franchised business is a considerable and long-term investment for a franchise owner. To avoid future dissatisfaction or even potential failure of business, all financial facts engaged in a start-up should be reviewed diligently (Hing 1995; Morrison 1996; Tuunanen 2002b). Franchisors normally estimate the expenses involved in starting a franchised business. Initial investment is a turnkey cost and it should include land and building, equipment, signage, inventory, initial franchise fee and working capital, etc. Among the US respondents, virtually all franchisors provided a dollar range as an estimate for the initial investment while in Finland a minority applied a euro range (see Table 8).

A payment that is also calculated in the initial investment is the initial franchise fee. It is a lump sum, normally paid immediately when the franchise contract is signed (Sen 1993). The initial franchise fee is a non-refundable, one time compensation to the franchisor for the right to make use of the business format (see e.g. Rubin 1978; Baucus et al. 1993). As with the initial investment, statistically significant differences were discovered between the samples. While the US franchisors preferred a variable sum for the initial franchise fee, the opposite emerged in Finland where eight out of ten studied franchisors collected a fixed sum.

A prospective franchisee has to be able to raise a sufficient amount of capital for the initial investment. For this purpose, some commercial banks have specialized departments and instruments for franchise financing (Stern and Stanworth 1994). Franchised businesses are considered to be less risky than independent small businesses (Hoy 1994). Partly because of the lower business risk bankers may issue a proportionally larger loan and offer a lower interest rate than for other business loans. Also franchisors may finance some part of the franchisees' initial investment although this is not the case every time. Franchisors are reluctant to carry the financial risk of the franchisees' performance (cf. Martin 1988; Norton 1988). A central tenet of franchising and indeed the franchisor's strategic incentive is that the franchisee contributes tangible (money and physical investment) and intangible (motivation, knowledge, skills) resources to the system (see e.g. Caves and Murphy 1976; Lillis et al. 1976; Rubin 1978; Brickley and Dark 1987; Thompson 1994; Dant 1995).

The most frequently used policy among the Finnish respondents was that the franchisor assisted the franchisee in raising money from a third party whereas in the US sample it was infrequently used. However, the results showed that the US franchisors offered finance for their franchisees slightly more frequently than in Finland (see Table 8).

In a franchise relationship, a franchisee is obligated to pay certain ongoing fees (Woll 1968-69). These fees are often a percent of the gross (or net) revenues paid weekly, biweekly or on a monthly basis (Agraval and Lal 1995; Combs and Castrogiovanni 1994; Lafontaine 1992; Lal 1990). Many of the franchisors in both countries required a specific percent of sales to be paid for royalties. A proportionally higher number of the Finnish franchisors applied a percentage range for royalties, but overall, the royalty usages were similar.

Most researched US franchisors also required franchisees to pay advertising fees as a percentage of sales. In Finland, fewer franchisors apply advertising fees. The average advertising fee percents employed were more or less equal in both countries. It should be noted that a franchise contract might also cover other fees such as leasing and training fees.

Table 8. Financial Aspects of Starting and Running a Franchised Outlet

ITEM		USA (n=114)	FINLAND (n=30)	Sig.
Initial investment	Fixed sum	1.8%	70.4%	
	€ or $ range	98.2%	29.6%	[.000]
Initial franchise fee	Fixed sum	7.0%	82.6%	[.000]
	Variable	92.1%	17.4%	
	Sum	0.9%	0%	
	None			
Finance from franchisor	Fully	0.9%	0%	
	Partially	36.8%	26.7%	
	No	62.3%	73.3%	
Finance from a 3rd party	Yes	23.7%	66.7%	[.000]
	No	76.3%	33.3%	
Ongoing fees: Royalties	Fixed %	92.9%	72.0%	
	Flat fee	1.8%	4.0%	
	%-Range	4.4%	24.0%	
	No	0.9%	0%	
The average royalty percentage (Md)		5.54 (5.0)	5.68 (6.0)	.901 (.035)
Ongoing fees: Advertising fees	No fee	9.6%	6.6%	
	Flat fee	4.4%	0%	
	% of Sales	86.8%	53.5%	
	%-Range	0%	6.6%	
	NA	0.9%	33.3%	
The average advertising percentage (Md)		2.13 (2.0)	1.72 (2.0)	.244 (.305)
Earnings claims	Yes	44.7%	100.0%	
	No	55.3%	0%	[.000]

Sig.: T-test (Mann-Whitney U-test) [Binominal test]

To be able to analyze the profitability of a franchised business, a prospective franchisee should obtain facts about the potential earnings (Justis and Vincent 2003). Nevertheless, franchisors may be very cautious and sensitive regarding the earnings claims. All projected earnings whether given in written, oral or visual form ought to be documented. It appeared that every surveyed Finnish franchisor supplied some kind of earnings claims, written or oral, for their potential franchisees. In this sense, an apparent distinction came out, as most of the US franchisors did not deliver such information in written form in the UFOC. Nonetheless, it should be noted that results concerning this issue are not comparable since in the USA any claim of sales, earnings, cost, etc. must be disclosed in the UFOC Item 19. This disclosure is voluntary under FTC regulations. Thus, the US franchisors may also be willing to disclose earnings information, yet not in the UFOC format.

5 Discussion and Implications

The small size of the US sample can be regarded as a limitation in the present analysis. At this early phase of the study, a cross-national comparison was conducted. Potential differences in the contracts between various industries, and between the different size and age of the franchise systems were not investigated. Moreover, in this cross-sectional study no consideration was given to the dynamics of contracting. Franchise contracts are not set for an indefinite time period: they are altered, modified and updated on regular basis – normally after the expiration of the initial term of the contract. These issues are possible subjects for further investigation. On the other hand, the cross-national research design may increase the value of the current study since multi-national studies are still virtually non-existent in the field of franchising.

The lesson learned from this study is that more differences than similarities may exist between the US and Finnish franchise contracts. Furthermore, this conclusion implies also that differences in contractual provisions of franchise agreements between the US and the EU countries are potential. The EU has regulations concerning franchise arrangements with which every member country must comply. This means that national legislation needs to be harmonized with the EU regulation. Notably, the EU regulation is drafted to address antitrust issues – it does not concern pre-sale disclosure. It should be also taken into account that the legal systems are dissimilar between the EU countries and the USA. This fact has a profound effect on how contracts are drafted.

Naturally, some of the dissimilarities found clearly hinge upon the two very diverse markets. Franchising is a relatively new phenomenon in Finland and therefore markets are in an evolving stage for franchise expansion, while in the USA franchising markets are saturating.

The implications of the research are relevant for both franchisors and prospective franchisees. The importance of a prudent franchise contract cannot ever be underestimated (Tuunanen and Hyrsky 2001). Sound agreements protect both a franchisor and a franchisee. The UFOC form applied in this study may serve as a systematic tool for a prudent inquiry on franchise offerings also for Finnish prospective franchisees[7]. By following the UFOC form Finnish franchisors could extend the openness and ensure that there is adequate information available for persons interested in becoming a franchisee.

Self-regulation may constitute a more favorable avenue for advancing healthy business practices than increasing the legal burden of franchisors. For instance, the *Finnish Franchising Association* could establish a suggested form for member franchisors detailing relevant disclosure information and proceedings. Well-established and functioning self-regulation could also diminish the need for the future franchise regulation. For franchisors a new regulation always involves a risk of additional costs. It is questionable whether extended regulation would prevent or decrease legal disputes. Despite extensive franchise regulation in the US, franchise-related litigation is still frequent. Poorly designed regulation may also hurt the whole franchising sector by making it less appealing as a vehicle for setting up and growing businesses. [8]

Nevertheless, self-regulation might be an ineffective measure. Seven out of ten (72%) Finnish franchisors do not hold membership with the national franchise association whose member chains obey the "non-coercive and non-sanctioned" Ethical Code. This fact implies that the majority of the Finnish franchisors have not necessarily paid enough attention to pre-sale disclosure. It should also be noted that the franchise contracts of the member franchisors of *Finnish Franchising Association* are reviewed by franchising specialized attorneys authorized by the FFA. A nation-wide survey of nearly 500 Finnish franchise owners from 36 franchises across various industries revealed that one fifth of them perceived that the information they received from the franchisor during initial franchise contract negotiations were either insufficient or incorrect. The study established a clear connection between pre-sale disclosure and post-sale satisfaction of franchise owner. In other words, dissatisfaction may stem from improper disclosure and dissatisfaction may turn to friction between the contractual parties and even voluntary turnover of the franchise owner (Tuunanen 2002).

---

[7] Elango & Fried (1997, p 77) see the UFOCs under-utilized source of significant information in the past academic franchising studies.

[8] Interestedly, Australian experiences are quite contrary. The mandatory *Franchising Code of Conduct* was introduced in 1998. Following the introduction, there were fewer substantial disputes, greater resolution of disputes through mediation than litigation, fewer franchise agreement terminations and fewer transfers of existing agreements. The Code also promoted trust, commitment, communication, power balance and mutual goals of the parties across various phases of the franchise relationship. A potentially correlated drawback was that the growth rate of franchisors and franchised units slowed down. (Lim & Frazer 2002). Terry (2003) came to rather similar positive conclusions concerning the experiences of the Australian franchise regulation. The Australian franchising regulation can be obtained from
http://scaleplus.law.gov.au/html/pastereg/2/1466/pdf/TradePracIndCodeFran98.pdf

Franchise regulation is a very contemporary and hotly debated issue. Terry (2003) has traced franchise regulation from 16 nations[9]. In most cases the legislation is of recent origin – in the 1990's – and in most cases the regulation concerns only prior disclosure not the relationship between the parties. He stated also that there is a global trend towards franchising regulation[10] (Terry 2003). This is supported by the UNIDROIT, which introduced the *Model Franchise Disclosure Law* in September 2002[11]. There is a growing interest towards pre-sale franchise disclosure also in Finland. Finnish *Ministry of Trade and Industry* set up a task force to explore general contractual models applied in inter-firm cooperation. In the final report substantial emphasis was placed on franchise agreements. The report raised important contractual provisions and outlined the core issues that a potential franchise owner should learn before entering into the relationship. (Ministry of Trade and Industry 2002)

If a franchise regulation concerning pre-sale disclosure is inevitable for ensuring ethical conduct and sound infrastructure for franchising in Finland, there are several issues, which need to be considered. First, the existing regulation from other countries should be scrutinized. Nevertheless, due diligence is necessary since there are favorable (e.g. Australian) as well as negative (e.g. the US) experiences emerging from franchise regulation. Through investigation best practices can be learned and applied. Second, the prospective regulation should be designed in a close collaboration with the franchise community and its shareholders. A smooth transition could be achieved by starting with a voluntary self-regulation for a certain period of time, say two years. After the transition period the regulation could be revised and subsequently implemented as a mandatory procedure.

Knowledge produced in this research is vitally important for the international franchising community - consultants, attorneys, accountants, franchise managers and small business policy makers. The findings are of particular interest for franchisors that are looking for penetration into foreign markets since franchise contracts need to be reviewed and altered to comply with country or region specific legislation and regulations. Along with these, characteristics of the target market and the prevailing culture cannot be omitted from the consideration. One beneficial route for the future study is to extend the investigation to other countries.

---

[9] The countries are: Albania, Australia, Brazil, Canada and Ontario, China, France, Indonesia, Japan, Korea, Malaysia, Mexico, Romania, Russia, Spain and Venezuela.

[10] Argentina, Italy, Philippines, Sweden, Tunisia, Belgium are considering, introducing or preparing franchise specific regulation.

[11] UNIDROIT, the *International Institute for the Unification of Private Law* is an independent inter-governmental organisation. Its purpose is to study needs and methods for modernizing, harmonizing and co-ordinating private and in particular commercial law as between States and groups of States. It was established in 1926 as an auxiliary organ of the League of Nations and it has presently 59 member states from the five continents. Member states represent a variety of different legal, economic and political systems as well as different cultural backgrounds. The Model Franchise Disclosure Law can be downloaded at http://www.unidroit.org/english/franchising/modellaw/modellaw.e.pdf

References

1. Agraval D, Lal R (1995) Contractual Arrangements in Franchising: An Empirical Investigation. Journal of Marketing Research 32 (May 1995):213-221
2. Baucus DA, Baucus MS, Human SE (1993) Choosing a Franchise: How Base Fees and Royalties Relate to the Value of the Franchise. Journal of Small Business Management 31(2):91-104
3. Brickley JA, Dark F (1987) The Choice of Organizational Form: The Case of Franchising. Journal of Financial Economics 18:401-420
4. Brickley JA, Dark F, Weisbach MS (1991) The Economics Effects of Franchise Termination Laws. Journal of Law and Economics 34(1):101-132
5. Brickley JA, Misra S, Van Horn RL (2003) Contract Duration: Evidence from Franchise Contracts. The Proceedings of the 17th International Society of Franchising Conference. February 14-16, 2003. San Antonio
6. Castrogiovanni GJ, Justis RT, Julian SD (1993) Franchise Failure Rates: An Assessment of Magnitude and Influencing Factors. Journal of Small Business Management (2):105-114
7. Caves RE, Murphy II WF (1976) Franchising: Firms, Markets, and Intangible Assets. Southern Economic Journal 42:572-586
8. Commission Regulation (EC) No 2790/1999 of 22 Dec. 1999 on the application of article 81(3) of the Treaty to categories of vertical agreements and concerted practices. Official Journal of the European Communities, L336:21-25
9. Combs JG, Castrogiovanni GJ (1994) Franchisor Strategy: A Proposed Model and Empirical Test of Franchise Versus Company Ownership. Journal of Small Business Management 32(2):37-48
10. Dandridge T, Falbe C (1994) The Influence of Franchisees Beyond Their Local Domains. International Small Business Journal 12(2):39-49
11. Dant RP (1995) Motivation for Franchising: Rhetoric Versus Reality. International Small Business Journal 14(1):10-32
12. EFF (2002) The European Code of Ethics for Franchising. Retrieved September 4, 2002, from http://www.eff-franchise.com/Code%20of%20ethics%20text.htm
13. Elango B, Fried VH (1997) Franchising Research: A Literature Review and Synthesis. Journal of Small Business Management 35(3):68-81
14. Hadfield GK (1990) Problematic Relations: Franchising and the Law of Incomplete Contracts. Stanford Law Review 42:927-992
15. Hing N (1995) Franchisee Satisfaction: Contributors and Consequences. Journal of Small Business Management 33(2):12-25
16. Hofstede G (1980) Culture's Consequences: International Differences in Work-Related Values. London, Great Britain: Sage
17. Hoy F (1994) The Dark Side of Franchising or Appreciating Flaws in an Imperfect World. International Small Business Journal 12 (2):26-38
18. Inaba FS (1980) Franchising: Monopoly by Contract. Southern Economic Journal (April):65-72
19. IFA (2002) The International Franchise Association Code of Ethics. Retrieved January 3, 2003, from http://www.franchise.org/welcome_about/code.asp
20. Justis RT, Chan P, Haynes JB (1991) Franchising Disclosure: A Review. The Proceedings of the 5th Annual International Society of Franchising Conference. February 9-10, 1991. Miami

21.Justis RT, Tuunanen M, Chen Y, Castrogiovanni GJ (2003) Disclosing the Activities of Franchisors. The Proceedings of the 17th International Society of Franchising Conference. February 14-16, 2003. San Antonio
22.Justis RT, Vincent WS (2001) Achieving Wealth Through Franchising: A Comprehensive Manual to Finding, Starting, and Succeeding in a Franchise Business. Adams Media Corporation, Holbrook
23.Justis RT, Vincent WS (2003) Earnings Claims: How Much Money Can I Make? The Proceedings of the 17th International Society of Franchising Conference. February 14-16, 2003. San Antonio, TX, USA
24.Justis RT, Judd RJ (1998) Franchising. Dame Publications Inc., Houston
25.Kaufmann PJ, Eroglu S (1999) Standardization and Adaptation in Business Format Franchising. Journal of Business Venturing 14(1):69-85
26.Koiranen M (1998) Spread of Franchising: A Multinational Comparison Based on the Notions Innovation Diffusion. Asia Pacific Journal of Marketing and Logistics 10(2):50-65
27.Koiranen M, Hyrsky K (1996) Lift-off: Finnish Business Format Franchising. Franchising Research an International Journal 1(2):16-21
28.Lafontaine F (1992) Agency Theory and Franchising: Some Empirical Results. Rand Journal of Economics 23(2):263-283
29.Lal R (1990) Improving Channel Coordination Through Franchising. Marketing Science 9(4):299-318
30.Leblebici H, Shalley CE (1996) The Organization of Relational Contracts: The Allocation of Rights in Franchising. Journal of Business Venturing 11(5):404-418
31.Lillis C M, Narayama CL, Gilman JL (1976) Competitive Advantage Variation Over the Life Cycle of a Franchise. Journal of Marketing 77-80
32.Lim J, Frazer L (2002) Introducing Franchising Regulation: An Analysis of the Australian Franchising Code of Conduct. Journal of Marketing Channels 2(10):39-56
33.Martin RE (1988) Franchising and Franchise management. The American Economic Review 78(5):954-968
34.Mathewson GF, Winter RH (1985) The Economies of Franchise Contracts. Journal of Law and Economics 28:503-526
35.Ministry of Trade and Industry (2002) Cooperation of Enterprises and Franchising – Administration of Contractual Risk and Contractual Guidance (in Finnish). Edita Publishing Ltd., Helsinki
36.Morrison KA (1996) An Empirical Test of a Model of Franchisee Job Satisfaction. Journal of Small Business Management 34(3):27-41
37.Norton SW (1988) An Empirical Look at Franchising as an Organizational Form. Journal of Business 61:197-217
38.Reynolds PD, Hay M, Camp MS (1999) Global Entrepreneurship Monitor 1999 Executive Report. Kaufman Center for Entrepreneurial Leadership at the Ewing Marion Kauffman Foundation
39.Rubin PH (1978) The Theory of the Firm and the Structure of the Franchise Contract. The Journal of Law and Economics 21:223-233
40.Scherer FM, Ross D (1990) Industrial Market Structure and Economic Performance. 3rd edn, Boston, MA: Houghton Mifflin Company
41.Sen KC (1993) The Use of Initial Fees and Royalties in Business Format Franchising. Managerial and Decision Economics 14:175-190
42.Spinelli S (1994) Franchising. In The Portable MBA in Entrepreneurship. (ed) Bygrave WD. John Wiley & Sons. NY.
43.Stadfeild LS (1992) Comment on Proposed US Franchise Legislation: A Search for Balances. Commercial Law Journal 97(4):540-566

44. Stern P, Stanworth J (1994) Improving Small Business Survival Rates via Franchising – the Role of Banks in Europe. International Small Business Journal 12(2), 15-25
45. Terry A (2003) Franchise Sector Regulation: The Australian Experience. The Proceedings of the 1st EMNet –conference on "Economics and Management of Franchising Networks", Vienna, Austria. June 26-28, 2003
46. Thompson RS (1994) The Franchise Life Cycle and the Penrose Effect. Journal of Economic Behavior and Organization 24(2):207-218
47. Tommila M, Elo H (2001) A Franchise Agreement Does Not Open up Easily to a Franchisee (in Finnish). In: R Granström, Tuunanen M (eds) Franchising in Finland 2002 (in Finnish). Finnish Franchising Association, Lohja, pp 65-67
48. Tuunanen M, Hyrsky K (2001) Entrepreneurial Paradoxes in Business Format Franchising: An Empirical Survey of Finnish Franchisees. International Small Business Journal 19(4):47-62
49. Tuunanen M (2002a) Franchising Statistics 2002(in Finnish). In: R Granström, Tuunanen M (eds) Franchising in Finland 2003(in Finnish). Finnish Franchising Association, Lohja, pp 32-37
50. Tuunanen M (2002b) An Ounce of Prevention Is Worth a Pound of Cure: National Franchisee (Dis-) satisfaction study. Journal of Marketing Channels 10(4):57-89
51. Tuunanen M (2003) Compilation of Finnish Franchising Statistics. In: Alon I and Welsh DHB (eds) International Franchising in Industrialized Markets: Northern and Western Europe. CCH Publishing Company, Chicago
52. Tuunanen M, Koiranen M (1998) Finnish Franchising in the 1990s and Beyond. In: Virtanen M (ed) Proceedings of the Conference on Growth and Job Creation in SME's. Helsinki School of Economics and Business Administration, Small Business Center, Mikkeli, (M-80):367-383
53. Webster's Dictionary (1993) New Jersey: Gramercy Books
54. Windsperger J (2002) Allocation of Decision and Ownership Rights in Franchise Relationship. Journal of Marketing Channels 2(10):19-38
55. Woll M (1968-69) Sources of Revenue to the Franchisor and Their Strategic Implications. Journal of Retailing 44(4):14-20
56. World Economic Forum (2002) Global Competitiveness Report 2002-2003. Retrieved January 3, 2003, from http://www.weforum.org/site/homepublic.nsf/Content/Global+Competitiveness+Programme/Reports/Global+ Competitiveness+Report+2002-2003#ExecutiveSummary

A Comparison of Finnish and United States Franchisee Satisfaction

Frank Wadsworth, CFE[1], Mika Tuunanen[2], Doug Haines[3]

[1] School of Business, Indiana University Southeast
4201 Grant Line Road, New Albany, Indiana, United States
fwadswo@ius.edu
[2] University of Jyväskylä
School of Business & Economics
P.O. Box 35 FIN-40351 Jyväskylä
Finland
mptuunan@econ.jyu.fi
[3] Department of Business
College of Business & Economics
University of Idaho
Moscow, Idaho 83844-3178
dhaines@uidaho.edu

Abstract. This paper investigates, using a multi-dimensional model, differences between franchisee satisfaction in Finland and the United States. Comparison of Finnish and American franchisee satisfaction levels is made across eight dimensions of franchisee satisfaction. Data was collected using a postal survey of Quick Service Restaurant (Hamburger) franchisees in Finland and the United States. Results show franchisees in Finland and the United States are overall equally satisfied. Data analysis revealed that for four of the eight dimensions, franchisees in both countries have statistically equal levels of satisfaction. However, for the other four dimensions, a statistical difference exists between franchisee perceptions in the two countries. United States franchisees are more satisfied than Finnish franchisees with the financial, entrepreneurial control, communication and franchise contract dimensions.A multiple regression model of franchisee satisfaction is able to explain 89 percent of the variation of franchisee general satisfaction with the variation of seven dimensions; financial, relation, support services, brand image, entrepreneurial control, contract and training.Future research comparing franchisee satisfaction among various countries should be undertaken to comprehend differences in franchisee satisfaction between countries. Models explaining cross-cultural differences should be employed to explain different results for different countries.

1 Introduction

A franchisor considering how to improve the effectiveness of their system might be concerned about how to improve franchisee satisfaction and whether satisfaction impacts performance. A prospective franchisee might wonder whether they would be satisfied in a particular franchise system. Franchisee satisfaction is an important construct in franchising. Some studies have explicitly investigated franchisee satisfaction (Hunt and Nevin 1974; Hing 1995; Morrison 1996: Wadsworth and Haines 2000) and operationalized the construct with single or multiple item measures. Franchisee satisfaction is an antecedant or consequence depending on the context. The purpose of this manuscript is to compare franchise satisfaction in a cross-cultural setting.

2 Literature Review

Franchisee satisfaction may reasonably be viewed in the general context of channel relationships and channel satisfaction. Examinations of channel member satisfaction usually focus on the satisfaction of the downstream channel member. Channel member satisfaction is more often measured and modeled as an outcome, consequence or "terminal value" determined by other constructs such as power and dependence (Frazier and Summers 1984, 1986; Lusch 1976; Skinner, Gassenheimer and Kelly 1992), conflict and cooperation (Gaski 1984). Measures of channel member satisfaction include single item, overall satisfaction measures Ping (1994) and multi-item measures that address various asserted dimensions of the satisfaction construct (Gassenheimer, Sterling and Robicheax 1996; Gassenheimer, Davis and Dahlstrom 1998; Reukert and Churchill 1984; Schul, Little and Pride 1985).

Two fundamental dimensions of satisfaction are satisfaction with economic and non-economic aspects of the relationship (Geyskins, Steenkamp and Kumar 1999). In their meta-analysis, Geyskins, Steenkamp and Kumar (1999) suggest that the channel satisfaction literature may be reasonably organized into these two dimensions. This suggests an overriding economic dimension for alternative dimensions such as satisfaction with products, financial considerations (Ruekert and Churchill 1984), profits, new product opportunities, and growth potential (Gassenheimer, Sterling and Robicheaux 1996; Gassenheimer, Davis and Dahlstrom 1998). Non-economic aspects could include social interaction and cooperation (Ruekert and Churchill 1984), franchise administration, service support, policies and reward systems (Schul, Little and Pride 1985) and treatment by headquarters and local sales representatives, fairness and honesty, and concern for channel member's goal accomplishment (Gassenheimer, Sterling and Robicheax 1996; Gassenheimer, Davis and Dahlstrom 1998).

Some have suggested that the franchisor-franchisee relationship might be considered an employer-employee relationship so that job-satisfaction dimensions apply (Morrison 1996). Salesperson job satisfaction is an antecedent of organizational commitment (Brown and Peterson 1993). Job satisfaction is a consequence of role perceptions (Brown and Peterson 1993). In their meta-analysis of salesperson job satisfaction, Brown and Peterson (1993) noted that job satisfaction is not related to performance either as a consequence or a determinant. They suggest that sales performance is a terminal value for sales people. Using a job satisfaction model, Morrison (1996) examines franchisee satisfaction in terms of non-economic dimensions.

A franchisee makes a long-term investment or purchase decision when they elect to begin a relationship with a franchisor. In this sense, the franchisee is a customer of the franchisor and has entered into an agreement that might be characterized more as an agreement for service rather than product. One perspective in the service satisfaction literature suggests that customer characteristics and expectations are important in determining perceived service quality and satisfaction (Parasuraman, Zeithaml and Berry 1994; Hing 1995).

Recent franchisee satisfaction research has considered economic and non-economic dimensions (Elango and Fried 1997), franchisee and franchisor characteristics, and expectations (Hing 1995; Morrison 1996). Economic dimensions of franchisee satisfaction can be broadly categorized as reward systems, perceptions of the franchisor's contribution to the franchisee's financial success, expectations for future success and growth, and satisfaction with cooperative advertising and promotion programs (Elango and Fried 1997). Non-economic factors include autonomy, fairness, operations support, training, control systems, and communications (Elango and Fried 1997). Morrison (1996) also suggests that characteristics of the franchisee such as extraversion and subjective well being contribute to franchisees' job satisfaction. Recognizing that franchisee characteristics and expectations contribute to franchisee satisfaction, Hing (1995) suggests that franchisors more carefully and completely screen potential franchisees to ensure higher levels of franchisee satisfaction.

A number of limitations exist with respect to past literature. First, past studies have not examined franchisee satisfaction across different cultures. Second, some past studies borrow scales without adapting the scale to a franchising context.

A goal of the franchisee satisfaction measure is to be specific enough to distinguish franchisee satisfaction from other types of satisfaction, yet capture the franchisee satisfaction domain of most franchise systems. In the context of this paper, franchisee satisfaction measures should be generalizable across different cultures.

3 Franchisee Satisfaction Measure

An eight-dimension measure of franchisee satisfaction exists (Wadsworth and Haines 2000; Haines and Wadsworth 2001) but has not been tested in a cross-cultural setting. Wadsworth and Haines used Churchill's (1979) measure development procedure in designing their measure. The eight factors are: Relationship, Financial, Training, Support Services, Fees, Brand Image, Entrepreneurial Control, and Franchise Contract. Advisory Council is a new dimension that has only been used in the 2001 survey.

4 Data Collection

Data was collected using a postal survey of Finnish and U.S. Quick Service Restaurants. The procedures have been discussed elsewhere (Wadsworth and Haines 2000; Tuunanen 2001) and need not be repeated here. This study used the data from 21 United States and 45 Finnish Quick Service Restaurant (Hamburger) franchisees.

5 Results

Results are discussed in the following order. First, we examine results of statistical tests designed to examine for differences between countries on the eight franchisee satisfaction dimensions and the general franchisee satisfaction dimension. Following the single dimension analysis, we examine dimension reliability consistency across studies and the two countries. Last, we examine the regression analysis results and implications from our study.

Examining each dimension of franchisee satisfaction separately to determine if a statistical difference exists between the Finland and the United States franchisees showed that four of the dimensions had no statistical differences (Table 1). Franchisee satisfaction with Relationship, Support Services, Brand Image, Training, and the General Franchisee Satisfaction measures do not differ between Finland and the United States. However, statistical differences do exist between Finland and the United States on Financial, Entrepreneurial Control, Communication, and Franchise Contract (Table 1). For every one of the dimensions with a statistical difference, United States franchisees are more satisfied than their Finnish counterparts.

Table 1. ANOVA Results: Differences between Factor Scores

Factor	F	Sig
Entrepreneurial Control	5.994	.017
Financial	4.891	.031
Franchise Contract	3.752	.057
Communication	2.990	.089
Brand Image	2.136	.149
Support Services	1.740	.192
Training	1.476	.229
General Satisfaction	.388	.536
Overall, how would you rate your franchise system	.242	.624
Relational	.046	.830

NOTES.---*F* F-Value, *Sig* Level of Significance between Mean Scores for Each Country

Table 2. Coefficient Alpha Values for the Eight Factor Solution Dimensions[1]

Factor	WH (2000)	Finland (1999)	U.S. (1999)	HW (2001)
Relationship	.95 (5)	.87	.84	.91
Financial	.85 (3)	.90	.91	.88
Training	.89 (5)	.87	.90	.90
Fees	.81 (3)	.72	.93	.79
Brand Image	.86 (5)	.88	.82	.82
Entrepreneurial Control	.89 (9)	.79	.86	.86
Franchise Contract	.86 (8)	.78	.72	.85
Advisory Council	Not included	Not included	Not included	.86

NOTES.---Number of items in parentheses. *WH2000* Wadsworth and Haines (2000) *HW* Haines and Wadsworth (2001)

Table 2 shows the consistent reliability of the measure dimensions across time, studies and countries. Dimensions are remarkably consistent across time, studies and countries. These results give us confidence in the validity of the measure and its generalizability.

Regression results are shown in Tables 3. When examining results separately for each country, they do not share dimensions that are significant predictors of general franchisee satisfaction. For Finland, franchisees' satisfaction with Relation, Brand Image, and Entrepreneurial Control are predictive of their general franchisee satisfaction. For the United States, franchisees' satisfaction with Financial and Contract dimensions were predictive of their general franchisee satisfaction. When the data across the countries were combined to predict general franchisee satisfaction, Financial, Relation, Support Services, Brand Image, Entrepreneurial Control, Contract and Training dimensions were significant predictors.

[1] The use of a coefficient alpha with a three-item scale is questioned by some researchers

Table 3. OLS Regressions Explaining Franchisee Satisfaction by Individual Dountry and Across Countries

	Country		
Independent variables	Finland	United States	Combined
Financial	.166	.696	.276
	(1.58)	(2.73)**	(2.92)***
Relationship	.310	-.096	.288
	(2.15)**	(-.49)	(2.46)**
Brand Image	.318	.104	.403
	(2.73)***	(.58)	(4.58)***
Entrepreneurial Control	.237	.205	.239
	(2.97)**	(1.02)	(2.78)***
Communication	.003	-.201	.151
	(.23)	(-1.27)	(1.25)
Franchise Contract	.190	.853	.387
	(1.26)	(3.04)**	(3.34)**
Training	.119	.004	.162
	(1.21)	(.287)	(2.01)**
Country			.167
			(1.01)
Constant	-1.241	-1.915	-1.855
	(-3.25)***	(-3.53)***	(-4.40)***
R^2	.885	.937	.890
Adj R^2	.862	.893	.871

NOTES.--- Value of t statistics in parentheses. Significance levels: *** P< .01; ** P< .05; * P< .10.

6 Conclusions

This study undertook to compare franchisee satisfaction across two different cultures. Franchisees in the two cultures did differ on their satisfaction with the Financial, Entrepreneurial Control, Communication, and Franchise Contract dimensions. Reliability analysis showed that franchisee satisfaction dimensions are generalizable across time, studies and cultures. Regression analysis revealed that the dimensions are able to explain almost 90% of the variation of general franchisee satisfaction with seven of the eight dimensions.

Limitations of the chosen research method include the use of a single data collection method rather than two or three methods. Either an observational or other communication method such as in-depth interviews or existential phenomenology might lead to a different conceptual model. A second limitation is the use of the franchisee satisfaction measure in a single category of a single industry rather than across multiple categories or industries. A third limitation is the small sample size used in this study.

A number of future directions are suggested by this study. First, additional testing of the franchisee satisfaction measure with other franchise industries and systems is recommended. Testing is necessary to confirm the reliability and validity of the measure. Second, continued testing of the instrument over time should be used to determine if the satisfaction construct indicants are stable over time and cultures. Finally, the goal of future research would be to place the franchisee satisfaction construct into a nomological network which will allow other researchers to use and confirm its appropriateness. In particular, for cross-cultural work, the use of variables that could potentially explain difference across cultures would be important to increasing our understanding of what makes franchising successful in one culture but perhaps not be as successful in another culture.

References

1. Brown SP, Peterson RA (1993) Antecedents and Consequences of Salesperson Job Satisfaction: Meta-Analysis and Assessment of Causal Effects. Journal of Marketing Research 30(1):63-78
2. Churchill GA, Jr. (1979) A Paradigm for Developing Better Measures of Marketing Constructs. Journal of Marketing Research 16(February):64-73
3. Churchill GA, Jr. (1995) Marketing Research: Methodological Foundations, 6th edn. Fort Worth, Texas, Dryden Press
4. Elango B, Fried VH (1997) Franchising Research: A Literature Review and Synthesis. Journal of Small Business Management 35(3):68-82
5. Frazier GL, Summers JO (1984) Interfirm Influence Strategies and Their Application Within Distribution Channels. Journal of Marketing 21(Summer):43-55
6. Frazier GL, Summers JO (1986) Perceprions of Power and Its Use Within a Franchise Channel of Distribution. Journal of Marketing Research 23(May):169-76
7. Gaski JF (1984) The Theory of Power and Conflict in Channels of Distribution. Journal of Marketing 48(Summer):9-29
8. Gassenheimer JB, Sterling JU, Robicheaux RA (1996) Long-Term Channel Member Relationships. International Journal of Physical Distribution Logistics Management 26(5):94-117
9. Gassenheimer JB, Davis EJC, Dahlstrom R (1998) Is Dependent What We Want to Be? Effects of Incongruency. Journal of Retailing 74(2):247-272
10. Geyskens I, Steenkamp J-BEM, Kumar N (1999) A Meta-Analysis of Satisfaction in Marketing Channel Relationships. Journal of Marketing Research 36(2):223-239

11.Haines DC, Wadsworth FH (2001) Overall Franchisee Satisfaction: A Predictive Model. Proceedings of the 15th Conference of the International Society of Franchising Las Vegas, NV
12.Hing N (1995) Franchisee Satisfaction: Contributors and Consequences. Journal of Small Business Management 33(2):12-26
13.Hunt S, Nevin J (1974) Power in a Channel of Distribution: Sources and Consequences. Journal of Marketing Research 11(May):186-93
14.Lusch RF (1976) Sources of Power: Their Impact on Intrachannel Conflict. Journal of Marketing Research 13(November):382-390
15.Morrison K (1996) An Empirical Test of a Model of Franchisee Job Satisfaction. Journal of Small Business Management 34(3):27-42
16.Parasuraman A, Zeithaml VA, Berry L (1994) Reassessment of Expectations as a Comparison Standard in Measuring Service Quality: Implications for Further Research. Journal of Marketing 58(January):111-124
17.Ping JR, Robert A (1994) Does Satisfaction Moderate the Association Between Alternative Attractiveness and Exit Intention in a Marketing Channel?. Journal of the Academy of Marketing Science 22(4):364-372
18.Ruekert RW, Churchill GA, Jr. (1984) Reliability and Validity of Alternative Measures of Channel Member Satisfaction. Journal of Marketing Research 21(May):226-233
19.Schul LP, Little TE, Jr., Pride WM (1985) Channel Climate: Its Impact on Channel Members' Satisfaction. Journal of Retailing 61(2):9-38
20.Skinner SJ, Gassenheimer JB, Kelly SW (1992) Cooperation in Supplier Dealer Relations. Journal of Retailing 8(Summer):174-193
21.Tuunanen M (2001) An Ounce of Prevention is Worth a Pound of Cure: Findings from National Franchisee (Dis-)Satisfaction Study in Finland. Proceedings of the 15th Conference of the International Society of Franchising Las Vegas, NV
22.Wadsworth FG, Haines DC (2000) Franchisee Satisfaction: A Measurement Approach. Proceedings of the 14th Conference of the International Society of Franchising San Diego, CA
23.Wadsworth FH, Jones W (1996) Franchisee Satisfaction Survey Report. Proceedings of the 3rd Annual Convention of the American Franchisee Association Washington, D.C.

Finnish Franchisee Training Program - Findings from the First Ten Programs 1999-2001

Jenni Torikka

School of Business and Economics, University of Jyväskylä
P.O. Box 35 (MaE), FIN-40351 Jyväskylä, Finland
jentori@econ.jyu.fi

Abstract. The Finnish franchisee training program is a unique training because it is given to prospective franchisees by a third party. The program aims to find people interested in franchising and to give them the essential skills and knowledge a franchisee needs. Additional goal is to help the trainees to choose a franchise. In total, more than 200 trainees graduated from the first ten programs held in 1999-2001. The graduates comprise the samples of the current study. The data was collected in two separate phases. The present study explores the potential differences of the samples. The purpose of the research is to analyze the effectiveness of the franchisee training program by describing the career shifts of the trainees.

Acknowledgement. I would like to express my gratitude to professor Frank Hoy for his insightful comments on earlier version of the paper. I also wish to thank my advisor, research fellow Mika Tuunanen for his assistance and support.

1 Introduction and Theoretical Background

The need for new franchisees continues to be the most severe growth barrier for franchise chains in Finland. Franchisors face problems in finding and recruiting proper franchise owners for their systems. Indeed, while entrepreneurship is appreciated in the society, only few people will set up a business. Generally taken, the situation is the same in whole Europe except the southern parts of the continent (cf. Green Paper: Entrepreneurship in Europe). In Finland, recently formed government has set the promotion of entrepreneurship as a top priority in its program. For this purpose, the Ministry of Trade and Industry has launched an implementation plan for the Entrepreneurship Policy Programme. The programme is to remove the obstacles to entrepreneurship and to utilize the potential provided by entrepreneurship for boosting growth and improving employment. The programme consists of five sub-sectors. Two of the five that are related to this study are "education and training of entrepreneurs and business consultancy" and "start-up, growth and internationalization of enterprises".

In order to allocate the scarce public resources in a best possible and productive way to promote entrepreneurship, the activities under the policy programme should be evaluated and their results reported. Franchisee training program is one of the government funded activities to foster entrepreneurship. To develop the training and to assess the inputs-outputs relationship, it is essential to gauge its effectiveness. Objective information on the outcomes of the training is therefore valuable to the government, the Ministry of Trade and Industry and other small business policy makers as well as to franchisors and prospective franchisees.

To be able to evaluate the impact of public policies their objectives should be specified in a quantitative manner in the form of targets. However, many governments do not follow that (Storey 2000). The Finnish government has set a concrete objective for its entrepreneurship policy. There is a need for 90,000 new small business owners by the year 2010. The figure is based on two things. First, the government has set an employment goal of 100,000 new jobs and 30,000 new enterprises are required to reach that goal. Second, 60,000 enterprises will undergo a transition of ownership from one generation or owner to other during this decade. The set clear target enables the impact of the policy to be evaluated. Whatsoever, a precondition for that is measuring the influence of the activities under the policy programme. This way also the successfulness of the policy can be judged. (see Storey 2000). The current study aims to analyze the effectiveness of the franchisee training program and in that way contribute to evaluating the impact of the entrepreneurship policy.

The study is related to 'creation of the franchising relationship', which is one of the three main streams of franchising research mentioned by Elango and Fried (1997). They suggest topics for future research and bring up a need for studies on training.

The paper begins with an introductory section that starts off with a brief overview of franchising in Finland. The origin of the franchisee training program, the organizing parties, trainees, and the program itself are introduced. Following, research design is described and the results of the survey are presented. The paper concludes with a discussion of the results, implications and recommendations for future research.

1.1 Franchising in Finland

Franchising is a relatively new phenomenon in Finland. The emergence of first business format franchises dates back to the late 1970's. Nevertheless, a breakthrough appeared a decade later when a stream of franchises was started and the national franchising association was established (Tuunanen and Hyrsky 2001). During the last decade the amount of franchises operating in Finnish markets has been growing around 10-15% yearly. The 2002 statistics indicate there being 164 franchisors with close to 3,900 franchisee-owned and over 1,800 company-owned outlets. Majority of the franchises are service (n=67) and retailing chains (n=69). In addition, 28 franchises operate in the fast food, café and restaurant sector. Three quarters of the franchises originate from Finland.

According to 2002 statistics, franchising employs nearly 38,000 people and generates a gross annual turnover of 3.54 billion EUR. In comparison, according to Statistics Finland the gross annual turnover of retailing in 2002 was 23.1 billion EUR. Franchising accounts for 2.5% of the gross domestic product (GDP). Despite a slight economic downturn, the upward progress of Finnish franchising is expected to continue for several reasons. For instance, the growth of franchising continued despite the years of recession in the early 90's[1]. Franchisors operating in the market also indicated that there was a need for 460 new franchisees in the year 2002. Moreover, there is room for new franchises particularly in consumer and business-to-business services, while the retail sector has reached a stable state. The fast food, café and restaurant sector is faced with saturated and mature markets. In addition, one out of four franchises indicated being in the "market entry – phase" of their lifecycle. (Tuunanen 2002)

In understanding the context of the franchisee training program, it is essential to recognize the differences between forms of franchising. In Europe, only Business Format franchising is regarded as franchising. In North America, Product Distribution and Trade Name franchising are also regarded as franchising. Consequently, when discussing franchising in this article, only Business Format franchising is considered. For the purpose of this article, the following definition given by the Finnish Franchising Association is employed.

> *"Franchising is a relationship which involves a contractual and long-term collaboration between two independent firms, a franchisor and a franchisee, in which the franchisor grants for payment a right to the franchisee to make use of the franchisor's business format in a pre-described and controlled manner at a certain location or area." (Finnish Franchising Association 2000, p 7)*

1.2 Background of the Program

Franchising started to arouse interest among Finnish small business policy makers after the mid 90's. In 1997 the Ministry of Labour initiated a research project "Franchising Entrepreneurship in Finland in year 2000". The project was partly funded by the European Social Fund (ESF) and its primary goal was to estimate the quantitative and qualitative development of Finnish franchising in the next three years. In their research report, Eräheimo and Laakso (1997) predicted that franchising would create 15,000 new jobs by the end of year 2000. In addition, at that time there was a need for 1,000 new franchisees in existing franchises. Eräheimo and Laakso (1997) also found that an essential threat to the projected growth estimates was a lack of franchising knowledge among new small business owners as well as among the public and private enterprise advisors. The project laid a foundation for the birth of a novel franchisee training program.

---

[1] Relationship between unemployment and new firm formation is a controversial issue that has received academic attention (see e.g. Bannock and Stanworth 1990; Tervo and Niittykangas 1994; Orser and Hogarth-Scott 1998). In broad terms, time-series studies tend to show that entrepreneurship could be induced by high unemployment while cross-sectional studies have indicated the reverse.

The franchisee training program was developed to find people interested in franchising and to give them the essential skills and knowledge a potential franchisee needs. Another goal of the program was to help the trainees to buy a franchise. The organizing parties behind the training are the Finnish Employment and Economic Development Centres (T&E Centres)[2] in the three major cities Helsinki, Turku and Tampere. A private company specialized in franchise consulting took responsibility for the implementation. The training programs are partly supported by the ESF. The rest of the finance is provided by the T&E Centres. Programs are complimentary for the trainees, only a nominal fee of 170 EUR to cover studying materials is charged. Also, some franchisors have sponsored training programs occasionally. The first two training programs were organized in 1999 in the capital city of Helsinki. By the end of the year 2001, ten programs had been completed with close to 200 participants finishing the program. This study will concentrate on the first three years when the programs were organized uniformly. From the beginning of 2002 the format of the training was changed considerably. The programs are still ongoing and the 17th training was launched in October 2003.

The programs are being advertised in national and regional newspapers and those interested can also learn more about them through the T&E Centres and local employment offices. The participants in the programs go through a selection process that includes a written application and interviews. In this sense, the program acts as a preliminary screening tool. Targeting, screening and recruiting potential franchisees may be a slow, costly and tricky process (cf. Macmillan 1996). The matter is pertinent for franchisors that presently face difficulties in finding and recruiting qualified franchisees. Indeed, lack of proper candidates is perceived by the franchisors as the most severe factor restraining the growth of franchising (Macmillan 1996; Tuunanen 2002).

Franchisee recruitment has received continuous academic attention (see footnote 3). It is assumed that prudent recruitment enables future prosperity of the franchise relationship and franchisee performance. Related, the previous research has established two tenets. First, from a franchisor's standpoint, it is vital to select best potential franchisees who possess desirable personality traits (e.g. motivation

---

[2] The Ministry of Trade and Industry, the Ministry of Labour, and the Ministry of Agriculture and Forestry supply their regional services from one outlet – the Employment and Economic Development Centres (T&E Centre). Fifteen centres across the country provide a comprehensive range of advisory and development services for businesses, small business owners, and private individuals. Tasks of the centres cover for instance: support and advise for small and medium-sized enterprises at the various stages of their life cycles, promotion of the technological development in enterprises and assistance in export and internationalisation, implementation of regional labour policies, planning and organising of adult training within the official labour policy framework, promotion and development of farming and fisheries and rural enterprise activities. The centres contribute and have specialised in EU funding. Each centre also develops EU co-operation in its own area.

or need for achievement, risk-taking propensity, internal locus of control, etc.) and personal characteristics (e.g. age, gender, ethnicity, education, work experience, business experience, health, financial resources, etc.) that are most suitable to the business. Second, from a franchisee's standpoint, it is essential to select the "right" franchise offering by seeking adequate information and evaluating, analyzing and comparing various franchise offerings. Any failure in recruitment may lead to franchisee dissatisfaction that again may result in lack of commitment, under-performance, diluted brand value and even to his or hers voluntary turnover[3]. Hence, the franchisee training programs serve both franchisors and future franchisees by minimizing their individual deficiencies.

1.3 Franchisee Training Program

The backgrounds of the trainees were heterogeneous. A part of them had regular full-time or part-time jobs, some were students, some were unemployed looking for a job and some even ran their own business when entering into the program. Despite the dissimilar starting points of the participants, a common feature uniting them was the interest in making a career choice[4]. Approximately 20-25 participants were selected for each program.

The programs were promoted via newspaper ads to reach people interested in franchising. Furthermore, they were introduced to franchisors to get them involved in programs. Franchisors were given a chance to introduce their franchise offerings and to meet the trainees. This way the theory was combined with real life business practice. However, franchisors interest was truly awakened when the first graduates contacted them. They wanted to know where those skilful applicants had learned about franchising. Especially for franchisors recruiting new franchisees, participation in the programs has been an efficient avenue for finding capable candidates. A noteworthy feature of the Finnish market is a shortage of events where franchisors could meet potential franchisees. Most often franchisors seek potential franchisees via advertising in national newspapers. The domestic market is small with 5.2 million inhabitants. Unlike in larger EU countries or the USA, there are no franchise expositions. A further indication of the significance of franchisee training programs is that in a franchise relationship the franchisor is responsible for arranging initial and on-going training for the franchisees. Nevertheless, most franchisors do not have enough resources to arrange in-depth comprehensive training for their new franchisees (Libart ltd. 1998).

---

[3] (Bernstein 1968-1969; Wattel 1968-1969; Tatham et al. 1972; Hunt 1977; Knight 1984; Brannen 1986; Weinraugh 1986; Schell and McGillis 1990; Withane 1991; Justis et al. 1993; Schell and McGillis 1992; English and Hoy 1995; Hing 1995; Kaufman and Stanworth 1995; Stanworth 1995; Mcmillan 1996; Morrison 1996; 1997; Stanworth et al. 1996; Price 1997; Jambulingam and Nevin 1999; Tuunanen 2001; Clarkin and Swavely 2003)

[4] Price (1997, pp 249-290) has applied career approach to franchisee buying decisions.

For the trainees the program is approximately five months period of reflection and decision-making, during which many of them decide whether they want to be franchisees. A typical training program consists of 20-25 day classroom instruction periods, distant learning, and self-studying exercises, and individual consultation.

Top franchising experts (e.g. consultants, attorneys) and professionals in various business areas (e.g. accounting, human resources, and marketing) have served as lecturers for the training programs. Each program teaches a standard curriculum. A detailed example of the curriculum is presented in Table 1. The lecturers aim to provide the participants with a realistic view of the time, financial and skills demands of franchise ownership. During the course of the lectures, the advantages and disadvantages of franchising are discussed[5]. According to Tuunanen and Hyrsky (2001), the advantages that franchisees encounter in operating their businesses are actually the same ones that motivate people to buy a franchise. These business boons and motivational factors include "recognized trade name", "proven business concept", "ease of entry", "ongoing franchisor support", "training" and "reduced risk of failure". By covering the various facts and requirements involved in franchise ownership, the programs' purpose is to inform and prepare the trainees for the difficulties and risks that many new franchisees are likely to confront[6]. Examples of such risks are lack of finance or under-capitalization, financial management, marketing, staffing, legislation and regulations, etc.

The training starts with classroom lectures and a self-studying period which in total last between 9-14 weeks. This phase includes 3-5 one-week pauses for distant learning and assignments. Classroom instruction is normally given 2-4 days per week. Assignments relate to various topics (e.g. book keeping, value added tax, payroll, general taxation) requiring completion of exercises. Every trainee is expected to choose one franchise according to his or her own preferences and to compose a detailed case analysis of it. The goal of the analysis is to learn to evaluate various franchise offerings and to gather the necessary information for deciding whether to buy the franchise or not.

Based on the participant's needs and wishes, she or he may receive personal consultation lasting up to two days. Trainees can meet with a franchising consultant, a franchise attorney and a career tutor. Generally, the first consultation meeting takes place after the classroom and self-studying phase. It involves a feedback interaction and discussion on the trainee's career path and options. At this point the trainee and the consultant together design the following action. Those who clearly indicate interest in buying a franchise receive further advice and guidance as to the negotiations with the franchisor, the franchise agreement,

[5] For franchisee advantages see e.g. Hunt 1977; Knight 1986; Peterson and Dant 1990; Dant 1995; Stanworth et al. 1995; Stanworth and Kaufmann 1996.

[6] see e.g. Hunt 1977; Carman and Klein 1986; Justis et al. 1993; Tuunanen and Hyrsky 2001.

start-up investments, financing, spreadsheet and other relevant issues related to the franchise offering and business plan.

Table 1. An Example of the Curriculum

Day	Topic
1	Operating as a franchise owner
2	Franchising versus independent small business ownership
3	Self-evaluation and decision to initiate a venture
4	How to analyze and valuate various franchises?
5	Case studies: Franchisors introduce their business offerings
6	Principles of franchisor-franchisee relationship and co-operation
7-8	How to run a franchise outlet?
9	Marketing in a franchise system and local store marketing
10	Customer relationship management
11	Laws and regulations related to franchising
12	Accounting in a franchised business
13	Principles of financial planning
14	Principles of corporate and value added taxation
15	Procurement and inventory management in a franchise system and local store
16	Business communication and franchise owner's interaction skills
17-18	Human resource management and franchisee as an employer
19	Time management and coping with stress
20	Wrap-up of the class-room instruction & orientation to self-studying and personal consultation

Because of their various backgrounds, the learning needs of the trainees are different. Some need a lot of personal consultation in planning their future careers, whereas some only want small amount of help to be better prepared for the negotiations with the franchisor they have chosen. Every participant's individual needs are taken into account via tutoring that is available throughout the program.

1.4 Effectiveness of Entrepreneurship Education

The article aims to contribute to the discussion on the effectiveness of entrepreneurship education and training[7]. The know-how invested in the franchise

[7] For the framework of the study, theories dealing with the evaluation of labour market training and employment programs (e.g. Kirkpatrick 1983; LaLonde and Maynard 1987; Mikkonen and Räisänen 1995), educational effectiveness (e.g. Vaherva 1983; Mikkonen 1997) and entrepreneurship education (e.g. Gibb 1993; Curran and Stanworth 1989) were reviewed.

package is transferable, teachable and learnable. This is a unique and core feature in characterizing franchising as a method of starting a business (see e.g. Stanworth et al. 1996). The article reports the results of a study assessing the effect of the franchisee training program on participants' career choices and their opinions about franchise ownership. Scholars of different disciplines, say pedagogy, economics and psychology, have shown that the effectiveness of education is a multifaceted and controversial phenomenon. For instance, as Orser and Hogarth-Scott (1998, pp. 61-67) have found, the assessment of education and the perceived value of its outcomes may be dependent upon the stakeholders (i.e. trainers, delivery agents, public policy-makers, business owners and employment equity groups) vested interest in the education. To highlight the nuances of the concept and the difficulty of measuring it, the following descriptions are given.

> *"...it is possible to define the effects of education as versatile and multidimensional phenomena on the dimensions of time. We can examine the primary or immediate, secondary and even tertiary effects of education, which by the end of education can be seen in the functioning of those educated and the surrounding society and which last as long as the following generation. Analysis-models derived from different fields of science emphasize further that impact-analysis cannot be limited merely to outputs, but we have to simultaneously take into consideration the costs and other inputs of education, educational process and immediate results, which all have to be brought into relation with the final goal oriented outcomes." (Vaherva 1983, p. IV)*

A slightly different point of view is provided by Garavan and O'Cinneide (1994, p. 5) who comment on the assessment of entrepreneurship education and training programs as follows.

> *"If entrepreneurship education and training is to be effective, the contention is that it must be so not only through factual knowledge and the limited skills acquirable in the classroom, but also through the stimulation of new ventures, the success of those ventures and the increasing capacity of the entrepreneur to pursue even greater success."*

When applying the view of Garavan and O'Cinneide for the present study, it is possible to come up with two questions: Can the program help "to make new franchisees"? And are the new franchisees successful in their ventures?[8] In this context, it has to be noted that due to the limitations of a cross-sectional analysis, the findings on the effectiveness of the training are preliminary. Furthermore, as a consequence of these limitations, it is difficult to measure success at the current phase of the study. In the forthcoming follow-up study, success could be measured for instance, through the following criteria: Does the franchisee continue his or her business after the first critical years of operation? Is the franchisee's business

---

[8] Research findings by Evans and Leighton (1990) had shown that previously unemployed people who started their own business were not as successful as those who were employed just before initiating their ventures. This is interesting since a considerable number of the participants of the franchisee training program were unemployed prior to entering the program.

profitable and growing? In the franchisor's opinion, is the franchisee's overall performance average, above or below the average in the particular franchise system? And finally, is the franchisee satisfied with his or her business?

2 Research Design

The research data were gathered in two phases and therefore, there are two samples, I and II[9]. The present study explores potential differences of the samples and the analysis pertains to the achieved results of the training programs. Consequently, the effectiveness of the training can be gauged and verified. The effectiveness of the program was measured through changes in the trainees' employment status and trainees' intention to purchase a franchise. Moreover, participants' overall satisfaction with the program was measured, since satisfaction is frequently used as a first level measure of the effectiveness of education indicating participants' reactions to the training[10].

The background and contact information of the participants were gathered in collaboration with the organizing parties. All graduated participants of the first ten training programs were chosen as respondents. In order to pass the program it is required for a trainee to take part in lectures and turn in self-study exercises. Few trainees had decided to discontinue the training. The first two surveyed programs were carried out in Helsinki in 1999 and the following three in 2000 in Turku, Tampere and Helsinki respectively. These five programs comprised the first sample of the study. The second sample included the five programs arranged in 2001. Three of them took place in Helsinki and one each in Turku and Tampere. The ten programs were organized uniformly and the same curriculum was applied.

In the initial data gathering phase all 100 graduated participants of the training programs 1-5 were surveyed. Ninety usable responses were received and hence, the response rate was 90%. In the latter phase, all graduated participants (N=114) of the programs 6-10 were sampled. Eighty-six acceptable responses and a response rate of 75% were obtained. At both times, quantitative and qualitative data were gathered through mailed questionnaires and phone interviews.

In both phases, all graduated participants of the chosen five programs were sampled simultaneously even though the training programs were arranged at different times and in different cities. Consequently, depending on the time of training, informants were surveyed six to twenty four months after they had completed the training. This issue could be regarded as a methodological limitation of the study, since the results i.e. effectiveness of the training, may

---

[9] The study concerning the first five training program is published in Torikka and Tuunanen 2003. The present study is a replication of the initial study. The reproduction of the study enables more reliable analysis on the outcomes of the training.

[10] See e.g. Kirkpatrick 1983; Vaherva 1983; Robinson and Robinson 1989; Mikkonen 1997.

depend upon the length of the time passed from the completion of the program. To find out whether the samples were similar, an investigation on the possible differences in the backgrounds of the trainees was done. Potential differences between the samples could limit the comparability of the results i.e. effectiveness of the training. The analyses showed no significant differences between the two samples. The organizing parties had employed similar lines of recruitment for all ten programs.

As Table 2 shows, the background variables of the two groups were fairly identical. Nearly half of the respondents were female, so both genders were almost equally represented. The mean age of the respondents in Sample I was 42 and 41 years of age in Sample II. In addition, there were less married people and some more people who had divorced in Sample II than in Sample I, but the differences were non-significant. Moreover, the education levels of the respondents were strikingly similar in both samples.

Table 2. Description of the Samples

Background variable		**Sample I (n=90) %**	**Sample II (n=86) %**	**Combined Sample I+II (n=176) %**
Gender	Female	51	53	52
	Male	49	47	48
Age	21-30 years	11	14	13
	31-40 years	28	34	31
	41-50 years	39	38	39
	51-60 years	22	12	16
	61-70 years	0	2	1
Marital Status	Married	52	45	48
	Long term relationship	24	28	26
	Single	16	14	15
	Divorced or widowed	8	13	11
Highest Level of Education Completed	Elementary school	4	5	5
	High school	4	6	5
	Vocational education * (vocational school or polytechnic)	74	73	73
	University	18	16	17

* In Finland there are vocational education institutions or polytechnics. The education runs between 2-4 years depending on the profession, specialization and the particular institution.

Table 3 further shows that the entry statuses of the trainees did not vary much between the samples. The main dissimilarity can be found in the number of unemployed persons, which was lower in Sample II. However, the difference was rather small, a mere 6 percent points.

Table 3. Trainees' Employment Status

Job Status upon Entry into the Training	I %	II %	I + II %	Job Status upon Completion of the Survey	I %	II %	I + II %
Unemployed	41	35	38	Unemployed	11	6	9
Salaried Employee	41	43	42	Salaried Employee	49	44	46
Small Business Owner	11	12	11	Small Business Owner	16	24	20
Franchisee	0	0	0	Franchisee	13	15	14
Student	5	6	6	Student	7	1	4
Other*	2	4	3	Other*	4	10	7

* Status not known.

3 Results

3.1 Career Decision Making

By examining changes in the trainees' employment status, it is possible to measure some effects of the program. First, trainees were asked about the impact of the program on their career choices made after passing the program. Nearly 60% of the Sample I respondents stated that the program had an effect on their decisions while the corresponding figure among Sample II respondents was 74%. Every fifth (21%) of the Sample I respondents and every fourth (26%) of the Sample II respondents felt the program had a strong or even very strong effect on his or her career decision. In addition, more than one third (37%) of the Sample I and almost half (48%) of the Sample II participants viewed the training having moderate or slight effect on their career decision-making. The effect was measured by a scale ranging from one to five - "the training had no effect on my career decision" to "the training had a very strong effect on my career decision". The T-test showed a significant difference (.001) between the samples. The training had a stronger effect on graduates' career decisions in the Sample II.

Since the training program was aimed at also the unemployed, one of the major goals was to assist them to employ themselves or find a job. The number of unemployed decreased by equal proportions in samples I and II. More importantly, entrepreneurial activity increased dramatically among the participants. Four new independent start-up businesses occurred in Sample I and eleven in Sample II. The amount of established new franchise businesses was also a bit higher in Sample II.

A more detailed analysis of the changes in trainees' professional statuses is illustrated in Figure 1. Identical information is given in Table 4.

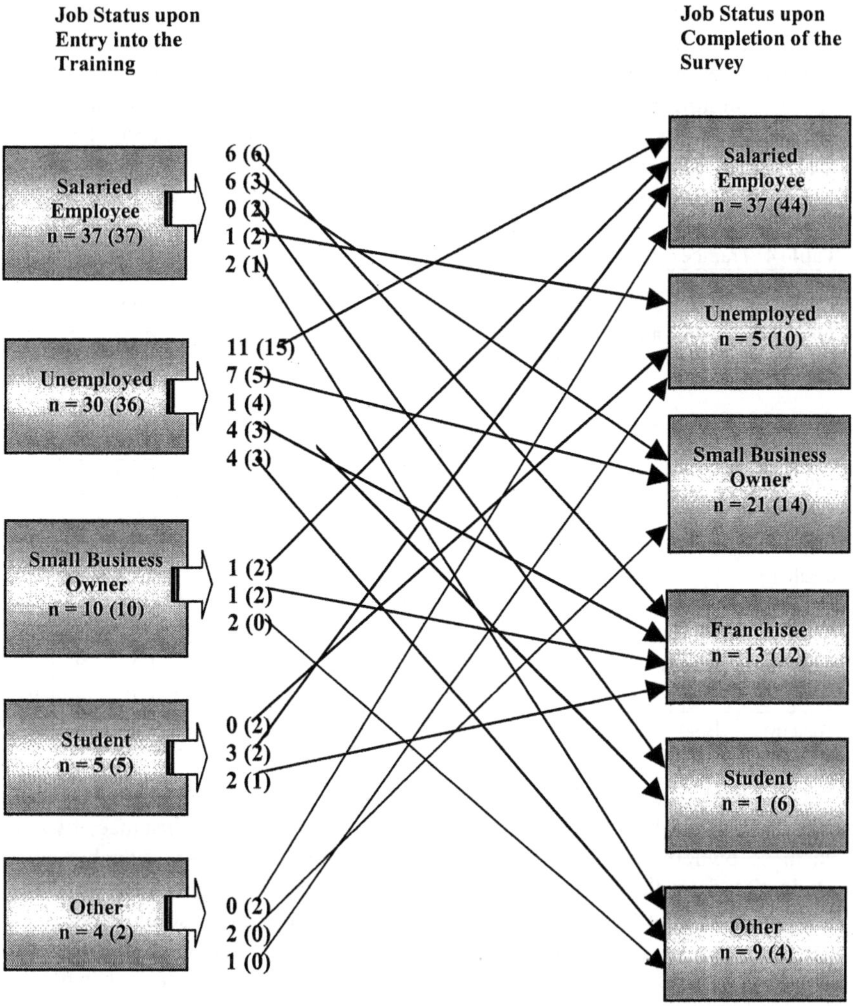

*Sample I in

Fig. 1. Trainees' Career Shifts

The arrows in the Figure 1 present career paths when a career shift took place. In order to separate the two samples, the numbers describing Sample I are in brackets. Sixteen different career paths emerged in both samples and in total fifty-five shifts in Sample I and fifty-four shifts in Sample II occurred. A couple of the paths stood out since so many people followed them, e.g. fifteen unemployed in Sample I and eleven in Sample II found a salaried job in either public or private sector. Meanwhile, six persons, who had either a full or part-time job at the time of entering the training, became franchisees afterwards. Interestingly, the same career-decision was made by equal amount of persons in both samples. Also, six trainees in Sample II who previously were salaried employees decided to establish stand alone businesses. Likewise, in Sample I, five previously unemployed decided to employ themselves and started an independent business, whereas four opted to continue their studies in vocational schools, polytechnics, or university after the training program. In comparison, seven persons in Sample II who were looking for jobs prior to the training, set up their own businesses while four became franchisees after the program.

Table 4. Trainees' Career Shifts

Job Status upon Entry into the Training			Job Status upon Completion of the Survey											
			Salaried Employee		Unemployed		Small Business Owner		Franchisee		Student		Other	
	I	II	I	II	I	II	I	II	I	II	I	II	I	II
Salaried Employee	37	37	23	22	2	1	3	6	6	6	2	0	1	2
Unemployed	36	30	15	11	6	3	5	7	3	4	4	1	3	4
Small Business Owner	10	10	2	1	0	0	6	6	2	1	0	0	0	2
Student	5	5	2	3	2	0	0	0	1	2	0	0	0	0
Other	2	4	2	0	0	1	0	2	0	0	0	0	0	1
Total (n)	90	86	44	37	10	5	14	21	12	13	6	1	4	9

Conversely, in several occasions career choices were rather individual and the paths varied slightly as only few people followed them. For instance, two small business owners in Sample I and one in Sample II became franchisees after graduation from the training. Similarly, three students, one in Sample I and two in Sample II became franchisees. The illustration shows that those 25 persons, 12 in Sample I and 13 in Sample II who bought a franchise after finishing the program had very dissimilar entry statuses. What should be noted though, is that twelve of those twenty-five had a job at the time of entering the training. It might have been easier for people who had jobs to gather the funds to start a franchised business. Additionally, some franchisors might prefer recruiting employed people to franchisees and avoid recruiting unemployed. Nonetheless, as there were 13 people with other kind of entry statuses who also became franchisees, it appears that the training can be effective for people having heterogeneous backgrounds.

No career shifts happened in 35 cases (39%) in Sample I and 32 cases (37%) in Sample II. Once more, the results between the samples seemed to be similar. In 23 of these cases in Sample I and in 22 in Sample II the trainee was a salaried employee. Twelve small business owners, six in Sample I and six in Sample II continued operating their businesses also after the program. Interestingly, in two occasions in Sample I and one in Sample II, a small business ownership was discontinued during the training and the trainee found a salaried job. One sixth (16%) of the unemployed people belonging to Sample I and every tenth (10%) belonging to Sample II remained unemployed also after the training.

3.2 Intention to Buy a Franchise

The second measure employed in analyzing the effectiveness of the training programs was trainees' intention to purchase a franchise. In Sample I, one fifth (20%) of the participants indicated that they were seriously interested in buying a franchise in the future. In similar vein, a group of equal size (21%) expressed being not interested in it. Interestingly, 59% of the trainees were still unsure of their future decision. In Sample II, there were more of those, who were uninterested in buying a franchise (15%) than those who were interested (12%). But, the figures were evidently much lower than in Sample I. On the other hand, the number of trainees who could not indicate their future decision was even greater than in Sample I, namely, two thirds (69%).

3.3 Satisfaction

Participants' satisfaction was measured via two scales. First one, overall satisfaction, was quantified by asking how did the training meet participants' initial expectations (see Table 5). A five-step Likert –type scale ranging from "Surpassed my expectations considerably" to "Fell short of my expectations considerably" was employed. Eighty-two percent of the Sample I respondents rated the program at "3" or above (met or surpassed expectations.) More than one third (36%) felt the program exceeded their expectations slightly or considerably. Only every sixth (18%) trainee rated the training as falling short of his or her expectations. The mean score of the overall satisfaction in Sample I was 3.26. To compare, in Sample II, nine out of ten (92%) respondents told the program had met or surpassed their expectations. Additionally, 46% felt that the training exceeded their expectations slightly or considerably. Less than every tenth (8%) trainee perceived that the training fell short of his or her expectations. The mean score of the overall satisfaction in Sample II was 3.52 and consequently, there was a significant difference (Sig. .056) between the samples in favor of the second sample.

Table 5. Trainees' Overall Satisfaction with the Program

How did the training meet your initial expectations?				
Scale	Alternatives	I %	II %	I + II %
5	Surpassed my expectations considerably	11	14	13
4	Surpassed my expectations slightly	25	32	28
3	Met with my expectations	47	46	46
2	Fell short of my expectations slightly	14	8	11
1	Fell short of my expectations considerably	3	0	2

The second scale pertaining to trainees' satisfaction was intention to recommend the program to others. The scale was dichotomous having the options: "Yes, I would recommend the program" or "No, I would not recommend the program". Nine out of ten (90%) of Sample I respondents opted for recommending the training for potential participants. Participants' overall satisfaction and their post-course intention had a strong and significant correlation (Contingency Coefficient .605; Sig. .000) with each other. Ninety percent of those who were satisfied with the program were likely to recommend it. Similarly, the respondents of Sample II appreciated the program and almost all of them (98%) were ready to recommend the training for potential participants. In contrast to Sample I, in Sample II the overall satisfaction of the participants and their post-course intention had a low and non-significant correlation (Contingency Coefficient .242; Sig. .152) with each other. Surprisingly, there were six graduates who expressed that the training fell short of their expectations but still they were ready to recommend it. Ninety-nine percent of those were contented with the program were likely to recommend it.

4 Discussion and Implications

Nearly one sixth of the respondents (n=12) purchased a franchise and eight informants started their own, independent businesses of the Sample I respondents. Moreover, six people continued running their existing businesses. Almost an equal amount (n=13) of respondents became franchisees and fifteen informants established their own, independent company in the Sample II. As in Sample I, six persons continued running their existing businesses. To summarize, the figures indicate that more than one fourth (29%) of the respondents of Sample I and over one third (39%) of the respondents of Sample II were involved in entrepreneurial activities at the time of the study. Twenty-three percent of the Sample I and 17 percent of Sample II respondents found a salaried job after passing the program. Moreover, a clear majority, nearly 60% of the respondents of Sample I and 74% of the respondents of Sample II confirmed the program had had an effect on their employment and career choices.

The results showed that the programs 6-10 were even more successful than earlier programs in fostering entrepreneurial activity among the participants. However, Sample II included less of those who intended starting a franchised business in the future compared to Sample I. Also, there were even more of those who were unsure about their upcoming career decision in Sample II. Within both samples, unemployment rate decreased by the same proportion. Nonetheless, results of the training programs were parallel and no remarkable differences were recorded between the samples.

Even though a majority of all the respondents (82% of the Sample I and 92% of the Sample II respondents) were pleased with the program, satisfaction is not necessarily a straightforward indicator of the effectiveness of the training. However, it is often used as a first level measure of the effectiveness of education. By the same token, it is recommended to assess what the participants have learned. Secondly, have any changes in their behavior occurred and further, have they been able to apply the learned skills in practice. The bottom-line effects of the training are results of the first three levels – satisfaction (reactions), learning and behavior. Measuring the bottom-line effects is demanding, time consuming and requires following the whole process and determining the expected or desired outcomes already beforehand. (Vaherva 1983; Mikkonen 1997) On the other hand, the assessment of education and the perceived value of its outcomes might differ depending upon the stakeholder (Orser and Hogarth-Scott 1998). In this cross-sectional study, the effectiveness of the program was gauged through direct changes in the participants' employment status.

The average franchise outlet in Finland employs five full-time and six part-time employees. Further, the annual sales average of a franchised outlet is close to 450,000 EUR (Tuunanen 1999). When taking these and indirect impacts of the created new businesses into account the outcomes of the training program have been positive and significant - particularly in comparison to inputs into the program. In this light, the training programs ought to be considered as a social and economic investment.

Occasionally, a trainee might come to the conclusion that franchising is not suitable for him or her. This should also be regarded as a positive outcome, since it will spare both the trainee and the potential franchisors from future frustration and disappointments. Another issue related to program outcomes is intrapreneurship or corporate entrepreneurship (Pinchot 1985; Kuratko and Hodgetts 1998). The program should not solely aim at training would-be franchisees or self-employed persons. The training should also be seen as an avenue available for stimulating intrapreneurial attitudes and behaviors among the trainees.

Moreover, the training can be seen as a neutral small business policy intervention that does not bias competition and markets. It applies to both growing and mature franchises due to the franchisee turnover and withdrawals that create new entrepreneurial career opportunities. Furthermore, the training is available to those interested in franchising. Although there is a selection process for the applicants, majority of them are approved. However, the program should be extended outside the three large cities. Programs should be started also elsewhere in Finland to increase the volume of graduates and to balance the regional development. Especially in areas where there is no large employer/s and the density of entrepreneurial activity is high there might be fruitful soil for extensions of the program (Stanworth et al. 1989). Nevertheless, the franchisee training programs serve to satisfy the strong current demand for new skilful franchisees.

The program serves both the franchisors and franchisees. It is of special interest to franchisors who can focus on business specific training while the program provides invaluable general business acumen. On the other hand, the nature of the program highlights the responsibility of the trainees or prospective franchisees for conducting information searches and analyzing franchise offerings. In Finland, there are no franchise specific laws or regulations such as in the USA. There is the ethical code[11] that concerns the members of the Finnish Franchising Association (FFA) as part of the European Franchise Federation. As regards the training programs, the role of the FFA is well worth considering. Thus far, the FFA has not been involved in executing the programs, but its participation might enhance the status of the training. A noteworthy fact is that many of the franchisors who have been involved in the programs are not members of the FFA. Therefore, the effect of the FFA's participation on the program status is not self-evident. In future, one possibility could be that the training programs would be granted a right to give out certified degrees of continuing education.

When discussing the effectiveness of the franchisee training program, an important question remains to be answered: What is the actual impact of the program on new business formation? Would those graduates, who became franchisees or established a stand alone business, have done that without the training?[12] Basically, individuals who met the prerequisites of the program might from the outset have been more interested and suitable for small business ownership. This is an issue that has been raised in connection with many employment and entrepreneurship education programs. Studying those trainees who became entrepreneurs might shed some light on this subject.

The possible limitation of the current study is its cross-sectional nature. Moreover, in both phases all graduated participants of the chosen five programs were sampled simultaneously even though the training programs were arranged at different times. Nevertheless, no statistically significant differences between the samples were found. Generally, the achieved outcomes of the both samples were surprisingly alike. What should be taken into account is that potential differences between the results of the training programs may still stem from several reasons that were not gauged in this survey. Different backgrounds of the trainees, location of the training program (the city) and nuances between the trainee groups might be intervening factors. Therefore, the comparability between the training programs is

---

[11] The same ethical code binds the members of *the European Franchise Federation*. See www.franchising.fi/esittely/saannot.htm for the Code of Ethics of *the Finnish Franchise Association* and www.eff-franchise.com/Code%20of%ethics%20text.htm for the European Code of Ethics for Franchising.

[12] This is in line with Storey (2000). He determines the effect of a policy as the difference between what actually happened and what would have happened in the absence of policy.

inevitably questionable. With regards to assessing the impact of a public policy, Storey (2000) brings up the difference between monitoring and evaluating. In the current study the effectiveness of the training was gauged by investigating participants' career choices and their opinions about franchise ownership. When applying Storey's notion, the study could be regarded as monitoring and not evaluation, since no control group existed. Notably, no international academic research in the field of franchisee training was found. Further absorption to evaluation and educational effectiveness studies could provide more advanced indicators and measures for future research.

The effectiveness of the franchisee training program is well worth studying already because of the unique nature of the program. No international academic research on a similar type of program was found. The present study will continue as a longitudinal investigation with the existing respondents. The aim is to deepen the information by utilizing qualitative methods and more sophisticated questionnaires. When assessing educational effectiveness, follow-up and longitudinal studies are essential, since career choices are rather complex and involve long-term decision making processes. In addition, as an implication of their extensive franchising literature analysis Elango and Fried (1997) mentioned the need for qualitative and prescriptive franchising research. What further supports conducting a follow-up study is that the opening of many franchised outlets might be delayed, say for a year or two, if a proper site location cannot be found. Another intention is to study the success of those trainees who purchased a franchise. It would also be worth examining how the franchisors' view and appreciate those applicants who have passed the training program. Actually, investigation on franchisors' views on performance of those franchisees who graduated from the franchisee training program versus franchisees who did not take the program, would provide a control group for the study (cf. Storey 2000). Similarly, financial performance of the companies of those graduates who established stand alone businesses could be compared to statistical data on equal size companies in general.

References

1. Bernstein LM (1968-1969) Does Franchising Create a Secure Outlet for the Small Aspiring Entrepreneur? Journal of Retailing 44(4):21-38
2. Bannock G, Stanworth J (1990) The Making of Entrepreneurs. Small Business Research Trust, London
3. Brannen KC (1986) The Coexistence of Franchising and Entrepreneurship: A Look at Franchisee Characteristic. Proceedings of the 1st Society of Franchising Conference, Omaha, Nebraska
4. Carman JM, Klein TA (1986) Power, Property, And Performance in Franchising: A Review And Integration of Theory. Research in Marketing 8:71-130
5. Clarkin JE, Swavely SM (2003) How Franchisors Choose Franchisees: A Comparison of Prospective Franchisee Evaluation Criteria. Proceedings of the 17th Annual International Society of Franchising Conference. San Antonio, Texas

6. Commission of the European Communities (2003) Green Paper: Entrepreneurship in Europe. Retrieved September 14, 2003, from http://europa.eu.int/comm/enterprise/entrepreneurship/green_paper/green_paper_final_en.pdf
7. Curran J, Stanworth J (1989) Education and Training for Enterprise. Some Problems of Classification, Evaluation, Policy and Research. International Small Business Journal 7(2):11-22
8. Dant RP (1995) Motivation for Franchising: Rhetoric Versus Reality. International Small Business Journal 14(1):10-32
9. Drucker PF (1985) Innovation and Entrepreneurship. Harper & Row, New York
10. Elango B, Fried VH (1997) Franchising Research: A Literature Review and Synthesis. Journal of Small Business Management:68-81
11. English W, Hoy F (1995) Are Franchisees Actually Entrepreneurs? Proceedings of the 8th Society of Franchising Conference, Las Crobas, San Juan, Puerto Rico
12. Eräheimo T, Laakso H (1997) Franchising Entrepreneurship in Finland in Year 2000 (in Finnish). Edita Oy, Helsinki
13. European Franchise Federation (1972) The European Code of Ethics for Franchising www.eff-franchise.com/Code%20of%20ethics%20text.htm (as of 5th April, 2002)
14. Evans DS, Leighton LS (1990) Small Business Formation by Unemployed and Employed Workers. Small Business Economics 12(4):319-330
15. Finnish Franchising Association (2000) Franchising in Finland 2001(in Finnish). In: Tuunanen M, Granström R, Karojärvi I (eds) Franchising in Finland 2001 (in Finnish). Lohja
16. Finnish Franchising Association (1996) The Code of Ethics of the Finnish Franchising Association (in Finnish). www.franchising.fi/esittely/saannot.htm (as of 5th April, 2002)
17. Garavan TN, O'Cinneide B (1994) Entrepreneurship Education and Training Programmes: A Review and Evaluation – Part 1. Journal of European Industrial Training 18(8):3-12
18. Gibb A (1993) The Enterprise Culture and Education. Understanding Enterprise Education and its Links with Small Business, Entrepreneurship and Wider Educational Goals. International Small Business Journal 11(3):11-24
19. Hing N (1995) Franchisee Satisfaction: Contributors and Consequences. Journal of Small Business Management 33(2):12-25
20. Hunt SD (1977) Franchising: Promises, Problems, Prospects. Journal of Retailing 53(3): 71-84
21. Jambulingam T, Nevin JR (1999) Influence of Franchisee Selection Criteria on Outcomes Desired by the Franchisor. Journal of Business Venturing 14(4):363-395
22. Justis RT, Olsen JE, Chan P (1993) Using Marketing Research to Enhance Franchisee/ Franchisor Relationships. Journal of Small Business Management 31(2):121-127
23. Kaufmann PJ, Stanworth J (1995) The Decision to Purchase a Franchise: A Study of Prospective Franchisees. Journal of Small Business Management 33(4):22-33
24. Knight RM (1984) The Independence of the Franchisee Entrepreneur. Journal of Small Business Management 22(2):53-61
25. Knight RM (1986) Franchising From the Franchisor and Franchisee Points of View. Journal of Small Business Management 24(3):8-21
26. Kirkpatric DL (1983) A Practical Guide for Supervisory Training and Development, 2nd edn. Management Institute, University of Wisconsin-Extension, USA
27. Kuratko DF, Hodgetts RM (1998) Entrepreneurship. A Contemporary Approach, 4th edn. The Dryden Press, Fort Worth, pp 53-91

28.LaLonde R, Maynard R (1987) How Precise are Evaluations of Employment and Training Programs: Evidence from a Field Experiment. Journal of Applied Social Research 11(4):428-451
29.Libart ltd (1998) An overview on franchisee instruction in franchise systems (in Finnish). Libart ltd, Helsinki
30.Macmillan A (1996) Aspects of Franchisee Recruitment. Special Studies Series No. 8. International Franchise Research Centre, London
31.Mikkonen I (1997) Manpower Training as Part of Labor Market Education. Effectiveness of Education at Individual Level (in Finnish). Labor Policy Studies n:o 174., Ministry of Labour, Helsinki
32.Mikkonen I, Räisänen H (eds) (1995) Evaluating Labor Market Training – Outcome and Effectiveness. Labor Policy Studies number 122., Ministry of Labour, Helsinki
33.Morrison KA (1996) An Empirical Test of a Model of Franchisee Job Satisfaction. Journal of Small Business Management 34(3):27-41
34.Morrison KA (1997) How Franchise Job Satisfaction and Personality Affects Their Performance, Organizational Commitment, Franchisor Relations, and Intention to Remain. Journal of Small Business Management 35(3):39-67
35.Orser B, Hogarth-Scott S (1998) Case Analysis of Canadian Self-employment Assistance Programming. Enterpreneurship and Regional Development 10(1):51-69
36.Peterson A, Dant RP (1990) Perceived Advantages of the Franchise Option from the Franchisee Perspective: Empirical Insights from a Service Franchise. Journal of Small Business Management 28(3):46-61
37.Pinchot G (1985) Intrapreneuring. Why You Don't Have to Leave the Corporation to Become an Entrepreneur. Harper & Row, New York
38.Price S (1997) The Franchise Paradox: New Directions, Different Strategies. Cassell, London
39.Robinson D, Robinson J (1989) Training for Impact; How to Link Training to Business Needs and Measure the Results? Jossey-Bass Publishers, San Francisco
40.Schell B, McGillis S (1990) Personality and Attitudinal Predictors of Commitment for Franchisees. Journal of Small Business & Entrepreneurship 7:40-63
41.Schell B, McGillis S (1992) Type A Traits, Innovativeness, Cognitive Complexity and Attitudinal Predictors Affecting Franchisees Job-Involvement Levels. Journal of Small Business & Entrepreneurship 9(3):47-59
42.Stanworth J (1995) Developing a Diagnostic Questionnaire as an Aid to Franchisee Selection. International Franchise Research Centre Special Studies Series No. 6, June 1995. University of Westminster Press, London
43.Stanworth J, Kaufmann PJ (1996) Similarities and Differences in U.K. and U.S. Franchise Research Data: Towards a Dynamic Model of Franchisee Motivation. International Small Business Journal 14(3):57-70
44.Stanworth J, Kaufmann PJ, Purdy D (1995) The Blenheim/University of Westminster Franchise Survey: A Comparison of U.K. and USA Data. International Franchise Research Centre, Special Studies, N:o 5, March. University of Westminster Press, London
45.Stanworth J, Price S, Purdy D, Zafiris N, Gandolfo A (1996) Business Format Franchising: Innovation and Creativity or Replication and Conformity? Franchising Research: An International Journal 1(2):29-39
46.Stanworth J, Stanworth C, Granger B, Blyth S (1989) Who Becomes an Entrepreneur? International Small Business Journal 8(1):11-22
47.Storey D (2000) Six Steps to Heaven: Evaluating the Impact of public Policies to Support Small Business In Developed Economies. In: Sexton DL, Landström H (eds)

The Blackwell Handbook of Entrepreneurship. Blackwell Business and Nova Southeastern University, pp 176-193
48.Tatham R, Bush R, Douglas R (1972) An Analysis of Decision Criteria in Franchisor/ Franchisee Selection Process. Journal of Retailing 48(2)
49.Tervo H, Niittykangas H (1994) The Impact of Unemployment on New Firm Formation in Finland. International Small Business Journal 13(1)
50.Torikka J, Tuunanen M (2003) Finnish Franchisee Training Program – An Exploratory Study. In: Alon I, Welsh DHB (eds) International Franchising in Industrialized Markets: Northern and Western Europe. CCH Inc, Chicago
51.Tuunanen M (1999) Research results on Finnish franchisees (in Finnish). In: Granström R, Karojärvi I, Tuunanen M (eds) Franchising in Finland 2000 (in Finnish). Lohja, pp 89-96
52.Tuunanen M (2001a) Franchising Statistics 2001 (in Finnish). In: Granström R, Tuunanen M (eds) Franchising in Finland 2002 (in Finnish). Lohja, pp 18-21
53.Tuunanen M (2001b) An Ounce of Prevention Is a Worth Pound of Cure: Findings from National Franchisee (Dis-)Satisfaction Study in Finland. Proceedings of the 15th International Society of Franchising Conference, Las Vegas
54.Tuunanen M (2002) Franchising Statistics 2002. In: Granström R, Tuunanen M (eds) Franchising in Finland 2003 (in Finnish). Lohja, pp 32-37
55.Tuunanen M, Hyrsky K (2001) Entrepreneurial Paradoxes in Business Format Franchising: An Empirical Survey of Finnish Franchisees. International Small Business Journal 19(4):47-62
56.Vaherva T (1983) Educational Effectiveness, An Attempt at a Conceptual Analysis and a Frame of Reference (in Finnish). Research Reports A 1/1983, Department of Education, University of Jyväskylä
57.Wattel H (1968-1969) Are Franchisors Realistic and Successful in Their Selection of Franchisees? Journal of Retailing 44(4):54-68
58.Weinrauch JD (1986) Franchising an Established Business. Journal of Small Business Management 24(3):1-7
59.Williams DL (1999) Why Do Entrepreneurs Become Franchisees? An Empirical Analysis of Organizational Choice. Journal of Business Venturing 14(1):103-124
60.Withane S (1991) Franchising and Franchisee Behavior: An Examination of Opinions, Personal Characteristics, and Motives of Canadian Franchisee Entrepreneurs. Journal of Small Business Management 29(1):22-30

Part G:

Regulation of Franchise Agreements

Antitrust Implications of Franchise Agreements

Kai Hüschelrath

WHU Graduate School of Management, Institute for Industrial Organization
Burgplatz 2, 56179 Vallendar, Germany
hueschel@whu.edu

Abstract. It seems plausible that franchise agreements can be an efficient way to solve a firm's distribution problem with certain products, services or concepts in certain environments. Notwithstanding the fact that the motivation to create franchise agreements are mainly efficiency driven and simultaneously welfare enhancing, it is clear that such strategies normally influence competition in upstream, downstream and/or 'adjacent' markets. Therefore, as far as some degree of market power is involved, there is the potential of an abusive use of franchise agreements to further increase a dominant firm's markups. Such behavior normally harms competition and social welfare. Against this background, it seems important to discuss the essential antitrust implications of franchise agreements. First, a brief overview of the evolution of antitrust regulations concerning franchise agreements in the United States of America and the European Union is given. Afterwards it is argued first, why and how firms choose certain franchise agreements including certain restrictions (the so-called 'vertical restraints') to distribute their products. Second, it is shown through examples, why and under which circumstances such agreements might get into difficulties with antitrust regulations. Third, some major challenges for antitrust policy are assessed; these simultaneously highlight avenues for further research.

1 Introduction

„I've been coming to these meetings for six years and have been paying close attention to antitrust since 1955 ... and I want to tell you that in the 20 years that I've been following antitrust, or have been trying to, I don't think they've changed a single word in the Sherman Act or the Clayton Act. But every year when I come to these meetings those same words mean something different" (Ray Burch 1973, Former President of the International Franchise Association).

The question for the determinants of firm boundaries have triggered an extensive discussion in economics and management research during the last couple of decades. As far as the horizontal boundaries are concerned, cost considerations are presumed as one important determinant. With respect to the vertical boundaries, theoretical and empirical research has shown that the balance between investment incentives (specific assets) and performance incentives has a high explanatory value (Cabral 2000, pp 40ff). This means that both complexes together determine the efficient degree of vertical integration, that is the degree which minimizes the sum of production and transaction cost.

In addition to the two polar options of 'market' and 'integration', several hybrid organizational forms have emerged to reach the desired efficient solution for certain transactions within certain environments. Besides, for example licenses, concessions, or commission affiliations, franchise agreements can be interpreted as one further solution to this general problem of vertical organizational structure (see Rubin 1978 for a formal treatment).

Notwithstanding the fact that the motivations to create franchise agreements are mainly efficiency driven and simultaneously welfare enhancing, it is clear that such agreements normally influence competition in upstream, downstream and/or 'adjacent' markets. Hence, as far as some degree of market power is involved, there is the potential of an abusive use of franchise agreements to increase a dominant firm's markups in its 'own' brand market (harming intra-brand competition) or leveraging market power into related brand markets (harming inter-brand competition) as well as 'adjacent' markets. The resulting welfare losses are the main reason why franchise agreements are of interest for public policy makers in general and for antitrust economists and agencies in particular.

Based on these introductive considerations, it seems to be important to discuss the essential antitrust implications of franchise agreements, not only from an antitrust economists' point of view, but also from the view of the franchise transactors, aiming at designing and maintaining an efficient and 'antitrust-proved' franchise agreement. To reach this goal, this paper is structured as follows. Section 2 gives a brief overview of the evolution of antitrust regulations concerning franchise agreements in the United States of America and the European Union. Section 3 focuses on a characterization of the basic economic interrelation between franchise agreements and antitrust. First, it is shown why and how firms choose certain franchise agreements and restrictions (the so-called 'vertical restraints'[1]) to distribute their products, services or concepts. Second, it is argued why and under which circumstances such agreements might get into difficulties with antitrust regulations. Section 4 concludes and provides avenues for further research.

2 Antitrust Regulations and Franchising

Franchise agreements are subject to a multitude of different regulations. Besides the existing general laws and other regulations that are applicable to every interfirm business action (e.g. contract law, agency law, corporate law or even competition law), franchise agreements additionally underlie a franchise-specific legislation in certain countries. Furthermore, a number of franchise associations adopted so-called 'Code of Ethics' to regulate the behavior of their members (see UNIDROIT 2002 for an overview).

---

[1] "A vertical restraint is a restriction imposed by manufacturers or wholesalers on those to whom they sell their products" (Kay 1990, p 551).

The following remarks will concentrate solely on antitrust regulations of franchise agreements (especially general antitrust law and certain antitrust guidelines[2]), without denying that the borders - especially to general contract law problems - are often rather thin.

2.1 United States of America

In the United States, franchise agreements underlie two major general antitrust codes: the Sherman Act and the Clayton Act.[3] Section 1 of the Sherman Act states that "[e]very contract, combination in the form of trust or otherwise, or conspiracy, in restraint of trade or commerce among the several States, or with foreign nations, is declared to be illegal". Furthermore, in Section 2, monopolization as well as attempts to monopolize are banned. The Clayton Act specifies the Sherman Act in many respects. As far as franchise agreements are concerned, the Act, for example, prohibits certain tying and exclusive dealing arrangements.

In addition to these general antitrust laws, competition authorities in the US issue certain guidelines (with changing degrees of influence on case decisions). For example, concerning franchising, in 1985 the Department of Justice issued Vertical Restraints Guidelines which were dominated by the so-called 'Chicago antitrust view' on vertical restraints. Consequently, the potential of anti-competitive behavior (such as the increased possibilities to facilitate collusion among competitors or to exclude rivals) was acknowledged, but it was also pointed out " ... that such restraints may also promote competition by allowing a manufacturer to achieve efficiencies in the distribution of its products and by permitting firms to compete through different methods of distribution" (Cann 1986, p 500). Based on this argumentation, the Guidelines stated that intra-brand competition generally represents little anti-competitive threat. Antitrust policy should therefore focus on an analysis of inter-brand competition, namely, the extent of competition in the market from other brands and from other distribution concepts.

Furthermore, in 1986, the Federal Trade Commission (FTC 1986) issued 'Disclosure requirements and prohibitions concerning franchising and business opportunity ventures' as part of a subchapter on Trade Regulation Rules. These regulations deal with the information a franchisor is required to supply the prospective franchisee in order for the franchisee to obtain all the information necessary to evaluate the franchise. Simultaneously, the regulations uncover several unfair or deceptive acts or practices concerning franchising, combined with advice for franchisees on how to avoid these problems.

[2] The third level of antitrust 'regulations' - the case decisions - which might have a binding effect (or at least an influence) on future cases, will be omitted here due to space limitations.

[3] The Robinson-Patman Act as well as the Federal Trade Commission Act, which might also be relevant for certain types of franchise agreements, are omitted here (see Scher 1991 and Makar 1994 for overviews).

2.2 European Union

The foundations of antitrust law in the European Union are codified in Article 81 and Article 82 of the European Community Treaty. Article 81 prohibits agreements (or practices) which prevent, restrict or distort competition. This article has been mainly used to catch a broad range of vertical restraints commonly found in franchising (see Field Fisher Waterhouse 2001), whereas Article 82 of the EC Treaty prohibits abuses of a dominant position.

The first kind of antitrust guidelines for franchise agreements in the European Union were (factually) created by the *Pronuptia de Paris GmbH* decision of the European Court of Justice in 1986 (see UNIDROIT 2002). The Court applied Article 81 of the EC Treaty and a Commission Regulation on exclusive dealing agreements. The decision contained certain conclusions of general applicability, especially that "... the franchisor must be in a position to protect certain interests vital to the business and to the identity of the network ... although the provisions must be essential for this purpose" (UNIDROIT 2002, p 1). Certain categories of clauses that restrain the franchisee especially (such as price determination clauses) were not considered acceptable by the court.

Following the Pronuptia decision and several further decisions on franchising cases, in 1988, the commission merged the case insights into a block exemption regulation for franchise agreements (see UNIDROIT 2002 and Field Fisher Waterhouse 2002 for further information). Besides definitions of franchising and the identification of different types of franchising, this regulation further indicates to which restrictions of competition the exemption shall apply, to which it shall apply notwithstanding the presence of certain obligations, to which it shall apply on certain conditions and to which it shall not apply (UNIDROIT 2002, p 2).

In 1995 the European Commission published a Green Paper on Vertical Restraints in EC Competition Policy which provides - besides other things - an economic analysis of vertical restraints in the single market and an analysis of the current community procedures and their institutional framework. One important finding of the Green Paper is that vertical restraints are no longer regarded as per se suspicious or per se pro-competitive. It is acknowledged that such a decision should depend on an analysis of the facts of the case in question, to decide which effects are outweighed by the other.

By the end of 1999, the Franchise Block Exemption (Regulation EC4087/88) was replaced by a new general Vertical Restraints Block Exemption Regulation (Regulation EC2790/1999), creating a new ‚safe harbour' exemption from the impact of Article 81 of the EC Treaty. It is important to note, that the regulation "... does not exempt vertical agreements containing restrictions which are not indispensable for the attainment of the positive effects of some vertical restraints, i.e. the improvement of economic efficiency" (UNIDROIT 2002, p 3). This leads to the fact that certain types of severely anti-competitive restraints, such as fixed resale prices or certain types of territorial protection are excluded from the benefits of the block exemption (see Field Fisher Waterhouse 2001 and Terhorst 2000 for a closer analysis). But it is important to note that the new regulation establishes no specific ban on several diverse forms of restraints. Furthermore, below a producer's market share of 30%, all restrains are deemed lawful. If the market share is above 30%, a case-by-case analysis is considered (see European Commission 2002, p 12).

3 Franchising and Antitrust Implications

The first section gives a broad understanding of the general motivations for franchisor and franchisee to let in franchise agreements. Such an overview provides an important basis for the subsequent antitrust analysis, especially as far as the question of welfare effects of a certain firm behavior is concerned. Afterwards, it is important to sketch certain implementation problems with an unrestricted (or 'pure') franchise agreement, which lead to the introduction of special contractual restrictions by the franchisor. Given this knowledge, the question of 'if', 'why' and 'how' certain parts of franchise agreements get into difficulties with antitrust law will be analyzed in greater detail in the next but one section.

3.1 Franchising as a Vertical Relationship

Franchise agreements organize the vertical relationship between two independent firms: a franchisor and a franchisee. The franchisor, the producer of a certain product or owner of a business concept sells this to the franchisee, subject to a specific contractual relationship and in return for set-up fees, license fees, royalties or other payments. The contracts will address questions such as prices to be charged, services offered, location and marketing effort (see Lipczynski and Wilson 2001, pp 289ff).

Why Do Transactors Use Franchise Agreements? It is well-known, that franchise agreements are not an omnipresent distribution strategy for every product in every industry. Quite the contrary is true: franchising is typically found in industries where services are provided that have to be produced locally (while the customer is present) and where large advantages in developing and maintaining a business formula or a brand name are existent (see Douma and Schreuder 2002, p 173 and Fulop and Forward 1997, p 607). This empirical observation leads to the conjecture that franchise agreements are the *most efficient governance structure* for *certain products* or services in *certain environments.*

To give an intuition about basic theoretical arguments which can fortify this conjecture, we consider a fully integrated local firm that has undertaken huge efforts to establish a brand name for its (locally produced) product or service. The fixed cost for establishing the brand name (interpreted as 'an implicit guarantee of a certain quality level') are largely sunk, but the marginal cost of expanding the brand name are almost zero. Therefore, it seems straightforward that it is in the profit-maximizing interest of the brand name owner to expand output, taking advantage of the large economies in the sale of brand name reputation (see Wainwright 2002, p 2).

During the growth process, the firm is subject to certain spatial and technological limitations. For example, in a spatial context, local demand will become saturated and market extensions are normally subject to specialized local information, which the manufacturers often do not have. Another internal growth restriction is technology driven, as the expansion of output might lead to diseconomies of scale, e.g. due to the growing complexity of in-firm coordination. With this respect, the growth of a fully integrated firm is associated with the standard economic problems in hierarchies, such as, for example, shirking by the employees. A thinkable solution to such problems would be intensive monitoring efforts (of the outlets) by the parent firm. Unfortunately, in a context of incomplete information, this often turns out to be problematic, as the necessary familiarity with local market conditions (to judge the efficiency of a specific outlet) is not existent.

Auxiliary to these general problems of internal growth strategies, Grimes (1996, p 108) identifies two further reasons, why franchising could be an efficient way of distribution. First, franchising raises the ability of the franchisor to acquire capital to build a network of dealer outlets. He can do this perhaps more quickly and/or at lower cost than would be possible in a vertically integrated business. This might create first-mover advantages in brand name recognition and product market competition. Furthermore, franchising requires a smaller financial investment by franchisors and a lower capital risk than a company-owned network (Fulop and Forward 1997, p 606ff). Second, franchise agreements allow harvesting the entrepreneurial energy and dedication that flows from investor-owned and - operated outlets. This would solve many typical hierarchical problems mentioned above (but would raise others explained below).

Besides these advantages for the franchisor, franchise agreements are also profitable for the franchisees, e.g. as franchising may lead to a business risk reduction through the trademarks or the franchisor assistance concerning training, advice and support. Furthermore, commercial banks might be more 'generous' in giving start-up financing, if a market-proven business concept from a well-known franchisor is the basis of the entrepreneurial idea (see Fulop and Forward 1997, p 608).

In a nutshell, "[f]ranchising is just one of many ways a firm can choose to distribute its product. The essential economic rationale for franchising is that it permits transactors to achieve whatever benefits of large scale may be available in, for example, brand name development and organizational design, while harnessing the profit incentive and retailing effort of local owners" (Klein 1995, p 10).

Why are Certain Restrictions Necessary to Stabilize Franchise Agreements? By signing a franchise agreement, it is in the first instance reasonable to assume that the franchisor and the franchisee have congruent general interests in maintaining a workable and efficient franchise relationship. The franchisor would like to distribute its products in the most efficient way and the franchisee expects a share from the 'joint' profit. However, theoretical research has shown that an unrestricted franchise agreement underlies some kind of *prisoner's dilemma,* meaning that it would be in the collective interest of all transactors, that everybody acts in the agreed way that maximizes joint profits. But as the following paragraphs will show, a single franchisee can raise its own short-run profits by deviating from the joint profit maximization solution. Such behavior normally harms the other transactors, jeopardizes the success of the whole franchise agreement and has at least the potential to harm social welfare. This is one reason why franchise agreements need some restrictions.[4]

The following more exact analysis of the drivers of such misbehavior can be structured according to the possible relationships in a franchise agreement: between manufacturers and retailers, between retailers and between manufacturers (see OFT 1997, Chapter 7).

As far as the first relationship – *manufacturer-retailer* – is concerned, one problem is the so-called *double marginalization*. This problem is created when not only the franchisor but also the franchisee has some degree of market power (e.g. due to the granting of exclusive distribution rights). In such a situation, the franchisee would not set prices equal to marginal costs (as it would be in the interest of the franchisor), but would set prices above the competitive level to exploit its retailer market power. As a consequence, from the view of the franchisor, the franchisee sells too little of the product and therefore reduces the profits of the franchisor. The economic problem behind this phenomenon is a vertical externality, as the franchisee only takes into account what is profit-maximizing for him and does not look at the negative consequences of its behavior for the franchisor.

Besides these diverging incentives in pricing, the same story can be applied to other aspects such as product quality or retailer service. "[A]s long as manufacturer and retailer both stand to gain from any increase in the quality or promotion of the manufacturer's product, then neither will individually have incentives to do the jointly profit maximizing amount of quality improvement or promotion" (OFT 1997, Paragraph 7.1.1.1).

Another form of 'moral hazard' in unrestrained franchise agreements is the so-called *input substitution*. This phenomenon arises when the retailer has the possibility of receiving a (substitutive) input not only from the monopoly manufacturer but also from a competitive adjacent industry. In such a case the retailer has (due to a shift in relative prices) an incentive to substitute towards the second (cheaper) input and therefore consumes too little of the manufacturer's input good. This happens because the retailer does not take the franchisor's marginal profit into account. One result for this is that the profit of the franchisor is shrinking. Another result is that a socially suboptimal input combination is realized at the retailer level (see Tirole 1995, p 179 ff, Blair and Kaserman 1978 for formal treatments).

Another justification for certain franchise restrictions lies in the fact that they would allow an incentive compatible *distribution of quasi-rents* (OFT 1997 and Klein and Murphy 1988). "Vertical restraints, by shifting some rents from manu-

---

[4] Some other justifications for the need of franchise regulation are more straightforward. For example, it seems reasonable, that certain franchise restrictions are necessary to protect the franchiser's intellectual property rights. Consequently, the franchisee should be prohibited from selling competing goods or services, "if the obligation is necessary to maintain the common identity and reputation of the franchised network" (European Commission 2002, p 23).

facturers to the dealers, have this effect [of an optimal distribution of quasi-rents] and thereby help to assure dealer performance of unspecified but essential elements of the contractual understanding." In other words, the manufacturer uses vertical restraints to decrease the short-run gain to non-performing dealers (by limiting their ability to expand output) and to increase the long-run gain to performing dealers (by creating a quasi-rent stream).

As far as the relationship *retailer-retailer* is concerned, free-riding incentives are a major problem. Klein (1995, pp 12ff) shows such an incentive with respect to quality: Given a common brand name ('an implicit guarantee of a certain quality level'), a *free-rider incentive* is created, because each franchisee has an incentive to reduce the quality of the product to save costs. This is the case, because the consequential reduction of the perceived quality is borne by all franchisees using the brand, e.g. the reduction in future demand is spread across the whole market. In other words, a single firm does not bear the full negative consequences of its behavior.

A closely related conflict could occur in businesses where some form of pre-sales services is provided. Free-riding franchisees might be able to cancel such services by relying on other firms to offer such initial services. This would reduce cost for the free-riding franchisee and would allow him to drop its retail price. The consumers take this into account and might get the pre-sales services for free from the rival and will buy the product afterwards from the free-riding franchisee. As a consequence, the franchisees with pre-sale service have to leave the market; with the subsequent result that no pre-sales services are no longer provided. This reduces total sales, joint profits and consumer welfare.

The third relationship in franchise agreements is *manufacturer-manufacturer*. This relationship defines inter-brand competition and underlies many of the vertical issues explained above. For example, given various brands of a product, advertising any particular brand would have positive spillover effects on other brands. This creates free-riding incentives between manufacturers and would lead to too little advertising in equilibrium, which regularly damages franchisors, franchisees and the consumers (see OFT 1997, Paragraph 7.1.1.2).

What Particular Restrictions are Suitable in Order to Solve the Franchising Problems? In economic terms, the connection between a franchisor and a franchisee is a principal-agent relationship. Accordingly, the principal (the franchisor) hires an agent (the franchisee) to perform an action (distributing products to the lowest possible cost) in a manner that the principal cannot fully control. The franchisor cannot perfectly observe the sales effort of the franchisee, which it can use to take advantage from.

The stabilization of the franchise agreement is in the interest of both transactors: the franchisor and the franchisee. However, due to the presence of individual incentives to deviate from such a 'pure' franchise agreement (because of higher short-run profits for the deviating firm), the question of ways to stabilize franchise agreements immediately occurs. Lipczynski and Wilson (2001, p 291) and the OECD (1993, p 10) identify three basic forms of vertical control, which have the potential to solve these problems. First, certain problems can be reduced (or even solved) by giving the franchisor *direct control* over the franchisee's decision (such as price-setting, quality and marketing effort). An obvious pre-condition for such solutions is that the franchisor is able to monitor the critical decisions of the franchisee.

Second, a *restructuring of incentives* can be determined to ensure that the objectives of both parties coincide. Thus the contract could specify a franchise fee plus buying the inputs at marginal costs so that the franchisee is committed to the maximization of aggregated profits.[5]

Third, *contracts* may be used to reduce potential externalities. Thus, to reduce competition between the franchisees (intra-brand competition), a franchisor may wish to offer exclusive territorial contracts or fix a minimum retail price ('vertical restraints'). Real franchise agreements might contain aspects of all three forms of vertical control.

It is important to note that several *empirical findings* corroborate this healing influence of certain vertical restrictions on several franchising problems explained above. For example, Brickley (1999) identifies (using US data) a positive correlation between the level of externalities present in the market and the level of restrictions included in the franchise agreement. In addition, Chaudey and Fadairo (2002) report – using a French dataset - that the choice of the degree of coercion in vertical contracts is positively correlated with the level of horizontal externalities.[6]

In a nutshell, it was shown that unrestricted franchising contracts contain several externalities and incentive problems, which endanger the benefits (and therefore the stability) of franchise agreements. To make franchise agreements workable, several contractual restrictions for the franchisee are necessary. Which restraints the contractors choose critically depends on the information situation, certain product characteristics, the market environment and also on the possible problems some restraints might get with antitrust rules.

3.2 Franchise Agreements and Potential Antitrust Conflicts

Despite the historical fact that antitrust laws have been motivated and legitimated by various arguments (brought forward by various communities), the economic profession nowadays sees the *central aim of antitrust laws* in maintaining and improving economic efficiency. Given this primary objective, antitrust is mainly interested in two *types of offences*, which comprise the potential to harm competition: exploitative and exclusionary (see Fox 2002 for an overview). 'Exploitative' means that firms (for whatever purposes) are doing some form of business together (e.g. form a cartel or a strategic alliance), while 'exclusionary' stands for

[5] This is the way franchising is often modeled in Industrial Organization theory (see Tirole 1995).

[6] Another form of empirical evidence is delivered by Salop (1993), who looked at the occurrence of free-rider justifications in court decisions in the US between 1977 and 1992. He found that in 97 antitrust cases, the courts mentioned free-riding justifications and in 49 cases, the courts accepted this justification for vertical restraints.

attempts by (usually) one firm to harm rivals by certain behavior with the aim of achieving a higher degree of market power.

For both types, theoretical as well as empirical research has shown that they could have either efficiency-enhancing or anti-competitive motives and effects. While several behaviors, such as, horizontal cartels or certain refusals to deal - are presumed to be detrimental to efficiency generally, others - such as strategic alliances or certain tying agreements - could be either supportive or detrimental to competition and efficiency.

This trade-off led to the development of two types of *control strategies*: per-se rules and the rule-of-reason. The per-se rule prohibits certain behavior generally, because the detrimental effects are assumed to be dominant, almost certain and easily identifiable by the firms (see Carlton et al. 1997, p 427). The rule-of-reason accommodates the more frequent case that the efficiency-enhancing effects of certain behaviors must be compared with the anti-competitive effects.

As such rule-of-reason assessments are very expensive, antitrust laws try to limit investigations into cases where the probability of an anti-competitive behavior is high and the potential harm to competition is presumed to be big. To differentiate between these and other cases, antitrust laws and authorities use a central initial indicator: the *level of market power*. If the firm in question has 'a certain degree' of market power (in the market identified as 'relevant') and if the usage of an anticompetitive strategy is likely, then the antitrust authority will investigate further.

Why Should Franchise Agreements be Subject to Antitrust Law and Antitrust Intervention? If antitrust is mainly interested in maintaining and enhancing economic efficiency, it seems questionable at first glance, why efficiency-enhancing vertical restraints should be subject to antitrust regulations. The central justification is the well-proved theoretical and empirical observation that vertical restraints are hybrids: They might have mainly pro-competitive effects, but it may be that they are mainly used for anti-competitive purposes. As the net welfare effects are unknown, antitrust analyses come into play.

What do these potential anti-competitive aspects look like? Generally speaking, franchise agreements contain the potential to harm competition by extending market power on the vertical (intra-brand) level and on the horizontal (inter-brand) level. Furthermore, as Kay (1990, pp 555ff) shows, vertical restraints may be used to extend monopoly power into a previously competitive ('adjacent') industry, e.g. by distorting the transfer price between the monopoly and competitive industries.

There are numerous other ways in which vertical restraints can be abused for anti-competitive behavior. For example, vertical restraints might raise switching or search costs as well as sunk costs. All these factors might discourage entry and maintain or even increase market power. If entry occurs anyhow, vertical restraints can be used to impede competitors, e.g. by acts of preventing a firm from acquiring an essential input ('foreclosure'). Furthermore, as theoretical research has shown, several vertical restraints might have the potential to ease horizontal cartelization in the product market. This small choice of aspects raises the conjecture that vertical restraints allow broad access to the 'toolbox of strategic behavior' for dominant firms in oligopoly markets (see examples later in this Section). In other words - and recapitulating - a franchisor could use vertical restraints (under the disguise of a franchise agreement) to enhance market power incurious of the regularly detrimental effects on competition and efficiency. These anti-competitive potentials provide an economically sound foundation for an application of antitrust rules.

Unsurprisingly, several critics challenge this reasoning (or at least the deduced conclusion). One older strand of arguments says that antitrust laws and intervention harm the development of efficient distribution structures. For example, Thompson (1969, pp 42ff) identifies a *franchisor's paradox* due to the fact that an integrated business enterprise is free to, for example, assign territories, select customers or fix prices for the sale of its products. However, a firm with identical business interests, which chooses to operate through a franchise structure, may find such obligations difficult to implement due to antitrust regulations.

This argumentation immediately raises the question of whether only inter-brand competition is the relevant task for antitrust policy. Rey and Stiglitz (1995, pp 431ff) show that this conclusion might be misleading. At least if (imperfect) competition among producers is taken into account, dominant firms might be able to reduce the effectiveness of inter-brand competition by manipulating intra-brand competition.

A related discussion surrounds this question: whether franchise agreements are *subject to antitrust law at all*. The basic argumentation by Klein (1999) says that because a franchsior has no market power over the franchisee before the franchise contract is signed, post-contractual competitive abuses are not of interest for antitrust law but for contract law. Several scholars and judges disagree with this view by articulating their concern that the limitation on such pre-contract analysis of franchisor market power would eliminate antitrust protection (Grimes 1999) and would lead to abuses of market power. Grimes (1996; 1999) fortifies this view by arguing that franchisors often have ex-post market power in dealing with franchisees because of the franchisee's sunk investments and the franchisor's power to confer benefits and impose costs on franchisees (Grimes 1996, p 155).

A third point which is brought forward against antitrust interventions stems from the discussion on whether and *how anti-competitive* the contractual restrictions in questions (the 'vertical restraints') really are. For example, the Chicago School contradicted the opinion that many vertical restraints are anti-competitive. Furthermore, even if such obligations have an anti-competitive impact, antitrust intervention would not be necessary "[b]ecause the market possesses remarkable self-correcting capacities" (Cann 1986, p 487f). Consequently, it was proposed that purely vertical restrictions (involving no dealer collusion) should be declared legal per se (see Posner 1981).

Especially recent research in game theory (see Tan 2001) and its application has been successful in showing that "[t]he Chicago approach correctly recognizes that vertical restraints may often serve wholly legitimate commercial purposes: but it underestimates the extent to which vertical restraints may be motivated by strategic objectives designed to change the structure of the industry, or to resist changes in the structure of the industry" (Kay 1990, p 560). More precisely, the idea of per-se legality is flawed by various models of strategic competition, which show that vertical restrictions can be introduced only for strategic purposes with the aim of disadvantaging rivals (see Williamson 1979 for an transaction cost approach).

Summing up, theoretical and empirical observations infer the general statement that franchise agreements should be subject to antitrust rules, because they could have either efficiency-enhancing effects or/and anti-competitive effects. Assuming a considerable harm of the potential anticompetitive effects and non-prohibitive enforcement cost, the rule-of reason approach seems to be the suitable antitrust reaction in such an environment (see below).

What Do Potential Franchising Antitrust Problems Look Like? In a study by Patrick Rey and Steven Brenner on behalf of the OECD (1993, pp 95 ff), the authors found that the following *vertical restraints* might be at odds with antitrust laws: Resale price maintenance (or vertical price restrictions), territorial or customer restrictions (or territorial exclusivity), tie-ins, exclusive dealing obligations, refusals to deal, obligations not to compete, minimum requirements and advertising restrictions.

It is far beyond the scope of this paper to give an overview of all these vertical restraints (see e.g. Chaudey and Fadairo 2002). But indispensable for further reasoning is a broad intuition of how these restraints heal certain franchising problems derived above. For example, the double marginalization problem can be solved by the imposition of e.g. resale price maintenance. If the price is fixed by the franchisor (and if he can monitor retail prices), the franchisee will not have the possibility of imposing the inefficient 'second marginalization' and, therefore, the problem is solved. Another example could be the problem of free-riding on pre-sales services. This externality can be internalized, for example, by the introduction of closed territories (see OECD 1993 for a complete overview).[7] A third example – the so-called tie-ins – will be analysed more exactly in the following paragraphs by giving a broad overview of definitions, likely pro- and anti-competitive effects as well as antitrust policy and case examples.

A tie-in results when a franchisor sells a good or service to a franchisee on the condition that the franchisee purchases a second good from the franchisor, which he does not want, or which he would prefer to purchase from another seller. An example for a tie-in could be the requirement of a fast food restaurant franchisor to buy not only the menu items (the tying good) but also to purchase the ingredients (the tied goods) from the franchisor.

The efficiency-enhancing potentials of tying are analyzed e.g. by Ahlborn et al. (2003, pp 43ff). They show, for example, that tying can reduce production and distribution cost through the realization of economies of scale and scope, can reduce transaction cost through reductions in search cost or can lead to product im-

[7] It is clear that most externality problems could be solved by vertical integration. But as was shown above, franchise agreements were just chosen because the disadvantages of vertical integration are dominant. In other words, the externalities have to be severe in order to outweigh the gains from vertical disintegration.

provement through value-enhancing combinations of certain inputs. Additionally, tying can help to ensure certain quality uniformity.

Besides these general efficiency-enhancing potentials, tying is a vertical restraint, which solves several of the incentive problems every franchise agreement is confronted with. For example, tying has the potential to reduce or even eliminate free-riding on quality by franchisees, because the franchisor delivers all inputs (with the optimal quality level) to the dealers (see Klein and Saft 1985). Furthermore, as Tirole (1995, pp 179ff) shows, tie-ins in combination with some form of resale price maintenance can solve the problem of input substitution.

As far as the potential harm of tie-ins is concerned, theoretical research investigates three main areas of interest: First, a focus lies on the ability of tying to achieve price discrimination (which could also be welfare-enhancing). Second, its ability to foreclose competition in the tied market is analyzed (see Whinston 1990). Recently, for example, Carlton and Waldman (2002) show that tying can also be used to preserve and extend a monopoly position in the tying market by deterring entry of efficient producers. All these models show that the occurrence and intensity of these anti-competitive effects depends on certain market characteristics, e.g. the level of market power in intra- and inter-brand competition. Such robust results of game-theoretic models should be part of a rule-of-reason approach sketched below.[8]

As far as antitrust policy and cases[9] are concerned, the subtitle of the survey by Ahlborn et al. (2003) 'A farewell to per se illegality' gives more than a hint about the past and actual judgment of tie-ins. After decades of a mainly sceptical view on tie-ins, the mainstream in Antitrust Law and Economics nowadays acknowledges the positive aspects of tie-ins and prefers the usage of a rule-of-reason approach. Ahlborn et al. (2003, pp 56ff) proposes a framework for tie-in cases and prefers the following three screens of analysis: 1. Is an anticompetitive effect possible? 2. Is an anticompetitive effect likely? 3. Are there offsetting efficiency benefits? (see Hylton and Salinger 2001 and McDavid and Steuer 1999 for other approaches).

What are the Major Challenges for Antitrust Economics Concerning Franchise Agreements? As explained above, business behavior with presumably pro- *and* anti-competitive effects is best dealt with by the rule-of-reason antitrust

---

[8] One example is provided by the European Commission (1995, p 3) by stating that "[T]he fiercer is interbrand competition, the more likely are the pro-competitive and efficiency effects to outweigh any anti-competitive effects of vertical restraints. Anti-competitive effects are only likely where interbrand competition is weak and there are barriers to entry at either producer or distributor level".

[9] The most influential case (on tying and related vertical restraints) in the United States is Kodak (1992). Pivotal pre-Kodak tying cases are Times-Picayune (1953), Northern Pacific (1958), Fortner (1969, 1977), and Jefferson Parish (1984). Influential post-Kodak cases are Queen City Pizza (1996), Wilson (1996, 1997) and Collins (1996). Further information on the cases provide Joseph (2001) and Thier (1998).

approach, at least as long as a general and considerable harm of the potential anti-competitive effects as well as non-prohibitive enforcement costs are assumed.

Despite this clear assertion, the consequential answers to the questions of design and implementation are complicated by at least two important characteristics: First, it may be that the same vertical restraint has a pro-competitive impact in one certain environment and an anti-competitive one in another environment. This complicates antitrust analysis as the case analysis and the following results critically depend on the correct assessment of the existing market environment (e.g. delineation of the relevant market, relevance of intra- and inter-brand competition, possibility to create impediments to entry, potentials for strategic behavior, etc.) and the role of a certain vertical restraint in the franchise agreement. A direct consequence of this is that the per-se illegality of certain vertical restraints - as currently practiced in the European Union - is flawed. Such a policy faces an inconsistency problem that stems from the fact that different vertical restraints might have the same (positive and/or negative) effects on competition, but are assessed differently by competition policy. Such a policy will provoke the inefficient substitution of one (prohibited) vertical restraint by another (permitted) one.

Second, different vertical restraints might be necessary to solve all franchise incentive problems. In other words, vertical restraints often interact in a complex way within one franchise agreement. Hence, the common isolation and analysis of one fragment of the whole franchise contract (e.g. tie-ins) might be misleading in examining its overall competitive impact. This leads to the determination that the popular way of analyzing franchise agreements by a 'disaggregated view' might be misleading, as the *mutual interdependences* are not discovered or assessed in a wrong way. An empirical study by Slade (1998) on a franchise tying case in the UK brewery industry might act as an example, where antitrust intervention might have led to welfare reductions. Slade investigates the fact of raised retail prices for beer after a decision of the Monopolies and Mergers Commission to divestiture brewer-owned public houses in the UK. She concludes that "[s]ince these [tying] practices interact with one another in complex ways, the piecemeal policy that was enacted probably made both consumers and brewers worse off ... It is highly likely that these restrictive measures were undertaken with little understanding of the ultimate ramifications for retail prices and industry profits" (Slade 1998, p 600).

Taking these challenges as given, a rule-of reason approach should be specified by the development of a general policy framework, which guides firms as well as antitrust authorities and rationalize antitrust enforcement. „What is needed is an approach that can accommodate important market differences: the characteristics of firms and markets that affect the probabilities of error, the error costs, and the implementation costs of alternative policy approaches" (Joskow and Klevorick 1979, p 218).

To reach these framework tasks, the first important step should exclude all franchising cases, in which antitrust violations are unlikely. In other words, the first framework stage has to answer the question 'Is anti-competitive conduct possible?'. If the answer is 'yes', the second stage of the framework is activated (see below). If the answer is 'no', no further antitrust efforts will be undertaken. The essential problem therefore is to discriminate between these two possibilities. Antitrust economics is fundamentally based on the belief that an assessment of market power is the best way to take up this desired separation.

Therefore, after the compulsory delineation of the relevant market, important market structure criteria have to be assessed, such as, the general status of competition, the number of sellers and buyers, the degree of product differentiation, barriers to entry or the role of buyer power. One possible outcome of this market structure analysis could be that an antitrust intervention is not necessary, because the franchisor underlies vigorous competition from other franchise systems or other distribution modes. Another argumentation, which would lead to the same conclusion, could state that anti-competitive effects of vertical restraints are less likely, because the buyers have significant (countervailing) buying power.

If some degree of market power (inter- and/or intra-brand) were identified, the antitrust authority would start further investigations in the second stage of the framework. The central question now is 'Is anti-competitive conduct plausible?'. To assess this question, a detailed analysis of market conduct is necessary. For example, concerning franchising, it seems to be pivotal to estimate the intensity of the franchise problems (inefficiencies), which could be solved by the introduction of vertical restraints. In this respect, an investigation into the information environment is essential, such as on what can be observed and enforced by the parties involved. Another important emphasis in the second stage should address the likelihood of forms of strategic behavior. The general antitrust challenge could therefore be described as 'find logical (theory-based) and likely (case-based) stories and show their basic mechanisms and interrelation'.

The third stage of a framework should contain some kind of efficiency defence, because it might be unclear if overwhelming pro-competitive effects are perhaps able to more than outweigh the anti-competitive effects. Such a stage might also contain answers to the question of whether the observed vertical restraints are essential for the success of the franchise agreement. In other words, it should be checked if less restrictive (but reasonable) alternatives to the observed vertical restraints are existent (see Ferris 2001 for several proposals).

Summing up, the major challenge for antitrust economics is to provide the antitrust authorities with theory-based stories which allow the extraction of the possible pro- and anti-competitive effects. Unfortunately, such 'stories' cannot be deterministic in the sense of 'If you extract this sign, you always have to react like that!' Game-theoretic models especially deliver insights rather than clear and deterministic answers to antitrust questions. In this respect, Ahlborn et al. (2003, p 56ff) are perfectly right when they state that "[u]nfortunately, the game-theoretic models … do not provide a universally valid set of conditions that could be used by competition authorities as a safe checklist in their rule-of-reason analyses. What these models do suggest is a series of screens for determining whether antitrust authorities should investigate …". Fortunately, some important insights of game-theoretic (and other) models - like the pivotal role of market power for predicting market conduct - are so robust, that - in this regard - antitrust authorities can set their mind to rest.

4 Conclusions

"There are many types of transactions which profit-seeking individuals might find worthwhile in the marketplace; Products and markets have sufficiently diverse characteristics so that a large number of arrangements might be profit maximizing. Thus, it would be surprising if there were in fact sharp distinctions between interfirm and intrafirm transactions; rather we would expect hybrid cases where markets allow various types of optimal blends. In fact, we do observe such mixed cases" (Rubin 1978, p 223). Franchise agreements can be interpreted as such a 'mixed case' on the continuum between 'markets' and 'hierachies'.

The aim of this paper was to give an overview of the basic interrelation between antitrust and franchise agreements. After sketching some pivotal antitrust regulations concerning franchising in the United States of America and the European Union and giving a broad overview of some essential reasons why firms engage in franchise agreements, the first major economic result shows that franchise agreements contain some kind of prisoner's dilemma: It would be in the collective interest of all franchise transactors that everybody acts in the agreed way which maximizes joint profits. But due to spill-overs, free-riding incentives and related inefficiencies, a single franchisee can raise its own short-run profit by deviating from the joint profit maximization solution. Such behavior normally harms the other transactors, jeopardizes the success of the whole franchise agreement and has at least the potential to harm social welfare. Therefore it was stated that franchise agreements need some contractual restrictions, e.g. the so-called 'vertical restraints', to reduce or eliminate such inefficiencies.

Notwithstanding these efficiency-enhancing effects of 'vertical restraints' (as part of a complex franchise contract), it was found that they also contain the potential to act in an anti-competitive way by reducing or eliminating competition on the manufacturer level and/or the retailer level. Which of these effects dominate and which restraint(s) will be chosen was found to be dependent on the vertical and horizontal market structures as well as the information environment (e.g. what can be observed and enforced by the manufacturers, or the relevance and scope of externalities in the relevant market).

Given these hybrid effects of vertical restraints on competition and efficiency, it was deduced that franchising strategies should underlie antitrust rules. The use of a rule-of-reason approach was identified as the appropriate antitrust reaction aiming at assessing the significance of pro- and anticompetitive effects. The desirable design of a corresponding policy framework was asserted as quite challenging, because of at least two characteristics: First, vertical restraints are only one part of a multi-part (complex) franchise contract with a multitude of mutual interdependences. As a consequence, it might be misleading to extract and evaluate one certain vertical restraint in its competitive effects, taking all the other contract parts as given. Second, especially game-theoretic research often delivers particular insights rather than clear and deterministic antitrust recommendations.

Taking these challenges as given, the major objective for antitrust economics in the future presumably lies in the further development of investigation tools, because the sound design and committing implementation of the resulting frameworks - not only with respect to franchising strategies - would enhance the general calculability of antitrust decisions for the firms, would reduce erroneous antitrust decisions (which harm social welfare) and would therefore promote the central aim of antitrust law and antitrust intervention, namely, the protection and the improvement of economic efficiency.

References

1. Ahlborn C, Evans D, Padilla J (2003) The Antitrust Economics of Tying. Unpublished Working Paper, AEI-Brookings Joint Center for Regulatory Studies, Washington D.C.
2. Blair R, Kaserman D (1978) Vertical Integration, Tying, and Antitrust Policy. American Economic Review 68:397-402
3. Brickley J (1999) Incentive Conflicts and Contractual Restraints. Evidence from Franchising. Journal of Law and Economics 42:745-774
4. Cabral L (2000) Introduction to Industrial Organization. MIT Press, Cambridge
5. Cann W (1986) Vertical Restraints and the "Efficiency" Influence. American Business Law Journal 24:483-540
6. Carlton D, Gertner R, Rosenfield A (1997) Communication among Competitors: Game Theory and Antitrust. George Mason Law Review 5:423-440
7. Carlton D, Waldman M (2002) The Strategic Use of Tying to Preserve and Create Market Power in Evolving Industries. Rand Journal of Economics 33:194-220
8. Chaudey M, Fadairo M (2002) Vertical Restraints: Anticompetitive Tools or Market Failure Palliatives? Unpublished Working Paper, Saint-Etienne
9. Douma S, Schreuder H (2002) Economic Approaches to Organizations. Prentice Hall, Harlow
10. European Commission (1995) Green Paper – Vertical Restraints in EU Competition Policy. Executive Summary, Brussels, available at http://europa.eu.int/en/record/green/gp9701/vrsumen.htm
11. European Commission (2002) Competition Policy in Europe. The Competition Rules for Supply and Distribution Agreements. Luxembourg
12. Federal Trade Commission - FTC (1986) Disclosure Requirements and Prohibitions Concerning Franchising and Business Opportunity Ventures. Washington D.C.
13. Ferris J (2001) Alternative Approaches to Vertical Restraints: Theoretical Models and Current Practices. Unpublished Working Paper for the Canadian Competition Bureau, Ottawa
14. Field Fisher Waterhouse (2001) The new Regime for Franchising in Europe. London, available at www.ffwlaw.com/practice_area/franchising/franchise.htm
15. Field Fisher Waterhouse (2002) The Treatment of Franchising by the Law of the European Community. London, available at www.ffwlaw.com/practice_area/ franchising/ franchise.htm
16. Fox E (2002) What is Harm to Competition? Exclusionary Practices and Anticompetitive Effect. Antitrust Law Journal 70:372-411
17. Fulop C, Forward J (1997) Insights into Franchising – A Review of Empirical and Theoretical Perspectives. Service Industries Journal 17:603-625
18. Grimes W (1996) When Do Franchisors Have Market Power? Antitrust Remedies for Franchisor Opportunism. Antitrust Law Journal 65:105-155

19. Grimes W (1999) Franchise Antitrust Claims: The Vacuum in Federal Leadership. The aai Column, available at www.antitrustinstitute.org/recent/46.cfm
20. Hylton K, Salinger M (2001) Tying Law and Policy: A Decision Theoretic Approach. Unpublished Working Paper, Boston
21. Joseph R (2001) Franchise Supply Systems and the Law of Antitrust "Tying". Unpublished Working Paper, Chicago
22. Joskow P, Klevorick A (1979) A Framework for Analyzing Predatory Pricing Policy. Yale Law Journal 89:213-270
23. Kay J (1990) Vertical Restraints. European Economic Review 34:551-561
24. Klein B (1995) The Economics of Franchise Contracts. Journal of Corporate Finance 2:9-37
25. Klein B (1999) Market Power in Franchise Cases in the Wake of Kodak: Applying Post-Contract Hold-Up Analysis to Vertical Relationships. Antitrust Law Journal 67:283-326
26. Klein B, Saft L (1985) The Law and Economics of Franchise Tying Contracts. Journal of Law and Economics 28:345-361
27. Klein B, Murphy K (1988) Vertical Restraints as Contract Enforcement Mechanisms. Journal of Law and Economics 31:265-297
28. Lipczynski J, Wilson J (2001) Industrial Organization – An Analysis of Competitive Markets. Prentice Hall, Essex
29. Makar S (1994) Antitrust and Franchising. Holland & Knight Working Paper, Jacksonville
30. McDavid J, Steuer R (1999) The Revival of Franchise Antitrust Claims. Antitrust Law Journal 67:209-241
31. OECD (1993) Competition Policy and Vertical Restraints: Franchising Agreements. Paris
32. Office of Fair Trading – OFT (1997) Competition in Retailing. London
33. Posner R (1981) The Next Step in the Antitrust Treatment of Restricted Distribution: Per Se Legality. University of Chicago Law Review 48:6-26
34. Rey P, Stiglitz J (1995) The Role of Exclusive Territories in Producers' Competition. Rand Journal of Economics 26:431-451
35. Rubin P (1978) The Theory of the Firm and the Structure of the Franchise Contract. Journal of Law and Economics 21:223-234
36. Salop S (1993) Exclusionary Vertical Restraints Law: Has Economics Mattered? American Economic Review – Papers and Proceedings 83:168-172
37. Scher I (1991) Franchising and the Robinson-Patman Act: Some Problems and Solutions. Antitrust Law Journal 60:479-489
38. Slade M (1998) Beer and the Tie: Did Divestiture of Brewer-Owned Public Houses Lead to Higher Beer Prices? Economic Journal 108:565-602
39. Tan G (2001) The Economic Theory of Vertical Restraints. Unpublished Working Paper, University of British Columbia, Vancouver
40. Terhorst G (2000) The Reformation of the EC Competition Policy on Vertical Restraints. Northwestern Journal of International Law & Business 21:343-378
41. Thier S (1998) An Analysis of Tying Arrangements in Franchising Contracts. Journal of Corporation Law 23:563-580
42. Thompson D (1969) Franchise Operations and Antitrust Law. Journal of Retailing 44:39-53
43. Tirole J (1995) The Theory of Industrial Organization. MIT Press, Cambridge
44. UNIDROIT - International Institute for the Unification of Private Law (2002) Legislation and Regulations Relevant to Franchising. available at www.unidroit.org/english/franchising/annex.htm

45.Wainwright K (2002) Dual Organizational Structure of Franchise Contracts. Unpublished Working Paper, Simon Fraser University, Burnaby
46.Whinston M (1990) Tying, Foreclosure and Exclusion. American Economic Review 80:837-859
47.Williamson O (1979) Vertical Market Restrictions: Antitrust Ramifications of the Transaction Cost Approach. University of Pennsylvania Law Review 127:953-993

List of Contributors

Janet E. L. Bercovitz
The Fuqua School of Business
Duke University
USA

Magali Chauday
CREUSET
Université Jean Monnet Saint Etienne
France

Gérard Cliquet
Center for Research on Economics and Management
Université de Rennes 1
France

Evelien Croonen
University of Groningen
Faculty of Management and Organization
The Netherlands

Krista Duniach-Smith
Faculté d'Administration et Gestion
Université Montpellier I
France

Thomas Ehrmann
Center for Entrepreneurship
University of Muenster
Germany

Muriel Fadario
CREUSET
Université Jean Monnet Saint Etienne
France

Mukul P. Gupta
Marketing Area
Management Development Institute
India

Doug Haines
College of Business & Economics
University of Idaho
USA

George W. J. Hendrikse
Rotterdam School of Management
Erasmus University Rotterdam
The Netherlands

Kai Hüschelrath
Institute for Industrial Organization
WHU School of Management
Germany

Regina Jarmalaite
Stockholm School of Economics in Riga
Latvia

Minh-Ngoc Nguyen
Center for Research on Economics and Management
Université de Rennes 1
France

Seth W. Norton
Department of Business and Economics
Wheaton College
USA

Rozenn Perrigot
Center for Research on Economics
and Management
Université de Rennes 1
France

Irina Sekundo
Stockholm School of Economics
In Riga
Latvia

Georg Spranger
Center for Entrepreneurship
University of Muenster
Germany

Jenni Torikka
School of Business and Economics
University of Jyväskylä
Finland

Mika Tuunanen
School of Business and Economics
University of Jyväskyla
Finland

Luis Vázquez
Department of Economics
and Business
Universidad de Salamanca
Spain

Frank Wadsworth
School of Business
Indiana University
USA

Josef Windsperger
Center for Business Studies
University of Vienna
Austria

Anne Yvrande-Billon
ATOM
Université de Paris I
France

Printing and Binding: Strauss GmbH, Mörlenbach

9 783790 802023

GPSR Compliance

The European Union's (EU) General Product Safety Regulation (GPSR) is a set of rules that requires consumer products to be safe and our obligations to ensure this.

If you have any concerns about our products, you can contact us on ProductSafety@springernature.com

In case Publisher is established outside the EU, the EU authorized representative is:

Springer Nature Customer Service Center GmbH
Europaplatz 3
69115 Heidelberg, Germany

Batch number: 10725973

Printed by Printforce, the Netherlands